BOLLINGEN SERIES XLVIII

# THE GOTHIC CATHEDRAL

Otto von Simson

# THE
# GOTHIC CATHEDRAL

Origins of Gothic Architecture and
the Medieval Concept of Order

BOLLINGEN SERIES XLVIII

PRINCETON UNIVERSITY PRESS

THIS VOLUME IS THE FORTY-EIGHTH IN A SERIES OF BOOKS
SPONSORED BY BOLLINGEN FOUNDATION

*Second edition, revised, with additions, 1962*
*First Princeton/Bollingen Paperback edition, 1974*
*Third edition, with additions, 1988*
*Second printing, expanded edition, 1989*

Princeton University Press books are printed on acid-free
paper, and meet the guidelines for permanence and durability
of the Committee on Production Guidelines for Book
Longevity of the Council on Library Resources

*Library of Congress Catalog Card No. 87-36886*

ISBN 0-691-01867-7 (paperback edn.)

ISBN 0-691-09959-6 (hardcover edn.)

MANUFACTURED IN U.S.A.

*Original cloth edition designed by Andor Braun*

5  7  9  10  8  6

*To My Mother*

WE SPEAK of the Middle Ages as an epoch of faith. Within the last decades, the history of ideas has given a more precise meaning to this term by clarifying the extent to which faith and doctrine have left their imprint upon all aspects of medieval thought, scientific as well as metaphysical.

Is the same influence traceable in medieval art, and, if so, can we define the manner in which Christian experience impinged upon the vision, perhaps even upon the technique, of the medieval artist? Medieval writers derive the norms of beauty and the laws that ought to govern artistic creation from the immutable values of a transcendental order. Are such statements pious commonplaces, mere theory that has remained remote from the practice of the workshop, and from the living experience of a work of art? Or have the hands of those who created the masterpieces of medieval art actually been guided by theological vision? And, if such is the case, can we, working with the inadequate tools of historical research and confronted with the terse testimony of medieval sources, still determine the kind of co-operation that existed between theologian and artist? The longer I studied medieval art, the more indispensable it seemed to me to find answers to the above questions. For an understanding of ecclesiastical architecture these questions seem to have a particular relevance.

Even if we consider only the architectural system of the cathedral, we would be mistaken in viewing it as a work of "nonobjective" art in the strict modern sense of this term. The cathedral, as we shall see, was designed as an image, and was meant to be understood as one. It remains, nevertheless, quite true that ecclesiastical architecture represents the reality of which it is symbol or image in a manner that differs radically from that of painting or sculpture. Architecture is not the image of objects that our eye may encounter in nature; it has no "content" that we could distinguish from architectural style. For this very reason, the impact of ideas upon the life of artistic forms appears, I think, even more directly in architecture than it does in the other arts, and the origins of Gothic, perhaps the most creative achievement in the history of Western architecture, can only be understood, as this book sets out to show, as the singularly sensitive response of artistic form to the theological vision of the twelfth century.

*

Parts of this book, in somewhat altered form, have previously appeared in *Measure*, I (1950), in the *Journal of the Society of Architectural Historians*, XI (1952), and in *Studien und Texte zur Geistesgeschichte des Mittelalters*, edited by J. Koch, III (1953).

The appendix, in which Professor Ernst Levy reports on his measurements of the towers of Chartres Cathedral, offers, I think, a most valuable addition to our knowledge of the architectural proportions used in the Middle Ages.

I am indebted to Robert M. Hutchins and John U. Nef, founder and chairman, respectively, of the Committee on Social Thought of the University of Chicago, the framework of which has provided me with working conditions that any scholar might consider ideal. And I am keenly aware of the advice and assistance I have received from my colleagues and students in the art department and other units of the University of Chicago.

The Social Science Research Committee at the University of Chicago has generously extended to me the financial assistance required for my research. For an additional grant I am indebted to the Bollingen Foundation.

M. Jean Maunoury, chief architect of the Département of Eure-et-Loir and of the Cathedral of Chartres, assisted me in innumerable ways, putting at my disposal his architect's knowledge of the great edifice under his care. M. Jean Porcher, keeper of the Cabinet des Manuscrits of the Bibliothèque Nationale, has, with that kindness which so many scholars have experienced, made available to me manuscripts as well as printed literature that otherwise would have remained beyond my reach. M. Georges Viollon is responsible for a number of photographs, including the color plates. Professor Ulrich A. Middeldorf, of the German Institute of Art History, at Florence, kindly provided the print for plate 7.

I am also grateful for photographs and other illustrations made available by the various institutions, authors, and firms to which acknowledgment is made in the lists of plates and text figures.

I am keenly aware that this book could not have been written without the help of my wife, the most understanding critic an author could hope to have.

O. S.

*Chicago, summer, 1955*

## PREFACE TO THE SECOND EDITION

THE FIRST edition of this book appeared five years ago. Scholarship has not stood still in the interval. It seems to have reinforced rather than invalidated the theses I have presented. Nevertheless, in order to take into account several important recent studies that bear on my argument, I have availed myself of the opportunity to make some alterations and additions. These are mainly in the form of a section of addenda, to which references have been inserted at the relevant points in the text, and a postscript to chapter 7, besides several textual revisions on pages 80, 154 f., 203, 207 ff., and 214. To illustrate some of the new material I have added four plates, 33, 34, 43, and 44.

One major change in this edition is the omission, at his request, of Professor Ernst Levy's appendix on the proportions of the South Tower of Chartres Cathedral. He felt that his conclusions had been superseded by the findings of a distinguished architect and student of "Gothic geometry," Colonel Leonard Cox. I have yielded to Ernst Levy's request all the more reluctantly as I do not yet know the results of Leonard Cox's study. I should add, however, that I am much indebted to Colonel Cox for a number of criticisms that have enabled me to improve the text of the present edition, and I should also add that Ernst Levy, whose study remains available both in my first edition and in a special printing (in *Publications in the Humanities* [*No. 20*] *from the Department of Humanities*, Massachusetts Institute of Technology, Cambridge, 1956), has put all students of Chartres Cathedral in his debt by his painstaking and exact measurements, some of which I have been able to use in the present text.

O. S.

*Paris, fall, 1961*

THE SECOND edition of this book appeared in 1962. After a number of re-prints—the last in 1984—the publisher has decided that a new edition would be useful. I am delighted to have an opportunity to add a new section—almost a new chapter—on the rose windows of Chartres (pp. 218 ff.), which I have come to consider more and more as one of the greatest and possibly the most characteristic achievements of the master of the cathedral. A number of new plates illustrate this theme.

The decision to bring out a new edition has, on the other hand, confronted me with a certain dilemma. Although I believe the conclusions presented in this book still stand, twenty-five years is a long time. Were I to write the book afresh today, I might formulate certain propositions slightly differently, not least be-cause I have been able to profit from the results of recent scholarship. The pub-lisher and I have decided, however, to let the text stand as it is, but to use this preface to call the reader's attention to some works that bear on my argument.

There is first of all the remarkable book *Experiments in Gothic Structure* (Cambridge, Mass., 1982) whose author, Professor Robert Mark, who is an engineer as well as an architectural historian, has used models of epoxy plastic for the analysis of a number of major Gothic churches with a view to deter-mining the effects of dead load and wind pressure upon these great structures. Using techniques available only since the last war, the analyses provide infor-mation that allows us for the first time to assess the Gothic architect's (empirical) knowledge of statics. Mark is thus able to give precise answers regarding the relation between structure and style, function and design, in some of the great masterpieces of Gothic architecture, and while I am not sure that his general conclusions—Mark tends to accept the "rationalist" interpretation of Viollet-le-Duc—are borne out by his own findings (see my review of his book in *JSAH*, LIV, 1985), these findings are important enough. Thus, contrary to what I and others believed (see below, p. 203), the upper flying buttresses of Chartres Ca-

thedral are indispensable in order for the structure to withstand wind pressure
and are part of the original design.

Jean Bony's long-awaited volume *French Gothic Architecture of the Twelfth
and Thirteenth Centuries* (Berkeley and Los Angeles, 1983) has at last appeared.
His masterful analysis of Chartres Cathedral should be read as a necessary sup-
plement to my own. No less interesting is his comparison of the cathedral with
St.-Yved at Braine, which is almost contemporary with Chartres, and in some
aspects of the elevation strikingly similar. In his interesting monograph *St.
Yved* (Cologne, 1984), Bruno Klein has argued not only that this church is earlier than Chartres but that it anticipates the great achievements of the cathedral,
which he therefore relegates to a rather modest place in the history of Gothic
architecture. In fact, however, the chronology of St.-Yved is uncertain. And as
to the elevations of the two churches, as Bony points out, the master of St.-Yved
remains far behind and is more "old-fashioned" than the architect of Chartres
(see my own observations below, p. 224).

An approach very different from Bony's is attempted in *Die gotische Architektur in Frankreich 1130–1270* (Munich, 1985). The authors, D. Kimpel
and R. Sukale, seek to understand Gothic architecture in terms of sociological,
political, and economic considerations. Some oddities, such as a section entitled
"Gothic as Cultural Imperialism," may have seemed inevitable to the authors
and need not concern us here. As regards Chartres Cathedral, some conclusions
are offered that require correction. The omission of the gallery is not considered
within its architectural context—the novel treatment of clerestory and side
aisles—but unconvincingly explained in terms of alleged religious practices.
Again, we are told that the tripartite elevation in that majestic sanctuary—cathedral of one of the wealthiest dioceses of France and a royal cathedral and great
pilgrimage center to boot—is to be understood as "a demonstration of modesty."
Absurdities such as these would not be worth mentioning were it not that the
authors may have misunderstood my observations on Cistercian austerity and its
contribution to early Gothic (see below, pp. 47–50, 56–58). The reader of
Kimpel's and Sukale's book is rewarded, however, by the fine illustrations contributed by A. and J. Hirmer, who have kindly permitted me to use their splendid view of the northern transept rose and lancet windows.

A year after the first edition of the present book was published, there appeared M. D. Chenu's magisterial study *La théologie au douzième siècle* (Paris, 1957). Chapter 3 of this work is devoted to what Chenu calls "la mentalité symboliste" of this period, and he observes that "the symbolist method we shall explore is intelligible only in connection with the poetry and art of the century." Chenu adds that what artists and theologians of the twelfth century had in common, the differences between their experiences and disciplines notwithstanding, was a conviction that there is a mysterious affinity between the physical world and the world of the sacred. The following pages concern precisely that symbolist mentality of Abbot Suger and his architect with which we have to familiarize ourselves if we are to understand both Suger's writings on his new church and the church's style—the first Gothic. As regards the influence of Hugh of St.-Victor on Suger and the iconographic program of his portal, see now G. R. Zinn, "Suger, Theology and the Pseudo-Dionysian Tradition," a paper presented at the Suger symposium in New York in 1981 and published in the *Acts* of that symposium. See also my interpretation of the Sainte-Chapelle in Paris, perhaps the most perfect realization of "Dionysian" aesthetics: "Opere superante materiam: Zur Bedeutung der Sainte-Chapelle zu Paris," in *Mélanges Jacques Stiennon* (Lièges, 1982).

My observations on Sens Cathedral ought now to be supplemented by the important essay "La cathédrale Saint-Etienne de Sens: Le parti du premier maître et les campagnes du XII^e siècle" (*BM*, CXL, 1982, pp. 81–168), by J. Henriet.

In the earlier editions of this book I had reproduced E. Gall's ground plan of the choir of St.-Denis. D. von Winterfeld has kindly made available to me his corrected version of that plan published in "Gedanken zu Sugers Bau in St.-Denis," in *Festschrift Gosebruch* (Munich, 1984).

I may finally mention that I have discussed Gothic architecture in France during the twelfth and thirteenth centuries in my volume *Das hohe Mittelalter*, Vol. VI of *Propyläen Kunstgeschichte* (Berlin, 1972).

*Berlin, spring, 1987*                                        O. S.

# CONTENTS

LIST OF PLATES

PLATES

*Following page 12:*

A. Design for a monument to King Edward VI of England. From Gough Maps 45, no. 63, Bodleian Library, Oxford
   P: Bodleian Library

*Following page 162:*

1. Christ in the Heavenly City. From the Bible historiée of Jean de Papeleu, 1317. Bibliothèque de l'Arsénal, MS. 5059, fol. 1
   P: Service Photographique de la Bibliothèque Nationale, Paris

2. Abbey of St.-Étienne, Caen. Nave (1064–1120)
   P: Archives Photographiques, Paris

3. Abbey of St.-Étienne, Caen. Choir (*c.* 1200)
   P: Archives Photographiques, Paris

4. Noyon Cathedral
   P: Archives Photographiques, Paris

5. Cathedral of Notre Dame, Paris
   P: Archives Photographiques, Paris

6a. God as architect of the universe. From the Bible moralisée, Vienna. Austrian National Library, cod. 2554, fol. 1
    P: Austrian National Library

6b. Reims Cathedral. Tomb of Hugh Libergier (d. 1263)
    P: Archives Photographiques, Paris

## LIST OF TEXT FIGURES

For full references, see List of Works Cited

# INTRODUCTION

THIS essay seeks to understand Gothic architecture as an image, more precisely, as the representation of supernatural reality. To those who designed the cathedrals, as to their contemporaries who worshiped in them, this symbolic aspect or function of sacred architecture overshadowed all others. To us, it has become the least comprehensible.

The term Gothic cathedral evokes in all of us a mental image as clear and definite as that produced by any other type of building. No other monument of a culture radically different from our own is as much a part of contemporary life as is the cathedral. We may feel no closer to medieval civilization than we do to ancient Greece or Egypt; indeed, our modern world came into existence as a revolt against the intellectual order of the Middle Ages. But the Gothic cathedral, the expression of that order, is intact and in use today; it is not the romantic ruin of a past beyond recovery, but still the center of nearly every European town and, in dubious imitations, of many American cities as well.

At the same time we have become curiously blind to the cathedral. Gothic has become a convention because the cathedrals have been accessible too long. The vision that originally challenged the material resources, the technical ingenuity, the consummate artistry of an entire age, has long since become a commonplace of respectable church building and an object of archaeological classification.

This statement may appear exaggerated or even false. The Gothic sanctuaries of France move the thousands who visit them every year as deeply as do few other works of art. And the scholarship of a century has yielded penetrating insights into the aesthetic and constructive aspects of Gothic architecture. Yet neither the just definition nor the sensitive appreciation of style and design can quite explain the cathedrals. What experience did these great sanctuaries inspire in those who worshiped in them? And what theme did those who built them wish to convey? It will be best to let two medieval witnesses answer these questions.

In 1130 the new choir of Canterbury Cathedral was dedicated. The ceremony, which was attended by the king as well as the entire hierarchy of his realm, seemed to contemporaries more splendid than any other of its kind "since the dedication of the Temple of Solomon." The assembly chanted the liturgical "Awesome is this place. Truly, this is the house of God and the gate of Heaven, and it will be called the court of the Lord." Upon hearing these words, and beholding the new choir, at that moment ablaze with innumerable lights, King Henry I "swore with his royal oath 'by the death of God' that truly [the sanctuary] was awesome." [1]

The remark was provoked by the sight of one of the great architectural masterpieces of the time and sums up the impression that it made not only upon the king but also upon his contemporaries. The cathedral was the house of God, this term understood not as a pale commonplace but as fearful reality. The Middle Ages lived in the presence of the supernatural, which impressed itself upon every aspect of human life. The sanctuary was the threshold to heaven. In the admiration of its architectural perfection religious emotions overshadowed the observer's aesthetic reaction. It was no different with those who built the cathedrals.

Fourteen years after the dedication of the choir of Canterbury Cathedral another choir was dedicated that was of epoch-making significance for the history of architecture: the choir of the French abbey of St.-Denis, the edifice that became the prototype of the Gothic cathedrals. Its builder, the Abbot Suger, sensed the significance of his achievement; he attempted to define its meaning for the benefit of his contemporaries and of posterity. To this end he composed a treatise in which he described the new building and interpreted the important elements of its design. The little work, unique in its kind, is of inestimable value for us who seek to understand Gothic architecture; yet in the sense of modern art criticism it is anything but an aesthetic analysis. In its opening passages the author unfolds before us a mystical vision of harmony

1. Luard (ed.), *Annales Monastici*, IV, 19 (*RBSS*, XXXVI, 4); cf. Salzman, *Building in England*, p. 366. (See List of Works Cited for full references.)

that divine reason has established throughout the cosmos. The treatise ends with the account of the consecration ceremony that Suger had arranged with calculated splendor and that he now describes as a spectacle in which heaven and earth, the angelic hosts in heaven and the human community in the sanctuary, seemed to merge.

What has his church to do with these two visions? Obviously, it is understood as their image. Every word of Suger's interpretation seeks to battle down that very sense of detachment which is characteristic of purely aesthetic observation, and to lead visitors to the new sanctuary on to the religious experience that art had revealed to Suger himself. Indeed, as my subsequent analysis of Suger's writings will show, the design of this church, Suger's creation of Gothic form, originated in that experience.

This attitude toward sacred architecture differs widely from our own. The two testimonies, the first by a visitor to a medieval sanctuary, the second by the builder of one, complement each other and indicate clearly that the cathedral meant to medieval man what it does not mean to us. As the "symbol of the kingdom of God on earth," the cathedral gazed down upon the city and its population, transcending all other concerns of life as it transcended all its physical dimensions. What then was the vision in which the cathedral originated, and what exactly is the connection between that vision and Gothic form? These are the questions I have tried to answer in the present work. Before doing so, however, it will be useful briefly to consider what distinguishes the medieval attitude toward art from our own.

The simplest way of defining this difference is to recall the changed meaning and function of the symbol. For us the symbol is an image that invests physical reality with poetical meaning. For medieval man, the physical world as we understand it has no reality except as a symbol. But even the term "symbol" is misleading. For us the symbol is the subjective creation of poetic fancy; for medieval man what we would call symbol is the only objectively valid definition of reality. We find it necessary to suppress the symbolic instinct if we seek to understand the world as it is rather than as it seems. Medieval man conceived the symbolic instinct as the only reliable guide to such an understanding. Maximus the Confessor, a thinker we shall meet again later, actually defines what he calls "symbolic vision" as the ability to apprehend within the objects of sense perception the invisible reality of the intelligible that lays beyond them.

Each world view will obviously ascribe widely differing functions to artistic activity and experience. The modern mind has severed the symbol, the image, from all metaphysical moorings; for Nietzsche art is a lie, the consequence of the artist's heroic will to "flee from 'truth' " and to create the "illusion" that alone makes life livable. The Middle Ages perceived beauty as the "splendor veritatis," the radiance of truth; they perceived the image not as illusion but as revelation. The modern artist is free to create; we demand of him only that he be true to himself. The medieval artist was committed to a truth that transcended human existence. Those who looked at his work judged it as an image of that truth, hence the medieval tendency to praise or condemn a work of art in terms of the ultimates of religious experience.

This standard was valid above all for sacred architecture. Within its walls God himself was mysteriously present. The medieval sanctuary was the image of heaven. King Henry I and Abbot Suger both describe it as such.

The Gothic age, as has often been observed, was an age of vision. The supernatural manifested itself to the senses. St. Hildegard of Bingen wrote a quaint, Platonizing interpretation of the cosmos that both she and her contemporaries (including the Pope and St. Bernard of Clairvaux) understood to have been revealed to her inner eyes by God. The Abbot Suger was convinced that the design of his church had been inspired by a celestial vision. In the religious life of the twelfth and thirteenth centuries, the desire to behold sacred reality with bodily eyes appears as a dominant motif.[2] Architecture was designed and experienced as a representation of an ultimate reality. But in what sense was it an image of that reality? The medieval answer to this question is essential to our understanding of the medieval mind and of medieval art.

Within the last decade or so, scholars and critics have become increasingly interested in the symbolic significance of sacred architecture.[3] Professor

2. Cf. Dumoutet, *Le Désir de voir l'Hostie*, and, for further literature, Sedlmayr, *Die Entstehung der Kathedrale*, p. 541.

3. Two interpretations of this kind deserve special mention in our present context. The first is Sedlmayr's *Die Entstehung*, a work rich in fruitful observations and yet, I believe, erroneous in its conclusions, with which I shall take issue in the immediately following pages

and throughout this book. The second work is R. Wittkower's *Architectural Principles in the Age of Humanism*. The only flaw in this brilliant exposition of the symbolism of Renaissance architecture is the author's belief that the idea of reproducing in the sanctuary the harmony of the cosmos by means of proportions corresponding to the musical consonances originated in the Renaissance. As I shall show, the same idea pre-

Sedlmayr, in a felicitous *aperçu*, has insisted that architecture, like sculpture and painting, must be understood as a "representational" art. For such an understanding of architecture, however, it is not sufficient to know the "what," the theme that is represented; we have to grasp as clearly as possible the "how" by which a religious vision was translated into an architectural form or style. As regards the Gothic cathedral, much harm has been done by the attempt to get from the visible form to its symbolic significance by a kind of naturalistic short cut. Since the Gothic age in general was interpreted—questionably enough—as an era of incipient "realism," [4] the Gothic cathedral was described as an "illusionistic image" of the Celestial City as evoked in the Book of Revelation. As if the illusionistic rendering of sense experiences could have been a concern of medieval art! Had it been, medieval art would have been neither the child nor the mouthpiece of its age.

The medieval mind, as I have just recalled, was preoccupied with the symbolic nature of the world of appearances. Everywhere the visible seemed to reflect the invisible. What made possible this co-ordination of the two spheres was not the naïve vesting of the invisible with the attributes of sense phenomena, but rather the relative indifference of medieval man to an object's sensuous appearance if he, as theologian, artist, or "scientist," sought to understand its nature. This tendency toward abstraction is as manifest in medieval art as it is in medieval thought.

More specifically, the tie that connects the great order of Gothic architecture with a transcendental truth is certainly not that of optical illusion. If it were, the sanctuary could not also have been understood as an "image" of Christ and even, as in a beautiful metaphor of St. Bonaventure, of the Blessed Virgin.[5] Such comparisons appeared ridiculous and mutually exclusive as long as it was taken for granted that a symbol, in order to be acceptable, had to be a naturalistically convincing image of the reality it was meant to represent. It

vailed in the theory and practice of medieval architecture. In the theory of proportions as in so many other respects, a continued tradition links the "Renaissance" with the Middle Ages, the rediscovery and imitation of the classical orders of architecture notwithstanding.

Within recent years, two authors have again sought to interpret the Gothic cathedral in terms of a presumed analogy or affinity between scholastic thought and Gothic art: Drost, *Romanische und gotische Baukunst*, and Panofsky, *Gothic Architecture and Scholasticism*. Neither of the two works is to my mind convincing.

4. See especially Mayer, "Liturgie und Geist der Gotik."

5. "De Purif. B. V. Mariae Sermo IV" (*Opera omnia*, Quaracchi, 1801, IX, pp. 649 ff.).

may well be that the general reaction against naturalistic reproduction that characterizes modern art has also made us more sensitive to the delicate process by which an experience of mind or soul may be realized in a work of art. The way in which the medieval imagination wrought the symbols of its visions appears, more clearly perhaps than in the conventional imagery of Christian iconography, in the strange designs by which an Avignon cleric, Opicinus de Canistris, sought to represent the Christian cosmos. When he represents the universal Church as "edificium templi Dei," he blends the female allegory of Ecclesia into a geometrical pattern that looks much like the ground plan of a church and helps one understand how the medieval mind envisaged the symbolic relation between the temple and the shape of man.[6] Opicinus was an eccentric; his drawings can hardly claim to be works of art. They are nevertheless characteristic of the mode by which the Middle Ages created its symbols. In the pages that follow I have tried not only to explore the meaning of the Gothic cathedral as a symbol but also to recapture the "how," the process by which the symbolic instinct transformed vision into architectural form.

This subject has imposed a number of limitations on this study. I have concentrated on the analysis of architecture, discussing even such important parts of the Gothic cathedral as sculpture and stained glass only inasmuch as they belong to the architectural system or clarify its meaning. Moreover, in order not to blur the understanding of either the style or its message, I have confined myself to the first period of Gothic art, which begins with St.-Denis and culminates with Chartres. Only these two monuments are dealt with at length.

Finally, I shall have to meet the objection that what I describe as the main aspects of the first Gothic art is no adequate definition of what we are accustomed to call Gothic, a stylistic tradition that continued to exist, with countless ramifications in regional schools, for more than three centuries after Notre Dame of Chartres had been completed. May the cathedral of the second half of the twelfth century—a period which in so many of its manifestations is still Romanesque—really be considered the embodiment of Gothic, as I state it to be in the present book?

This objection may be answered by a general observation. The life of art forms is governed by two conflicting principles, one creative and original, the

6. See Salomon, *Opicinus de Canistris*, Pl. 27, ill. 19; also text, pp. 302 ff.

other bound by tradition and conservative. An eminent Spanish art historian, J. Puig y Cadafalch, has on occasion explained this phenomenon in terms of the analogy between style and language. Both are media through which a culture, during several generations, expresses itself, a fact that accounts for the static, retardatory character by which the imagery of languages and the styles of art tend to limit the creative scope of the individual artist and poet. This enduring matrix is broken only if a universal experience receives expression at the hands of a great artist or poet. In that event, the poet creates, as T. S. Eliot has remarked, a new language, the artist a new style. In language as in art, these are the creative moments, when both become transparently meaningful symbols of life. But the great poet and artist have pupils. The echoes of their voices will be heard for centuries to come. The more universally meaningful their message, the sooner it will become the property of all, the sooner the personal creation will become style, increasingly conventionalized until a new insight demands emancipation.

In no other art is the traditional element so powerful as in religious architecture, the work of entire communities and often of generations. Here a fresh and creative vision, in its formative impact upon society, may amount to an act of state. But for this very reason such vision will have to contend with the particular resistance of ingrained traditions, as well as with the limitations of technical skills and material resources that happen to be available. It is profoundly significant that it took a man who was at once a great prelate and a statesman of genius, Suger of St.-Denis, to overthrow Romanesque architecture and to establish the Gothic in its place.

Once created, Gothic became the conservative "language" of Christian architecture throughout the Western world. It is this language, with its local dialects, that we think of if we speak of Gothic. What concerns me here, however, is not the structure of the language, but the reason of its origin and the meaning of its message. The Gothic cathedral originated in the religious experience, the metaphysical speculation, in the political and even the physical realities, of twelfth-century France, and in the genius of those who created it. I have tried to seize this singular nexus of living forces in Gothic form that is its lasting expression. But let us begin by looking at this form.

# GOTHIC DESIGN
# AND THE
# MEDIEVAL CONCEPT
# OF ORDER

# I. GOTHIC FORM

W H A T is Gothic? The decisive feature of the new style is not the cross-ribbed vault, the pointed arch, or the flying buttress. All these are constructive means (developed or prepared by pre-Gothic architecture) but not artistic ends. The masters of the Angevin school handle the ribbed vault with a skill that is un-surpassed by their Gothic contemporaries; yet we would not call the great twelfth-century churches of Angers or Le Mans Gothic. Nor is soaring height the most characteristic aspect of Gothic architecture. Whoever has stood in what remains of the great abbey of Cluny—epitome of all that is Romanesque—will have realized that its effect of immense height is the very thing that the Gothic masters, during the first century at least, deliberately abstained from producing.[1] Two aspects of Gothic architecture, however, are without prece-dent and parallel: the use of light and the unique relationship between structure and appearance.

By the use of light I mean more specifically the relation of light to the ma-terial substance of the walls. In a Romanesque church, light is something distinct from and contrasting with the heavy, somber, tactile substance of the walls. The Gothic wall seems to be porous: light filters through it, permeating it, merging with it, transfiguring it. Not that Gothic interiors are particularly bright (although they are generally much more luminous than their Romanesque predecessors); in fact, the stained-glass windows were such inadequate sources of light that a subsequent and blinder age replaced many of them by grisaille or white windows that today convey a most misleading impression. The stained-

1. "*At mox surgit basilica ingens*—'and sud-denly a giant basilica surges up' says the chron-icler as he passes with the visitor from the nar-thex at Cluny to the nave." Conant, *Benedictine Contributions to Church Architecture*, p. 29. It is this effect of the immense that also displeased St. Bernard in Cluniac architecture. Gothic architecture, as has been pointed out many times, remains in its proportions commensurable with the size of man. See, e.g., Viollet-le-Duc, *Dictionnaire raisonné de l'architecture française du XI<sup>e</sup> au XVI<sup>e</sup> siècle*, V, 143 ff.

glass windows of the Gothic replace the brightly colored walls of Romanesque architecture; they are structurally and aesthetically not openings in the wall to admit light, but transparent walls.[2] As Gothic verticalism seems to reverse the movement of gravity, so, by a similar aesthetic paradox, the stained-glass window seemingly denies the impenetrable nature of matter, receiving its visual existence from an energy that transcends it. Light, which is ordinarily concealed by matter, appears as the active principle; and matter is aesthetically real only insofar as it partakes of, and is defined by, the luminous quality of light. We shall see in a later chapter how clearly impressions such as these convey medieval speculations about the nature of light, matter, and form.

In this decisive aspect, then, the Gothic may be described as transparent, diaphanous architecture.[3] During the first century after its emergence, this aesthetic principle was developed with complete consistency and to its ultimate consequences. The gradual enlargement of the windows as such is not the most important manifestation of this process. No segment of inner space was allowed to remain in darkness, undefined by light. The side aisles, the galleries above them, the ambulatory and chapels of the choir, became narrower and shallower, their exterior walls pierced by continuous rows of windows. Ultimately they appear as a shallow, transparent shell surrounding nave and choir, while the windows, if seen from the inside, cease to be distinct. They seem to merge, vertically and horizontally, into a continuous sphere of light, a luminous foil behind all tactile forms of the architectural system.

We find the same principles at work even in details: in the Romanesque the window opening is a void surrounded by heavy, solid framing. In the Gothic window, the solid elements of the tracery float, as it were, on the luminous window surface, its pattern dramatically articulated by light.

The second striking feature of the Gothic style is the new relationship between function and form, structure and appearance. In Romanesque or Byzantine architecture structure is a necessary but invisible means to an artistic end, concealed behind painted or stucco ornaments. If an early medieval writer

2. See the significant observation of Grodecki, "Le Vitrail et l'architecture au XIIe et au XIIIe siècle" (*GBA*, series 6, XXXVI, 1939), that stained-glass windows, during the thirteenth century, are kept more somber as their surfaces are enlarged.

3. The term "diaphanous" is first applied to Gothic architecture by Jantzen, "Über den gotischen Kirchen..."

describes a church, he speaks at great length of its paintings but usually fails to say a word about the architecture.[4] And, indeed, the entire edifice was often but a scaffold for the display of great murals or mosaics. There is good reason to suppose that in the case of the famous church of St.-Savin, architectural structure itself was actually modified for the sake of the murals.[5] Quite the opposite is true of Gothic architecture. Here ornamentation is entirely subordinated to the pattern produced by the structural members, the vault ribs and supporting shafts; the aesthetic system is determined by these. With the advent of the Gothic the art of the mural declines. It has been suggested that its flowering was, to some extent at least, owing to the technical imperfection of Romanesque building; that paintings on walls and vaults vanished as such imperfections that had to be covered up were overcome.[6] And Suger of St.-Denis actually spent a good deal of money on having the walls of the old nave of his church, the masonry of which was in poor condition, painted over with murals.[7]

But great art is never just compensation for poor workmanship or poor engineering; and the building skills even of the early Middle Ages were far more highly developed than was long believed. Even the Carolingian mason displayed the most perfect craftsmanship where necessary, that is, where the masonry remained visible. Since, however, the walls were, in the interior of the sanctuary at least, covered with murals or mosaics, a much cruder technique was used in these places.[8]

In Gothic architecture, on the other hand, the structure of the edifice acquires an aesthetic dignity that had been unknown in earlier times. The wonderful precision, for example, with which every single block was cut and

4. Hubert, L'Art pré-roman, p. 199.

5. Deschamps and Thibout, La Peinture murale en France, pp. 75 ff.

6. Cf. Duprat, "La Peinture romane en France," II (BM, CII, 1944), with reference to the findings of Puig y Cadafalch and Folch y Torres regarding Catalonian wall painting.

7. " . . . propter antiquarum maceriarum vetustatem et aliquibus in locis minacem diruptionem, ascitis melioribus quos invenire potui de diversis partibus pictoribus, eos aptari et honeste depingi tam auro quam preciosis coloribus devote fecimus." Suger, De rebus in administratione sua gestis, p. 186.

That in the Gothic sanctuary construction takes over the aesthetic function of the Romanesque mural is clearly stated in Gervase's comparison of the new eastern arm of Canterbury Cathedral—the first Gothic edifice in England —with the Romanesque structure that preceded it: "there was a ceiling of wood, decorated with excellent painting, but here is a vault beautifully constructed of stone and light tufa." Gervasii monachi Cantuarensis opera historica, p. 27. Gervase's account is transcribed in Willis, Architectural History of the Conventual Buildings of the Monastery of Christ Church in Canterbury.

8. See Hubert, pp. 88 ff.

set in the Gothic vault—leaving no ragged joints that had to be concealed—suggests not only perfect craftsmanship (and the availability of equally perfect building material) but also a novel delight in and esteem for the tectonic system for which the Romanesque, by and large, seems to have had no eyes.[9] Gothic wall painting never conceals, but on the contrary underscores, the architectural skeleton. Even the stained-glass windows submit in composition and design increasingly to the pattern of the stone and metal armature in which they are embedded.[10]

This development, to be sure, cannot be understood, as was once believed, as a triumph of functionalism. Architectural form reveals function inasmuch as it reveals the actual physical interplay of weights (or thrusts) and support. Such interplay is very much in evidence in the Greek temple and not at all in a Byzantine church. The picture is somewhat ambivalent in Gothic architecture. Here it is not easy to determine whether form has followed function, or function form. The latter actually seems to be true for the most conspicuous members of the Gothic system, vault rib and respond. True, the aesthetic possibilities of the vault rib were fully understood and utilized only after it had been used by the Gothic builder as a technical device.[11] But a "false" rib, without any practical function, was used for ornamental purposes under the half domes of Romanesque and indeed of Roman apses before ribs were used in the same place as actual supports.[12] Similarly, responds seem at first to occur, in Norman architecture, without structural function.[13] Moreover, neither rib nor respond is

9. Cf. Bond, *An Introduction to English Church Architecture*, I, 319 ff.

10. Cf. Dyer-Spencer, "Les vitraux de la Ste-Chapelle de Paris" (*BM*, XCI, 1932), and Grodecki, *Vitraux des églises de France*, Paris, 1947, pp. 12 ff.

11. An illuminating example of this dual function of Gothic rib construction is that of Morienval. The cross-ribbed vault over the ambulatory (soon after 1122), the oldest of its kind in existence, had a purely technical function. In the presbytery, on the other hand, as Ricôme's excellent analysis reveals ("Structure et fonction du chevet de Morienval," *BM*, XCVIII, 1939), the cross-ribbed vault has been employed in the full realization of its aesthetic and symbolic significance. Forms are much more elegant here than in the ambulatory, and

remains of ancient coloring suggest how the "fonction spirituelle" of this "véritable dais de pierre" which rose over the relics of the titular saint was effectively underscored by decorative means. Cf. also Sedlmayr, *Die Entstehung der Kathedrale*, p. 211.

12. See Formigé (*BM*, LXXVII, 1913), p. 26; Vallery-Radot (*BM*, CII, 1945); also *CA*, *Avignon*, 1909, I, 121 ff., and II, 275 ff. For further literature on the use of ribs in Roman architecture, see Sedlmayr, pp. 189 f.

13. Gall, *Die Gotische Baukunst in Frankreich und Deutschland*, I, 26 ff.; Bony, "La Technique normande du mur épais" (*BM*, XCVIII, 1939); Sedlmayr, p. 172. In some cases at least, the Norman responds terminated conically and thus can hardly have had any structural function.

ever purely "functional." The ribs certainly help maintain the vault, but are by
no means so indispensable as was once thought.[14] The responds are so frail that
without the bracing walls between them they could not support themselves, let
alone the vault.[15] The main weight of the latter rests, of course, on the flying
buttresses that are not even visible from the inside of the edifice. Finally, even
the shape of the unequivocally structural members in the Gothic system is deliberately modified, often at the expense of functional efficiency, for the sake
of a certain visual effect. Thus the massive thickness of walls and piers is never
allowed to appear; where it might become visible, as through the openings of     *Plates 2, 3*
gallery arcades, tympana and colonnettes placed in these openings create the
illusion, not of a wall, but of a membrane-thin surface. Again, the true volume
of the supports is concealed behind, or seemingly dissolved into, bundles of frail,
soaring shafts.[16]

And yet, we cannot enter a Gothic church without feeling that every
visible member of the great system has a job to do. There are no walls but only
supports; the bulk and weight of the vault seem to have contracted into the
sinewy web of the ribs. There is no inert matter, only active energy. However,
this cosmos of forces is not the naked manifestation of tectonic functions, but
their translation into a basically graphic system. The aesthetic values of Gothic
architecture are to a surprising extent linear values. Volumes are reduced to
lines, lines that appear in the definite configurations of geometrical figures. The
shafts *express* the principle of supporting by the dynamics of their vertical lines.
The ribs *represent* the statically important ridges where the two "tunnels" of a
groined vault interpenetrate but are not essential to its maintenance. In fact,
it can be shown how the cross-rib was preceded and prepared by the architect's inclination to see and conduct the ridges of a groined vault not as the
interpenetration of curved surfaces but as the intersection of straight lines. At
this "intermediary" stage—since *c.* 1080—the ridges are no longer allowed to

14. For a summary and bibliography of the
controversy over Gothic "rationalism," which
was started by Abraham's *Viollet-le-Duc et le
rationalisme . médiéval*, see Kubler, "A Late
Gothic Computation of Rib Vault Thrusts"
(*GBA*, XXVI, 1944).

15. On the technical function of the Gothic

respond, see Choisy, *Histoire de l'architecture*,
II, 310 ff., 349 ff.; cf. Seymour, *Notre Dame of
Noyon in the Twelfth Century*, pp. 134, 156 f.

16. See the analysis of Notre Dame, Dijon,
by Abraham, pp. 102 ff.; note also the reduced
volumes of supporting members in the nave of
Notre Dame, Paris, compared with those of the
older choir: Aubert, *Notre-Dame de Paris*, p. 41.

describe the sinuous lines prescribed by the vault but are "arbitrarily" adjusted so as to mark a straight line. An architectural member as conspicuous as is the cross-ribbed vault is thus largely not the cause but the creation of the geometrical "graphism" of Gothic design.[17]

It is no longer necessary to insist on the overwhelming importance of this geometrical element in Gothic design. It constitutes the very principle of its order and aesthetic cohesion. But it is also the medium through which the architect conveyed an image of the structural forces joined together in his building.

"Their design," Bony has written with regard to the configuration of lines of the Gothic system, "transcribes, with some freedom of interpretation, what is going on behind them, and expresses what was believed by the architects to be the theoretical framework of the building." [18] In this sense, however, Gothic is indeed functionalist, especially so when we compare it with Romanesque.[19] And this singular "geometrical functionalism," as we may perhaps call it, is all the more remarkable if we recall the idea to which the Christian sanctuary is to give expression.

The church is, mystically and liturgically, an image of heaven.[20] Medieval theologians have, on innumerable occasions, dwelt on this correspondence. The authoritative language of the dedication ritual of a church explicitly relates the vision of the Celestial City, as described in the Book of Revelation, to the building that is to be erected. As if to stress this symbolic significance of the church edifice, the Heavenly Mansions are, in the representations of the Last Judgment on Romanesque portals, occasionally represented as a basilica

17. Bilson, "The Beginnings of Gothic Architecture: Norman Vaulting in England" (*RIBA Journal*, VI, 1899; IX, 1902), "Les Voûtes d'ogives de Morienval" (*BM*, LXXII, 1908); Frankl, *Frühmittelalterliche und romanische Baukunst*, p. 106 (with reference to the groined vaults in the side aisles of Jumièges); Bony, "Gloucester et l'origine des voûtes d'hémicycle gothique" (*BM*, XCVII, 1938); Sedlmayr, p. 192.

18. *French Cathedrals*, p. 7.

19. Gall, *Niederrheinische und normännische Architektur*, pp. 9 ff., similarly calls "Diese Verbindung des dekorativen mit dem tektonischen Charakter der Bauformen . . . besond-

ers bezeichnend für das 'gotische' Denken, das alle Formen nach dieser Richtung hin umbildete."

20. The passage in Rev. 21 : 2–5 forms the Epistle read during the dedication rite. See Andrieu, *Le Pontifical romain au XIIᵉ siècle*, pp. 192 f. Cf. Sedlmayr, pp. 103 ff., and Simson, "Birth of the Gothic" (*Measure*, I, 1950), p. 285. The first historian to recognize the symbolic relation between the Gothic cathedral and the Celestial City was Didron. He pointed out that the angels on the flying buttresses of Reims Cathedral "assimilent [the cathedral] à la Jérusalem divine bâtie sur terre." *Manuel d'iconographie chrétienne*, p. 261.

(Conques); and the monastic painter, illuminating his manuscript with a picture of heaven, "could think of no more appropriate image of this vision than    *Plate 1*
the apse of a church." [21] In the Romanesque sanctuary this symbolic significance
is conveyed by the monumental representation of Christ in majesty, surrounded
by his heavenly court, which usually adorns the apse, and occasionally even by
images of the Heavenly City (St.-Chef; S. Pietro at Civate).[22] Such images suggest the spiritual reason for the "antifunctionalism" of Romanesque and
Byzantine art: the mystical experience that murals or mosaics are to help in-
voke within the faithful is emphatically not of this world; the celestial vision
depicted is to make us forget that we find ourselves in a building of stone and
mortar, since inwardly we have entered the heavenly sanctuary.[23]

A particularly striking example of this intention occurs in the two-storied
church at Schwarzrheindorf, the magnificent sepulcher of its builder, the Archbishop of Cologne, Arnold of Wied (d. 1156). While the murals of the upper
church depict mainly scenes from the Book of Revelation, those of the lower
church were inspired by the Vision of Ezekiel, which, in some respects an Old
Testament counterpart to the Apocalypse of St. John, also contains a vision of
heaven under the image of an edifice, i.e., of a temple. The pictorial cycle in the
lower church at Schwarzrheindorf, one of the most impressive of the Middle
Ages, seeks to make us see the entire sanctuary as the setting for Ezekiel's
eschatological image. The four central vault compartments surrounding the
octagonal opening that connects upper and lower church contain in four scenes
the vision of the new temple. The eastern compartment shows a churchlike
edifice with open doors that reveal Christ standing inside, his right hand raised
in the gesture of benediction. The composition represents the eastern gate
through which the Lord has entered his sanctuary (Ezek. 43 f). An inscription
"Porta Sanctuarii" or "Sanctuarium" seems to have explained this meaning.[24]
The onlooker could not fail to notice that this representation appeared over the

21. Puig y Cadafalch, *La Géographie et les
origines du premier art roman*, p. 399.
22. See also the titulus quoted by Hubert,
pp. 108 f.
23. On the illusionistic character of Byzantine decoration, see Demus, *Byzantine Mosaic
Decoration*. Quite similarly, the *Majestas* in the

apse of St.-Céneri-le-Gérei conceals the spherical surface of the apse. *CA, Angers et Saumur*,
1910, II, ill. opp. p. 162.
24. See Neuss, "Das Buch Ezechiel in
Theologie und Kunst" (*BGAM*, I, II); Clemen,
*Die romanische Monumentalmalerei in den Rhein-
landen*, pp. 271 ff.; Verbeek, *Schwarzrheindorf*.

entrance from the crossing to the sanctuary of the church. The scene thus designated this part of the building as a mystical image of the Lord's eternal sanctuary in the Heavenly Jerusalem.

Such great pictorial evocations of the mystical significance of the church edifice no longer have a place in the Gothic sanctuary. In the interiors of cathedrals as well as abbeys, imagery now occupies a less conspicuous place. The builder has become far more important than the painter, and nothing can disturb the singular convergence of structural and aesthetic values achieved by the geometrical functionalism of the Gothic system. Such convergence seems to have been noted and demanded even by contemporaries who were not architects. Around 1200, a chronicler reports the collapse of the Romanesque transept tower of Beverley Minster. He blames the calamity upon the architects, whom he accuses of having sacrificed solidity and structural strength to *decor* and pleasing appearance. The verdict suggests an awareness of the possible conflict between form and function, and of the need to subordinate the former to the latter, that strikes one as "Gothic." In Gothic architecture, whatever its technical shortcomings may have been, the distinction between form and function, the independence of form from function, have vanished. Are we to conclude that this artistic achievement marks, as was once believed, the advent of a more secular spirit, a lessening of the religious impact upon the artist's imagination, and that the evolution of Gothic design was inspired by the eschatological meaning of the sanctuary to a less extent than other medieval styles, or that the architect was less intent upon invoking it? On historical grounds this is very unlikely. Gothic architecture was created, as I shall try to show in the next chapter, in response to a powerful demand for an architecture particularly attuned to religious experience, a fact that has recently led to a brilliant and provocative attempt to interpret all important elements of Gothic architecture as almost literal representations of features of the Heavenly Jerusalem as described by St. John.[25]

Such an interpretation, to be sure, encounters serious difficulties. Some passages of the Biblical text said to be "depicted" in the Gothic system defy,

25. Sedlmayr, *passim*. See my review in *Kunstchronik*, IV, 1951. See also Deschamps and Thibout, pp. 1 ff.; also the descriptive terms quoted in Hubert, pp. 108 ff. The report on Beverley Minster is in Raine (ed.), *The Historians of the Church of York* (RBSS, LXXXL, 1), p. 345.

in point of fact, all architectural representation. Other images are couched in terms that can be, and have been, translated with equal plausibility into the contradictory languages of many different styles.

It is, for example, quite true to say that the Gothic architect sought to represent the splendor of the city that, according to the Book of Revelation, was of "pure gold, like to clear glass." But so did the Romanesque builder. Early medieval writers have often described sanctuaries that elicited their admiration; there are few of these descriptions that do not stress the "splendor," the "radiance," the dazzling glitter of these ancient basilicas. And in his account of the Trinité at Fécamp, the chronicler likens this Romanesque church to the Heavenly Jerusalem precisely because "it is resplendent with gold and silver." [26]

The Book of Revelation, moreover, is by no means the only source from which Christian imagination drew its picture of the world to come. The Temple of Solomon—likewise evoked in the dedication rite—and the Temple of Ezekiel were, as the example of Schwarzrheindorf shows, also understood as images of heaven. They, no less than the Heavenly City, were looked upon as archetypes of the Christian sanctuary and actually inspired the medieval builder. A miniature in the famous *Liber Floridus* from St.-Bertin (*c.* 1120) depicts "Jherusalem Celestis" as a medieval cathedral. The image, however, appears directly above the Biblical passage (II Chronicles, 2) that recounts how Solomon built the Temple. The twofold relationship makes it quite clear that the church was conceived as an image of the Celestial Jerusalem, but that the Celestial Jerusalem in turn was thought to have been prefigured in the Solomonic Temple.[27] (Conversely, Jean Fouquet represents the Temple of Solomon as a Gothic cathedral.)

But, it must be asked, in what sense were these Biblical descriptions prototypes of medieval architecture? The liturgy applies them metaphorically to every sanctuary, regardless of style or design; external appearance may be a token, but is certainly not the cause, of that mystical correspondence between

26. Mortet and Deschamps, *Recueil de textes relatifs à l'histoire de l'architecture* . . . , I, 243 ff.

27. See Rosenau, *Design and Medieval Architecture*, Pl. 1b. Another vision that influenced medieval ideas about the Heavenly City is the Book of Enoch; its description of the heavenly palace as "built of crystals," having walls "like a mosaic crystal floor," may not be unconnected with Gothic predilection for the replacement of walls by glass. See Dillmann (tr.), *The Book of Enoch*, p. 80; also Ruegg, *Die Jenseitsvorstellungen vor Dante*, I, 226.

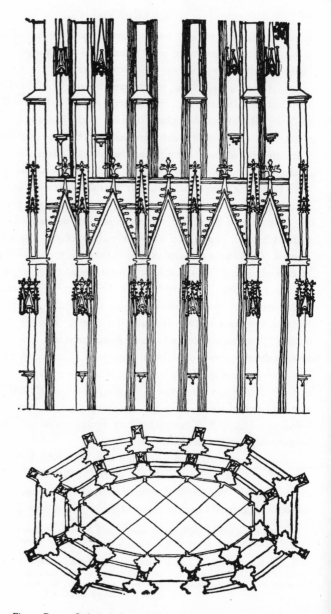

Fig. 1. Prague Cathedral. Ground plan and elevation for a sepulchral chapel

*Design for a monument to King Edward VI of England*

The sepulchral structures reproduced here and on the opposite page are in many respects comparable. The peculiar way in which (left) the Gothic architect represents architecture is underscored by the Renaissance design. The English artist renders columns, architrave, etc. as tangible bodies clearly distributed and related in space. His Gothic predecessor perceives all architectural members as mere configurations of lines on a surface. We encounter the same geometrization of optical values in Gothic architecture actually built.

A

visible structure and invisible reality. The unchanging texts of the liturgy determine the limits within which the builder's imagination must move in order to remain attuned to the religious experience of the Church; but these texts cannot explain the changes of styles in ecclesiastical architecture.

However, if the supernatural truth that the liturgy conveys is immutable, the artistic means of representing this truth are not. The scope of the architect's vision is challenged and circumscribed by the technical skills and the building materials that happen to be available in a given region; the climate of ideas changes from epoch to epoch. Above all, ecclesiastical art reflects the changing views that different ages have held regarding the possibility of representing transcendental truth in a work of art; a fresh religious experience usually yields a new answer to this question. This is eminently true for the Gothic age. What distinguishes the cathedral of this epoch from preceding architecture is not the eschatological theme but the different mode of its evocation. If we seek to understand the birth of Gothic architecture, it is not sufficient to ask *what* the Gothic cathedral represents. The questions on which our attention must focus are how the Gothic cathedral represents the vision of heaven, and what was the religious and metaphysical experience that demanded this new mode of representation.

The evidence of Gothic architecture itself will lead us to an answer. With few exceptions, the Gothic builders have been tight-lipped about the symbolic significance of their projects, but they are unanimous in paying tribute to *geometry* as the basis of their art. This is revealed even by a glance at Gothic architectural drawings, such as the thirteenth-century Reims palimpsest [28] or the great collections of the Prague and Vienna cathedral lodges; [29] they appear like beautiful patterns of lines ordered according to geometrical principles. The architectural members are represented without any indication of volume, and, until the end of the fourteenth century, there is no indication of space or perspective.[30] The exclusive emphasis on surface and line confirms our impres-

*Fig. 1 and*<br>*Plate A*

---

28. First published by Didron, "Dessins palimpsestes du XIIIᵉ siècle (*AA*, V, 1846); see Hahnloser, "Entwürfe eines Architekten um 1250 aus Reims" (*XIIIᵉ Congrès international d'histoire de l'art*).

29. See Tietze, "Aus der Bauhütte von St. Stephan" (*Jahrbuch der kunsthistorischen Samm-*

*lungen* (new series, IV, V); and Kletzl, *Plan-Fragmente aus der deutschen Dombauhütte von Prag*.

30. Kletzl, *Plan-Fragmente*, pp. 11 ff. Contrary to Colombier's suggestion (*Les Chantiers des cathédrales*, p. 65), perspective is certainly not a characteristic aspect of Gothic archi-

sions of actual Gothic buildings. As to the principles or formulae used in developing these architectural systems and in determining the proportions among their different parts, recent research has elucidated at least all basic aspects of this question which less than a century ago appeared insoluble.[31]

With but a single basic dimension given, the Gothic architect developed all other magnitudes of his ground plan and elevation by strictly geometrical means, using as modules certain regular polygons, above all the square.[32] The knowledge of this way of determining architectural proportions was considered so essential that it was kept a professional secret by the medieval lodges. Only toward the end of the fifteenth century—and of the cathedral age—was it made public by Matthew Roriczer, the builder of Regensburg Cathedral. He teaches "how to take the elevation from the ground plan" by means of a single square. From this figure Roriczer derives all proportions of his edifice, in this case a pinnacle, inasmuch as its dimensions are related to one another as are the sides of a sequence of squares, the areas of which diminish (or increase) in geomet-

tectural drawings. Cf. Ueberwasser, "Deutsche Architekturdarstellung um as Jahr 1000" (*Festschrift für Hans Jantzen*). The *trecento* drawing of the interior of a chapel in Christ Church Library, Oxford (No. A 1, IV), may or may not be a very rare example of a sketch after an existing building as Degenhart has tentatively suggested in "Autonome Zeichnung bei mittelalterlichen Künstlern" (*MJ*, III Folge, I, 1950). It clearly is the work of a painter; no architect would at that time have handled perspective in this fashion. For architectural representation in the Romanesque age, see Ueberwasser, "Deutsche Architekturdarstellung."

31. See Viollet-le-Duc, *Lectures on Architecture*, Lect. IX. Cf. also his *Dictionnaire*, VII, 537 ff.

32. See above all the important contributions of Ueberwasser: "Spätgotische Baugeometrie" (*Jahresbericht der öffentlichen Kunstsammlung Basel* (n.s., 25–27); *Von Maasz und Macht der alten Kunst;* "Nach rechtem Maasz"; and "Beiträge zur Wiedererkenntnis gotischer Baugesetzmässigkeiten" (*ZK*, VIII, 1939). Also Texier, *Géometrie de l'architecture;* Jouven, *Rhythme et architecture* (it should be noted that

Texier and Jouven are or were Architectes-en-Chef des Monuments Historiques); Fischer, *Zwei Vorträge über Proportionen; RDK*, arts. "Architekturtheorie" and "Architekturzeichnung"; and Colombier, p. 70. Nearly all older works, including Dehio's *Untersuchungen über das gleichseitige Dreieck als Norm gotischer Bauproportionen*, are now obsolete, since they were undertaken on the basis of inexact measurements and drawings. On the other hand, Thomae's criticism, *Das Proportionenwesen in der Geschichte der gotischen Baukunst*, though correct in refuting individual errors of interpretation, is marred by the author's ignorance of medieval thought. See Kletzl's review of the book in *ZK*, IV, 1935. As for the technical methods by which the medieval architect and even his "scientifically" untrained assistants were able to execute these mathematical proportions, see the interesting paper by Funck-Hellet, "L'Équerre des maîtres d'oeuvres et la proportion" (*Les Cahiers techniques de l'art*, II, 1949). The author stresses the important function of the *équerre*, or square, the instrument that indeed figures so conspicuously as the builder's tool in nearly all images of medieval architects.

*Fig. 2. Ground plans and elevations of Gothic canopy supports*
Medieval drawings

rical progression. Proportions thus obtained the master considers to be "according to true measure." [33]

It was not only the late Gothic architect or the German lodges that made this modular use of the square. Perhaps the most important single piece of evidence regarding the principles of Gothic design is the famous model book by the Picard architect, Villard de Honnecourt, who was active in the second quarter of the thirteenth century. He too teaches how to halve the square for the purpose of determining the "true" proportions of a building, in this case the ground plan of a cloister.[34]

This canon of proportions did not remain confined to theory. Villard de Honnecourt in another drawing shows its application in the towers of Laon Cathedral. It appears likewise in a number of medieval ground plans of Gothic steeples studied by Maria Velte. Here not only the recesses of the different stories, but the dimensions of every single detail, be it the keystone or the width of the walls, hang proportionately together, as do the sides of a series of squares the areas of which increase in geometrical progression.[35] In the famed Church of Our Lady at Trier, as Ernst Gall has recently shown, all proportions are determined by the same formula.[36] Again, the façade of Notre Dame of Paris is composed of a sequence of four squares developed "according to true measure." If one compares this façade with the earlier but generally similar

*Plates 4, 5*   façade of Noyon, he is tempted to say that the development of Gothic from its beginning to the classical maturity reached by the mid-thirteenth century is marked by the increasing clarity with which the geometrical principle is realized.[37] Of course, geometrical formulae were also used by pre-Gothic architects and by sculptors and painters as well. Here, however, they seem to have been practical rather than artistic devices, of which the observer usually remains unconscious. Nowhere do they determine the aesthetic appearance as they

33. See Frankl, "The Secret of the Medieval Masons" (*AB*, XXVII, 1945); also Colombier, p. 68. The *Fialenbüchlein* is published in Heideloff, *Die Bauhütte des Mittelalters in Deutschland*, pp. 105 ff.

34. The model book has been reproduced by Lassus, *Album de Villard de Honnecourt*, and Hahnloser, *Villard de Honnecourt*. My references are to Hahnloser, Pls. 18, 39.

35. Velte, *Die Anwendung der Quadratur und Triangulatur bei der Grund- und Aufrissgestaltung der gotischen Kirchen*. See, however, the review of this book by J. S. Ackerman in *AB*, XXV, 1953.

36. Gall, "Über die Maasze der Trierer Liebfrauenkirche . . . " (*Form und Inhalt*).

37. Cf. Seymour, *Notre Dame of Noyon*, pp. 139 ff.

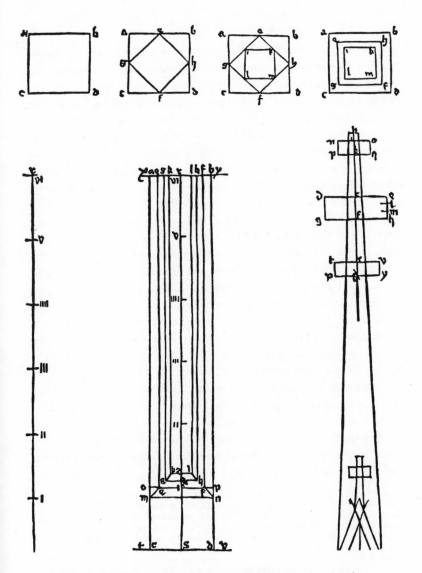

Fig. 3. Matthew Roriczer. Ground plan and elevation of a pinnacle

do in the Gothic system.[38] We shall return to this point in the last chapter.

Why this extraordinary submission, so alien to our own notions concerning the nature of art and of the freedom of artistic creation, to the laws of geometry? One reason often given is a practical one: measuring units varied from place to place, yardsticks were unknown or unusable; this must have recommended a system of proportions that could be translated by purely geometrical means from the small-scale architectural drawing or model into the large dimensions of the actual building. This explanation is but partially valid, however. Standardized and generally accepted measuring units were certainly in use during the twelfth and thirteenth centuries in other professions, for example, the uniform measures and weights employed by all the towns represented at the great fairs.[39] The architect Villard de Honnecourt, moreover, on one occasion does supply absolute measures in feet, both in Roman numerals and in the accompanying text, in his model book.[40] But he uses these arithmetical measures only in a technical drawing; in his architectural designs he relies exclusively on geometry. Furthermore, the proportion "according to true measure," whatever the facility of its practical execution, occurs, as Ueberwasser has shown, in Gothic paintings and engravings, where the problem of translating one dimension into another did not enter.

The Gothic artist would have overthrown the rule of geometry, had he considered it, as most modern artists would, a fetter. It is clear, on the other hand, that he did not use his geometrical canons for purely aesthetic reasons either, since he applied them where they are invisible to the observer. Thus, all the ribs under the vault of Reims Cathedral circumscribe, according to Viollet-le-Duc, equilateral triangles, a fact no visitor to the church is likely to notice. And even such purely technical data as the width of a wall or buttress were

38. Where the geometrical grid obtrudes in such Romanesque works, we experience its effect as unpleasant. See, e.g., Hubert, "Les Peintures murales du Vic et la tradition géométrique" (*Cahiers archéologiques*, I, 1945), Pl. XV.

39. See Levasseur, *Histoire du commerce de la France*, I, 86.

40. Hahnloser, t. 59, pp. 159 f. The famous Carolingian monastery plan in St.-Gall represents a special case. While the church is laid out geometrically *ad quadratum*, measurements in feet have been entered upon the plan that yield entirely different proportions. The only possible explanation, it seems to me, is that the plan represents an ideal *exemplum* and as such follows the "perfect" proportions based on the square. The numerical dimensions given, on the other hand, are to guide those who wish to translate the plan into reality. And this reality is entirely different from the ideal scheme. The Gothic builder would not have deviated so widely from his geometrical model. For the interpretation of the St.-Gall plan, see Reinhardt, *Der St. Galler Klosterplan*, pp. 18 ff.

determined by the formula "according to true measure." Again, the Gothic builders show what F. Bond has called "a sneaking fondness" for the square bay, even though the adoption of the pointed arch had rendered the square bay obsolete as a vaulting unit.[41] In short, the alternative of technical or aesthetic does not make sense in medieval terms. Fortunately, at least one literary document survives that explains the use of geometry in Gothic architecture: the minutes of the architectural conferences held during 1391 and the following years in Milan.

The Cathedral of Milan had been begun in 1386. But after a few years difficulties became apparent and it was decided to call in foreign advisers from France and Germany. In the discussions between them and their Italian colleagues, the minutes of which have survived, two points stand out that are of paramount importance for our present inquiry. First, the reliance on geometric figures—attested by the German architect, Matthew Roriczer, of the fifteenth century, and the thirteenth-century French architect, Villard—is emphatically confirmed by the Italian document of the intervening century. The question debated at Milan is not whether the cathedral is to be built according to a geometrical formula, but merely whether the figure to be used is to be the square (which had already determined the ground plan) or the equilateral triangle.

The second and even more interesting aspect of the Milan documents is that they suggest the reason for this reliance on geometrical canons. The minutes of one particularly stormy session relate an angry dispute between the French expert, Jean Mignot, and the Italians. Overruled by them on a technical issue, Mignot remarks bitterly that his opponents have set aside the rules of geometry by alleging science to be one thing and art another. Art, however, he concludes, is nothing without science, "ars sine scientia nihil est." [42] The terms "art" and "science" do not mean what they mean today. Art for Mignot and his contemporaries is the practical know-how gained from experience, science the ability to account for the reasons that determine sound architectural procedure by rational and, more precisely, geometrical means. In other words, architecture that is scientific and good must invariably be based on geometry;

41. Bond, *Introduction*, p. 321.
42. *Annali*, esp. I, 68 ff., 209 f. The best study of the much discussed passage is that of Ackerman, "Ars sine scientia nihil est" (*AB*, XXXI, 1949). See also Frankl, "Secret."

unless he obeys the laws of this discipline, the architect must surely fail. This argument was considered unassailable even by Mignot's opponents. They hasten to affirm that they are in complete agreement as regards this theoretical point and have nothing but contempt for an architect who presumes to ignore the dictates of geometry. And it is taken for granted by both sides that the stability and beauty of an edifice are not distinct values, that they do not obey different laws, but that, on the contrary, both are comprehended in the perfection of geometrical forms.

Thus, the Milan document answers our question regarding the function of geometry in Gothic architecture. I think it also provides the clue to the reasons underlying what seems an almost superstitious belief in mathematics. Jean Mignot's juxtaposition of *ars* and *scientia* recalls, like a faint echo, the distinction that occurs almost a millennium before in the most influential aesthetic treatise of the Christian Middle Ages. To this work, to the world view it expounds, and to the tradition it created, we must now turn.

## 2. MEASURE AND LIGHT

IN THE first book of his treatise *De musica*, St. Augustine defines music as the "science of good modulation."[1] Before telling us what good modulation is, he explains why music, properly understood, is a science. He does not deny that music can be produced by instinct or practical skill, just as music can be appreciated by one who just "knows what he likes." Such understanding of music, however, creative or receptive, is but of a low order, according to Augustine. Vulgar performers and vulgar audiences have such an understanding; even a singing bird has. In fact, there is little difference between man and beast in regard to this kind of musical knowledge, which Augustine contemptuously calls *art*.[2] The true understanding of music, on the other hand, which knows the laws that are of its very essence, applies them in musical creation, and discovers them in a composition, is what Augustine calls the *science* of music, and he goes on to explain the nature of this science as mathematical.[3]

The science of good modulation is concerned with the relating of several musical units according to a module, a measure, in such a way that the relation can be expressed in simple arithmetical ratios. The most admirable ratio, according to Augustine, is that of equality or symmetry, the ratio 1:1, since here the union or consonance between the two parts is most intimate. Next in rank are the ratios 1:2, 2:3, and 3:4—the intervals of the perfect consonances, octave, fifth, and fourth. It is to be noticed that the pre-eminence of these intervals, for Augustine, is not derived from their aesthetic or acoustic qualities. These, rather, are audible echoes of the metaphysical perfection that Pythag-

---

1. "Musica est scientia bene modulandi (*PL*, XXXII, 1083).
2. II, 19 (*PL*, XXXII, 1111).
3. On Augustine's aesthetics, see especially H. Edelstein, *Die Musikanschauung Augustins* *nach seiner Schrift "De musica"*; K. Svoboda, *L'Esthétique de Saint Augustin et ses sources;* and H. I. Marrou, *Saint Augustin et la fin de la culture antique* (with exhaustive bibliography), esp. pp. 197 ff.

orean mysticism ascribes to number, especially to the four numbers of the first *tetractys*. Without the principate of number, as Augustine calls it, the cosmos would return to chaos. Taking up the Biblical passage "thou hast ordered all things in measure and number and weight," [4] the Bishop of Hippo applied Pythagorean and Neoplatonic number mysticism to the interpretation of the Christian universe, thus establishing the cosmology that remained in force until the triumph of Aristotelianism. Augustine shares with Plato both distrust of the world of images and belief in the absolute validity of mathematical relationships. These views form the basis of Augustine's philosophy of art. His postulates about the function of the arts in the Christian commonwealth, and even, one may say, their style, left their imprint on Christian art for a thousand years. This influence may be formulated as follows:

1. The principles of good musical modulation and its appreciation that Augustine established in *De musica* are mathematical principles and therefore apply, in his opinion at least, to the visual arts as they do to music. On the monochord, the musical intervals are marked off by divisions on a string; the arithmetical ratios of the perfect consonances thus appear as the proportions between different parts of a line. And since Augustine deduces the musical value of the perfect consonances from the metaphysical dignity of the ratios on which they are based, it was natural for him to conclude that the beauty of certain visual proportions derives from their being based on the simple ratios of the first *tetractys*. The place Augustine assigns to geometry among the liberal arts, like the place he assigns to music, is caused by what the Middle Ages called the "anagogical" function of geometry, that is, its ability to lead the mind from the world of appearances to the contemplation of the divine order. In the second book of his treatise *On Order*, Augustine describes how reason, in her quest for the blissful contemplation of things divine, turns to music and from music to what lies within the range of vision: beholding earth and heaven, she

---

4. Wisd. of Sol. 11:20b. It was not difficult to find in the Biblical phrase justification and confirmation of the Pythagorean theory of a symphonic universe based on numbers. According to the ancient legend, Pythagoras had discovered that perfect consonances were produced according to the proportion of weights (of hammers beating on a piece of iron), the same proportion as that between the segments of the monochord that yield those consonances. See Macrobius, *Commentarius ex Cicerone in somnium Scipionis*, II, 1; Chalcidius, *Platonis Timaeus interprete Chalcidio*, XLV; Boethius, *De musica*, I, 10 (*PL*, LXIII, 1176 f.).

realizes that only beauty can ever satisfy her, in beauty figures, in figures proportion, and in proportion number.[5]

2. The aesthetic implications are clear. Augustine was nearly as sensitive to architecture as he was to music. They are the only arts he seems to have fully enjoyed; and he recognized them even after his conversion, since he experienced the same transcendental element in both.[6] For him, music and architecture are sisters, since both are children of number; they have equal dignity, inasmuch as architecture mirrors eternal harmony, as music echoes it.

Consistent with this view, Augustine uses architecture, as he does music, to show that number, as apparent in the simpler proportions that are based on the "perfect" ratios, is the source of all aesthetic perfection. And he uses the architect, as he does the musician, to prove that all artistic creation observes the laws of numbers. The architect, if he is a mere practitioner rather than a "scientist" of his art, may be unaware of the fact that he is instinctively applying mathematical rules. No beautiful edifice is conceivable, however, unless these rules have been applied and unless their presence is apparent to the observer.

We should by no means overlook the positive aspects of this aesthetics: its underlying distrust and depreciation of the imitative in art, and indeed of all imagery, kept alive sensibility for the "nonobjective" values in artistic design and thus constituted a powerful counterweight to the overwhelming pictorial and illustrative concerns of medieval art. At the same time, however, Augustinian aesthetics, further elaborated by Boethius, confined the entire creative process, from the first design to the completed composition, within the rigid limits not only of metaphysical doctrine but of certain mathematical laws. Feeling, aesthetic sensibility, according to Boethius, have an altogether subordinate function: they can at best arrive at a dim, confused notion of harmony, which reason alone can realize and represent. In short, the artist is not free to trust his intuition in the matter of proportion, the loftiest aesthetic principle of all; and he is not even free to choose between the mathematical formulae upon

5. *De ordine*, II, 39 ff. (*PL*, XXXII, 1013 f.)
6. *De libero Arbitrio*, II, 42 (*PL*, XXXII, 1263 f.). Augustine's definition of all artistic imagery as false or illusionary in Plato's sense is in *Soliloquiorum*, II, 18 (*PL*, XXXII, 893). Cf. Svoboda, p. 50.

which his proportions are to be based, since Augustinian (and Boethian) aesthetics recognize only the "perfect" ratios of Pythagorean mysticism.[7]

3. For medieval art, the greatest significance of this philosophy of beauty lies elsewhere. While disparaging imagery, while stripping the arts of nearly all their sensuous life, while imposing upon artistic creation authoritative regulations that for centuries were more generally and more timidly observed than we often realize, it was precisely this philosophy that invested Christian art with an extraordinary dignity. True beauty, according to Augustine, is anchored in metaphysical reality. Visible and audible harmonies are actually intimations of that ultimate harmony which the blessed will enjoy in the world to come. The place that harmony and proportion came to assume in the art and contemplation of the Christian West is not altogether unlike that which the icon, the sacred image, occupies in the art and thought of the Eastern Church. Here, and under the enduring inspiration of the Greek tradition, the ideal of ultimate beauty remained a visual one; it centered in the image of man. In the West, and under the influence of Augustine, beauty was conceived in musical terms, and even ultimate bliss as the enjoyment of an eternal symphony. And as the icon is thought to partake of the sacred reality it represents, so, according to Augustinian aesthetics, the musical consonances in visual proportions created by man partake of a sacred concord that transcends them.

Hence, the contemplation of such harmonies can actually lead the soul to the experience of God; hence, also, the truly regal place, the lofty mission, that the medieval Church assigned to the creation and enjoyment of artistic work of this kind. Recurrent iconoclastic waves have sought to limit this mission of medieval art without ever impairing it. On the contrary: the Christian iconoclast judges art from the viewpoint of ultimate theological reality; his attack has therefore always elicited the attempt to create a religious art in harmony with that reality. During the Christian Middle Ages every criticism of this kind has been followed by a style of ecclesiastical art more perfectly attuned to the religious experience of that generation.

7. See Augustine, *De vera religione*, XXX and XXXII (*PL*, XXXIV, 145 ff.). Riegl, *Spätrömische Kunstindustrie*, ch. 5, was the first to analyze Augustine's aesthetics in relation to the art of his time. He sees in this relationship a historical parallel only and does not explore either the metaphysical background of Augustinian aesthetics or the metaphysical reasons that account for the influence of these aesthetics upon medieval art. For the passages in Boethius, see *De musica*, II, 34; V, 1 (*PL*, LXIII, 1195, 1285 ff.).

This is particularly true for architecture, which, in the solemn language of its forms, conveys insights that transcend the world of imagery. In order to evoke those sentiments of reverence and awe that seemed to convey an intimation of the divine presence (sentiments that are so clearly conveyed in the words of King Henry I quoted in the Introduction), the ecclesiastical builder of the twelfth century relied increasingly on the Augustinian aesthetics of number and proportion.

The validity of this aesthetics remained unquestioned. In the *Retractions*, that singular work in which a renowned author at the end of his life examines his entire literary output with an eye not only to posterity but to eternity, Augustine himself spoke once more of the views he had expressed in *De musica*. Although he found much of the treatise unacceptable, he reaffirmed his belief that number may guide the intellect from the perception of created things to the invisible truth in God.[8]

Augustine's authority shaped the Middle Ages. The passage from the Wisdom of Solomon, "thou hast ordered all things in measure and number and weight," and the interpretation he had given to it became, as has rightly been observed, the keyword of the medieval world view. E. R. Curtius has recently shown how this world view, through number composition, is reflected in the content as well as the form of medieval poetry; [9] Manfred Bukofzer and others have traced its impact upon the development of medieval music.[10] It is not yet sufficiently realized that this impact is equally manifest in the visual arts, above all in architecture.

In a sense, this is true for the Middle Ages in general. In the second quarter of the twelfth century, however, Augustine's philosophy of beauty was seized upon by two powerful intellectual movements in France. The first of these centered in the group of eminent Platonists assembled at the Cathedral School of Chartres; the second movement, antispeculative and ascetic, emanated from the great monastic houses of Cîteaux and Clairvaux; its personification was St. Bernard. French civilization in the twelfth century may almost be described as

8. *Retractationum*, I, 11 (PL, XXXII, 600 ff.).
9. *European Literature and the Latin Middle Ages*, pp. 501 ff. Cf. H. Krings, "Das Sein und die Ordnung" (*DVLG*, XVIII, 1940); also V. F. Hopper, *Mediaeval Number Symbolism*, pp. 98 f.
10. "Speculative Thinking in Medieval Music" (*Sp*, XVII, 1942); cf. Spitzer, "Classical and Christian Ideas of World Harmony" (*Traditio*, II, 1944; III, 1945).

the synthesis of these two trends, which, though distinct, are nevertheless connected by close intellectual and personal ties, above all by the common heritage of St. Augustine. We must look more closely at the aesthetic views of the two movements. Their influence was such that they could not but affect contemporary art. Indeed, Gothic art would not have come into existence without the Platonic cosmology cultivated at Chartres and without the spirituality of Clairvaux.

The Platonism of Chartres was in many respects a true Renaissance movement.[11] The men who gathered there in the second quarter of the twelfth century were primarily interested in theological and cosmological questions, to be solved by means of a synthesis of Platonic and Christian ideas. These early scholastics approached their task in a spirit of tolerance and respect for the thought of antiquity that often reminds one of the "universal theism" of the fifteenth century; yet theirs was a strange Platonism indeed. It was almost entirely based on one single treatise, the *Timaeus*. Of this treatise but a fragment was available, of this fragment not the Greek original but only a garbled translation along with two commentaries, by Chalcidius and Macrobius, that viewed Plato's cosmology through the lenses of an eclectic and confused Neoplatonic mysticism. The Platonic fragment (and the two mediocre commentaries) were approached by the theologians of Chartres with nearly the same awe and respect as was the Book of Genesis. Both these works, it was believed, were in substantial agreement in what they revealed about the creation of the universe, indeed, about the Creator himself. If one considers that the theology and cosmology of Chartres resulted largely from the interpretation of two documents as different as Plato and the Bible, but approached with the notion that they must not contradict each other and that the interpreter must not contradict

11. On the School of Chartres, see Hauréau, *Mémoire sur quelques chanceliers de l'école de Chartres;* Clerval, *Les Écoles de Chartres au moyen-âge;* Poole, *Illustrations of the History of Medieval Thought and Learning,* ch. 4, and "The Masters of the School of Paris and Chartres in John of Salisbury's Time" (*EHR,* XXV, 1920); Liebeschuetz, "Kosmologische Motive in der Bildungswelt der Frühscholastik" (*Vorträge der Bibliothek Warburg,* 1923–24); Paré, Brunet, and Tremblay, *La Renaissance du XII° siècle. Les écoles et l'enseignement,* pp. 30 ff.; Haskins, "Some Twelfth Century Writers on Astronomy: the School of Chartres" (*Studies in the History of Science*), and *The Renaissance of the Twelfth Century,* pp. 101 ff., 135 f; Taylor, *The Mediaeval Mind,* I, ch. XII, 3; Parent, *La Doctrine de la création dans l'école de Chartres;* Gilson, *La Philosophie au moyen-âge,* pp. 259 ff. See also the stimulating, if somewhat one-sided, account in Heer, *Aufgang Europas,* pp. 297 ff.

either, one can but marvel at the wonderful and daring speculative system that resulted.

The aspects of the theology and cosmology of Chartres that interest us most in our present context are, first, the emphasis on mathematics, particularly geometry; and second, the aesthetic consequences of this thought. The masters of Chartres, like the Platonists and Pythagoreans of all ages, were obsessed with mathematics; it was considered the link between God and world, the magical tool that would unlock the secrets of both. The most influential exponent of the system, Thierry of Chartres,[12] hoped to find, with the help of geometry and arithmetic, the divine artist in his creation; [13] he went further and sought to explain the mystery of the Trinity by geometrical demonstration. The equality of the Three Persons is represented, according to him, by the equilateral triangle; the square unfolds the ineffable relation between Father and Son. Thierry recalls that Plato, "like his master Pythagoras," identified the metaphysical principles of monad and dyad with God and matter, respectively. God is thus supreme unity, and the Son is unity begotten by unity, as the square results from the multiplication of a magnitude with itself. Rightly, Thierry concludes, is the Second Person of the Trinity therefore called the first square.[14] It has been said that, under Thierry's influence, the School of Chartres

---

12. See Hauréau, *Notes et extraits de quelques manuscrits latins de la Bibliothèque Nationale*, I, 49, for the letter in which Thierry is called "utpote totius Europae philosophorum praecipuus"; also the dedication to Thierry of Bernard Silvestris' *De mundi universitate*, p. 5. On Bernard's relations to the School of Chartres, see Parent, p. 16.

13. See Hauréau, *Notes*, pp. 64 ff., in which Thierry introduces the passage from Wisd. of Sol. 11:20b as the primordial principle of creation: " . . . creatio numerorum rerum est creatio. . . . Prior igitur generatio numerorum facit tantummodo tetragonos, vel cubos, vel circulos, vel spheras, quod aequalitates dimensionem custodiunt. . . ." Even more significant is the following passage from *De sex dierum operibus:* "Adsint igitur quattuor genera rationum, quae ducunt hominem ad cognitionem creatoris, scilicet arithmeticae probationes et musicae et geometricae et astronomicae quibus instrumentis in hac theologia breviter utendum

est, ut et artificium creatoris in rebus appareat et, quod proposuimus, rationabiliter ostendatur" W. Jansen, "Der Kommentar des Clarembaldus von Arras zu Boethius' *De Trinitate*" (*Breslauer Studien zur historischen Theologie*, VIII, 1926), p. 108 *; cf. pp. 125 ff., 12 * and 62 *.

14. "Unitas ergo in eo quod gignit, Pater est, in eo quod gignitur Filius est. . . . Sed unitas semel tetrago natura prima est. . . . Sed haec tetrago natura est generatio Filii et, ut verum fateor, tetrago natura haec prima est generatio. . . . Et quoniam tetrago natura prima generatio Filii est et Filius tetragonus primus est." "Bene autem tetragonus Filio attribuitur quoniam figura haec perfectior ceteris propter laterum aequalitatem indicatur et, sicut in omnibus trianguli lateribus quaedam aequalitas est, triangula namque latera habet aequalia, ita quoque Filius essendi est aequalitas." *Librum hunc*, Jansen, p. 13 *. Almost identical is the passage by Thierry's pupil, Clarembaldus; see Jansen, p. 62 *.

attempted to change theology into geometry.[15] The attempt, which appears so strange to us, conveys a glimpse of what geometry meant to the twelfth century.

More daring than this theology, more dubious from the standpoint of orthodoxy, and more significant for the art historian is the cosmology of Chartres and the philosophy of beauty that it engendered.[16] In the *Timaeus* Plato describes the division of the world soul according to the ratios of the Pythagorean *tetractys*. The aesthetic, especially musical, connotations of this idea are underscored by Chalcidius, who points out that the division is effected according to the ratios of musical harmony.[17] He, as well as Macrobius,[18] insists that the Demiurge, by so dividing the world soul, establishes a cosmic order based on the harmony of musical consonance.

It was easy to fuse this notion with the Augustinian idea of a universe created "in measure and number and weight." As a result, the creation appeared as a symphonic composition. It is so described in the ninth century by Johannes Scotus Erigena,[19] and the idea was seized upon by the School of Chartres. William of Conches,[20] the teacher of John of Salisbury, and Abelard, who

15. "So ist (am Ende des) zwoelften Jahrhunderts die Theologie zur Mathematik, zur Geometrie geworden." Baumgartner, "Die Philosophie des Alanus de Insulis" (*BGPM*, 1896, II, 112). It is interesting to note that daring speculations of this kind did not arouse, at this time at least, the suspicions that other rationalist interpretations of Christian doctrine incurred. Clarembaldus of Arras (d. after 1170) wrote a fierce polemical treatise, *De Trinitate*, directed against Abelard and Gilbert de la Porrée and paying warm tribute to St. Bernard. The treatise, however, is almost a copy of the *Librum hunc*, which, according to Jansen (pp. 26 * ff.), is a work of Thierry.

16. On the aesthetics of the School of Chartres, see de Bruyne, *Études d'esthétique médiévale*, II, 255 ff.

17. *Platonis Timaeus*, XL–XLVI, pp. 106 ff. Another authority for this notion is Boethius; see *De musica*, I, 1 (*PL*, LXIII, 1168).

18. *Commentarius*, II, 1. See Schedler, "Die Philosophie des Macrobius und ihr Einfluss auf die Wissenschaft des christlichen Mittelalters" (*BGPM*, XIII, 1916); and for a critical summary of the Macrobius studies of Schedler and Duhem, Stahl, *Macrobius, Commentary on the Dream of Scipio*, pp. 39 ff. The

essentially musical character of Plato's cosmology is beyond question. Ahlvers, *Zahl und Klang bei Plato*, pp. 39 ff., suggests convincingly that even Plato's preference for his elementary triangles originates in the mysticism of the perfect consonances. See also the passage in Pseudo-Apuleius—who likewise influenced the twelfth century—"Musicen vero nosse nihil aliud esse, nisi cunctarum rerum ordinem scire, quaeque sit divina ratio sortita. Ordo enim rerum singularum in unum omnium artifice ratione collatus concentum quendam melo divino dulcissimum verissimumque conficiet." *Asclepius*, XIII (*Opera omnia*, ed. Hildebrand, II, 294).

19. *De divisione naturae*, II, 31; III, 3 and 6; and V, 36 (*PL*, CXXII, 602, 630 ff., 965). On Erigena's concept of music, see Handschin, "Die Musikanschauung des Johan Scotus Erigena" (*DVLG*, V, 1927). On Erigena's influence on the School of Chartres, see Parent, p. 48. The idea of the cosmic symphony occurs once more in a magnificent passage in the *De anima* of the Platonizing William of Auvergne. See below, p. 125.

20. See Flatten, *Die Philosophie des Wilhelm von Conches*, pp. 126 ff.: "Item (anima mundi) dicitur constare ex musicis consonantiis . . .

seems to have studied mathematics under Thierry and whose cosmological views are those of the School of Chartres,[21] both identify the Platonic world soul with the Holy Ghost in its creative and ordering effect upon matter; and they conceive this effect as musical consonance. The harmony it establishes throughout the cosmos is represented, however, not only as a musical composition but also as an artistic one, more specifically, as a work of architecture. The ease with which the transition from the musical to the architectural sphere is here effected will not surprise us in view of the sistership of the two in Platonic and Augustinian thought. But for the theologians of Chartres, the notion of the cosmos as a work of architecture and of God as its architect has a special significance, since they assume a twofold act of creation: the creation of chaotic matter and the creation of cosmos out of chaos. Since the Greek word *kosmos* signified ornament as well as order, it was plausible to view matter as the building material, the creation proper as the "adorning" of matter by the artful imposition of an architectural order. In the Platonic cosmology, moreover, the masters of Chartres could detect the design and method according to which the divine architect had built the universe, the cosmic temple, as Macrobius calls it.[22]

In the *Timaeus* the primary bodies of which the world is to be composed are conceived as building materials [23]

ready to be put together by the builder's hand. This composition is effected by means of fixing the quantities in the perfect geometrical proportions of squares and cubes ($1:2:4:8$ and $1:3:9:27$)—the same proportions that also determine the composition of the world soul. According to this composition the world's body, consisting of the four primary bodies, whose quantities are limited and linked in the most perfect proportions, is in unity and concord with itself and hence will not suffer dissolution from any internal disharmony of its parts; the bond is simply geometrical proportion.

In this view, the perfect proportions, the beauty of which we may admire in musical and architectural compositions, also acquire an explicit technical or

quia res secundum convenientias harum consonantium dicuntur esse dispositae." Cf. Parent, pp. 22, 42 ff.

21. *Theologia Christiana*, V (*Opera*, ed. V. Cousin, II, 379 ff.). On Abelard's relation to the School of Chartres, see Poole, *Illustrations*, pp. 314 f.; and Liebeschuetz, "Kosmologische Motive," p. 115.

22. *Commentarius*, I, 14 (p. 539). On the

twofold act of creation, see Parent, p. 42. For a similar notion, see Hugh of St.-Victor, *De sacramentis Christianae fidei*, I, 1, 6 (*PL*, CLXXVI, 169).

23. For the following, see Cornford, *Plato's Cosmology*, II, 59 ff. For the tradition and study of Platonic dialogues during the twelfth century, see Klibansky, *The Continuity of the Platonic Tradition during the Middle Ages*, p. 27.

tectonic function: they chain and knit together the different elements of which the cosmos is composed. William of Conches quite correctly interprets the Platonic passage in this sense.[24] Here, then, perfect proportion is thought to account for both the beauty and the stability of the cosmic edifice.

What was the significance of these views for the history of architecture? They were, in the first place, bound to affect the concept of what an architect is. The term architect is rarely used during the earlier Middle Ages; where it does occur, it denotes either clerics responsible for a building—regardless of whether they merely commissioned it or were actually interested and experienced in architecture—or simple masons. On the basis of this evidence, Professor Pevsner concluded a few years ago that the professional architect, in the classical sense (which is also the modern one), hardly existed in the Middle Ages.[25] Pevsner suggested that the revival of the term in the mid-thirteenth century coincided exactly with the sociological change that transformed the humble master mason into the architect of the thirteenth century, no longer considered a mere craftsman but the "scientist" or *theoreticus* of his art.

There may be a good deal of truth in all this. We shall see in Chapter 4 how wrong it would be to impute to medieval building practices our own notions of a highly specialized professionalism. But surely Professor Pevsner is wrong when he seeks to connect the changing significance of the term "architect" with the introduction of Aristotle's *Metaphysics*—where the term is defined in our sense—to Western thought after 1200. Quite apart from the writings of Vitruvius, known and respected since Carolingian times,[26] it was Augustine

24. Flatten, p. 119. We still find this cosmology in the *Roman de la rose*. See Paré, *Le "Roman de la rose" et la scholastique courtoise*, vv. 16, 747 (pp. 197 ff.); 20, 312 (pp. 53 ff.).
25. "The Term 'Architect' in the Middle Ages" (*Sp*, XVII, 1942); Colombier, *Les Chantiers des cathédrales*, ch. IV; Swartwout, *The Monastic Craftsman*, p. 35.
26. On Vitruvius in the Middle Ages, see Sandys, *A History of Classical Scholarship*, I, 481 ff.; Manitius, *Geschichte der lateinischen Literatur des Mittelalters*, III, 118, 550, 710 ff.; II, 274 f., 313, 499, 763 ff.; Mortet, "La Mesure des colonnes à la fin de l'époque romaine," "La Mesure et les proportions des

colonnes antiques d'après quelques compilations et commentaires antérieurs au XIIᵉ siècle," and "Observations comparées sur la forme des colonnes à l'époque romaine" (*BEC*, LVII, 1896, and LIX, 1898); Haskins, *Renaissance*, p. 330; Juettner, *Ein Beitrag zur Geschichte der Bauhütte und des Bauwesens im Mittelalter*, pp. 22 ff.; Koch, *Vom Nachleben des Vitruv*, pp. 14 ff.; also the recent observations of Beseler and Roggenkamp, *Die Michaeliskirche in Hildesheim*, with regard to the probable use made, in the building of St. Michael's, Hildesheim, of Vitruvius, a Carolingian manuscript of which was owned by the abbot of this great monastery. Swartwout, p. 4, is certainly wrong in asserting

who kept alive the classical definition of the architect. His distinction between the mere practitioner and the true architect who deliberately applies scientific principles occurs in at least three different treatises, all studied and admired throughout the Middle Ages. While this definition permitted the medieval application of the term "architect" to even the mere craftsman, it left no doubt that only the "scientist" who had mastered the liberal arts was truly entitled to it. Boethius, moreover, had illustrated the intellectual distinction by a metaphor that was bound to have its effect upon the social status of the medieval artist. He had compared the practical execution of a work of art to a slave, the science that should guide such work to a ruler. This meant, of course, that what counted in a work of art was not the humble knowledge of the craft but the theoretical science that laid down the laws to which the craft had to conform. It is no wonder, therefore, that we find so many "architects" among medieval ecclesiastics: the "science" of architecture was a purely theoretical one—the development of the plan in accordance with geometrical laws—and the knowledge of the quadrivium that it required was for a long time and with relatively few exceptions the privilege of clerics.[27]

But it was the School of Chartres that dramatized the image of the architect (a century before Aristotle's *Metaphysics* could have done so) by depicting God as a master builder, a *theoreticus* creating without toil or effort by means of an architectural science that is essentially mathematical. The Platonists of Chartres, moreover, also defined the laws according to which the cosmic edifice had been composed. Toward the end of the twelfth century, Alan of Lille (Alanus ab Insulis) described the creation of the world. To Alan, the *doctor universalis*, the thought of Chartres owes perhaps its widest influence and diffusion. According to him, God is the artful architect (*elegans architectus*) who builds the cosmos as his regal palace, composing and harmonizing the

that Vitruvius was never taught in monastic schools. The evidence adduced by Mortet (in the papers listed) shows to what extent architectural instructions, at least in the Vitruvian tradition, were considered part of the geometrical curriculum.

27. There are, of course, notable exceptions, such as the nobleman Ailbert, who studied the liberal arts at the Cathedral School of Tournai, even becoming master of this school and subsequently a renowned architect who, in 1108, built the Church of Rolduc. See Rolland, "La cathédrale romane de Tournai et les courants architecturaux" (*Revue belge d'archéologie et d'histoire de l'art*, III, 1937). For the Boethian passage just quoted, see *De musica*, II, 34 (*PL*, LXIII, 1195).

variety of created things by means of the "subtle chains" of musical consonance.[28]

The first Gothic cathedrals were rising when these lines were written. It is most unlikely that the views of Alan, who fully deserved his dual fame as a poet as well as a thinker, did not reflect—if they did not actually influence—the aesthetic philosophy and the architectural practice of his age. A later thinker, Alexander of Hales (d. 1245), actually uses the example of the *coementarius*, who "measures and numbers and weighs" in composing his building, to illustrate the harmonious composition of everything beautiful.[29] The architecture of the twelfth and thirteenth centuries offers ample evidence, as we shall see, that the "musical proportions" employed by Alan's divine builder were indeed considered the most nearly perfect by the medieval architects also.

The aesthetic aspects of this philosophy of proportions were taken over from Augustine. He, as well as his pupil, Boethius—for the School of Chartres

28. *De planctu naturae* (PL, CCX, 453). Mathematical notions dominate Alan's cosmology and aesthetics throughout. De Bruyne (*Études*, II, 292) has called attention to the pre-eminent place that Alan assigns to *concordia;* see also his description of arithmetic in the sculptor's workshop, *Anticlaudianus*, III, 4 (PL, CCX, 514), and his reference to the Creator as "Omnia sub numero claudens sub pondere sistens / Singula, sub stabili mensura cuncta coercens," V, 5 (PL, CCX, 534). For a similar image, see Bernard Silvestris (*De mundi universitate*, I, 1, 18 ff.; 2, 78 ff.), who may be identical with the Bernard who appears around 1156 as Chancellor of the School of Chartres; cf. Poole, "Masters," and Parent, p. 16. On Alan and his influence, see Hauréau, *Mémoire;* Baumgartner, "Die Philosophie des Alanus de Insulis" (BGPM, II, 1896); Huizinga, "Über die Verknüpfung des Poetischen mit dem Theologischen bei Alanus de Insulis" (*Mededeelingen der Kgl. Akademie van Weetenschappen, Afdeeling Letterkunde*, LXXIV); Cornog, *The Anticlaudian of Alain de Lille*, pp. 9 ff. On Alan's relation to the School of Chartres, see Parent, p. 110, and Raynaud de Lage, *Alain de Lille, poète du XIIᵉ siècle*, pp. 69, 165. The image of the "house of nature" composed according to the consonances of music appears elsewhere. See the *Metamorphosis*

*Goliae Episcopi*, p. 21. For an illustration of the idea, see Muetherich, "Ein Illustrationszyklus zum Anticlaudianus des Alanus ab Insulis" (MJ, III, series 2, 1951). The image also occurs, in a purely theoretical and allegorical context, in Gerhoh of Reichersberg, *Opusculum de aedificio Dei*, I (PL, CXCIV, 1191 ff.): ". . . potentissimum fabrum, cujus filius Christus esse non dubitatur, qui in Evangelio filius fabri appellatur"; "Haec Domus tunc coepit aedificari, quando creavit Deus coelum et terram." Interpreting the creation of Eve as a type of the Church, Gerhoh continues: "mulier vero, quoniam Ecclesiam significat, non plasmari sed aedificari dicitur, ut videlicet, cum eam a Domino aedificatam audias, mulierem cogitans, aedificium intelligas." On Gerhoh, see Manitius, III, 61 ff.

29. *Summa universae theologiae*, I, Inq. I, Tract. 1113, 110 (ed. Quaracchi, I, 172). On the authenticity of this part of the *Summa*, see ibid., IV, 1 (pp. ccclv ff.). Robert of Melun, on the other hand, takes pains to point out that the creation of the world ought not to be imagined "eo modo quo lapis in fundamento domus iacitur,' since God not merely uses but creates the primordial matter. The distinction only shows how current the architectural image was. *Sententie*, I, I, 19 (*Oeuvres*, ed. R. M. Martin, Louvain, 1947, III, 1, p. 211).

and the Middle Ages in general the greatest mathematical authority [30]—taught, moreover, how to visualize the perfect consonances in geometrical terms. Boethius points out that the proportions of double and half, triple and third— those, in other words, that yield the perfect consonances on the monochord— are as readily perceived visually as they are acoustically, for, he continues, echoing Plato, "the ear is affected by sounds in quite the same way as the eye is by optical impressions." [31] Boethius does not confine this doctrine of synesthesia only to proportions of line or surface; he discovers "geometrical harmony" in the cube, since the number of its surfaces, angles, and edges, $6:8:12$, contains the ratios of octave, fifth, and fourth.[32]

But the Platonists of Chartres expounded not only the aesthetic excellence of these proportions but their technical importance as well. We have seen that they maintained, with the *Timaeus*, that the indissoluble stability of the cosmos is grounded in perfect proportion.

It is here that the necessary impact of this cosmology upon the architecture and architectural procedure of the twelfth and thirteenth centuries becomes apparent. Since art is an image of nature, Professor de Bruyne asks, "Must not the ideal church be constructed according to the laws of the universe?" In other words, application of the "perfect proportions," determined by rigid geometrical means, became a technical necessity as well as an aesthetic postulate if the building was to be stable as well as beautiful.

We now understand why the High Middle Ages defined and practiced architecture as applied geometry; [33] why the experts at Milan paid the same

30. Parent, p. 111, calls Boethius, with Plato, the most important source of the thought of Chartres.

31. *De musica*, I, 32 (*PL*, LXIII, 1194). The classical tradition of representing numbers by geometrical figures was also known to the Middle Ages. See Macrobius, *Commentarius*, II, 2; and esp. Boethius, *De arithmetica*, II, 6 (*PL*, LXIII, 1121).

32. ". . . Omnes autem in hac dispositione symphonias musicas invenimus." *De arithmetica*, II, 49 (*PL*, LXIII, 1158). For antecedents of this notion, see Cantor, *Vorlesungen über Geschichte der Mathematik*, p. 154.

33. See Dominicus Gundissalinus, *De di-*

*visione philosophiae* (*c.* 1140–50), in which every artist or craftsman is defined as "secundum geometriam practicans. Ipse enim per semetipsum format lineas, superficies, quadraturas, rotunditates et cetera in corpore materiae, que subiecta est arti suae" (*BGPM*, 1906, IV, 102 ff.). That Gundissalinus is merely describing common practice is obvious on every page of Villard de Honnecourt's model book. For the definition of architecture as applied geometry, see also the curious *Constituciones artis gemetriae secundum Euclydem* (British Museum Bibl. Reg. 17A1), a late fourteenth-century poem in which the art of geometry is treated as a synonym for the mason's art. The poem begins, "Hic incipiunt astonishing tribute to this discipline as had Augustine and Boethius; why the evidence of Gothic architecture itself seems to indicate that all statical problems were actually solved by purely geometrical methods.[34] And we also understand the lofty claim that the great architects of the Gothic period meant to convey *Plate 6b* in having themselves depicted, compass and measuring rod in hand, as geometricians.[35] Boethius had singled out the mason's stone ax as symbolic of an art

constitutiones artis gemetrie secundum Euclyde" and describes the mason's craft as derived from geometry and the most noble of all crafts. Similarly, the Cooke MS., also in the British Museum (Add. MS. 23198), dating from 1430–40 but copying an older work. Its author "used a treatise . . . on geometry, purporting to give a history of that science and emphasizing its application to masonry." Geometry, according to him, is the indisputable principle of all the sciences. And since the mason's craft is applied geometry, it is also the most important of the arts. Both documents have been published by Knoop, Jones, and Hamer, *The Two Earliest Masonic MSS.* See also Ghyka, *Le Nombre d'or*, II, 65; Harvey, *The Gothic World*, pp. 28, 37, 47. Hugh Libergier, on his tomb in Reims Cathedral, appears in an architectural frame composed of a rectangle "according to true measure" and an equilateral triangle. He is represented, moreover, with the tools of the geometrician (see below, p. 225, n. 102). His proportion compass seems to be based on the golden section. Colombier's denial that the proportion compass existed prior to the Renaissance (pp. 66 f.) is unfounded. The proportion compass was already known to the Romans. See the instrument, from Pompeii, in the Museo Nazionale at Naples, reproduced by Moessel, *Vom Geheimnis der Form und der Urform des Seins*, p. 374. Libergier's compass is clearly quite different from that represented on one of the stalls of St. Peter's at Poitiers (Colombier, fig. 14).

34. It is significant that where arithmetical problems did arise, as they did during the building of Milan Cathedral, a professional mathematician had to be called in. See Frankl, "The Secret of the Medieval Masons" (*AB*, XXVII, 1945), and the illuminating appendix to this article by Panofsky. It is difficult to say whether or not the method used for computing rib-vault thrusts by a Spanish sixteenth-century architect, Rodrigo Gil de Hontanon (see Kubler, "A Late Gothic Computation of Rib-Vault Thrusts" [*GBA*, XXVI, 1945]), represents medieval practice. Advanced Gothic may have invited rule-of-thumb calculations of this type.

35. See the remarks of Ueberwasser, *Von Maasz und Macht der alten Kunst*. Notes 27 and 33, above, show to what extent even the social position of the master was determined by the dignity that the Platonic world view ascribed to geometry. It is quite true that the Middle Ages themselves drew a sharp distinction between the simple practice and the speculative knowledge of geometry. See Mortet, "Note historique sur l'emploi de procédés matériels et d'instruments usités dans la géometrie pratique du moyen-âge" (*Congrès International de Philosophie*, 2nd session, Geneva, 1904, pp. 925 ff.). Every mason was in a sense a practitioner of this discipline; the architect, however, had to master it "scientifically." It is significant that the geometrical knowledge exhibited, and even the problems posed, by Villard de Honnecourt are no different from what a scholar like Adelard of Bath has to say in his characterization of the different arts, *De eodem et diverso* (*BGPM*, IV, 1906, pp. 23 ff.). That knowledge, however, and the metaphysical framework from which it was inseparable, could be acquired in cathedral and monastic schools only. Pevsner, p. 558, quotes Hugh of St.-Victor (*PL*, CLXXVI, 760) and Otto of Freising (*MGH SS*, XX, 396 ff.) as witnesses to the fact that the twelfth century excluded the craftsman, even the architect, "ab honestioribus et liberioribus studiis," and considered his profession as fit for "plebei et ignobilium filii" only. Can we attribute general sociological significance to these statements? I have earlier (n. 27) cited the example of a nobleman who, early in the twelfth century, became an architect, having previously studied the quadrivium. It is quite likely that it was precisely his knowledge of the liberal arts that raised the architect, even socially, high above the simple artisans who worked under

that can only create a "confused" shape, whereas he chose precisely the compass to represent an art that truly "comprehends the whole." [36] And it was with the compass that God himself came to be represented in Gothic art and literature as the Creator who composed the universe according to geometrical laws.[37] It is only by observing these same laws that architecture became a science in Augustine's sense. And in submitting to geometry the medieval architect felt that he was imitating the work of his divine master.

*Plate 6a*

We do not grasp this all-important connection by calling the cathedral an image or a symbol of the cosmos; the term "symbol" has become too vapid today. Designed in an attempt to reproduce the structure of the universe, not unlike the great scientific experiments of the modern age in this respect, the cathedral is perhaps best understood as a "model" of the medieval universe. That may give us a better idea of the speculative significance of these great edifices, a significance that transcends their beauty and practical purpose as a place of public worship.

Above all, however, the cathedral was the intimation of ineffable truth. The medieval cosmos was theologically transparent. The Creation appeared as

him. It is as scientists, not as practitioners, of geometry that the great Gothic architects had themselves depicted, and we recall with what insistence the masters at Milan referred to geometry as a science. Rziha's thesis (*Studien über Steinmetz-Zeichen*, p. 38) that the signs of the master masons are derived from geometrical figures seems entirely convincing to me. The medieval architect could not have expressed more succinctly the abiding principle of his profession. Finally, it may be worth noting that it is a theologian of the School of Chartres, William of Conches, who, already in the twelfth century, defines architecture along with medicine (which was taught at Chartres and which he himself had studied there) as an "honest" profession, at least "his quorum ordini conveniunt." See Holmberg, *Das Moralium Dogma des Guillaume de Conches*, p. 48.

36. *De musica* V, 1 (*PL*, LXIII, 1287). For the meaning of "aciculus" as the stonemason's tool, see *Thesaurus linguae latinae* and Du Cange, *Glossarium mediae et infimae latinitatis; Editio nova*, s.v. "asciculus."

37. The earliest painted representation

known to me is the famous miniature in the Bible moralisée, No. 15, in Vienna (Cod. 2554, fol. 1). The codex was executed for Thibault V, Count of Champagne (1237-70), or for his wife, Isabella, a daughter of Louis IX. See *Beschreibendes Verzeichnis der illuminierten Handschriften in Österreich*, VIII, 7, p. 14. See also Rushforth, *Medieval Christian Imagery*, p. 150. The image was probably inspired by Proverbs 8:27: "When he prepared the heavens, I was there: when he set a compass [circle] upon the face of the depth." It is significant that the passage does not seem to have found a reflection in the iconography of the creation until the thirteenth century. Attention may also be called to the representation (after Ezekiel 40:3) of Christ as an architect, rebuilding Jerusalem after the Captivity, in the relief under the statue of Ezekiel on the west façade of Amiens Cathedral. See Durand, *Description abrégée de la cathédrale d'Amiens*, p. 60; Lefrançois-Pillion, *Maîtres d'oeuvre et tailleurs de pierre des cathédrales*, p. 159; and Katzenellenbogen, "Prophets of the West Façade of the Cathedral of Amiens" (*GBA*, series 6, XL, 1952).

the first of God's self-revelations, the Incarnation of the Word as the second.[38] Between these two theophanies medieval man perceived innumerable mystical correspondences, and only he who understood these correspondences understood the ultimate meaning and structure of the cosmos. Accordingly, the musical harmony that the Platonists of Chartres discovered in the universe was primarily not a physical but a metaphysical principle, maintaining the order of nature but far more clearly present in the world to come. For Adam's fall on earth had obscured the theological order of the cosmos, its origin and end in what in Augustinian terms is the "unison" with God. That order, however, is still manifest in the harmony of the heavenly spheres. Hence the medieval

Plate 7

38. "Duo enim simulacra erant proposita homini, in quibus invisibilia videre potuisset: unum naturae et unum gratiae. Simulacrum naturae erat species hujus mundi. Simulacrum autem gratiae erat humanitas Verbi. . . . Per simulacra igitur naturae, creator tantum significabatur, in simulacris vero gratie praesens Deus ostendebatur. . . . Haec est distantia theologiae hujus mundi ab illa, quae divina nominatur theologia. Impossibile enim est invisibilia, nisi per visibilia demonstrari." Hugh of St.-Victor, *Commentaria in hierarchiam caelestem*, I, 1 (*PL*, CLXXV, 926). Elsewhere Hugh develops this idea further by dwelling on the parallelism between the works of creation and redemption. See *De sacramentis Christianae fidei*, I, 1, 28 (*PL*, CLXXVI, 204). This parallelism in turn suggests to him the idea of man as a microcosm, a center of the universe: "Necesse autem fuit ut visibilium conditio ita ordinaretur, quatenus homo in eis foris agnosceret quale esset invisibile bonum, quod intus quaerere deberet, hoc est, ut sub se videret, quid supra se appeteret." *Eruditionis Didascalicae*, VII (*PL*, CLXXVI, 811 f.). The whole idea may not be without significance for the symbolism of church architecture. The cathedral, as we have seen, is an image of the cosmos. But it is also an image of Christ, who had himself compared his death and resurrection to the destruction and rebuilding of the Temple. Consistent with this idea, the Middle Ages perceived in the church edifice an image of Christ crucified; see Mortet and Deschamps, *Recueil*, I, 159 f. It is this correspondence which accounts for the anthropomorphism of terminology that, for example, prompts Peter of Celle to refer not only to the chevet of his church as *caput*, but to the nave as its *venter* (*PL*, CCII, 610). In Vitruvius, moreover, the medieval builder found the notion that the temple, in its proportions, ought to follow the proportions of the human body (III, 1): "ecclesiae forma humani corporis partionibus respondet," writes Durandus of Mende (*Rationale Div. Offic.*, I, 14), and in the fifteenth century Francesco di Giorgio rendered this notion explicit by inscribing the human figure into the ground plan of a church. See Wittkower, *Architectural Principles in the Age of Humanism*, p. 13. The idea that the church can be at once the image of Christ and heaven appears paradoxical to us. But already in the *Clavis Melitonis* we find the correlation of Temple, Christ, and heaven (Pitra, *Spicilegium Solesmense* III, 184), and the symbolic triad recurs frequently in the Middle Ages. The symbolism is rendered possible by the parallelism between creation and redemption: between the cosmos and Christ, who is both the Word Incarnate and the perfect man in whom the universe centers. Attention has been called to the similarity between thirteenth-century representations of the microcosm and contemporary representations of Christ on the Cross. See Singer, "The Scientific Views and Visions of St. Hildegard" (*Studies in the History and Method of Science*, I, 37 f.). The theology of measure and number and weight found in proportion the link between macrocosm and microcosm, and it was in virtue of its proportions that the church could be understood as an image of Christ as well as of the cosmos.

inclination, familiar to every reader of Dante, to connect the realm of the stars with the celestial habitations of the blessed. The same tendency explains the seemingly dual symbolism of the cathedral, which is at once a "model" of the cosmos and an image of the Celestial City. If the architect designed his sanctuary according to the laws of harmonious proportion, he did not only imitate the order of the visible world, but conveyed an intimation, inasmuch as that is possible to man, of the perfection of the world to come.

This symbolic interconnection between cosmos, Celestial City, and sanctuary is well explained in a passage of Abelard, whose ties with the School of Chartres were mentioned earlier, and whose titanic claim to encompass with his reason everything that is on earth and in heaven so deeply shocked St. Bernard.[39] After identifying the Platonic world soul with world harmony, he first interprets the ancient notion of a music of the spheres as referring to the "heavenly habitations" where angels and saints "in the ineffable sweetness of harmonic modulation render eternal praise to God." [40] Then, however, Abelard transposes the musical image into an architectural one: he relates the Celestial Jerusalem to the terrestrial one, more specifically to the Temple built by Solomon as God's "regal palace." [41] No medieval reader could have failed to notice with what emphasis every Biblical description of a sacred edifice, particularly those of Solomon's Temple, of the Heavenly Jerusalem, and of the vision of Ezekiel, dwells on the measurements of these buildings. To these measurements Abelard gives a truly Platonic significance. Solomon's Temple, he remarks, was pervaded by the divine harmony as were the celestial spheres. What suggested this notion to him is the fact that the main dimensions of the Temple, as given in I Kings 6, yield again the proportions of the perfect consonances. (The length, width, and height of the edifice are given as 60, 20, and

---

39. The impassioned passage depicts the great enemy as a caricature of a microcosmic man: "Qui dum omnium quae sunt in coelo sursum, et quae in terra deorsum, nihil, praeter solum, Nescio, nescire dignatur; ponit in coelum os suum, et scrutatur alta Dei, rediensque ad nos refert verba ineffabilia, quae non licet homini loqui et dum paratus est de omnibus reddere rationem." *Tract. de erroribus Abaelardi*, I (*PL*, CLXXXII, 1055).

40. Abelard, *Theol. Christ.*, I, 5 (*Opera, ed.* V. Cousin, Paris, 1859, II, 384).

41. Abelard found the source of this analogy in the Bible: "Thou hast commanded me to build a temple upon thy holy mount . . . a resemblance of the holy tabernacle, which thou hast prepared from the beginning." Wisd. of Sol. 9:8. See also Pitra, III, 183: "Tabernaculi nomine coelum designatur." For Solomon's Temple as a type of the Heavenly City, see Sauer, *Die Symbolik des Kirchengebäudes*, p. 109.

30 cubits respectively; those of the cella as 20, 20, 20; those of the aula as 40, 20, 30; and those of the porch as 20 and 10.) [42]

Now, the mention of the Temple of Solomon, the mystical image of heaven, in this connection is very significant. The Temple, as already mentioned, was considered a prototype of the Christian sanctuary; as such, it is frequently mentioned in medieval documents.[43] A famous masonic poem even insists that Solomon actually "taught" architecture in a manner "but little different from that used today" and that this science was directly transmitted to France.[44] In particular, the dimensions of the Solomonic Temple seem to have been viewed as ideal, because divinely inspired, proportions for the Christian sanctuary also. It is a striking and moving testimony to this conviction that a renowned Renaissance architect, Philibert Delorme—whose knowledge of Gothic building practices, however, was profound—voices toward the end of his life his regret that he neglected in his projects those admirable proportions which God, "the great architect of the Universe," revealed to Noah for the ark, to Moses for the Tabernacle, and to Solomon for the Temple.[45]

So far as I know, Abelard is the first medieval writer to suggest that the proportions of the Temple were those of the musical consonances and that it was this "symphonic" perfection that made it an image of heaven. The passage reflects most revealingly the influence of Platonic cosmology upon Christian eschatology of the twelfth century. The Biblical description of the Heavenly City is pervaded and transfigured by the vision of an ineffable harmony. The mystical contemplation of the age, no less than its philosophical speculation, seems to be under the spell of an essentially musical experience. Is not the same trend reflected in monumental art? The Gothic sanctuary, as we have seen, replaces with the graphic expression of the structural system the painted representation of heaven that adorned the Romanesque apse. In the singular perfection of its proportions, this ordered system presented an object of mystical

42. On the proportions of the Solomonic Temple as likely models for those used by medieval church builders, see Trezzini, *Retour à l'architecture*, p. 16.

43. It was pointed out earlier that the liturgy itself compares the Christian church to the Solomonic Temple (see above, p. 11). See also the sequence *In dedicatione ecclesiae*, ascribed to Adam of St.-Victor: "Rex Salomon fecit templum . . ." (*Analecta Hymnica*, LV, p. 35); Walter of Châtillon's "Templum veri Salomonis dedicatur hodie . . ." (Strecker, *Die Gedichte Walters von Châtillon*, p. 13); and Pitra, III, 184 ff. Equally telling are the frequent references in masonic documents to the building of the Solomonic Temple (see above, n. 33).

44. The Cooke MS. as cited above, n. 33.

45. See the quotation below, p. 228, n. 108.

contemplation that for the Platonists must have surpassed by far the beauty of those naïve paintings. Whereas the Romanesque painter could but deceive the senses with the *illusion* of ultimate reality, the Gothic builder applied the very laws that order heaven and earth. The first Gothic, in the aesthetic, technical, and symbolic aspects of its design, is intimately connected with the metaphysics of "measure and number and weight." It seeks to embody the vision that the Platonists of Chartres had first unfolded, no longer content with the mere image of truth but insisting upon the realization of its laws. Seen in this light, the creation of Gothic marks and reflects an epoch in the history of Christian thought, the change from the mystical to the rational approach to truth, the dawn of Christian metaphysics.

The musical mysticism of the Platonic tradition was, at this time, not the exclusive property of Chartres. Owing to the authority of Augustine, it played an important part in the spirituality of the Cistercian movement and of its leader, Bernard of Clairvaux. As was stated at the beginning of this chapter, this movement contributed as much to the formation of French civilization in the twelfth century as did the School of Chartres. And its influence upon the arts of the time, if not greater, was certainly far more direct and is, therefore, more palpable for us. Thierry of Chartres, though considered by many the most renowned philosopher of Europe, wielded neither the enormous political and spiritual influence of his contemporary, St. Bernard, nor a pen as fiercely polemical as was that of the Abbot of Clairvaux. It is time to consider Bernard's thought in its impact upon the philosophy and practice of art during the twelfth century.

Bernard's artistic views are usually described as those of a puritan. They are, in point of fact, Augustinian. No other author exerted a greater influence upon Bernard's theological formation than Augustine. He considered the Bishop of Hippo the greatest theological authority after the Apostles; with Augustine, Bernard writes at the height of his controversy with Abelard, he wants to err, as well as to know.[46] And musical mysticism could claim Augustine as its greatest spokesman. It not only permeated his cosmological and

46. *Tract. de Bapt.*, II, 8 (*PL*, CLXXXII,    1036); see Martin, "La Formation théologique
de St. Bernard" (*ABSS*, I, 234 ff.).

aesthetic speculations but reached to the core of his theological experience. Thus, in his treatise *De Trinitate*, Augustine meditates on the mystery of redemption by which the death of Christ atoned for man's twofold death of body and, through sin, of soul. As the Bishop of Hippo ponders this "congruence," this "correspondence," this "consonance" of one and two, musical experience gradually takes hold of his imagination, and suddenly it dawns upon him that *harmony* is the proper term for Christ's work of reconciliation. This is not the place, Augustine exclaims, to demonstrate the value of the octave that seems so deeply implanted in our nature—by whom if not by Him who created us?— that even the musically and mathematically uneducated immediately respond to it. Augustine feels that the consonance of the octave, the musical expression of the ratio 1:2, conveys even to human ears the meaning of the mystery of redemption.[47]

The wonderfully vivid passage suggests an aesthetic experience radically different from our own. It was not that the enjoyment of musical consonances subsequently led Augustine to interpret these as symbols of theological truth. On the contrary, the consonances were for him echoes of such truth, and the enjoyment that the senses derive from musical harmony (and its visual equivalent, proportion) is our intuitive response to the ultimate reality that may defy human reason but to which our entire nature is mysteriously attuned.

This experience determines the medieval attitude toward music. It accounts for the fact that the study and cultivation of music was looked upon with favor even, nay, especially, in monasteries of strict ascetic observation. A typical example is that of Othlon of St. Emmeram (1032–70). In embracing the most austere monastic ideal, he had renounced all his former humanistic

47. *De Trinitate*, IV, 2:4 (*PL*, XLII, 889). On the wide distribution of this work in the Middle Ages, see Wilmart, "La Tradition des grands ouvrages de St. Augustin," *Miscellanea Agostiniana*, II, 269 ff.; the library at Troyes (MS. 32) preserves the remains of the twelfth-century catalogue of the library of Clairvaux. It contained, of St. Augustine's works, the first part of the *Retractions*, *De Trinitate*, *De musica*, *De vera religione*, etc.; there were also works by Boethius (including the commentary by William of Conches), Johannes Scotus Erigena, Hugh of St.-Victor, and "Alani Cisterciensis." The core of this library, as Dom Wilmart points out, refutes the legend of paucity of books in Cistercian libraries. The collection at Clairvaux, moreover, was undoubtedly created by St. Bernard himself. "La bibliothèque de Clairvaux, telle que nous la voyons au terme du XIIᵉ siècle, ne peut qu'être la création du premier abbé de Clairvaux; il a dû lui-même fixer le programme selon lequel elle s'est peu à peu organisée et achevée." Wilmart, "L'Ancienne Bibliothèque de Clairvaux" (*Société académique . . . de l'Aube*, LV, LVI, 1916). Cf. H. d'Arbois de Jubainville, *Études sur l'état intérieur des abbayes cisterciennes*, p. 109.

interests. But arithmetic and music retained their hold over his imagination. In his writings he uses them to convey divine secrets to his fellow monks, to prepare them for the life in a world to come. Even the order prevailing among the heavenly hosts, he writes, corresponds to the intervals of the perfect consonances.[48]

Bernard's attitude toward music was quite similar. He was profoundly musical. The *Regulae de arte musica* by his pupil, the Abbot Guy of Charlieu, which occupy an important place in the history of twelfth-century music, were, as the author acknowledges, written at Bernard's request and actually embody his views.[49] The Abbot of Clairvaux was, as Father Luddy observes, an Augustinian even in musical matters.[50] Something of a composer himself, he was once invited by the abbot of another monastery to compose an office for the feast of St. Victor. Bernard's reply is noteworthy. What he demands of ecclesiastical music is that it "radiate" truth; that it "sound" the great Christian virtues. Music, he thinks, should please the ear in order to move the heart; it should, by striking a golden mean between the frivolous and the harsh, wholesomely affect man's entire nature.[51]

Now these are hardly the views of a puritan. Bernard must have responded to musical experience with unusual sensitivity. He is fond of describing even heavenly bliss in musical terms, as an eternal listening to, and participating in, the choirs of angels and saints.[52] In demanding that music be attuned to the

48. ". . . ut licet ibi pro meritis diversis alter quidem sanctus ad alterum quasi sesquioctavus, id est tonus integer, alter vero, ut sesquialter, id est diapente, et alius et sesquitertius, id est diatesseron ad alium referatur: tamen omnes sancti per claritatis concordiam, quasi per diapason, unum resonant, unum sapiant." "Omnia enim non solum in sonis proportione numerorum relativa coaptatis, verum etiam in rebus quibuslibet rite ordinatis consonantia efficitur; omnesque quod ordinatum constat, conveniens profecto et congruum efficitur: consonantiae hujus definitio videtur posse dici rerum dissimilium convenientia. Proinde si in qualibet convenientia est consonantia; omnis autem creatura, licet dissimilis sit invicem, Deo ordinante convenit; consonantia ergo habetur in omni creatura." *Dial. de tribus quaest.*, XLIII (*PL*, CXLVI, 117 ff.). Cf. Pietzsch, *Die Musik im Erziehungs- und*

*Bildungswesen des ausgehenden Altertums und frühen Mittelalters*, pp. 122 ff.

49. *SSM*, II, 150 f.; see also Coussemaker, *Histoire de l'harmonie au moyen âge*, pp. 56 ff.; 256 ff. Cf. Vacandard, *Vie de St. Bernard*, II, 101 ff.

50. "Bernard's ideas on church music correspond exactly with those of St. Augustine." Luddy, *Life and Teaching of St. Bernard*, p. 257. See also Vacandard, II, 101 ff., where Bernard is called a "plainchantiste distingué."

51. *Ep.* CCCXCVIII (*PL*, CLXXXII, 609 ff.); see also the *Exord. Magn. Cisterc. Dist.*, V, 20 (*PL*, CLXXXV, 1174).

52. Note such phrases as "in plateis supernae Sion melos angelicum auscultare" (*PL*, CLXXXIII, 1130); "angelorum admistus choris" (ibid., 1355); "martyrum inseri choris" (ibid., 1478). A similar vision occurs in a passage by Bernard's contemporary, Gottfried of

metaphysical and ethical experiences of Christian life, he did not restrict its creative scope but confronted it with a magnificent and typically Augustinian challenge. The importance of Bernard's musical ideas for our present inquiry lies in the fact that they also provide an indispensable clue to his convictions regarding religious art. For medieval experience musical and artistic composition were closely akin. That the laws of music embody a cosmic principle, that they "embrace everything" and extend to all the arts, was an axiom frequently expressed during the High Middle Ages.[53] To a man steeped, as Bernard was, in the Augustinian tradition, the presence of the "perfect" ratios must have been as evident in visible proportions as in audible consonances. And the meta-

*Plate 10*

Admont (d. 1165): "ipsi [the souls of the blessed] gratias agentes voce incessabili jucunda suae redemptionis gaudia laetissimo coelestis harmoniae concentu resonabunt in saecula" (*PL*, CLXXIV, 901). Such notions became commonplace. See the entirely musical description of heavenly bliss in Wolfram of Eschenbach's *Willehalm*, XXXI, 14 ff.

53. "Musica enim generaliter sumpta obiective quasi ad omnia extendit, ad deum et creaturas, incorporeas et corporeas, celestes et humanas, ad sciencias theoricas et practicas," *Speculum musicae* (a work of Jacobus of Liége, not Johannes de Muris), I, 1. Cf. Grossmann, *Die einleitenden Kapitel des 'Speculum Musicae,'* p. 58. Bukofzer, "Speculative Thinking," remarks that the passage "omnia in mensura et numero et pondere disposuisti" was "significantly enough quoted over and over by musical theorists." In the anonymous *Musica enchiriadis* (c. 860), the author inquires into the "deeper and divine reasons underlying musical harmonies" and finds them in the eternal laws of the cosmos. See Gerbert (ed.), *Scriptores eccles. de musica*, I, p. 159. Boethius' division of music into *musica mundana*, *musica humana*, and *musica instrumentalis* is the basis for all medieval speculation on this subject. In the first half of the twelfth century it is repeated by Adelard of Bath (*BGPM*, IV, 23) and Dominicus Gundissalinus (ibid., 95 ff.), and toward the end of the century by John of Salisbury (see below, p. 191). It is as an image of cosmic harmony that music was occasionally represented in Romanesque churches, as on the famous capitals of the Abbey Church of Cluny (most recent discussion by Meyer in *AB*, XXXIV, 1952), or in

the great pavement composition that once adorned the choir of St.-Remi at Reims (see Marlot, *Histoire de la ville, cité et université de Reims*, II, 542 ff.). The possibility of yet another, more obscure symbolic representation of music in Romanesque sculpture has recently been suggested by Schneider, *El Origen musical de los animales símbolos en la mitología y la escultura antiguas*. He believes that the animals carved in the twelfth-century capitals of certain cloisters in Catalonia represent musical notes that, when read in the order in which they appear on the capitals, yield the tune of a hymn in honor of the monastery's patron saint.

The magnificent pen drawing reproduced here (Pl. 10) illustrates the medieval idea of cosmic music. The figure of Aer is described by Baltrušaitis, probably correctly, as "the personification of the air, of the source of all harmony." "L'Image du monde céleste du IXe au XIIe siècle" (*GBA*, series 6, XX, 1938). However, the representation of Aer under the iconography of the microcosmos may find an explanation in the following passage from St. Hildegard of Bingen: "Aer . . . qui . . . naturali virtute sua creaturas terrarum temperat. . . . Anima, hominem quam vivificat, sed a Deo creatum esse intelligere facit, ipsaque aeri, qui inter coelum et terram medius videtur assimilatur" (*PL*, CXCVII, 845). The drawing is in the collection of the False Decretals in the Municipal Library at Reims (MS. 672). See *Catalogue générale des manuscrits des bibliothèques publiques de France*, Vol. XXXIX, and *Les Richesses des bibliothèques provinciales de France*, Vol. II, Pl. 26. The work was first reproduced by Didron (*AA*, V, 1844).

physical dignity of the ratios that he admired in musical composition he cannot have failed to respect in well-proportioned architecture.

The appraisal of Bernard's artistic tastes has relied far too exclusively on the opinions he expressed in writing, especially in the *Apologia ad Guillelmum*, his famous attack upon the ostentation of the Cluniac Order. In this polemical work he makes two specific points about art: he condemns as "monstrous" the anthropomorphic and zoomorphic imagery of Romanesque sculpture and demands their banishment from the cloister; and he inveighs against the "immense" height, the "immoderate" length, the "supervacuous" width of Cluniac churches as incompatible with the spirit of monastic humility.[54] [*See Add.*]

That these views became law for Bernard's own order, at least during his lifetime, is beyond question. The iconophobic bias he expressed in regard to the representational arts—he was a consistent pupil of Augustine even in this regard—led to the prohibition of illumination in Cistercian manuscripts and to the exclusion of all imagery, with the exception of painted crucifixes, from the churches of the order.[55] Bernard's concept of religious architecture was to have far greater repercussions, as we shall presently see.

But we do well not to overlook two aspects of his criticism. Consistent with the character and purpose of the *Apologia*, he bases his artistic postulates on the religious and, more specifically, ascetic ideals of monasticism. That is to say, he explicitly admits that nonmonastic sanctuaries, such as cathedrals, have to make concessions to the sensuous imagination of the laity; that "since the devotion of the carnal populace cannot be incited with spiritual ornaments, it is necessary to employ material ones," i.e., painted or carved images.[56] On the other hand, the sumptuousness of the Cluniac churches seems to Bernard incompatible not only with the ideals of monastic humility and (through the diversion of funds from charitable purposes) charity, but with the spiritual

54. XII, 28 ff. (*PL*, CLXXXII, 914 f.). To understand Bernard's utterances correctly, one has to bear in mind the circumstances under which the *Apology* was composed. Supporters of St. Bernard had attacked the luxury of Cluny. This attack had been rebuked with great dignity by Peter the Venerable. It is in answer to this rebuttal that Bernard wrote, at the insistence of his close friend William, Abbot of St.-Thierry, his *Apology*. See Leclercq, *Pierre le Vénérable*,

pp. 169 ff.

55. The extent to which these rules were actually observed, especially after Bernard's death, is quite another question. See Porcher, "St. Bernard et la graphie pure" (*MD*), and Green (*AB*, XXX, 1933, p. 241), who, however, still accepts 1134 as the date of the statute.

56. ". . . carnalis populi devotionem quia spiritualibus non possunt, corporalibus excitant ornamentis." *Apologia*, XII (*PL*, CLXXXII, 914).

education of the monk as Bernard envisaged it. To him the life of the Cistercian cloister was ideally an image and foretaste of paradise; he coined the term *paradisus claustralis*.[57] It is no coincidence that the names of so many foundations of the order refer to the realm of eternal beatitude.[58] Bernard sought to prepare his monks, even while in this life, for the mystical perception of divine truth, an ideal of spiritual contemplation in which the world of the senses had no place and where the relatively crude imagery of Cluniac painting and sculpture seemed to be without purpose, inadequate, and indeed confusing. Cistercian art criticism and Cistercian art must always be understood in the light of Cistercian asceticism and its definitions of prayer and contemplation.[59]

Quite as noteworthy is the second aspect of Bernard's criticism: it is very far from revolutionary. One could easily name half a dozen twelfth-century authors who have similarly deprecated ostentatious building by ecclesiastics.[60] What is more, Cluny itself might at this time have subscribed to such criticism. When the *Apologia* was written, the great phase of Cluniac art had passed. It had coincided with a period of wealth unprecedented in the history of the abbey. Not only did that wealth decline, but an acute economic crisis developed early in the twelfth century.[61] To meet this emergency, the abbot, Peter the Venerable, decided upon a radically new policy. The closing down of the great artistic workshops seems to have been one of the first steps. And in enjoining

57. *PL*, CLXXXIII, 663. It is of particular interest that in speaking of *paradisus claustralis* St. Bernard quotes Gen. 28:17, "How dreadful is this place! this is no other but the house of God, and this is the gate of Heaven," which his audience knew from the dedication rite to refer to the Christian basilica. On the meaning of the term, see Gilson, *La Théologie mystique de St. Bernard*, pp. 108 ff. The image of the *paradisus claustralis* was frequently used by Bernard's followers; cf. *PL*, CLXXXIV, 525, 1058; also Leclercq, "Prédicateurs bénédictins aux XIᵉ et XIIᵉ siècle" (*RM*, XXXIII, 1943).

58. E.g., Locus Coeli, Vallis Paradisi, Vallis Lucis, Nova Jerusalem, Paradisus S. Mariae, Hortus Dei, Vallis Coeli, Beatitudo, Castrum Dei. See Laurent, "Les Noms des monastères cisterciens" (*ABSS*, I, 168 ff.).

59. See Dimier's important paper, "La Règle de Saint Bernard et le dépouillement architectural des cisterciens" (*BRA*).

60. See, e.g., Ailred of Rievaulx, *Speculum*

*Charitatis*, II, 25 (*PL*, CXCV, 572); the passage is also quoted in Dimier, *Recueil de plans d'églises cisterciennes*, p. 25. On Ailred, cf. Powicke, "Ailred of Rievaulx and His Biographer, Walter Daniel" (*BJRL*, VI, 1921, pp. 331, 413 f.). For other critics of ecclesiastical building, see Mortet, "Hugue de Fouilloi, Pierre le Chantre, Alexandre Neckam et les critiques dirigées au douzième siècle contre le luxe des constructions" (*Mélanges Bémont*); one may add the names of Guigue I, prior general of the Carthusians (see Mortet and Deschamps, *Recueil*, II, 39), Abelard (ibid., p. 45), Walter of Châtillon. See Wilmart, *Gautier de Châtillon*, p. 137, also the passage (Strecker, p. 167) "plures reedificant Babilonis murum per quos domus domini fit spelunca furum."

61. See Duby, "Le Budget de l'abbaye de Cluny" (*A*, VII, 1952), and Leclercq, *Pierre le Vénérable*, pp. 145 ff.

upon his monks a life far more austere than that which they had been accustomed to lead, the abbot quite justly stressed the ascetic and spiritual ideals of the monastic life that seemed to demand the sacrifice of comfort and splendor. His views, if less radical, were in basic agreement with those of his fiery friend at Clairvaux, and it would be rash, I think, to ascribe them to the latter's influence.

It is not surprising that the celebrated monastery should have met the economic challenge by falling back on its lofty spiritual tradition, or that this development should have had immediate repercussions in the artistic sphere. Far more remarkable is the fact that the great Romanesque art that had its fountainhead in Cluny was moribund even at the time of the economic crisis, not because it was expensive but because it no longer corresponded to the taste of the age, which, from the early twelfth century, underwent a profound change.

By 1130 or so this trend had become crystallized. In sculpture and monumental painting, in book illumination and the goldsmith's art, a new style emerged that contrasted sharply with the style of the preceding period. The wild, ecstatic restlessness of line, the exuberance of gesture and action, and the ardent expressionism that were the heritage of the schools of Reims and Winchester gave way to a much calmer and firmer mode of composition. Straight lines meeting at right angles were now preferred to undulating curves. Artistic thinking was in simple forms, powerfully outlined and clearly set off from one another. We encounter a new sense for tectonic values. Figures and scenes tend to become serene, quiet, monumental.[62]

*Plates 8, 9*

62. See the remarks of Wormald, "The Development of English Illumination in the Twelfth Century" (*Journal of the British Archaeological Association*, 3rd series, VII, 1942). Also Boeckler, "Die romanischen Fenster des Augsburger Domes und die Stilwende vom 11. zum 12. Jahrhundert" (*Zeitschrift des deutschen Vereins für Kunstwissenschaft*, X, 1943). In sculpture, this trend finds its most authoritative expression in Chartres West. But it has close contemporary parallels in Germany (e.g., the Freudenstadt lectern) and in Italy; see Beenken, *Romanische Skulptur in Deutschland*, pp. 120 ff., and Krautheimer-Hess, "Die figurale Plastik der Ostlombardei von 1100 bis 1178" (*Mar-burger Jahrbuch*, IV, 1928). On the early manifestations of the new style in Lorraine, see Laurent, "Art rhénan, art mosan et art byzantin" (*Byzantion*, VI, 1931), and recently Swarzenski, *Monuments of Romanesque Art*, pp. 26 ff. Laurent qualifies his observations by stating (pp. 91 f.): "il existe à l'époque romane un mouvement général qui pousse les artistes du nord vers la simplification et les solutions plastiques du problème de la forme. Ce mouvement est indépendant de Byzance." On the "formalism" of French art even during the twelfth century, see Boeckler, "Die Pariser Miniaturen-Ausstellung von 1954" (*Kunstchronik*, VIII, 1955). [*See Add. for p. 151.*]

The new style emerged almost simultaneously in France and England, in Germany and Italy. Its earliest manifestations seem to have occurred in Lorraine, and the impression caused by Byzantine art was certainly a powerful and important factor. But this impression cannot explain the new style any more than the impression made by Japanese prints can explain the new manner of a Toulouse-Lautrec or Degas. In the late nineteenth century, as in the early twelfth, it was an inner affinity that led to the "discovery" of the model; the particular appreciation of, and sensibility for, the qualities of that model, the ability to re-create certain aspects of its aesthetic structure, were part of an original and creative act that has nothing to do with copying or imitation.

When St. Bernard wrote his indictment of Cluniac art, the new style of the twelfth century was emerging everywhere. None of its creations show that "ridiculous monstrosity," that "rich and amazing variety of forms," castigated by the Abbot of Clairvaux. On the contrary, one cannot help feeling that both the *Apologia* and the art of the 1130's speak the aesthetic language of one and the same generation; that Bernard's criticism lent literary support to a youthful artistic movement for whose taste the preceding style—which Bernard seems to have identified with Cluny—had become outmoded. This style, however, was still firmly entrenched in many centers of religious art. Professor Boeckler has recently observed that the taste for the "bizarre and extravagant, for exaggerated motion and distorted proportions," survived with particular tenacity in France, where the great monasteries continued to produce sculptures and book illuminations whose elegant formalism attests a highly sophisticated taste rather than deep religious emotion. Such formalism obviously must have been distasteful to St. Bernard. The favor it enjoyed in a Benedictine house like Liessiés, with which his own Clairvaux maintained frequent contacts, may well account for the fierce tone of Bernard's polemics. These polemics, however, are but the negative and relatively unimportant aspect of the abbot's influence upon ecclesiastical art.

There is good reason to think that the saint himself may not have insisted too zealously on the observation of his prohibitions even in art works executed in his own monastery. The great Bible of Clairvaux, which was probably executed upon St. Bernard's orders and certainly represents "the purest type of Cistercian manuscript art," evades the regulations of the famous Article 82 of the Statutes of Cîteaux [63] and occasionally even introduces grotesque animal heads—as if the *Apologia* had never been written. This fact alone should put us on our guard against accepting this polemical treatise as a complete expression of Bernard's views on art. If his temper was fiery, his mind was not narrow, certainly not in aesthetic matters. He has criticized art forms that appeared to him incompatible with his spiritual vision. But the art he demanded and called into existence as responding to that vision reveals a taste of rare grandeur and an almost infallible judgment in aesthetic matters. If Bernard's criticism of Romanesque art was not always fair, his own Cistercian art was, generally speaking, as good as what he had condemned, and indeed often far superior. In the calligraphy inspired by the Abbot of Clairvaux an eminent student finds "une sûreté de goût de plus en plus rare, un sens élevé de ce qui est véritablement précieux." [64] Bernard's most remarkable and in fact epoch-making artistic contribution, however, lies in the field of architecture.

*Plate 13b*

*Plate 12*

There can be no doubt that the Abbot of Clairvaux took an active part in developing the design of Cistercian architecture, although we do not know the exact extent of his supervision; nor can there be any doubt that the distinct style evolved under his direction was one of the major events in the history of medieval architecture. The churches built or commissioned by St. Bernard are neither "puritanical" nor humble, but on the contrary "worthy of the greatest architects of his age." [65] It ought to be emphasized at this point that what is peculiarly Cistercian or Bernardian about these edifices is not their plan but their style. Practically every single element of the early Cistercian church can be found in other types of ecclesiastical architecture. It is the spirit of the Bernardian sanctuary that puts it apart. Details of plan and construction that

63. The Bible is now in Troyes (MS. 27). Of course we do not know the exact date of either the Bible or Article 82 ("Litterae unius coloris fiant et non depictae"). There is good reason to suppose that the article was not composed until the very end of St. Bernard's life and inserted in the Institutes only after his death. See recently Porcher, p. 19, and Lieftinck, "De librijen en scriptoria der West-vlaamse Cisterciënser" (*Mededeelingen van de Koninklijke vlaamse Academie voor Wetenschappen, Letteren en schone Kunsten van Belgïe, Klasse der Letteren XV*), pp. 7, 87.

64. Porcher. Cf. Wenzel, "Die Glasmalerei

der Zisterzienser in Deutschland" (*BRA*).

65. The monk Achardus built under Bernard's direction: "Achardus . . . jubente et mittente beato Bernardo . . . plurimorum coenobiorum initiator et extructor" (*PL*, CLXXXV, 1078). See also Eydoux, "Les Fouilles de l'abbatiale d'Himmerod et la notion d'un plan bernardin" (*BM*, CXI, 1953).

"Saint Bernard lui-même [M. Aubert asks] lors de la reconstruction de son abbaye à Clairvaux [*i.e.*, Clairvaux II, built 1135–1145] n'acceptera-t-il pas un ensemble de vastes et beaux bâtiments dignes des plus grands architectes d'alors" (*MD*, Preface, p. 15)?

were taken over from older Benedictine architecture were transformed in a way that creates a unique and unmistakable mood.

In view of Bernard's ascetic ideals, the elimination of figurative sculpture and painting from the churches of his order was inevitable. Nevertheless, Bernardian architecture is far more than "expurgated Romanesque." The disappearance of the representational arts seems to have cleared the way for an unexcelled purity and perfection of construction and architectural proportion. And in this respect Cistercian building appears closely related to the broad artistic current just mentioned. Bernard was motivated solely by religious considerations. But his asceticism, including its iconophobic implications, agrees very well with the marked preference for sober, "abstract" forms, for architectonic values, that appear even in the style of book illuminations of this time. Cistercian architecture as well as the style of mid-twelfth-century sculpture and painting may to some extent be understood as the reaction against Romanesque "expressionism"; both cultivate certain values that one might call "cubist," were it not that this term, inadequate like all definitions taken over from another period, failed to take account of the element of proportion that is the most conspicuous aesthetic achievement of Cistercian architecture.

We do not yet know all the geometrical canons used by the Cistercian builders.[66] Yet the use of such canons is strikingly evident in every one of their churches. Augustine's "perfect" ratio of $1:2$ generally determines the elevation.[67] In the abbey of Fontenay (1130–47), the best surviving example of early *Plate 11* Cistercian architecture—Bernard himself may have been responsible for its plan—the octave ratio determines the ground plan as well.[68] Moreover, the bays of the side aisles are of equal length and width, and the same dimension is marked off vertically by a stringcourse. We thus obtain a spatial "cube" in

66. On the much-discussed question of a Cistercian church plan, see recently Lambert, "Remarques sur les plans d'églises dits cisterciens" (*BRA*).

67. Focillon, *Art d'Occident, le moyen-âge, roman et gothique*, p. 162. Rose, *Die Frühgotik im Orden von Cîteaux*, p. 34, suggests that the same proportion usually determines the relation of the width and height of the nave. Similarly Hahn's dissertation, *Die Kirche der Zisterzienser-Abtei Eberbach im Rheingau und die romanische*

*Ordensbaukunst der Zisterzienser im 12. Jahrhundert* (summary in *Nassauische Annalen*, LIV, 1953, p. 160), with regard to Eberbach. [*See Add.*]

68. This ratio determines the relation between the length of the church *in opere* and the total width of the transept; between the length and width of the transept and between nave and side aisle. See Bégule, *L'Abbaye de Fontenay*, and *L'Abbaye de Fontenay et l'architecture cistercienne*.

each bay, an aesthetic impression that recalls the "geometrical harmony" of Boethius. The same "cubic" tendency appears in the central nave.

The austere façade, today stripped of its porch, again describes a square if we include the buttresses and the upper stringcourse. The distance between the upper and lower stringcourses is determined "according to true measure." [69] One may ask if medieval preference for this proportion may be, in part at least, connected with the Augustinian preference for the octave and with the role of the square in the thought of nearly all the Christian Platonists: the proportion "according to true measure" [70] may be defined as the geometrical expression of the octave ratio in terms not of the rectangle, 1 : 2 (relegated by Boethius to the "dyadic" order of matter, a fact that induced the twelfth century to consider "two" the symbol of sin), but of the square, the geometrical representation of the Godhead. [71] The ratios of the other perfect consonances are similarly present

69. The façade, including buttresses, is 10.88 m. wide. So is the nave, including the main piers. The length of the double bays, between the pilasters that support the transverse arches, is again 10.88 m.; however, the fourth bay from the entrance is about 40 cm. longer than the others. The side aisles, including the walls and the piers of the nave are 5.38–5.40 m. wide and long, and I measured the same height to the stringcourse. In the foregoing measurements, it will be noted, the distances that yield the squares of the ground plan are not determined by the intervals between the centers of piers or walls. The architect has instead used either the inner or the outer face of piers and walls as his line of direction. This method of setting out agrees with findings elsewhere. See below, p. 215, n. 79; Forsyth, *The Church of St. Martin at Angers*, pp. 74 ff.; also Texier, *Géometrie de l'architecture*, p. 63, who stresses the importance of the "réglage des volumes réels extérieurs et intérieurs" in Romanesque buildings as contrasted with the dimensions of Gothic edifices, which he thinks are determined by the intervals between axes. See, however, below, pp. 208 ff., my findings regarding the Cathedral of Chartres, and Bachmann, in his review of Velte's *Die Anwendung der Quadratur und Triangulatur bei der Grund- und Aufrissgestaltung der gotischen Kirchen* (ZK, XV, 1, 1952), who seems to accept that author's thesis "dass man nicht von Pfeilerkern

zu Pfeilerkern messen muss, sondern von Kämpfer zu Kämpfer."

70. Medieval predilection for the proportion "according to true measure" (the rectangle 1 : $\sqrt{2}$) was inherited from Vitruvius, who (VI, 3) teaches how to give an atrium this proportion; moreover, he (IX, Preface, 2 ff.) singles out Plato's demonstration of how to double a square as one of those few extraordinary achievements which have bettered human life and therefore deserve the gratitude of mankind. For his demonstration (*Meno*, 82 ff.), Plato used the same figure employed by the architects who taught "how to take the elevation from the ground plan" according to "true measure." The device, as we have seen, must have recommended itself by the simplicity of its application. Nevertheless the extraordinary praise that Vitruvius bestows on Plato for the solution of that simple geometrical problem may well have confirmed the Middle Ages in the conviction of the metaphysical perfection of the rectangle "according to true measure." On the tradition of Vitruvius in medieval building, see also Frankl, "Secret," and Texier, p. 10.

71. See de Bruyne, I, 15; and Hugh of St.-Victor: ". . . unitas, quia prima est in numeris, verum omnium significat principium. Binarius, quia secundus est, et primus ad unitate recedit, peccatum significat quo a primo bono diviatum est." *De scripturis et scriptoribus sacris*, XV (*PL*, CLXXV, 22). See above, n. 13.

in Fontenay: besides the 1:1 ratio of the crossing, the ratio of the fifth, 2:3, regulates the relation of the width of the crossing to its length, including the choir, and also the relation between the width of the crossing and the total width of nave plus side aisles. Finally, the ratio of the fourth, 3:4, determines the relation between the total width of nave plus side aisles and the length of the transept including chapels. In no other style of Christian architecture are the Augustinian "perfect" ratios so much in evidence as in the churches of the Cistercian Order.[72]

\*

The affinity between the second characteristic aspect of Gothic architecture—luminosity—and the metaphysical trend of the time is perhaps even more striking than in the case of proportion. In the consistent and dramatic development the Gothic builder gave to this aspect, he unquestionably paid tribute to the taste or, rather, to the aesthetic urge of his age. For the twelfth and thirteenth centuries light was the source and essence of all visual beauty. Thinkers who differ as widely as do Hugh of St.-Victor and Thomas Aquinas both ascribe to the beautiful two main characteristics: consonance of parts, or proportion, and luminosity.[73] The stars, gold, and precious stones are called beautiful because of this quality.[74] In the philosophical literature of the time, as in the courtly epic, no attributes are used more frequently to describe visual beauty than "lucid," "luminous," "clear." [75] This aesthetic preference is vividly reflected in the decorative arts of the time with their obvious delight in glittering objects,

72. For similar measurements, though the author reaches somewhat different conclusions, see Hahn. Hahn's findings for Eberbach are of special interest in view of the fact that he shows this church to have been begun *c.* 1145 rather than a generation later, as was commonly believed. [*See Add.*]

73. Hugh, *Erud. Didasc.*, VII, 12: "Quid luce pulchrius, quae cum colorem in se non habeat, rerum ipsa quodammodo illuminando colorat?" See *PL*, CLXXVI, 821 (cf. de Bruyne, II, 213 ff.); and Thomas Aquinas, *Summa Theologiae*, I, 39, 8c: "perfectio . . .

debita proportio sive consonantia . . . claritas. . . ." Cf. Coomaraswamy, "Medieval Aesthetics" (*AB*, XVII, 1935):

74. See Baeumker, "Witelo" (*BGPM*, III, 2, 1908), pp. 464, 499 f. On the question of the authorship of the treatise *De intelligentiis*, which Baeumker had originally attributed to Witelo, see him in *Miscellanea Francesco Ehrle*, I.

75. Cf. Weise, *Die Geistige Welt der Gotik*, pp. 447 ff., 477 ff.

76. Cf. Heckscher, "Relics of Pagan Antiquity in Medieval Settings" (*JWCI*, I, 1937/38), p. 212.

shiny materials, and polished surfaces.[76] The development of the stained-glass window, impelled by the astonishing idea of replacing opaque walls by transparent ones, reflects the same taste. And in the great sanctuaries of the twelfth and thirteenth centuries luminosity is a feature demanded and singled out for praise by contemporaries; they note with pleasure the more lucid structure, *structuram clariorem*, of the new Cathedral of Auxerre [77] or, in the case of Suger's choir of St.-Denis, the substitution of a bright church for a dark one.[78]

If such medieval impressions of Gothic architecture coincide with our own, they originate in, and were experienced as part of, a comprehensive world view to which we have become strangers. The medieval experience and philosophy of beauty—we have already noted it in the case of musical consonance—are not exclusively or even primarily derived from sense impressions. It is even doubtful that we may speak of medieval aesthetics, if we define aesthetics as the autonomous philosophy of beauty. To the medieval thinker beauty was not a value independent of others, but rather the radiance of truth, the splendor of ontological perfection, and that quality of things which reflects their origin in God. Light and luminous objects, no less than musical consonance, conveyed an insight into the perfection of the cosmos, and a divination of the Creator.[79]

According to the Platonizing metaphysics of the Middle Ages, light is the most noble of natural phenomena, the least material, the closest approximation to pure form. For a thinker like Grosseteste, light is actually the mediator between bodiless and bodily substances, a spiritual body, an embodied spirit, as he calls it.[80] Light, moreover, is the creative principle in all things, most active in the heavenly spheres, whence it causes all organic growth here on earth, and weakest in the earthly substances. But it is present even in them, for, asks St. Bonaventure, do not metals and precious stones begin to shine when we polish

77. Mortet and Deschamps, *Recueil*, I, 101: "ut ecclesia quo more veterum usque tunc fuerat subobscura, in lucem claresceret ampliorem." The work of reconstruction was carried out under Bishop Hugh of Noyers (1183–1206).

78. "Ut . . . ex tenebrosiore splendidam redderent ecclesiam." *Sugerii vita*, in Suger, *Oeuvres complètes* (Lecoy de la Marche, ed.), p. 391.

79. For the following, cf. de Bruyne, III, ch. 1, "L'Esthétique de la lumière," and

Baeumker, "Witelo." For classical antecedents, see also Bultmann, "Zur Geschichte der Lichtsymbolik im Altertum" (*Philologus*, XCVII, 1948).

80. See Baur, "Das Licht in der Naturphilosophie des Robert Grosseteste"; also Sharp, *Franciscan Philosophy in Oxford*, pp. 20, 23; Muckle, "Robert Grosseteste's Use of Greek Sources" (*Medievalia et Humanistica*, III, 1945), pp. 41 f.; Birkenmajer, "Robert Grosseteste and Richard Fournival" (ibid., V, 1948), pp. 37 f.

them, are not clear windowpanes manufactured from sand and ashes, is not fire struck from black coal, and is not this luminous quality of things evidence of the existence of light in them? [81] According to the medieval thinkers, light is the principle of order and value. The objective value of a thing is determined by the degree to which it partakes of light. And in experiencing delight at the sight of luminous objects, we grasp intuitively their ontological dignity within the hierarchy of beings. The reader will find in Dante's *Paradiso* the greatest poetical exposition of medieval light metaphysics. The poem might be described as a great fugue on the single theme, "la luce divina e penetrante per l'universo secondo ch'e degno" (31:22 ff.), "the divine light penetrates the universe according to its dignity."

Such views embody a very ancient, half-mythical experience of light. Their philosophical articulation originates with Plato. In the sixth book of the *Republic*, the good is defined as the cause of knowledge as well as of being and essence, and then compared to sunlight, which is "not only the author of visibility in all visible things but generation and nourishment and growth."

In that passage sunlight is perhaps no more than a metaphor; but Plato's followers gave it a very different meaning. For the Neoplatonists, this brief sentence was the seed out of which they developed an entire epistemological system. Light was now conceived as the transcendental reality that engenders the universe and illuminates our intellect for the perception of truth.

These ideas were adopted by Christianity. St. Augustine developed the notion that intellectual perception results from an act of illumination in which the divine intellect enlightens the human mind. The father of a Christian philosophy in which light is the first principle of metaphysics as well as of epistemology is an Eastern mystic, Denis, the so-called Pseudo-Areopagite, of whose identity and strange afterlife in medieval France more will be said later. This thinker blends Neoplatonic philosophy with the magnificent theology of light in the Gospel of St. John, where the divine Logos is conceived as the true Light that shineth in darkness, by which all things were made, and that enlighteneth every man that cometh into this world. Upon this passage the Pseudo-Areopagite bases the edifice of his own thought. Creation is to him an act of illumination, but even the created universe could not exist without light. If

81. Baeumker, "Witelo," pp. 40, 464, 499; Gilson, *La Philosophie de Saint Bonaventure*, pp. 263 ff.

light ceased to shine, all being would vanish into nothingness. From this metaphysical concept of light, the Pseudo-Areopagite also deduced his epistemology. The creation is the self-revelation of God. All creatures are "lights" that by their existence bear testimony to the Divine Light and thereby enable the human intellect to perceive it.[82]

It is a strange world view indeed that stemmed from these ideas. All created things are "theophanies," manifestations of God.[83] How is this possible when God is transcendental to His creation? Are His creatures not too imperfect to be images of Him? The Pseudo-Areopagite answered this question by pointing to the frailty of our intellect, which is incapable of perceiving God face to face. Therefore, God interposes images between Him and us. Holy Writ as well as nature are such "screens"; they present us with images of God, designed to be imperfect, distorted, even contradictory. This imperfection and mutual contradiction, apparent even to our minds, is to kindle in us the desire to ascend from a world of mere shadows and images to the contemplation of the Divine Light itself. Thus it is, paradoxically enough, by evading us that God becomes gradually manifest; He conceals Himself before us in order to be revealed. But of all created things light is the most direct manifestation of God. St. Augustine had occasionally remarked that Christ is *properly* called the Divine Light, not figuratively, as when we speak of Him as the Keystone.[84] In the thirteenth century a French theologian picks up the Augustinian dictum and declares that among corporeal things light is most similar to the Divine Light.[85]

The experience of the world and of God that underlies such views is difficult for us to relive. We are tempted to understand medieval definitions of light

82. The *Corpus areopagiticum* is printed in Migne, *Patrologiae cursus completus . . . series Graeca*, III. On Dionysian epistemology, see Gilson, "Le Sens du rationalisme chrétien" (in *Études de philosophie médiévale*); "Pourquoi St. Thomas a critiqué St. Augustin" (*Archives d'histoire doctrinale et littéraire du moyen âge*, I, 1926); and *La Philosophie au moyen-âge*, pp. 80 ff.

83. See Dionysius' pupil and commentator, Erigena: "Materialia lumina, sive quae naturaliter in caelestibus spatiis ordinata sunt, sive quae in terris humano artificio efficiuntur, imagines sunt intelligibilium luminum, super omnia ipsius verae lucis" (*PL*, CXXII, 139). See the comment on this passage by Panofsky, "Note on a Controversial Passage in Suger's *De Consecratione Ecclesiae Sancti Dionysii*" (*GBA*, 6th series, XXVI, 1944).

84. "Neque enim et Christus sic dicitur lux quomodo dicitur lapis; sed illud proprie, hoc utique figurate." *De Genesi ad litteram*, IV, 28 (*PL*, XXXIV, 315).

85. The author, however, writes "agnus" instead of "lapis"; see Baeumker, "Witelo," p. 374. Cf. Bonaventure: "Lux inter omnia corporalia maxime assimilatur luci aeterni." ibid., p. 394.

either in a pantheistic or in a purely metaphorical sense. The reader of the preceding paragraphs may occasionally have asked himself whether it is the physical light to which the Christian Platonists are referring or to a transcendental
light, only symbolically invested with the qualities of physical light. But it is
precisely this distinction that we have to disregard if we seek to understand the
medieval mind. At the basis of all medieval thought is the concept of *analogy*.
All things have been created according to the law of analogy, in virtue of which
they are, in various degrees, manifestations of God, images, vestiges, or
shadows of the Creator. The degree to which a thing "resembles" God, to
which God is present in it, determines its place in the hierarchy of beings. This
idea of analogy, as Gilson has stressed with reference to St. Bonaventure, was
by no means a poetical play with symbols but, on the contrary, the only epistemological method considered valid.[86] We understand a piece of wood or a stone
only when we perceive God in it, a medieval writer observes.[87]

Hence the connection between the "aesthetics of light" and the "metaphysics of light" of the Middle Ages. The Pseudo-Areopagite, in the solemn
opening sentence of his treatise on the *Celestial Hierarchy*, declares that the
divine splendor, in its emanations, always remains undivided and indeed unifies
those of His creatures that accept it.[88] In the aesthetics of the twelfth and thirteenth centuries this thought is appropriated: light is conceived as the form that
all things have in common, the simple that imparts unity to all.[89] As an aesthetic
value, light, like unison in music, thus fulfills that longing for ultimate concord,
that reconciliation of the multiple into the one, which is the essence of the
medieval experience of beauty, as it is the essence of its faith.

This metaphysical and theological vista that light and the luminous opened
to medieval man is closed to us.[90] The sunlight filtering through the transparent

86. Gilson, *La Philosophie de Saint Bonaventure*, pp. 198 ff.; cf. his *The Spirit of Medieval
Philosophy*, pp. 100 f.

87. Erigena, *Expositiones super Ierarchiam
caelestem*, I, 1 (*PL*, CXXII, 129). Cf. Gilson,
"Le Sens du rationalisme," p. 12.

88. "Quia omnis divinus splendor secundum
benignitatem varie in providentibus procedens,
manet simplex, et non hoc tantum, sed et coa-
dunat illa que splendorem accipiunt." Abbot
Hilduin's translation in Théry, *Études Diony-*

*siennes*, II. Cf. Erigena's translation (*PL*,
CXXII, 1037).

89. Baeumker, "Witelo," p. 434.

90. The most celebrated literary testimony
to the cult of luminosity in Gothic architecture
is the description of the Temple of the Grail
in Albrecht von Scharfenberg's *Younger Titurel*
(Hahn, ed., p. 33, vv. 330 ff.; Wolf, ed., pp.
18 ff.). See Wolf's criticism of the passage in
*Zeitschrift für deutsches Altertum*, LXXIX,
209 ff. Cf. de Bruyne, III, 131 ff.; Lichtenberg,
*Architekturdarstellungen in der mittelhochdeut-*

walls of a Gothic cathedral is for us either a physical phenomenon to be explained in terms of physics or an aesthetic one that may or may not awaken religious reflections within us. These different levels of experience have almost nothing in common with one another. It was just the opposite for the men and women of the Middle Ages. Christian theology is centered in the mystery of the Incarnation, which in the Gospel of St. John is perceived as light illuminating the world. The liturgy of the Church lent immediate reality to this image by celebrating Christmas, the feast of the Incarnation, at the time of the winter solstice. At some unknown date, but certainly before the end of the thirteenth century, it had become general custom to read the opening passage from the Gospel of St. John at the close of every Mass.[91] With its sublime theology of light it must have conveyed to those who listened a vision of the eucharistic sacrament as divine light transfiguring the darkness of matter.

In the physical light that illuminated the sanctuary, that mystical reality seemed to become palpable to the senses. The distinction between physical nature and theological significance was bridged by the notion of corporeal light as an "analogy" to the divine light. Can we marvel that this world view called for a style of sacred architecture in which the meaning of light was acknowledged as magnificently as it was in Gothic?

How much can actually be ascertained regarding the direct influence of the intellectual and spiritual movements we have studied in this chapter upon the creation of Gothic architecture? The question can only be answered with varying degrees of assurance: the historian must be on his guard not to mistake parallels or affinities for causes, and the influence of the School of Chartres upon architecture is far less palpable than is that of the Augustinianism of Clairvaux. For all we know, the Platonists of Chartres never formulated a system of aesthetics, let alone a program for the arts. We cannot even say with certainty that the aesthetic and technological consequences of their cosmology exerted a direct impact upon the new architectural style, the Gothic, that emerged around 1140. Yet such influence is eminently likely, even on the mere

*schen Dichtung;* Sedlmayr, "Die dichterische Wurzel der Kathedrale" (*Mitteilungen des österr. Instituts für Geschichtsforschung,* supp. vol. XIV, 1939).

91. Thalhofer and Eisenhofer, *Handbuch der katholischen Liturgik,* II, 236; cf. I, 376. See also the important remarks in Jungmann, *Missarum Solemnia,* II, 542 ff.

basis of circumstantial evidence. Gothic architecture, as we have seen, was conceived, and was defined at this very time, as applied geometry. The most famous mathematical school—certainly in the Christian West—was then Chartres. We know that the geometrical knowledge displayed by a Gothic architect such as Villard de Honnecourt was substantially that of the cathedral and monastic schools and was acquired in them. Here, however, the study of the quadrivium was intimately connected with the metaphysical and mystical speculations of the Platonic tradition. The student, if he later applied his geometrical knowledge to architecture, was bound to be influenced by the recollection of the aesthetic, technical, and symbolic properties that his teachers attributed to geometry.

Far more distinct and certainly far more tangible, thanks to the influence of St. Bernard, was the influence that Augustinian spirituality exerted upon the formation of Gothic. Even from a purely artistic point of view, Cistercian architecture, as the first radical and consistent application of the general aesthetic trend of the age to the art of building, could not fail to have far-reaching repercussions. It was even more important that St. Bernard linked aesthetic and religious experience in presenting Cistercian architecture as the only adequate expression of the new religious attitude of which he was the revered exponent.

The influence of Cistercian upon the first Gothic architecture is beyond question. The simultaneous emergence of the two, already pointed out by Bilson, is revealing.[92] Such important elements as the pointed arch, the sequence of identical, transverse oblong bays, the buttressing arches visible above the roofs of the side aisles, were employed by Cistercian architects before their adoption by the cathedral builders of the Île-de-France.[93] The picture is equally striking

92. Bilson, "The Beginnings of Gothic Architecture: Norman Vaulting in England" (*RIBA Journal*, VI, 1899; IX, 1902), pp. 267 ff.

93. See Dehio and Bezold, *Kirchliche Baukunst des Abendlandes*, I, 519, where the significance of all these innovations for Gothic architecture is stressed, although Dehio emphasizes the "unkünstlerische, vielmehr antikünstlerische Grundstimmung" of the Cistercians. Similarly negative is the judgment of Lambert, pp. 38 f. See, however, Rose, pp. 6 ff., who considers the introduction of Gothic into the Burgundian tradition the great achievement of Cistercian

architecture. Rose, p. 70, and Aubert, *Notre-Dame de Paris*, pp. 57, 99, stress the early use of the buttressing arch in Cistercian churches; Aubert also calls attention to the use of an ambulatory without chapels in Cistercian choirs before this device is employed in Paris Cathedral. The buttressing arches of the choir of Pontigny are of the same date as this part of the building, begun *c.* 1185; see Aubert, *L'Architecture cistercienne*, I, 189. It ought to be pointed out, however, that both the pointed arch and, after the catastrophe of 1125, the flying buttress were used in the great third church of

in England. Durham Cathedral had received its first ribbed vaults before the turn of the century. These, however, kept to the round arch. The pointed arch was introduced only in the ribbed vault of the nave, constructed 1128–33. "If we remember," observes Bony, "that the first Cistercian mission came to England in 1128 we shall realize that the year 1128 is not without significance." [94]

Even the crocket capital, perhaps the most impressive example of the subordination of ornament to function, has its predecessors in Cistercian architecture.[95] It is quite true that, generally speaking, St. Bernard's order did not invent new architectural forms but rather revived old ones; and it is characteristic that the Cistercians seem to have been influenced by the pristine architecture of the Cluniac Order.[96] But such borrowed elements were adapted to a comprehensive and unified design that produced a profound effect upon the cathedral builders of the Île-de-France.

It would be incorrect to describe the first Gothic as the child of Cistercian architecture, even though it is the child of St. Bernard. In criticizing the extravagance of Cluniac art, the Abbot of Clairvaux had pointed out himself that his postulates applied to monastic buildings only. To the secular cathedrals and their art, which was aimed at the edification of people living in the world and had to appeal to their imagination, he made important concessions.[97] And yet, Bernard's insistence that all religious art and music be attuned to religious experience, that their only justification is their ability to guide the mind to the perception of ultimate truth, confronted the cathedral builder with the same challenge as it did the monastic architect. The Abbot of Clairvaux had been scathing in his denunciation of certain types of imagery and decoration that to him appeared incompatible with the character of the sanctuary; they disappear from the first Gothic cathedrals, too. In some cases, as in the Cathedral of Tournai or in Chartres West, where they had been employed in an earlier phase of the building program, they are discontinued, perhaps under the personal

Cluny. See Conant, "Medieval Academy Excavations at Cluny" (Sp, XXIX, 1954), with bibliography of earlier reports. See also below, n. 96.

94. Bony, "French Influences on the Origin of English Architecture" (JWCI, XII, 1949).

95. On the importance of this capital for the development in England, see Bond, Gothic Architecture in England, pp. 416 f., 441.

96. Lambert, L'Art gothique en Espagne, pp. 39 ff., rightly stresses the influence exerted upon the earliest Cistercian plans by the architecture of Cluny. See above, n. 93.

97. See above, n. 56.

influence of St. Bernard.[98] Above all, however, we find the main aesthetic and technical features that characterize Cistercian architecture, the unadorned perfection of workmanship, the attention to proportion, equally present in the cathedrals of the Île-de-France. Cistercian and early Gothic architecture may thus be described as two branches growing from the same soil and realizing the same religious and aesthetic postulates, with the sole difference that the first is designed for the devotional life of the convent, the second for that of the diocese. [See Add.]

This interpretation is confirmed by the fact that since the second half of the twelfth century Cistercian and Gothic cease to be distinct stylistic branches, even in France. The Cistercian builders introduce Gothic in their native Burgundy, employing the design of the cathedrals in their own architecture; abroad they become the pioneers of Gothic.[99]

But it is only when we fix our attention on the group of monuments with which Gothic architecture came into existence, if we consider the personalities of those who created it and the historical moment in which that event took place, that we can grasp the actual link between the ideas we have considered and the new style. Metaphysical concepts do not readily spark the artist's imagination. The visions of Plato, Augustine, and Dionysius Areopagita had to acquire a peculiar relevance beyond the realm of abstract speculation before they could call forth artistic expression. The metaphysics of music acquired such significance by being absorbed into the religious movement led by St. Bernard. By being made the basis of the first cosmological system, Platonism dazzled the entire age. And by a singular concatenation of circumstances the Dionysian metaphysics of light in the twelfth century entered even into the political bloodstream of France. The birth of the Gothic results from the joined impact of these ideas. It is to this event that we must now turn.

98. See below, ch. 5, n. 14.

99. Rose, pp. 11 ff. The Cistercians introduce Gothic into Germany (Heisterbach) and Italy. They import noteworthy elements of Gothic architecture into England. See Gall, Niederrheinische und normännische Architek-
tur im Zeitalter der Frühgotik, pp. 86 ff.; Clasen, Die gotische Baukunst, p. 137; Enlart, Origines françaises de l'architecture gothique en Italie; Kroening's review of Paatz, Wesen und Werden der Trecento Architektur in Toscana (ZK VIII, 1939, 196 ff.); and Bond, Gothic Architecture.

# THE BIRTH OF THE GOTHIC

# 3. SUGER OF ST.-DENIS

No MISCONCEPTION has proved a greater obstacle to our understanding of Gothic architecture than its interpretation as the "logical" sequel to Romanesque, as the consistent development of stylistic principles and technical methods evolved during the preceding period. In point of fact, Gothic architecture is not the heir but the rival of Romanesque, created as its emphatic antithesis. The first Gothic art (as the French call it) originated around 1140, the culmination of those anti-Romanesque or anti-Cluniac tendencies in art that we observed in the preceding chapter. At that time, however, Romanesque art was still flourishing in many parts of Europe. It was perhaps the very power of this adversary that evoked, on the part of its opponents, an artistic answer as forceful and clear as was St. Bernard's polemic. This answer is Gothic architecture.

Great works of art—great works of the human mind in general—are always called forth by the dialectical process of what Mr. Toynbee has defined as the law of challenge and response. Such interaction, in the creation of a work of art, is the answer to a source or model or influence. But historians of art and literature are apt to overrate and oversimplify the role of such influences and hence to view the development of art as governed by a kind of Darwinian law, consistent, predictable, and inevitable. This is, of course, a sure way to overlook or misunderstand in a work of art all that is significant, original, authentic. A work of art is created because an individual or a group is compelled to convey an experience that is particularly his or theirs. Such an urge might very well have been provoked, and usually is, by contact with an influence or model that acts as a catalyst. Even so, the more significant a work of art, the more marked will be the elements of revolt, the destructive tendencies, even in regard to the work that served as a prototype. Conversely, transparency of influences, docility of their acceptance in a work of art, are nearly always signs of mediocrity. Since understanding a work of art means to participate in the singular expression of a singular experience, it is usually more important to grasp the element of "revolt" than the reflection of influences in it.

All this applies particularly to the genesis of Gothic architecture. None of its constituent elements were inventions. Romanesque architecture, especially that of Normandy and Burgundy, contributed a great deal. The first Gothic builders employed, co-ordinated, and transformed these elements and in so doing achieved an architectural system that was novel and anti-Romanesque precisely because of the novelty of the spiritual message that was to be conveyed.[1]

This view of the relationship between Gothic and Romanesque is confirmed by the geography as well as the chronology of the new style. The first Gothic is so remarkably identified with one limited territory, the Île-de-France —more exactly, the domain of the Capetian monarchy—that the late Henri Focillon suggested wisely, if somewhat paradoxically, that Gothic be defined as the Romanesque of the Île-de-France.[2] No other artistic style has been more closely linked to a political idea and its historical realization and growth. "We intend to demonstrate," observed Viollet-le-Duc a century ago, "that the French cathedral . . . was born with the monarchical power." [3] More recent scholarship has only confirmed this thesis.[4] Created in the very heart of Capetian power,[5] the Gothic advanced in the wake of its consolidation and expansion.

1. Bony, "La Technique normande du mur épais" (*BM*, XCVIII, 1939), asks whether Anglo-Norman architecture "n'aurait-elle donc été qu'un champ d'expériences préliminaires pour l'art gothique français?" This kind of teleological approach seems to me dangerous: Anglo-Norman architecture was not imperfect Gothic, but rather the realization of stylistical principles germane to itself. But Bony is surely right in stating: "seule l'Angleterre a poursuivi méthodiquement, après 1080, les expériences commencés en Normandie; seule elle a su les conduire jusqu'aux lisières de la pensée gothique. Sous quelque angle que l'on aborde le problème des origines du gothique français . . . c'est donc toujours vers la Normandie et l'Angleterre que l'on se trouve ramené."

2. Focillon, *Art d'Occident, le moyen-âge*,

*roman et gothique*, p. 140. See also Francastel, *L'Humanisme roman*, ch. VI, "Une École romane: Le Gothique."

3. Viollet-le-Duc, *Dictionnaire raisonné de l'architecture française du XIᵉ au XVIᵉ siècle*, II, 284 f.

4. See Lefèvre-Pontalis, *L'Architecture religieuse dans l'ancien diocèse de Soissons au XIᵉ et au XIIᵉ siècle*, pp. 68 f.: "But why did the new architecture make its first appearance in the Île-de-France rather than in another province? The cause is in our opinion above all a political one. . . ."

5. On the geographical and political definition of the Île-de-France, see Longnon, "L'Île-de-France, son origine, ses limites, ses gouverneurs" (Société de l'histoire de Paris, *Mémoires*, I, 1874), and *La Formation de l'unité française*, pp. 36 ff.

Every single one of the great cathedrals rose on territory subject to the French crown.

No other region has done more, architecturally speaking, to prepare the advent of the new style than Normandy. Yet Normandy did not begin to build Gothic until after its conquest by Philip Augustus. Again, the Cathedral of Le Mans, capital of Maine, was built in the Romanesque—or rather in the Angevin —style at a time when the first Gothic buildings had already made their appearance in the Île-de-France. Structurally the great cross-ribbed vault of Le Mans —like that of Angers Cathedral—is the equal of any Gothic vault. It is all the more significant that here, as in the other churches of this school, the organization of the walls, especially in the clerestory zone, shows no trace of the Gothic tendencies toward luminosity and the reduction of inert surfaces.[6] After the annexation of Maine by the French crown, however, the chapter of Le Mans Cathedral decided to build the Gothic choir that came to be considered perfect of its kind.

Those regions of modern France, on the other hand, that remained outside the orbit of Capetian power retained their Romanesque cathedrals. But in Provence, the appearance of Gothic sculpture (a manifestly alien element) since the last quarter of the twelfth century was owing to the increasingly close political ties between the episcopate of Provence and the French king; [7] the introduction of the art of France into this region ominously foreshadowed its conquest in the Albigensian Crusade. This political significance of the Gothic is even more apparent abroad. In Apulian Lucera the cathedral rises, a grim, ascetic monument to the victory of the French Charles of Anjou over the smiling "Romanesque" culture of the Hohenstaufen. Even in this form, so sadly different from its original spirit, the Gothic bespeaks its connection with the French monarchy.

These impressions are confirmed if we consider the development of Gothic elsewhere in Europe. Nowhere outside the sphere of French influences does it appear as a spontaneous development of Romanesque. Gothic was imported into Germany by the Cistercians more than half a century after its creation;

6. See Bilson, "Les Voûtes de la nef de la Cathédrale d'Angers" (CA, Angers, 1910): "Nothing so perfect and skillful as these vaults had been built" elsewhere during the first half of the century. See also the remarks of Ward, Medieval Church Vaulting, pp. 49 ff.

7. See Aubert, La Sculpture française au moyen-âge, p. 155.

it was considered a "French" style as late as the fourteenth century.[8] In England the new style appeared first in the Cathedral of Canterbury, begun in 1175 by William of Sens. Sens had received the exiled Thomas Becket with particular hospitality a few years before, a fact that may well account for the selection of the architect who reproduced the model of the Cathedral of Sens in many features of the English cathedral. In England, as well as in Germany and Italy, Gothic conflicted with powerful indigenous traditions and hence underwent transformations that changed it into something entirely different.

In short, Gothic is the style of the Île-de-France; it is so closely tied to the destinies of the Capetian monarchy and encouraged by the latter to such an extent that we must assume that Gothic was considered the expression of ideas with which the crown wished to be associated. If so, how did that association come about?

For an answer to this question we turn to the first Gothic sanctuaries and to the personalities of their authors. The Gothic appears first in three great churches, all within a limited area, all in places of particular importance to the French monarchy, all designed, if not executed, within a decade: the first Gothic cathedral is that of Sens; the first Gothic abbey is that of St.-Denis; the west façades of St.-Denis and, especially, of Chartres are the first manifestations of Gothic architectural sculpture. Responsible for these three buildings were the Bishops Henry of Sens and Geoffrey of Chartres, and the Abbot Suger of St.-Denis. These prelates were personal friends and shared the same convictions. As we inquire into the origin and meaning of Gothic architecture, we must try to understand the ideas of these prelates as well as the monuments that have kept their memories alive.

The most famous of the three men is Suger of St.-Denis. His personality is as fascinating today as it was to his contemporaries.[9] His career, which led

8. The Church of St. Peter at Wimpfen-im-Tal was constructed in 1259, *opere francigeno*, by a master who had recently returned from Paris. See Graf, *Opus francigenum*, p. 9; also Renan, *Mélanges d'histoire et de voyages*, p. 220, who asserts that Gothic was regarded as *opus francigenum* until the fourteenth century in Germany. See also de Mely, "Nos vieilles cathédrales et leurs maîtres d'oeuvre" (*Revue archéologique*, 5th series, XI, 1920).

9. See Doublet, *Histoire de l'abbaye de S. Denys en France*, pp. 226 ff.; Félibien, *Histoire de l'abbaye royale de Saint-Denys en France*, pp. 151 ff. Within recent years Suger's biography has been sketched twice, both times, characteristically, by art historians. See Panofsky, *Abbot Suger on the Abbey Church of St.-Denis and Its Art Treasures*, Introduction; and Aubert, *Suger*.

him from very humble origins to the regency of France, gave him scope for the application of an extraordinary variety of gifts. Suger's diplomatic skills called the young monk to the attention of his abbot. He was only in his twenties when he represented his monastery at the Council of Poitiers (1106) and subsequently before the pope.[10] In the years that immediately followed, Suger, as deputy of his abbot, showed equal ability as an administrator and as a resourceful and courageous military leader who defended with success his king's and his monastery's possessions against some rapacious feudatories of the land.[11] Those military accomplishments brought him again into immediate contact with King Louis VI, who had been educated with Suger at St.-Denis. What had started here as a friendship between two youths of very different origins developed into a tie that united the two men for the rest of their lives.[12] The king employed Suger, who from then never seems to have ceased being his sovereign's chief political adviser as his ambassador to the pope. It was during one of these missions to Italy, in 1122, that Suger learned of his election to the abbacy of St.-Denis.[13]

To understand the full significance of the appointment, we must bear in mind that this monastery was no ordinary Benedictine house. Even in the age of monasticism, even among the great monasteries of France, St.-Denis occupied a position of unparalleled power and prestige.[14] The old historians of St.-Maur have not unjustly called it the foremost of all French and perhaps of all European abbeys.[15] Medieval sources abound in references to its pre-eminence. They designate St.-Denis the mother of French churches and the crown of the realm.[16] No other ecclesiastical institution, perhaps no institution of any kind, was more closely identified with the Capetian monarchy.[17] St.-Denis was the shrine of

---

10. Suger, *Vie de Louis le Gros*, p. 23.

11. Suger, *De rebus in administratione sua gestis*, XXIII (*Oeuvres complètes de Suger*, pp. 184 f.); *Vie de Louis*, pp. 60 ff.; Félibien, pp. 139 ff.; Panofsky, *Suger*, p. 7; Aubert, *Suger*, pp. 7 ff.

12. Suger, *Vie de Louis*, p. 5. Louis VI says of Suger, "quem fidelem et familiarem in consiliis habebamus." Tardif, *Monuments historiques*, No. 391.

13. *Vie de Louis*, pp. 96 f.

14. See the imposing, though only partial,

list of the monastery's possessions and revenues in d'Ayzac, *Histoire de l'abbaye de St.-Denis en France*, I, 168 ff.; and Cartellieri, *Abt Suger von St. Denis*, pp. 175 ff., 186 ff. On the abbot's revenues, see d'Ayzac, I, 359 ff.

15. "Omniumque facile totius Galliae, et forsan Europae abbatiarum princeps" (*GC*, VII, 332).

16. *GC*, VII, 335; Doublet, pp. 170, 284, 410.

17. Luchaire, *Louis VI le Gros*, pp. cxlviii ff.; and Lavisse, *Histoire de France*, III, 1, pp. 20 ff.

the patron saint of France and of the royal house and the burial place of French kings since Merovingian times.[18] Long the recipient of munificent donations of the crown, the house was, as one of the "royal" abbeys, exempt from all feudal and ecclesiastical domination and subject only to the king.[19]

In the first half of the twelfth century, St.-Denis became the cornerstone of royal policy and the fountainhead of that idea of the Christian monarchy which established Capetian ascendancy throughout France, in some respects throughout Europe. The attainment of this place and influence was principally the work of Suger. To his high ecclesiastical position he brought that peculiar blend of gifts which characterizes the statesman. As an administrator he had both the knowledge of jurisprudence necessary to maintain and expand the vast possessions of his house and the sense of practical detail that prompted him to attend even to such matters as the provision of better plowshares for his tenants and the initiation of a competent program of forest preservation.[20] As a diplomat and politician, Suger had a rare sense for the possible, willingness to compromise, and above all a never faltering preference for peaceful accommodation. Louis VI was a ruler of very considerable gifts; but it is doubtful if he would have attained the stature that history has accorded him had he not had at his side a councilor always ready and often able to restrain his sovereign's rash and violent disposition, a disposition that he lived to deplore in his old age.[21] And among the ecclesiastical statesmen of the Middle Ages, Suger is one of the very few whom religious zeal did not make insensitive to the plight of the powerless, the humble, the vanquished, even if these had previously obstructed the course of his government.[22]

What welded these political and moral gifts together was the power of the imagination. A singularly lucid political vision unified his innumerable occupations. This vision, which he lived to see realized, stands behind the great artistic achievement—the Abbey Church of St.-Denis—that is the subject of this chap-

18. See Doublet, pp. 168 ff.; Crosby, *The Abbey of St.-Denis*, pp. 48 ff. Cf. also Schramm, *Der König von Frankreich*, pp. 131 ff.

19. Doublet, pp. 168 ff., 391, 441 ff., 655 ff. This, as we shall see, was partly the work of Suger.

20. Suger, *De admin.*, IV (*Oeuvres*, p. 160); cf. Panofsky, *Suger*, p. 8; Aubert, *Suger*, pp. 22 ff.; and Cartellieri, *Suger*, pp. 71 ff.

21. Suger, *Vie de Louis*, XXXII, 123.

22. See his intervention on behalf of the commune of Poitiers when, in addressing Louis VII, he used the memorable words: "Esto securus, quanto siquidem crudelitatis minus admiseris, tanto regie majestatis honorem divina potentia amplificavit." *Vie de Louis*, XXXII, 153.

ter. But as he himself wanted this monument to convey his political and religious ideas, we have to acquaint ourselves with these ideas first.

Suger's life falls within the epoch of European history that is marked by the struggle between *imperium* and *sacerdotium*, centering mainly in the issue of investiture. But the position of France differed profoundly from that of the German Empire. The Carolingian heritage that supplemented the modest Capetian possessions in the Île-de-France was mainly an ecclesiastical one.[23] Along the perimeter of its frontier, from Burgundy to Flanders and indeed to Normandy, the kingdom was ringed by a number of great bishoprics that, as "royal" sees, were subject to the French crown. The rulers of six—the archbishop of Reims, the bishops of Laon, Langres, Châlons, Beauvais, and Noyon —were dukes and counts of the realm and in this capacity great feudal lords whose possessions, added together, exceeded by far the size of the royal domain. As vassals of the king, the occupants of the "royal" sees swore fealty like all other feudatories. And since occupancy of the ecclesiastical fiefs was not hereditary, the king's right to nominate the bishops of them greatly increased his power.

Such composition of its dominion could not but affect the political character of the monarchy. As *Pairs* of France, the six prelates just mentioned made up one half of a college of twelve.[24] In the assemblies of the realm the hierarchy was prominently represented, its views often decisive. The archbishops of Reims and Sens, under whose ecclesiastical jurisdiction lay the greater part of all crown territories, were almost invariably present at these meetings. The more important assemblies coincided with the great feasts of the liturgical year and were customarily held in cathedral towns. In that event, not only the local bishop but his chapter and often his clergy would sit in the assembly, the ecclesiastical estate outnumbering the secular nobility.[25]

Such ecclesiastical influence had important effects on relations between the French crown and its neighbors. It was of added significance that the most powerful of the "royal" bishoprics were situated in foreign territory, French

23. For the following, see Schwarz, "Der Investiturstreit in Frankreich" (*Zeitschrift für Kirchengeschichte*, 1923); Fliche, "Y-a-t-il eu en France et en Angleterre une querelle des investitures?" (*RB*, XLVI, 1934); and Faw-

tier, *Les Capétiens et la France*, p. 71.
24. See de Manteyer, "L'Origine des douze Pairs de France" (*Études . . . Monod.*)
25. Luchaire, *Histoire des institutions monarchiques de la France sous les premiers Capétiens (987–1180)*, I, 254 ff.

enclaves that acted as spearheads of royal expansion and as thorns in the flesh of the territorial rulers. As an obvious act of self-preservation, many of these seized the opportunity that seemed to offer itself with the Gregorian and Cluniac reform. It is hardly surprising to find the Duke of Burgundy and the counts of Anjou, Troyes, and Chartres siding with the popes in their attempts to free the Church from royal domination. The capital cities of every one of them was spiritually ruled by a bishop whom the king of France had appointed.

This alignment of forces had induced Philip I to regard the reform movement with considerable hostility. But it soon became clear that its progress was irresistible. During the reign of Philip's son, Louis VI, the sees of Sens, Paris, and Chartres disregarded the king's fierce opposition and embraced the party of St. Bernard.[26] However, if the makings of a struggle with the Church, analogous to that which embroiled Germany and temporarily even England, ever existed in France, events soon propelled her political course in the opposite direction. In its climactic duel with the German emperor the papacy turned to France for protection and assistance.

Menaced by Henry V, Pope Paschal II entered France to begin a long sojourn there. In 1107 he had a very friendly interview with the aging Philip I and Prince Louis at St.-Denis. But he had previously visited Chartres and met its bishop, the great Yves, who above all was responsible for that definition of the relationship between Church and State that spared France a war of investiture.[27] Yves had occasion to remind the pope that more than any other Christian ruler the French king had been loyal to the Apostolic See; that no division between *imperium* and *sacerdotium* had ever rent France asunder.

These developments occurred during the formative years of Suger's life; he witnessed them at close range. He met Paschal II personally and accompanied him during much of his French journey. Before this pontiff the young monk earned his political spurs by pleading the case of his monastery against the Bishop of Paris, "manly, with sound reasoning and valid canonical argument"; the words are his own.[28] It is one of the few occasions on which Suger has

26. See Luchaire, *Louis VI*, p. clxxv, and below, p. 144.

27. Suger, *Vie de Louis*, IX, 24 ff. Cf. Fliche and Martin, *Histoire de l'Église*, VIII, 353.

28. *Vie de Louis*, IX, 24 ff.: " . . . contra dominum episcopum Parisiensem Galonem,

multis querimoniis ecclesiam beati Dionisii agitantem, in conspectu domini pape viriliter stando, aperta ratione et canonico judicio satisfecimus." For the background of this quarrel, see *Oeuvres*, XIV, 430 ff.

spoken with explicit praise of himself. In subsequent years, as the king's emissary to the Holy See and later as abbot of St.-Denis and first minister of Louis VI, Suger had a decisive share in formulating and putting into effect the policy that determined the relations between France and the Church. This policy was the implementation of the views of Yves of Chartres, whom Suger revered: a firm alliance with the pope against the emperor, and with the bishops against the predatory nobility of the kingdom; second, endorsement by the king of the basic ideas on ecclesiastical reform, and recognition by the pope of the king's continued domination of the "royal" bishoprics, a domination that, from now on, was usually exerted by less forceful, if equally effective, means than under Louis VI's predecessor.[29]

In the field of foreign relations, the results of this political course soon proved momentous. In 1119 Guy of Burgundy, Archbishop of Vienne, was elevated to the papacy. He took the name of Calixtus II. A son of the Count of Burgundy, he inclined toward the reform movement that had such powerful adherents in his own country. Dissatisfied with the compromising course of Paschal II, he had, when still archbishop, imperiously reprimanded the pope, convoked a synod of his see at Vienne, and from there hurled anathema against Emperor Henry V. As an uncle of Adelaide, queen of France, Calixtus was a relative of the French king. It is Suger who hints that these family ties had important political consequences.[30]

Of the four popes mentioned in Suger's writings, Calixtus is the one whom he esteemed by far the most. What drew the two men, whose temperaments differed so greatly, together was complete identity of political convictions and interests. Their close acquaintance developed into friendship. That Suger was raised to the abbacy of St.-Denis while representing France at the Holy See was hardly just a coincidence, even though Louis VI, to judge from his momentary ire about the monastery's vote, seems to have had no previous knowledge of it.[31] But his dissatisfaction about not having been consulted passed quickly enough; Suger found his sovereign all benevolence upon his return to France. If the elevation of Guy of Burgundy to the papacy was a fortunate event for

29. Imbart de la Tour, *Les Élections épisco-pales dans l'église de France*, pp. 439 ff.

30. *Vie de Louis*, XXVI, 94. On Calixtus

and the events mentioned, see Fliche and Martin, pp. 398 ff.; Luchaire, *Louis VI*, pp. cxxix ff.

31. Suger, *Vie de Louis*, p. 97.

St.-Denis as well as for France, the appointment of Suger to the abbacy of St.-Denis proved to be of equal advantage to the king and to the pope. As an intransigent champion of reform, Calixtus II almost immediately resumed the struggle of his predecessors with the empire. His family relations, political tradition, and above all the ecclesiastical policy of France made it inevitable that he should lean upon this power.

The European crisis quickly came to a climax. Like so many popes, Calixtus sought refuge in France. And before a council assembled at Reims, in the presence of the French king, he declared the emperor excommunicated as an enemy of the Church (October 30, 1119).[32] In this firm policy, which eventually induced Henry V to give in, Suger undoubtedly had his part. In 1123 he attended the first Ecumenical Council held in the Lateran, at which the emperor's ambassadors announced Henry's conciliatory terms to an assembly of more than three hundred bishops. The unusual tokens of the pope's esteem that Suger received on his departure suggest that Calixtus meant to signify his appreciation of French support in the negotiations he had so successfully terminated.[33]

But if Henry V had made his peace with Rome, he felt quite differently in regard to France. In August, 1124, the emperor, in league with his father-in-law, Henry I of England, decided to invade France. His enmity against Louis VI had long been festering, but Suger was probably right in feeling that what had precipitated hostilities was the open alliance of France and the papacy that had enabled Calixtus II to excommunicate the emperor at a council convoked on French soil.[34] The menace of the two-pronged attack that now was afoot seemed deadly. In this emergency Louis VI hurried to St.-Denis. In its ancient sanctuary the relics of the patron saint and his companions Rusticus and Eleutherius were solemnly exposed. Kneeling in prayer before them, the king invoked the intercession of St. Denis, his "special patron," whom he designated as "after God, the singular protector of the realm," promising the saint rich donations for his abbey in case of victory.[35]

32. Suger, *Vie de Louis*, p. 94.
33. Suger, *Vie de Louis*, p. 100.
34. Suger, *Vie de Louis*, pp. 101 ff. Cf. Luchaire, *Louis VI*, p. cxxxvi, and Kienast, *Deutschland und Frankreich in der Kaiserzeit*, p. 61.

35. "Et quoniam beatum Dionisium specialem patronum et singularem post Deum regni protectorem et multorum relatione et crebro cognoverat experimento, ad eum festinans, tam

These prayers completed, Louis VI rose to receive from the altar of the Apostle of France, "as from his Lord," the banner of St. Denis.[36] Actually, this vexillum was the standard of the Vexin, a fief of the abbey, the possession of which made the king the vassal of its abbot, or, in medieval terms, the vassal of the abbot representing the patron saint. On this occasion, the investment with the vexillum was to indicate that Louis VI considered himself the liege man of St. Denis, that he went into battle in the saint's cause, and that the banner was a token of the latter's protection.[37] After Suger had presented the vexillum to Louis, the king, before the chapter of the monks, formally acknowledged his vassalage, adding that he would render homage to the abbey if his royal authority did not forbid it.[38] Whereupon, probably still in front of the altar—like Bohemond of Antioch in Chartres Cathedral pleading for his Crusade [39]—the king appealed to the assembly to join him in the defense of the realm. The response was extraordinary. The contingents of Reims and Châlons, Laon and Soissons, Étampes and Paris, Orléans and St.-Denis, were swelled by the forces of great lords whose relations with the crown had long been hostile or cool. The dukes of Burgundy and Aquitaine, the counts of Anjou, Chartres, Flanders, and Troyes, now followed the royal summons.[40]

Of the events just mentioned, Suger has made himself the chronicler. He

precibus quam benefitiis precordialiter pulsat ut regnum defendat, personam conservet, hostibus more solito resistat, et quoniam hanc ab eo habent prerogativam ut si regnum aliud regnum Francorum invadere audeat, ipse beatus et admirabilis defensor cum sociis suis tanquam ad defendendum altari suo superponatur, eo presente fit tam gloriose quam devote." Suger, *Vie de Louis*, pp. 101 f.

36. "Rex autem vexillum ab altari suscipiens quod de comitatu Vilcassini quod ad ecclesiam feodatus est, spectat, votive tanquam a domino suo suscipiens . . . " Suger, *Vie de Louis*, pp. 101 f.

37. See Erdmann, "Kaiserfahne und Blutfahne" (Preussische Akademie der Wissenschaften, *Sitzungsberichte*, 1932). Cf. Doublet, pp. 230, 299 ff.; Schramm, pp. 139 ff.; and below, n. 58. The oldest existing identification of the vexillum with the oriflamme occurs in Gullaume le Breton's *Philippid*, XI, 32 ff. (Delaborde, ed., II, 319); the oldest pictorial representation is in the southern transept

window at Chartres.

38. ". . . evocatis inde cum abbate ejusdem monasterii Sugerio religiosis, et in pleno capitulo causam regni eorum devotioni commendans, dixit se more priscorum regum auriflammam velle sumere ab altari, affirmando quod hujus bajulatio ad comitem Vulcassini de jure spectabat, et quod de eodem comitatu, nisi auctoritas regia obsisteret, ecclesie homagium facere tenebatur." The passage occurs in the famous MS. lat. 5949 A of the Bibliothèque Nationale, which very probably represents, or is based upon, Suger's own carefully revised version of his *Life of Louis VI*. See *Vie de Louis*, p. 142, and the remarks of Molinier therein, pp. xxii ff.; also Waquet's translation, *Vie de Louis VI le Gros*, p. xxii.

39. Suger himself had witnessed the event; see *Vie de Louis*, IX, 23; cf. Lépinois, *Histoire de Chartres*, I, 81.

40. Cf. *Vie de Louis*, XXVII, 102 ff. and 143, for the revised account in the MS. Lat. 5949 A.

was a man of conspicuous literary interests and achievements. His infallible memory, his knowledge of classical authors, Horace and Lucan above all, astonished his monks no less than the modern reader.[41] A man of indefatigable energy, despite his frail health, he found the time to write a great deal. But among the monastic authors of his century he is probably the only one who did not compose a single theological treatise. It was to historical writing, as well as to his artistic interests, that he devoted the years of relative political retirement (1137–44).

These writings, above all his life of Louis VI and that of Louis VII, of which Suger himself was able to complete only the first chapters,[42] may well earn for their author, in addition to his many other titles, that of the first systematic historian since antiquity. The great archives of his monastery, depository of royal as well as ecclesiastical state papers, had aroused Suger's interest at an early age.[43] At the beginning of the twelfth century, a collection of chronicles was compiled at St.-Denis.[44] In view of Suger's interests it is not impossible that he himself may have begun this work while still a young monk, and that he directed and supervised its continuation in subsequent years. His own histories, admired, utilized, and supplemented by contemporaries as well as later historians,[45] seem to have been designed as only part of a much vaster project. There is good reason to believe that Suger himself planned to make his abbey, already the royal archive, the institute for the official historiography of the realm. In the following century, St.-Denis actually assumed this function.[46]

It is in Suger's historical writings that what I have called his political

41. See Panofsky, *Suger*, p. 13; Aubert, *Suger*, p. 51. "Quodque saepius in illo miratus sum," his biographer writes, "ita quaecumque in juventute didicerat, memoriter retinebat . . . Gentilium vero poetarum ob tenacem memoriam oblivisci usquequaque non poterat, ut versus Horatianos utile aliquid continentes usque ad vicenos, saepe etiam ad tricenos, memoriter nobis recitaret." Suger, *Oeuvres*, p. 381.

42. Also printed in *Vie de Louis*, pp. 165 ff. See Molinier's remarks therein, pp. xxxi; and his *Les Sources de l'historie de France*, p. 183.

43. "Cum aetate docibili adolescentiae meae antiquas armarii possessionum revolverem cartas." *De admin.*, III (*Oeuvres*, p. 160).

44. See Molinier in Suger, *Vie de Louis*, p. xvii; and his *Catalogue des manuscrits de la*

*Bibliothèque Mazarine*, II, 321 ff. Cf. Doublet, pp. 226 ff.

45. Odo of Deuil dedicated to Suger his history of the Second Crusade and invited the abbot to undertake the history of Louis VII as he had written that of his father. His own work, Odo hopes, will be of assistance to Suger in this undertaking (*MGH SS*, XXVI, 60; *PL*, CLXXXV, 120 ff.; and *De profectione Ludovici VII in Orientem*, p. 2). See Aubert, *Suger*, p. 113.

46. Molinier, *Catalogue*, and *Sources*, II, 23; Aubert, *Suger*, p. 114; Fawtier, p. 11, is less positive. See also Viard's introduction in his edition of *Les Grandes Chroniques de France publiées pour la Société de l'histoire de France*, I, xii ff.; and Curtius, "Über die altfranzösische Epik" (*Romanische Forschungen*, LXII, 1950).

vision, the ultimate goal of his statesmanship, becomes tangible. For the abbot of St.-Denis, as for Richelieu, historiography was a part of his statesmanship: justification of its actions, clarification of its principles, authoritative interpretation for the benefit of future generations. It is significant that the abbot destined certain chapters of his *Life of Louis VI* to be read in choir as part of the annual liturgical observation of the king's death.[47]

Suger's style is apt to obscure his achievement, at least for the modern reader. The *Life of Louis VI* is densely written; it abounds in grammatical inaccuracies; there are even obvious omissions of words. Composed in haste, unfinished and unpolished, parts of it constitute perhaps no more than a first draft, like Richelieu's *Mémoires*, intended for future revision. At least there is reason to believe that Suger himself went over the work in his last years, correcting and clarifying its style and reinforcing the main argument that inspires every sentence.[48]

This argument is clear. Despite his stylistic shortcomings, Suger is a writer with a distinct sense for the dramatic, occasionally even the melodramatic, as when he recounts the massacre of La Roche Guyon.[49] He has a keen eye for great personalities and great historical moments; he has an equal ability to bring them back to life. It is in this vein that he reinvokes the conflict among the major powers of his day, which he had witnessed and in which he had taken so decisive a part. It is a drama played on two levels, the political and the theological, the human and the divine, and Suger is continually trying to render visible the ties that connect the two spheres. Yet his work is no theodicy, no philosophy of history, as is that of his contemporary, Otto of Freising. Suger was not a spectator but an actor. He himself had forged and utilized the crises he chronicles, and it is this role, as well as his gifts as a historian, that irresistibly direct his narrative, and our eyes with it, toward the place where the historical and the providential intersect. This place is St.-Denis.

Suger's *Life of Louis VI* represents the rule of this king as the undeviating realization of the grand political design that was uppermost in Suger's own

47. See Martène, *Veterum scriptorum amplissima collectio*, IV, xxxvii ff. Cf. Doublet, p. 1281.

48. On this hypothesis and the arguments for and against it, see Waquet's translation of Suger, *Vie de Louis VI le Gros*, pp. 22 ff.

49. *Vie de Louis* (Molinier, ed.), XVI, 52 ff. Unless otherwise specified, succeeding references are to the Molinier edition.

mind. He passes over in silence those acts of his sovereign of which he disapproved and which he was unable to prevent, such as the persecution of the Archbishop of Sens and the Bishop of Paris. Instead, Suger depicts Louis VI as a deeply pious ruler whose every act, like an illustration of the Virgilian dictum, "parcere subjectis et debellare superbos," was designed to protect the law-abiding and meek and to punish, sword in hand, the proud and lawless.[50] For Suger, the meek and just are supremely represented by the clergy of France, the proud by its feudal oppressors. Thus the terrible Hugh du Puiset stands accused, in 1111, before a great assembly of "archbishops, bishops, clerics, and monks" led by the bishops of Sens, Chartres, and Orléans, whose lands he had devastated, "more rapacious than a wolf." [51] Hugh is condemned, and the ensuing war, in which Suger himself takes an active part, ends with the complete defeat of the scoundrel. Again, Suger dwells broadly on the campaign that Louis VI undertook ten years later to liberáte the Bishop of Clermont from his oppressor, the Count of Auvergne.

But throughout the entire narrative the Abbey of St.-Denis remains the focus of the great panorama. Suger begins by recounting the king's early love and devotion for his patron saint that continues throughout his entire life and prompts him to make rich donations to the abbey.[52] Before his death he desires to divest himself in St.-Denis of his royal insignia in order to exchange them for the habit of a monk.[53] The biography ends with the king's burial in the sanctuary, at the very place he had designated before his death (1137), and which, contrary to everyone's opinion, was almost miraculously found to be exactly large enough to receive his remains.[54]

These events, however, are but the framework for the crisis of 1124 and the position the abbey assumed at that moment. Their narration forms the most

50. *Vie de Louis*, XVIII, 62. The Virgilian passage is also quoted by St. Bernard to indicate the responsibilities of the Christian ruler. *Ep.* CCCLVIII (*PL*, CLXXXII, 564).

51. *Vie de Louis*, XXVIII, 106 ff.

52. "Altus puerulus, antiqua regum Karoli Magni et aliorum excellentiorum, hoc ipsum testamentis imperialibus testificantium, consuetudine, apud Sanctum Dyonisium tanta et quasi nativa dulcedine ipsis sanctis martyribus suisque adhesit, usque adeo ut innatam a puero eorum ecclesie amiciciam toto tempore vite sue multa liberalitate et honorificentia continuaret, et in fine, summe post Deum sperans ab eis, seipsum et corpore et anima, ut si fieri posset, ibidem monachus efficeretur . . . " *Vie de Louis*, I, 5. See n. 53.

53. *Vie de Louis*, XXXII, 124; Félibien, p. 168. On the significance of this act, cf. de Pange, *Le Roi très-chrétien*, p. 302.

54. *Vie de Louis*, XXXIII, 127 ff.; Félibien, p. 168; Doublet, p. 1277.

lively and intense part of Suger's history.[55] It is here that he has even altered slightly the facts and rearranged their sequence in order to make their significance, as he wanted it to be understood, more apparent to his readers. According to him, the estates had rallied behind their king at the Assembly of St.-Denis as they never had before. The impression caused by that show of determination to stand together in the defense of the realm was such that the emperor was overcome by fear and withdrew from French soil. The victory, Suger remarks, was as great as or even greater than if it had been won in the field of battle.[56]

And in a deeper sense Suger's presentation of the events of 1124 was far from untrue. For the prestige of the French monarchy the consequences of the Assembly of St.-Denis were considerable; they were momentous for the abbey itself. In reading Suger one feels that the tortuous course of political developments suddenly reveals a clear and simple pattern, a pattern that realized Suger's own vision. Church and monarchy now became inseparable allies. France rallied around her king in order to defend the cause of the kingdom, which, in view of the person and record of its attacker, the emperor, was also the cause of the Church. It characterizes the new relations between the French monarchy and the Church that even Bernard of Clairvaux now addressed Louis VI as "the first of kings." [57]

The great rally took place at St.-Denis. The banner of St.-Denis, which had marked the king as liege man of the Apostle of France, became, from now on, the official battle insigne of the royal arms, "St.-Denis" the battle cry. In the popular imagination the standard of the abbey merged with the oriflamme of the *Chanson de Roland,* the mythical banner of Charlemagne.[58] And it was only natural that the abbot who in that solemn hour had invested Louis VI with the vexillum should become the French prelate most intimately associated with the crown; that he should assume dignities that, in certain respects, placed him at

55. Compare the two versions in *Vie de Louis*, 101, 142.

56. ". . . superius fuit quam si campo triumphassent." *Vie de Louis*, XXVII, 104.

57. *Ep.* CCV (*PL*, CLXXXI, 462). See Olschki, *Der ideale Mittelpunkt Frankreichs im Mittelalter*, p. 18.

58. Schramm, p. 139; Erdmann, "Kaiserfahne." As was pointed out recently, there is no direct evidence that Suger himself was responsible for the identification of the vexillum of St. Denis with the oriflamme. See Loomis, "The Oriflamme of France and the War-cry 'Monjoie' in the Twelfth Century" (*Studies in Art and Literature for Belle da Costa Greene*). This momentous identification, however, became possible only in virtue of the political ideology of which Suger was the author. Cf. above, n. 37.

the head of the French hierarchy. In 1147, Louis VII embarked on the Second Crusade. Prior to the king's departure, a Royal Assembly held at Étampes nominated Suger regent of France. In announcing the result of the election, Bernard of Clairvaux presented the abbot of St.-Denis and the Count of Nevers to the Assembly with the Biblical metaphor that Bernard himself had made portentous in the political controversy of his age: "Behold the two swords."[59] In point of fact, both swords, the spiritual and the temporal power, subsequently passed into the hands of Suger.[60] During his regency the two spheres seemed to have merged.

France had been without a religious capital until this time.[61] From 1124 on, St.-Denis occupied this place. The danger of war over, Suger tells us, Louis VI proceeded to implement the vows he had made on the eve of the threatened invasion. In a public document of vast consequence to the future of the abbey, the king recalls how, in the face of the national peril, he had hastened to St.-Denis "after the custom of our ancestors." He calls the abbey the capital of the realm ("caput regni nostri"), since providence had placed in the hands of St. Denis and his companions the protection of the French dynasty.[62] The royal donation to the monastery that is then set forth is represented as a personal gift to the patron saint "for the salvation of our soul as for the benefit of the government and defense of the realm." [63] It is characteristic of the time that the document does not distinguish between the religious institution and the saint to whom it is dedicated. As the king's investment with the oriflamme made him a vassal of the sacred protector of France, so donations made to the monastery of St.-Denis were considered donations to the saint himself. Interference with such possessions were outrages against the sacred protector that were certain to draw his wrath upon the offender, just as charity on his behalf

59. The account of Odo of Deuil, *De Ludovici VII . . . profectione in Orientem* (PL, CLXXXV, 1209).

60. The Count of Nevers was later replaced by Raoul of Vermandois; but neither he nor the Archbishop of Reims, who assisted Suger, disputed the latter's authority. It is the abbot who in 1149 summons the Archbishop of Reims to the Assembly of Chartres. Suger's biographer states accurately, "dux novus gemino statim accinctus est gladio, altero materiali et regio, altero spirituali et ecclesiastico . . . " *Oeuvres*, p. 394.

61. Olschki, pp. 40 ff.

62. ". . . et nostram et antecessorum successorumque nostrorum protectionem in capite regni nostri, videlicet apud sanctos martyres dignatus est collocare." Tardif, No. 391, p. 217.

63. ". . . pro salute anime nostre quam pro regni administratione et defensione." Tardif, No. 391, p. 217.

ensured his benevolence.[64] It is easy to see what incalculable consequences such beliefs were bound to have for the fortunes of an institution identified, as was St.-Denis, with the patron of the entire kingdom. In the present case the king's donation was designed both to underscore the spiritual prestige of the abbey and to supply the house with the material means required for the adequate physical expression of that position.

Suger speaks of a twofold donation. Upon returning from his campaign, he says, Louis VI presented to the abbey the crown of his father, Philip I, which he had retained unjustly, since by right it belonged to St.-Denis. In point of fact, the king had made this present four years earlier, acknowledging on that occasion that "by law and custom" the royal insignia did belong to St. Denis, "our Lord and protector." [65] Suger's deviation from the chronological truth is characteristic. Actually, the presentation of Philip's crown to St.-Denis had taken place not under his abbacy but under that of his predecessor. He wished this act to appear as having been prompted by the political prestige that the abbey had attained in consequence of the events of 1124 with which his personality and his designs were so intimately connected. And it is true that in the light of these events even that earlier act took on a significance it may not have possessed before. We have seen how Louis VI, before his death, wished to divest himself of his crown in St.-Denis. His grandson, Philip Augustus, returned the insignia to the abbey immediately after his coronation.[66] From then on, St.-Denis seems to have been the traditional depository of the crown. This fact automatically assured to the abbot of the house a share in the royal consecration. There is some reason to believe, as we shall see, that it was Suger who first insisted on this privilege. His successors were able to exert it.[67]

Suger mentions but briefly a second royal grant that his abbey received in

64. Fournier, *Nouvelles recherches sur les curies, chapitres et universités de l'ancienne église de France*, p. 83; Lesne, "Histoire de la propriété ecclésiastique en France" (*Mémoires et travaux publiés par des professeurs des Facultés Catholiques de Lille*, fasc. VI, pp. 171 ff.).

65. Suger, *Vie de Louis*, XXVII, 105; cf. Molinier, ibid., Tardif, No. 379, p. 213. See also Félibien, p. 156; Crosby, *L'Abbaye royale de Saint-Denis*, pp. 8 f. It ought to be

observed, moreover, that the royal diploma of 1124 was, contrary to Suger's assertion, promulgated before, not after, the projected German invasion.

66. See *Recueil des historiens des Gaules et de la France*, XII, 216; Schramm, p. 133; Berger, "Annales de St.-Denis, généralement connues sous le titre de *Chronicon sancti Dionysii ad cyclos paschales*" (*BEC*, XL, 1879).

67. Schramm, p. 133 ff.; cf. Doublet, pp. 366 ff.

1124. The king, he says, restored to St.-Denis the "outer *indictum*."[68] The brief sentence records a donation of very great significance. The *indictum*, the famous Lendit, denotes a fair, one of the most famous of medieval France, held under the auspices of St.-Denis. Although only initiated in the mid-eleventh century, it was generally believed, in the Middle Ages, to be much older.[69] According to a legend, fabricated and fostered by the abbey, the Lendit (the term *indictum* signified the institution of a religious feast) had been established in honor of certain relics of Christ's Passion, which had been presented to St.-Denis by Charles the Bald, the emperor most closely associated with the house. (He himself had assumed the abbacy after the death of Abbot Louis, who was also imperial chancellor.) Charles the Bald was also said to have instituted the annual feast in honor of the relics. Such feasts, and the crowds of pilgrims they attracted, usually led to the establishment of annual fairs, which coincided with the feast and played an extremely important part in the economic life of the time. The Lendit is a good example. Established in 1048, the feast received added luster when in 1053 the chasses of St. Denis and his companions were opened and shown actually to contain the relics of these saints.[70]

As the fame of St.-Denis increased as a pilgrimage center, so did the economic success of the Lendit. Indeed, this success was such that Louis VI, at a time when his relations with the abbey were not yet cordial, resolved on a competitive enterprise.[71] Notre Dame of Paris had received a particle of the True Cross in 1109; the king instituted an *indictum* in its honor. This second Lendit, or "outer Lendit," as Suger calls it, was established in the plain of St.-Denis, between the abbey and Paris. Placed under the jurisdiction of the Bishop of Paris, its revenues went directly to the crown. For the Abbey of St.-Denis, this outer Lendit could only be a thorn in the flesh, taking away from its spiritual luster and diminishing its revenues. It was therefore an achievement of the first order when, in 1124, Suger was able to persuade the king to place the outer

68. "Indictum exterius in platea, interius enim sanctorum erat, libentissime reddidit . . . " *Vie de Louis*, XXVII, 105.

69. See Levillain, "Essai sur les origines du Lendit" (*RH*, CLV, 1927), and "Études sur l'abbaye de Saint-Denis à l'époque mérovingienne" (*BEC*, XCI, 1930); Lebel, *Histoire administrative, économique et financière de l'abbaye de Saint-Denis*, pp. 206 ff.; Crosby, *Abbey of*

*St.-Denis*, p. 58.

70. Doublet, pp. 219 ff.; Félibien, pp. 120 f.; Levillain, "Essai"; cf. also Huvelin, *Essai historique sur le droit des marchés et des foires*, pp. 146 ff.

71. Levillain, "Essai"; Roussel, "La Bénédiction du Lendit au XIVᵉ siècle" (*Bulletin de la Société de l'histoire de Paris*, XXIV, 1897).

Lendit, along with the territory in which it was held, under the jurisdiction of the abbey, granting to this house all revenues from the fair. To the monastery, the deed opened a source of large additional revenues. But the material aspect was not the most important one.

In his document Louis VI declares that Christ has deigned to ennoble the entire French realm by the relics of His Passion in honor of which the Lendit had been established.[72] It would have been impossible to state more emphatically the importance of these relics and their singular relation to the monarchy. The implication, of course, was that the relic of Paris Cathedral, which had rivaled the sacred treasures of St.-Denis as long as the outer Lendit rivaled the Lendit proper, was of but secondary significance. The appropriation of both feasts by the abbey denoted not only another victory in its century-old struggle for complete independence from the bishops of Paris, but established St.-Denis as the religious center of the kingdom.

To appreciate the full significance of this fact we must remember that the twelfth century was the age of pilgrimages and of the Crusades. These hazardous journeys to remote places satisfied the romantic sense of high adventure, the longing for the wonders of regions unknown, that possess the people of all times. But for medieval men and women the passing over the threshold that separates the known from the unknown, the customary from the wonderful, meant the passing from the human to the sacred sphere. At the goal of these pious journeys, as they set foot on the soil hallowed by Christ's Passion or entered the sanctuaries sheltering the relics of saints, crusaders and pilgrims experienced the palpable presence of the supernatural.

For Suger's generation, pilgrimages and crusades were no longer distinct. The Church herself presented the Crusades as armed pilgrimages undertaken in defense of the holy places and hence even more meritorious than ordinary pilgrimages.[73] Conversely, the most celebrated pilgrimage center of western Europe, Santiago de Compostela, and some of the major stations on the roads leading toward it were, in the imagination of pilgrims, rendered venerable by

---

72. "Regnum nostrum Indicti die insignis sue passionis dignatus est sublimare." Tardif, No. 391, p. 217.

73. The clerical author of the *Pseudo-Turpin* refers to Roland as a saint and martyr. Meredith-Jones, *Historia Karoli Magni et Rotholandi ou Chroniques du Pseudo-Turpin*, pp. 212, 202. See also Erdmann, *Die Entstehung des Kreuzzugsgedankens*, p. 306.

the memories of the Christian warriors who had fought and died here in the defense of their faith against the infidels. During the second half of the eleventh century, the wars against the Almoravides of Spain had engaged the flower of French chivalry. The military glory of these campaigns had received added luster from the Church, which promised heavenly rewards to the Christian fighters.[74]

It was an age whose favorite saints were knights, an age apt to look upon the Christian knight defending his Church as a saint. To this theme the *chanson de geste* gave wide popular appeal by evoking the memory of the Spanish campaign of Charlemagne as an exploit implementing the divine mission of the French nation in defense of the Christian faith.[75] These tales became intimately connected with the Compostela pilgrimage. They were circulated if not actually composed by the monks of the great monasteries that straddled the roads to Santiago and now claimed associations with the great events of the Carolingian legend. The monks of Lérins thus made St. Honoratus, the early Christian founder of their abbey, into a friend of Charlemagne.[76] It was not enough that the Roman necropolis of Aliscamp at Arles was hallowed by the tombs of several saints; legend asserted and was eagerly believed that the heroes of Roncevaux had been brought here and buried by Charlemagne.[77] And St.-Guilhem-le-Désert, foundation and tomb of the saintly Count William, became an important religious station on the road to Compostela.[78] All these sights were sanctuaries in a twofold sense: they invoked patriotic as well as religious sentiments. In the twelfth century the pilgrimage roads thus became the arteries, the main churches situated on these roads the centers, of the spiritual life of France; owing to the ancient glories they claimed in virtue of their connection with the Carolingian past, and because of the economic activities that such fame attracted, these same places became political and economic centers as well.

Suger was a child of his age. In 1123, after attending the Lateran Council, and despite his pressing obligations as abbot, he took the time to visit every one

74. Meredith-Jones, pp. 124 ff.; 248, 292.
75. For the following, see especially Bédier, *Les Légendes épiques: Recherches sur la formation des chansons de geste;* and Holmes, *A History of Old French Literature,* pp. 68 ff. [*But see Add.*

*for p. 90.*]
76. Bédier, I, 376.
77. Bédier, I, 369.
78. Bédier, I, 336 ff., 386; Holmes, pp. 101 ff.

of the famous pilgrimage centers of southern Italy.[79] The idea of the Crusade had an equally firm hold upon his imagination. He was only twenty-five when he heard Bohemond of Tarent, prince of Antioch, plead in the Cathedral of Chartres for the defense of the Holy Sepulcher. The thought never left Suger. His appointment as regent made it impossible for him to accompany his king on the Crusade of 1147. The failure of this enterprise, which he seems to have anticipated, troubled him deeply. In 1150, at the very end of his life, Suger himself with the support of St. Bernard prepared another crusade, on behalf of which he first appealed to the pope and, at two great assemblies held at Laon and Chartres, to the episcopate and chivalry of France.[80] The response was lukewarm, but Suger remained undaunted. When St. Bernard declined the actual leadership because of ill health, Suger, then a man of seventy, assumed the supreme responsibility himself.[81] And, the subsidies for which he had hoped being refused, he decided that his own monastery was to shoulder the enormous financial burden alone.[82] The illness to which he was to succumb seized him while his thoughts and his remaining energy were centered in this project of a crusade that would originate at, and return to, St.-Denis, thus linking the religious heart of France with Jerusalem, the navel of the world.

This last design suggests the light in which St.-Denis appeared to its abbot. His monastery had once been reformed by Cluny; [83] the two great houses shared many ideals and ambitions. But the historical constellation led Suger into open rivalry with Cluny. Like Santiago de Compostela, like the other pilgrimage churches under Cluniac influence or domination, St.-Denis was to become a pilgrimage center where the idea of the Crusade intermingled with the memory of Charlemagne. This design was dictated not only by the religious mood of the time but by the singular political position of Suger's monastery.

79. *Vie de Louis*, XXVI, 100.
80. *Vie de Louis*, IX, 21 ff. Cf. *Oeuvres*, p. 429; Félibien, p. 182.
81. *Recueil des historiens*, XV, 614, 523, 648; Luchaire, *Études sur les actes de Louis VII*, pp. 247 f., 175 ff.; Aubert, *Suger*, pp. 58 ff.; Suger, *Sugerii vita*, III (*Oeuvres*, pp. 398 ff.); Grousset, *Histoire des croisades et du royaume franc de Jérusalem*, II, 269.
82. "Et regi quidem Francorum parcendum judicans vel reversae nuper militiae, quod vix

paululum respirassent, convocatos super hoc negotio regni convenit episcopos, exhortans illos et animans ad praesumendam secum victoriae gloriam, quae potentissimis regibus non fuisset concessa. Quod cum frustra tertio attemptasset, accepto gustu formidinis et ignaviae illorum, dignum nihilominus duxit, cessantibus aliis, per se laudabile votum implere." *Sugerii vita*, III (*Oeuvres*, pp. 398 ff.).
83. Cf. d'Ayzac, I, 2 f.; Crosby, *Abbey of St.-Denis*, p. 20 f.

The growing ascendancy of the Capetian dynasty took place, as it were, in the historical and legendary shadow of Charlemagne. The idea that the rule of the Capetians represented a true *renovatio* of the Carolingian era animated both Louis VI and Louis VII.[84] The mouthpiece of this idea, if not its originator, was Suger himself. At the very beginning of his *Life of Louis VI* he represents the king as the legitimate heir of the great emperor.[85] In his speech before the Assembly of 1124, as recorded by Suger, Louis VI claimed that the French were entitled to rule Germany as well as France, the implication being that not the German emperor but the French king was the legitimate heir to the Carolingian tradition.[86] Such claims were sufficiently disturbing to be at least partly responsible for the decision of the Emperor Frederick I to have Charlemagne canonized (1165) and to fix his cult at Aachen.[87] In France these measures remained without effect. Her memories of the Carolingian dynasty converged in St.-Denis.

It was certainly not without significance that Louis VI's programmatic speech was delivered in this abbey. Here Charlemagne as well as his father, Pepin, had received the royal consecration. Charles Martel, Pepin, and Charles the Bald were buried in St.-Denis. Charlemagne and other members of his house had enriched the sanctuary with donations that Suger pointed out to its visitors three centuries later. These gifts included, or rather were said to include, the relics of the Lendit. Suger took particular care to make these relics a part of the Carolingian legend, and to use that legend in order to enhance the luster of the relics.

The means Suger employed to this end strike the modern reader as peculiar enough. We must not pass them over, since they are part of his statesmanship and, above all, allow us to grasp the political ideology of which the church of St.-Denis was to become the monumental expression.

We have already seen that Suger employed historiography as an instrument of politics. For this very reason history was for him not merely, nor even primarily, the documentation of fact, but rather the creation of political reality.

84. Olschki, pp. 18 ff.; Schramm, pp. 137 ff.; Fawtier, p. 57.; Kienast, pp. 128 ff.

85. See above, n. 52.

86. "Senciant contumacie sue meritum, non in nostra sed in terra sua, que jure regio Francorum Francis sepe perdomita subjacet." *Vie de Louis*, XXVII, 102.

87. See Becker, "Das Werden der Wilhelms- und der Aimerigeste" (*Sächsische Akademie der Wissenschaften, Philol.-hist. Klasse*, XLIV, 1, 1939, p. 52).

He was no more inclined than his contemporaries to let factual proof interfere with the flights of the imagination. To realize his political aims Suger had recourse to poetry and fable. Hence these aims appear not only in the official history he wrote or inspired, but in the popular tales of the jongleurs that were launched by the abbey and soon became the most effective means by which the great sanctuary established itself in the public mind.

"If," Joseph Bédier has written, "at the time of the First Crusade some misfortune had ruined the Abbey of St.-Denis and dispersed its community, several of our *chansons de geste*, including the most celebrated of them, would never have come into existence." [88] There can no longer be any question that monks of this institution furnished the jongleurs with the material for their epics and in some cases actually composed these themselves.[89] The jongleurs in turn claimed that they had found their stories recorded in the official chronicle of the kingdom, composed and preserved at St.-Denis.[90] And the affinities between these chronicles and some of the epics is such as to preclude any further doubt regarding their common source. This applies above all to those epics and legends in which St.-Denis is depicted as the spiritual center of France.

Such recourse to fiction for political purposes was, if not justified, at least rendered excusable by the habits of thought and belief which, in that age, shaped public opinion. Under Louis VI's predecessor, the relatively weak Philip I, the centrifugal tendencies that worked in the great feudal centers of France had not only been reflected but powerfully reinforced by *chansons de geste* in which the zeal of local patriotism extolled the religious and historical glories of those smaller capitals.[91] Under Louis VI, and to a large extent thanks to Suger's statesmanship, the power of the monarchy was gradually consolidated. The crown was successful in vindicating its claim to be superior even to the greatest lords of the realm. And it is this development which, since the time of Suger,

88. Bédier, IV, 122 ff.
89. Bédier, IV, 122 ff.; Olschki, pp. 52 ff.; Becker, pp. 55 ff.; Curtius, "Über die altfranzösische Epik." [*But see Add. for p. 90.*]
90. See the reference to the noble monk of St.-Denis in the introduction to the *Enfances Guillaume*, I, 3, and II, 16 (Henry, ed., pp. 3 f.), and comment on these passages in Becker, p. 55; also the reference to the "sancti Dionysii chronica regalis" in the dedicatory epistle addressed to Leoprand of Aachen by the author of the *Historia Karoli Magni et Rotholandi*, the so-called *Pseudo-Turpin* (Meredith-Jones, p. 87), and the editor's comment, pp. 260 ff. Cf. Gautier, *Les Épopées françaises*, I, 118; Olschki, pp. 52 ff.; Curtius, "Über die altfranzösische Epik."
91. Olschki, pp. 52 ff., and the critique of Olschki's thesis in Kienast, pp. 124 ff.

is again reflected in the *chanson de geste:* St.-Denis now appears as the capital of Carolingian France, a great pilgrimage center that is particularly close to the heart of Charlemagne.[92]

All this would be of no more than marginal interest in our present context were these legends but popularizations of historical fact. But for their audiences, if not their authors, no clear distinction separated fact and fiction. Thus what appears to us as only the legendary image of the great abbey, or as the product of wishful thinking on the part of its community, actually was designed as an instrument for the realization of those claims on which the ecclesiastical aspirations of the house rested.

This is particularly true for two literary works. The first of these is the Latin *Descriptio* of the legendary journey of Charlemagne to the Holy Land, and its popularization, the *Pèlerinage de Charlemagne.* Both have entirely remodeled the legend for the sole purpose of spreading the fame of those relics of the Passion which St.-Denis possessed and on behalf of which the Lendit had been instituted. Charlemagne is said to have recovered the relics in the Holy Land and to have brought them to Aachen. From there Charles the Bald transferred them to St.-Denis. The *Pèlerinage,* however, asserts that Charlemagne himself presented the relics to the monastery. To lend more vivid colors to this tale it is merged with the great national saga of the recent past: in the *Descriptio* the emperor's journey appears as a crusade; the Holy Land is depicted in the very condition in which the crusaders of 1096 had encountered it.[93]

The second work, no *chanson de geste,* though fully as fictitious, purports to be the life of Charlemagne and Roland, composed by the emperor's faithful friend, the Archbishop Turpin, who had been a monk and treasurer of St.-Denis before being raised to the see of Reims.[94] Many details of the origin of

92. Olschki, pp. 41 ff.

93. See Coulet, *Études sur l'ancien poème français du Voyage de Charlemagne en Orient,* especially pp. 216 ff.; Bédier, IV, 126 ff.; Holmes, p. 78 ff.; Adler, "The *Pèlerinage de Charlemagne* in New Light on Saint-Denis" (*Sp,* XXII, 1947); Cooper (ed.), *Le Pèlerinage de Charlemagne;* and Rauschen (ed.), *Descriptio qualiter Karolus Magnus, clavum et coronam a Constantinopoli.* For an interesting comparison of *Descriptio* and *Pèlerinage,* see now Walpole, "The Pèlerinage of Charlemagne" (*Romance*

*Philology,* VIII, 1955).

94. See Meredith-Jones, who publishes the texts of the Codex Calixtinus of the cathedral archives of Santiago de Compostela as well as the MS. Nouv. Fonds Latin 13774 of the Bibliothèque Nationale; Whitehill, *Liber Sancti Jacobi Codex Calixtinus:* I, 301 ff., contains the *Pseudo-Turpin* (see, however, Meredith-Jones's review of this edition, *Sp,* XXXII, 1948); and Smyser, *The Pseudo-Turpin, Edited from Bibliothèque Nationale, Fonds Latin, MS. 17656.*

this strange work are obscure and may remain so forever. It was composed in the mid-twelfth century; and in reviving the memories of the Spanish "crusade" of Charlemagne, the *Pseudo-Turpin*, as the work is commonly called, certainly lends powerful support to the claims of the Abbey of St.-Denis.[95] This appears most strikingly in Chapter 30.[96] Here we are told that Charlemagne returned from the "crusade" to St.-Denis. Upon his arrival there he convoked a great assembly in order to proclaim the singular privileges he had decided to accord the abbey. All of France is to belong to St. Denis. Her kings and bishops are to be subject to the abbot as the saint's representative. Without his consent neither king nor bishops may be consecrated. In short, the abbot of St.-Denis is to be primate of France. What renders the story more significant is that in an earlier chapter an identical imperial proclamation in favor of Santiago de Compostela is recorded.[97] And in this case the story comes fairly close to reflecting historical reality inasmuch as the Archbishop of Compostela, who owed his metropolitan dignity to Calixtus II, had, early in the twelfth century, actually asserted primatial claims over the Spanish Church.[98]

That the *Pseudo-Turpin* was considered an authentic historical work is certain. In 1180, Geoffrey, prior of St.-Pierre of the Vigeois, and a noted historian in his own time, sent a copy of this work to the religious of St.-Martial at Limoges. At this time the book was already famous. Geoffrey

95. Bédier, III, 91 f., and, following him, Whitehill in his introduction to his edition of the Codex Calixtinus, III, pp. xxvii ff., maintain the thesis that the work was composed as propaganda on behalf of Compostela and the other great sanctuaries on the pilgrimage roads to Santiago. Recent appraisals, however, stress increasingly the relation of the *Pseudo-Turpin* to St.-Denis: see Schramm, p. 142; Curtius' criticism (in "Über die altfranzösische Epik") of Haemel, "Überlieferung und Bedeutung des Liber S. Jacobi und des *Pseudo-Turpin*" (*Bayerische Akademie der Wissenschaften, Phil.-hist. Klasse*, 1950, p. 2); Walpole, "Philip Mouskés and the Pseudo-Turpin Chronicle" (*University of California Publications in Modern Philology*, XXVI, 1947); also Powicke's review of Smyser's edition (*Sp*, XIII, 1938, p. 365), where Powicke urges the exploration "of a fundamental problem—the relation of Pseudo-Turpin to the whole historical movement which

had its center in St.-Denis, and which had as its object the appropriation of the Carolingian legend. In this movement the Pseudo-Turpin may or may not have taken a leading part."

96. Meredith-Jones, pp. 216 ff., and the editor's remarks, p. 348. Whitehill, I, 338 ff.

97. Ch. 19 (Meredith-Jones, p. 168; Whitehill, I, 325).

98. Toward the end of the *Pseudo-Turpin*, the emperor's soul is saved through the intercession of St. James (Meredith-Jones, ch. 32, p. 229; Whitehill, I, 341 ff.; Smyser, ch. 35, p. 94). As Gaston Paris was the first to point out (cf. Smyser, p. 47), the episode is strikingly similar to a legend relating the rescue of King Dagobert by St. Denis and his companions. I wonder if *Pseudo-Turpin*'s reference to St. James as "headless" ("capite carens; sine capite") does not reflect the "Dionysian" origin of the legend. St. Denis, rather than St. James, is the headless martyr par excellence.

declares that he has had these "illustrious victories of the invincible Charles and the battles of the great Count Roland in Spain" transcribed with the greatest possible care, all the more so as heretofore these events had been known only through the tales of the jongleurs. In a few places, where the text had become illegible, the prior had ventured to mend the gaps by slight additions. But so certain is he of Turpin's authorship that he worries about the possible irreverence of such emendation and concludes by invoking the intercession of the archbishop, who is now in heaven, before the divine Judge.[99]

The *Pseudo-Turpin* as well as the *Descriptio qualiter Karolus* were taken even more seriously in St.-Denis. The two passages summarized above were eventually inserted in the French edition of the *Chronicles of St.-Denis*, proof that the great monastery considered both works media through which it "could communicate to the minds of a new and multiplying elite its vision of a Christian France."[100] Nor is this all. Before the end of the century a false decretal, purportedly by Charlemagne, set forth item by item the extraordinary privileges that the emperor, according to the *Pseudo-Turpin*, had granted St.-Denis, including the primatial dignity of its abbot.[101]

Indeed, if the two stories were assumed to be true, they were bound to add immensely to the prestige of the abbey. Both exalt St.-Denis as the shrine of relics particularly revered by Charlemagne himself: the chapter in the *Pseudo-Turpin* centers around the relics of the Apostle of France and his companions, the *Descriptio* around the relics of the Passion. Skillfully interweaving the motifs of Crusade, pilgrimage, and Carolingian myth, the two legends, moreover, depict St.-Denis not only as a great religious center like Santiago but also as the capital of the realm: from here the emperor departs for the Holy Land, and here he returns from Jerusalem as well as from his Spanish "crusade."

---

99. See Gautier, I, 101 f. On Geoffrey, see *HLF*, XIV, 337 ff.

100. Walpole, "Philip Mouskés," p. 387. See Viard (ed.), *Grandes Chroniques*, III, 4 ff.; III, 160 ff.; V, 7, pp. 288 ff. On the relationship between the *Grandes Chroniques* and the *Chroniques de Saint-Denis*, their source, see Viard's Introduction, I, xii f. Walpole's paper presents impressive evidence for the assumption that the *Pseudo-Turpin*, while rewritten and possibly composed in St.-Denis, and certainly used as propaganda on behalf of the political ideology formulated by Suger, was even at that time not considered sufficiently reliable history to be read by the highly educated clergy; and was therefore excluded, along with the *Journey*, from the official Latin history of the realm compiled in the monastery. See below, p. 88.

101. Printed in *MGH Dipl. Karol.*, I, 286 (428 ff.). See Buchner, "Das gefälschte Karlsprivileg für St. Denis . . . und seine Entstehung" (*Historisches Jahrbuch*, XLII, 1922), and Schramm, pp. 142 ff.

But for the French reader of the twelfth century these stories revived not only the great past of the abbey; the events recorded dovetailed so curiously with certain occurrences that readers themselves had witnessed that it may have been difficult not to see the present in the transfiguring light of the past. With the events of 1124, St.-Denis had, by the king's own declaration, become the national sanctuary of France. The campaign against the German emperor, which began and ended in St.-Denis, was something of a crusade in the eyes of Frenchmen. Suger, at least, presented it in this light and very probably was responsible for the ceremony in the abbey that climaxed in Louis VI's investment with the saint's standard, the same ceremony that preceded Louis VII's departure for the Crusade of 1147. In his history Suger claims that the emperor was not only ignominiously routed but that he soon afterward succumbed mysteriously, stricken by the wrath of the patrons of France whose repose he had sacrilegiously disturbed.[102] Suger's own position, moreover, since 1124 was such that it may well have inspired the primatial claims that the Carolingian legend raised on behalf of the abbot of St.-Denis. He had presented to Louis VI, as to the saint's liege man, the vexillum of St.-Denis. Suger's insistence that the crown insignia "belonged" by right to St.-Denis seems to imply the claim that the abbot of St.-Denis also be charged with the primate's function at the royal consecration. And during the years of his regency, Suger was in fact, if not in name, primate of France.

What rendered the account of these Carolingian "histories" so effective politically was the medieval inability to distinguish past and present, more exactly, the tendency to see in the historical past the justification for the political present. Suger himself, as we have seen, sought to make his contemporaries understand the design of his government as a renewal of the Carolingian age. The popular epic shows how successful he was or how well he understood his time: Professor Olschki has pointed out that the figure of the abbot of St.-Denis, as it appears in the *chansons de geste*, is not at all that of a prelate who was a contemporary of Charlemagne, but rather that of Suger himself, the great

---

102. *Vie de Louis*, XXVII, 105. "Imperator ergo theutonicus, eo vilescens facto et de die in diem declinans, infra anni circulum extremum agens diem, antiquorum verificavit sententiam, neminem nobilem aut ignobilem, regni aut ecclesie turbatorem, cujus causa aut controversia santorum corpora subleventur, anni fore superstitem, sed ita vel intra deperire."

ecclesiastical statesman of whom every jongleur had heard and whom many might even have seen in the presence of the king.[103]

Was Suger responsible for historical and poetical forgeries, the purpose of which was certainly to further the political aims of his abbey? The false decretal, at least, was not composed until after his death, and what we know of his personality makes deliberate falsification, in our sense, very unlikely. On the other hand, that the *Pseudo-Turpin* originated at St.-Denis is at least possible; that the *Descriptio* did is certain. The content and implications of both works are too close to Suger's own views to permit us to assume that he was ignorant of them. We cannot explain the poetic license with which they deal with historical truth for political purposes unless we bear in mind that what constituted reality for medieval man was not the palpable fact, but its transcendental meaning; in the light of ideas and beliefs every phenomenon appeared romantically transformed. It is this quixotic outlook that made Suger at once an unreliable reporter and a great artist. Such general considerations, however, are no adequate answer to the vexing question posed in the preceding paragraph. Professor Walpole has suggested, with arguments that cannot be easily dismissed, that whoever had general responsibility for the prodigious historical and "epical" activities carried on in St.-Denis during the second quarter of the twelfth century was aware of the borderline that separates historical fact from pious legend. That person in authority, of course, can only have been Suger. He knew the *Pseudo-Turpin* as well as the *Descriptio* and is, at least within the orbit of St.-Denis, by far the likeliest person to have been responsible for the distribution and even the commission of these masterpieces of ecclesiastical propaganda. But Suger was no less responsible, as we have seen, for the impetus given to historiography at St.-Denis. And there is no reason why we should not credit him—directly or indirectly—with the startling omission of the *Pseudo-Turpin* as well as the *Descriptio* from the history of the realm, even though both legends had originally been included in the collection of documentary "sources" on which the historical work was to be based.[104] Suger himself, as we have seen,

103. Olschki, pp. 53 ff. As regards the increasing importance of St.-Denis as a pilgrimage center, see Olschki, pp. 66 ff.; and for reflections, in the French epic, of the abbey's aspirations to assume a role in the coronation ceremonial, pp. 60 f.

104. See above, n. 100; also Lair "Mémoire sur deux chroniques latines" (*BEC* XXXV, 1874).

has occasionally slanted, in his own historical writings, the narrative of events in order to emphasize their meaning as he saw it and as he wanted his readers to see it with him. But he has not allowed political legend to enter his historical work—it is significant that he abstains, as Mrs. Loomis has pointed out,[105] from the momentous identification of the *vexillum S. Dionysii* with the oriflamme, even though his account of Louis VI's investment with the banner of St.-Denis was such that it invited the subsequent identification.

Does not the ability to distinguish between factual history and patriotic legend, yet skillfully to use both as the demands and limitations of a given audience might require, recall a similar distinction in quite another sphere? St. Bernard, as we have seen, banished all imagery from the cloisters of his order as unbefitting the spiritual elevation of his monks. He himself, however, conceded that the use of such imagery might be permissible and even necessary to arouse the religious fervor of a more "carnal" laity. Suger, it would seem, quite similarly employed legend in order to imprint upon the minds of the laity the cause to which he devoted his ecclesiastical career; but he excluded that same legend from the historical works that he wrote or commissioned for the benefit of the educated clergy. Legend and historiography, however, had the same purpose; both unfold the same ideology before us; it is only the means that differ.

When we consider together both Suger's writings with their peculiar political slant and the Carolingian legends mentioned, we grasp the abbot's "grand design" for St.-Denis as well as for France. And it is in the light of these literary activities that the great artistic project to which we shall turn now must be understood. Suger undertook the rebuilding of his church in order to implement his master plan in the sphere of politics. His vision as a statesman imposed itself upon the architectural project; he conceived it as the monumental expression of that vision. Not only as a shrine but as a work of art the sanctuary was to eclipse the great pilgrimage centers of western Europe; it was to bear comparison, as we shall see, with Constantinople and in a sense with Jerusalem. The new church is in a very real sense part of the "myth" of St.-Denis. Its architecture and the pictorial rhetoric of its sculpture and stained-glass windows are addressed to the same audience that Suger sought to reach as an author or

105. See above, p. 75, n. 58.

through the historical and epical works he commissioned in his monastery. It is most significant that among the celebrated windows with which he adorned the sanctuary two invoked his cherished ideas of crusade and pilgrimage. One represented the First Crusade, the other the journey of Charlemagne.[106] This legend thus received Suger's official sanction: visitors to the great church were not permitted to question the Carolingian origin of the cult of relics that called them to St.-Denis on the feast of the Lendit. [See Add.]

106. The windows are preserved in the drawings of de Montfaucon, Les Monumens de la monarchie française, I, 277, 384 ff., and Pls. 24, 25, 50–54. The inspiration of these windows by Suger has recently been maintained, convincingly I think, by Grodecki, "A Stained Glass Atelier of the Thirteenth Century" (JWCI, 1947, X, 92). That the window is based on the Pilgrimage of Charlemagne was pointed out by Bédier, IV, 172.

# 4. THE NEW CHURCH

SUGER seems to have conceived his plan to rebuild the church of his abbey immediately after the events of 1124. These events had bestowed upon his house an ecclesiastical position and religious significance that the old sanctuary was inadequate either to serve or to express. The abbot himself mentions, as one of the compelling reasons for his undertaking, the ever-increasing numbers of pilgrims eager to behold the relics of the Passion, crowds that the Carolingian church could no longer accommodate.[1] The royal edict of 1124 in favor of the Lendit was indeed bound to foster such growing veneration of the relics; and since that great festival was by the same proclamation put under the jurisdiction of the abbey, it also yielded to the latter the additional revenues required for an architectural project of extraordinary splendor. Suger records that he set aside 200 livres annually—something like $64,000 in modern currency—for the rebuilding of the choir and crypt. Of this sum, only one fourth was raised from ordinary revenues of the house: they were collected from one of its possessions in Beauce that Suger's administration had put back on its feet. The remaining 150 livres were to be contributed by pilgrims; it is characteristic that Suger, calculating his budget, could safely expect the receipt of 100 livres during the feast of the Lendit alone and the rest on the feast of the patron saint, which was likewise accompanied by a fair.[2]

For the west façade and narthex, Suger raised the required funds in a manner that, in its mixture of the shrewd and the humane, is characteristic of him: on March 15, 1125, Suger freed the inhabitants of the town of St.-Denis from the burdensome obligations of mortmain. He received from them in turn

---

1. Suger, *De consecratione ecclesiae sancti Dionysii*, II, 216; *De rebus in administratione sua gestis*, XV, 186.

2. *De consecr.*, IV, 226. For the means used to compute medieval figures into modern monetary values, see below, ch. 6, n. 43.

200 livres for the "renovation and decoration of the entrance," that is, the west façade of the abbey.[3] It is curious to note that the measure found a legendary echo—was it designed to pass as a precedent?—both in the *Pseudo-Turpin* and the false decretal of Charlemagne. Both documents assert that the emperor prescribed a general levy for the rebuilding of St.-Denis, in return for which all contributors who were still unfree were to be enfranchised. The patron saint himself was said to have appeared to Charles in a dream, promising that he would intercede for all benefactors. When this revelation was made public, the story continues, everyone paid willingly and thus acquired the title of *frankus S. Dionysii*, a term providing an etymological explanation of the name of the kingdom.[4] We do not know whether the legend was circulated in Suger's time for fund-raising purposes. But the idea that contributions to the saint's sanctuary were gifts to him personally, which he would reward by special favors to the donor, was certainly utilized by Suger, who believed in it as much as did his contemporaries. Besides the sums mentioned, the abbot received many substantial gifts specifically for the rebuilding of St.-Denis.

Thus, only half a year after the royal proclamation of 1124, Suger had begun raising the funds for his project. Yet years were to elapse before the work was actually begun. Around 1130 he seems to have spent a good deal of money on repairs of the old nave, an expense rendered superfluous by his eventual decision to rebuild the church entirely.[5] The west façade was not begun until 1137, the choir not until 1140. How are we to account for this astonishing delay?

Suger was certainly preoccupied with other responsibilities. St. Bernard of Clairvaux had long and passionately demanded that Suger reform his monastic community.[6] Although Bernard's criticism was aimed at Suger personally, it

3. The charter is printed in *Oeuvres complètes de Suger*, pp. 319 ff. For a different interpretation of the passage, see Crosby, *L'Abbaye royale de Saint-Denis*, p. 32.

4. Meredith-Jones, *Historia Karoli Magni et Rotholandi ou Chroniques de Pseudo-Turpin*, pp. 219, 339; cf. above, pp. 85 f.; also Buchner, "Das gefälschte Karlsprivileg für St. Denis . . . und seine Entstehung" (*Historisches Jahrbuch*, XLII, 1922), and Schramm, *Der König von Frankreich*, p. 143, who points out that St. Louis implemented the legend by offering, as a

"serf of St. Denis," the "census capitis proprii" upon the saint's altar. Cf. *Recueil des historiens des Gaules et de la France*, XX, 76.

5. Suger, *De admin.*, XXIV, 186.

6. *Ep.* LXXVIII (*PL*, XLXXXII, 191). See Félibien, *Histoire de l'abbaye royale de Saint-Denys en France*, pp. 158 ff.; Vacandard, *Vie de St. Bernard*, I, 178 ff.; Aubert, *Suger*, p. 17. Mabillon suggests, and nearly all historians have accepted his thesis, that St. Bernard's description of an abbot whom he saw "sexaginta equos et eo amplius, in suo ducere comitatu"

sheds light on the general situation: as we have seen, relations between the crown and the reform party had long been cool. The royal abbey, a monastic institution that also served as the king's residence and was filled with the turmoil and bustle of a ministry of state, seemed indeed to embody the very abuses that the reform strove to abolish. Suger did not allow his sympathy for this party to interfere with his political designs. He was on a diplomatic mission in Italy when he was elected abbot and, with seeming disregard for the state of his abbey, spent another six months of the following year (1123) in that country.[7] Yet he and St. Bernard were working from opposite sides toward the same goal: as the latter insisted on the ethical obligations of the Christian ruler, Suger forged the alliance between Church and Crown that was so impressively demonstrated at the Council of Reims and again, in 1124, at the Assembly of St.-Denis. Only then did the abbot of St.-Denis turn his attention to his monastery. Its reform, which he effected with wisdom and moderation, elicited, in 1127, the enthusiastic applause of St. Bernard.[8] We shall see that the latter's ideas of religious art did not remain without influence upon the design of Suger's church.

Yet for the time being Suger was unable to carry out his artistic plans. During the next decade, from 1127 to 1137, we find him continually in the king's presence, his most eminent and most intimate councilor. Affairs of state can hardly have left Suger much time or leisure for other projects. With the death of Louis VI, in 1137, Suger's position changed somewhat. It seems unnecessary to assume that with the ascent of Louis VII the abbot fell into disgrace.[9] He could not have been appointed regent of France in 1147 had his immense prestige ever been seriously impaired and had he not enjoyed the complete confidence of the young ruler. But the advent of a new monarch is usually the occasion for changing the guards. And Suger had been so close to Louis VI, his ascendancy throughout the kingdom so overwhelming, that Louis le Jeune was bound to desire a group of advisers that would grant more scope

refers to Suger. *Apologia ad Guillelmum*, XI, 27 (*PL*, CLXXXII, 913).

7. Suger, *Vie de Louis le Gros* (Molinier, ed.), XXVI, 100.

8. Cf. above, n. 6; also Félibien, p. 158. That Suger considered the reform of his monastery a spiritual prerequisite to the execution of his architectural plans may possibly be inferred from his brief reference to the "pacato habitaculo." *De consecr.*, I, 214.

9. Aubert, *Suger*, p. 96, actually speaks of a "disastrous disgrace." See the judicious remarks in Waquet's edition of Suger's *Vie de Louis VI le Gros*, p. ix.

to his own political initiative than the aging prelate was likely to surrender. However that may be, changing political and personal circumstances at last provided Suger with the leisure and perhaps the incentive to undertake several long-meditated projects designed to cast into an enduring and impressive mold the great political vision that had inspired every major action of his career. Suger's historical writings were all composed within the years after 1137.[10] So were his artistic projects, or at least that part of them which he lived to see completed.

Perhaps the most important reason for the delay that intervened between the planning and the execution of the church was that as a builder Suger had to start from scratch. When he conceived the great project he had at his disposal neither the materials nor the craftsmen; he could count neither on the artistic tradition nor on the technical skills that the building would require. We have seen that Suger started out by merely patching up the most dilapidated parts of the old building. Later he considered importing classical columns from Rome, like those he had admired in the Baths of Diocletian, "through the Mediterranean, thence through the English Sea and the tortuous windings of the River Seine." [11] Such wasteful projects, such piecemeal planning, such preoccupations with complicated means of importing architectural parts that were not available or could not be produced at home—all this indicates clearly that the idea of the new church did not spring full grown from Suger's mind. On the contrary, the design took shape but gradually and was constantly challenged by the nature and limitations of the skills and resources available. Suger mentions the fortunate discovery of a quarry near Pontoise "yielding very strong stone such as in quality and quantity had never been found in these regions." [12] And he himself had to set out in search of timber of sufficient strength for the tie beams of his new structure, his carpenters as well as forest wardens having insisted that logs of such size could not be found in the entire region.[13] Again, the craftsmen and artists, masons, sculptors, goldsmiths, stained-glass painters, had all to be

10. The *Life of Louis VI* was written after 1138 (cf. Molinier, ed., *Vie de Louis le Gros*, pp. xiii, 123); Suger's other works (excepting the testament of 1137) were written between 1140 and 1149; cf. Waquet, p. xi, and Panofsky,

*Abbot Suger on the Abbey Church of St.-Denis and Its Art Treasures*, pp. 144 f.
11. *De consecr.*, II, 219.
12. *De consecr.*, II, 219.
13. *De consecr.*, III, 221 f.

called in from abroad.[14] As Suger recalls his endeavors in this direction, it is apparent that he could not always be sure that he would succeed.

In retrospect, it seems to us almost providential that the Île-de-France did not possess, at this moment, an architectural school of its own. If it had, his task would have been much easier, his accomplishments perhaps more conventional. But here, as in all cultural respects, the Île-de-France had been entirely eclipsed by its neighbors, Burgundy and Normandy, where the Benedictine Order, under the patronage of the secular power, had developed magnificent systems of architecture. It reflects the weak and troubled political situation of France that, in the generation before Suger, the royal domain could not boast a single building of the first order. Within this vacuum, Suger planned and executed his church, which not only became the archetype of French cathedrals, but whose style—the Gothic—appears to us as the embodiment of medieval civilization.

Perhaps it was this very dearth of immediately available models that gave a freer rein to Suger's imagination. He had set his sights high indeed. Neither of the two ideal prototypes that were before his mental eye could be approximated within the traditions of Romanesque architecture. The first of these was Hagia Sophia at Constantinople, the second the Solomonic Temple. That he should have sought to emulate the great Byzantine church, or what he had heard of its splendors, is not surprising. The goals of the crusaders, which he was not destined to see himself, possessed his imagination all the more. He would ask travelers returning from Jerusalem for their impressions and eagerly listened to their descriptions. His own church was to bear comparison with even the greatest of pilgrimage centers; it was to be a compensation for what he had not himself seen. Suger was relieved when polite pilgrims told him that his abbey did not compare unfavorably with Hagia Sophia.[15]

Aside from this church, Suger admits to only one other source of inspiration: the Solomonic Temple. Although he does not dare to measure his own achievement against that of Solomon, he knows that both sanctuaries were built with the same purpose in mind, and that both have the same author—God himself, since the Temple built by Solomon under divine guidance is also the

14. *De consecr.*, II, 218.                    15. *De admin.*, XXXIII, 199; cf. XXV, 187.

model for the sanctuary.[16] We have seen in the preceding chapter how cosmological as well as mystical speculations prompted many a medieval builder to consider Solomon's Temple a kind of ideal prototype for his own work.[17]

But Suger had not seen either of these two lofty "models." Whether or not he had a clear notion of their design, the down-to-earth problems of construction were not answered by any available description of the two buildings. For the solution of these problems he had to rely on the knowledge available in his time, and, as we shall see, it was this knowledge that cast Suger's aesthetic vision into a definite form.

The question that presents itself and that we ought to answer at this point is: to what extent was Suger himself responsible for St.-Denis? Was he the architect? We can hardly assume that a man in Suger's position could have had either the time or the technical knowledge to carry out a building that, from the artistic as well as the constructive viewpoint, marked a revolution. We know, on the other hand, of several medieval prelates—the bishops Benno of Osnabrück and Otto of Bamberg, to mention but two—who were renowned architects in the strict sense of the term. And the knowledge of technical matters exhibited in Suger's writings, the responsibilities and initiative he assumed, are remarkable enough. He thinks about means of transportation, he himself procures the required timber, and he is completely familiar with the functions and technical properties of the cross-ribbed vault [18]—the great architectural novelty of his time. All this certainly surpasses by far the role that the man who merely commissions a building assumes in our own time, who usually leaves all questions regarding design and execution to the architect. But in the Middle Ages, and even much later, he who commissioned the building had often more architectural knowledge and nearly always more ideas to contribute than his modern counterpart. Hence, his responsibilities overlapped with those of the architect and contractor.[19]

16. *De consecr.*, II, 218.

17. "Conferebam de minimis ad maxima, non plus Salomonianas opes templo quam nostras huic operi sufficere posse, nisi idem ejusdem operis auctor ministratoribus copiose praeparareret. Identitas auctoris et operis sufficientiam facit operantis." *De consecr.*, II, 218.

18. *De consecr.*, V, 230; see Panofsky's comment, *Abbot Suger*, pp. 224 ff.; however, note Conant's cautious remarks in his review of Panofsky (*Sp*, XXVIII, 1953, p. 604).

19. On the entire question, see now the observations of Aubert, *Suger*, pp. 128, 133; also Salzman, *Building in England*, pp. 1 ff., and Colombier, *Les Chantiers des cathédrales*, pp. 58 ff.

It would be a great mistake to impute to Suger's age the notions and practices of contemporary professionalism. Within recent decades new techniques and building materials have demanded a great deal of scientific knowledge of the architect, have transformed the latter into something of an engineer, and have made us view the problems of architecture primarily as problems of engineering. To correct this one-sided view it is worth quoting a recent student of the subject: "Experience shows," writes M. du Colombier, "that a number of great architects were not professionals . . . what one expects of the architect is not the ability to execute a building himself but rather the knowledge of what is technically possible, the execution of which may then be delegated to others. And this knowledge, especially in the matter of stone construction, which has developed very slowly, is much simpler than the nonspecialist assumes. The opposite view has prevailed in our age, especially since the engineer assumed his role in building enterprises in order to apply new techniques like those of iron and ferro-concrete construction. . . . How different was the situation during an age that proceeded in purely empirical fashion." [20]

In other words, the Middle Ages, which talked so much about the science of architecture, actually built with practically no theoretical science at all. Or rather, mathematical or even metaphysical speculation, as we have seen, took the place of scientific knowledge. We have, therefore, no reason, Professor Coulton and his school notwithstanding, to mistrust medieval witnesses who identify the ecclestiastic "patron" as the architect of a building. The medieval bishop or abbot could rely on his mason to take care of the practical problems of the task; the ideas he himself provided were not of a technical but rather of an aesthetic and symbolic kind. Thus, between the patron and his chief mason there was no room for an architect in the modern sense. This vocation and position seem to re-emerge only with the Gothic cathedral and the structural problems these great edifices posed.

The general building practices just described explain Suger's share in the design and construction of St.-Denis, but they also make this share appear all the more astonishing. The crude empiricism mitigated by fantasy that characterizes medieval building was rendered possible by an extremely conservative attitude. Innovations are rare indeed. Important buildings would be imitated

20. Colombier, pp. 58 ff.

innumerable times (hence the significance of regional "schools" in the history of Romanesque architecture) and patrons often sent their masons to distant places in order to study sanctuaries of which they wished to build copies themselves.[21] By this method ancient architectural traditions and experiences were long preserved and new problems of construction avoided. It was quite otherwise in the case of Suger's St.-Denis. The controversy initiated by St. Bernard over religious architecture, with its implied criticism of the traditional "Romanesque," the great interest that the reconstruction of a church as important as St.-Denis was bound to arouse, especially the particular bent of Suger's own mind, impelled him to reject the architectural forms of the past and to strike out in entirely new directions. In order to do so, he had to assume a large share of the responsibility himself. He was able to do so because he possessed the knowledge as well as the enthusiasm of at least an amateur architect. The assistant or assistants he employed, perhaps lay brothers of his monastery, like those artists that are known to have existed at St.-Denis in the thirteenth and fourteenth centuries,[22] probably were to him what the contractor is to the modern architect. But Suger fails to mention any of them. He himself was the "leader" of the great enterprise, as he declares in one of the dedicatory inscriptions.[23] The ideas that guided him, the means he employed for their realization, appear when we look at the edifice itself.

The construction of Suger's St.-Denis progressed in three campaigns. He began with the west end of the church. The Carolingian sanctuary, terminated by Abbot Fulrad in 775 (though Suger thought it dated back to the times of King Dagobert I), possessed two apses, the small western apse (perhaps identical with the sepulcher built or completed by Charlemagne for his father, Pepin the Short) being flanked by two towers and one or two narrow passages leading into the church.[24] All these constructions had become dilapidated and

21. See the examples enumerated by Colombier, pp. 60 f.; also Krautheimer, "Introduction to an Iconography of Medieval Architecture" (*JWCI*, 1942).

22. See d'Ayzac, *Histoire de l'abbaye de St.-Denis en France*, II, 211 ff., 520 ff.; Voege, *Die Anfänge des monumentalen Stiles im Mittelalter*, p. 289; and Colombier, p. 39.

23. "Qui Suggerus eram, me duce dum fieret." *De admin.*, XX, 190. Crosby, *Abbaye*, p. 34, defines Suger's responsibility much as I

do.

24. See Crosby, "Excavations in the Abbey Church of St.-Denis, 1948" (American Philosophical Society, *Proceedings*, XCIII, 1949), 150 ff.; Panofsky, *Abbot Suger*, pp. 156 ff., 208 ff.; Aubert, *Suger*, p. 133. The exact disposition of this western part of the Carolingian church remains uncertain. See Crosby, *Abbaye*, p. 15.

were now torn down.[25] In their place and a little farther to the west, Suger erected first a façade flanked by two towers and provided with three portals *Plates 14, 19* ample enough to allow clergy and laity to circulate freely on the great festivals of the abbey. Behind this façade Suger built a narthex consisting of two bays and comprising three aisles on the ground level and three large chapels above *Plate 15* these. Both stories were covered with cross-ribbed vaults.[26] Between these western additions and the Carolingian nave a considerable interval remained. Suger therefore lengthened the old nave by about 40 per cent.[27] Under the arcades of this addition he placed those columns which he had thought of importing from Rome before the quarry at Pontoise had so unexpectedly yielded the material that enabled him to have new columns made. The constructions mentioned so far were completed in 1140, when Suger, as if under a sudden inspiration, interrupted work on the upper parts of the two towers of the façade in order to embark on the second campaign devoted to the choir.[28]

This structure, of far greater artistic significance and originality than the western part,[29] is one of the epoch-making buildings in the history of architecture. It was certainly the first Gothic edifice completed. Fortunately, enough of this part of Suger's church remains intact even today to enable us to assess his achievement. Above the ancient crypt, which was enlarged and its vaults heightened so as to serve as support for the floor of the upper structure, was erected the choir that filled its author with enthusiasm and pride. A double ambulatory, from which there radiated nine chapels, surrounded the choir. This description, the customary one, is not sufficiently precise. In point of fact, the outer ambulatory and its crown of chapels merge. Suger himself describes *Plate 16* them well as a unit—"circuitus oratoriorum." [30] The outer ambulatory expands, as it were, beyond the walls normally separating the chapels from one another.

25. Suger, *De consecr.*, I, 217.

26. Pending his final publication, see Crosby, "Fouilles exécutées récemment dans la basilique de Saint-Denis" (*BM*, CV, 1947); "Early Gothic Architecture—New Problems as a Result of the St. Denis Excavations" (*JSAH*, VII, 1948); "New Excavations in the Abbey Church of Saint Denis" (*GBA*, 6th series, XXII, 1944). Cf. also Anfray, *L'Architecture normande. Son influence dans le nord de la France*, pp. 48 f.

27. Crosby, *Abbey of St.-Denis*, fig. 92; Panofsky, *Abbot Suger*, p. 154.

28. ". . . turriumque differendo prosecutionem in superiori parte . . ." *De consecr.*, IV, 224.

29. Crosby, "Early Gothic," and Bony, "French Influences on the Origin of English Architecture" (*JWCI*, XII, 1949), believe that the choir is actually the work of a different master.

30. *De consecr.*, IV, 225.

What remains of these is no more than shallow segmental shells, just large enough for the altar that was placed in each one; the rest has been merged into the flowing current of the ambulatory. The spherical outer walls of each chapel were pierced by two tall windows that reduced the wall surface to the dimen-

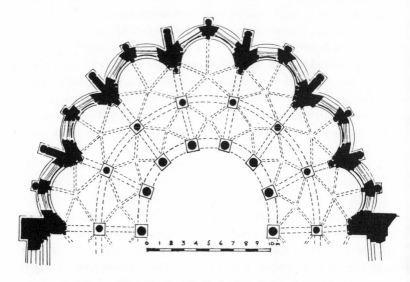

*Fig. 4. Abbey Church of St.-Denis. Ground plan of sanctuary*

sions of mere frames. And owing to the shallowness of the chapels, the light thus admitted floods into the ambulatory. In the words of Suger's description, at once ecstatic and accurate, "the entire sanctuary is thus pervaded by a wonderful and continuous light entering through the most sacred windows" [31] —Suger's celebrated stained-glass windows with which the history of Gothic glass may be said to begin. Although the upper part of Suger's choir no longer exists—it had to be torn down, and was replaced, in 1231, by Peter of Montreuil's masterpiece—we know, again from Suger's description, that it was covered by a cross-ribbed vault, as were the ambulatories and chapels. In this

31. ". . . illo urbano et approbato in circuitu oratoriorum incremento, quo tota sacratissimarum vitrearum luce mirabili et continua interiorem perlustrante pulchritudinem eniteret." *De consecr.*, IV, 225.

entire eastern part of the building, the round arch, which still dominates the west façade, has been replaced by the pointed arch.[32]

Suger completed the choir in three years and three months.[33] Had the service of an architect of genius become available to him? The abruptness with which the work on the façade was momentarily abandoned in favor of the choir, the swiftness with which the latter was completed, above all the masterful way of its execution, suggest that Suger by this time had at his side a man capable of realizing every one of his wishes. In 1144 the choir was consecrated.

There remained, between the eastern and western ends of the church, the nave. It was this part of the basilica which, according to a legend firmly believed by Suger himself, had been hallowed by the miraculous consecration that Christ in his own person had bestowed upon its walls.[34] This belief was undoubtedly the reason why Suger had at first not envisaged the reconstruction of the nave. As we have seen, he wasted considerable expense not only on necessary structural repairs but on adorning the nave with murals that no longer corresponded with the taste for "transparent walls." He had even taken great trouble to align his new additions, "by the application of geometrical and arithmetical rules," with the old part of the church in such a way that their dimensions would exactly coincide.[35] Yet the two aesthetic values that Suger placed above all others in a work of art—luminosity and concordance of parts—made the old nave with its darkness and heavy forms appear obsolete, its obsoleteness unbearable as soon as the choir had been completed. It seems that this made Suger resolve to demolish the ancient structure after all; he embarked on the third and last

---

32. For the reconstruction of the choir, see Crosby, *Abbey of St.-Denis*, figs. 86, 87; and Panofsky, *Abbot Suger*, p. 221. Cf., however, Crosby, *Abbaye*, p. 46, where the view is maintained that the supports are too frail to allow the assumption of a gallery.

33. "Quod quidem gloriosum opus quantum divina manus in talibus operosa protexerit, certum est etiam argumentum, quod in tribus annis et tribus mensibus totum illud magnificum opus, et in inferiore cripta et in superiore voltarum sublimitate, tot arcum et columnarum distinctione variatum, etiam operturae integrum supplementum admiserit." *De admin.*, XXVIII, 190. Suger mentions three years and three months because of the trinitarian symbolism.

In point of fact, it took Suger three years and eleven months to complete the choir entirely. See Panofsky, *Abbot Suger*, p. 166; Aubert, *Suger*, p. 144.

34. See below, n. 127.

35. *De consecr.*, IV, 225. Cf. Panofsky, *Abbot Suger*, p. 222, and Forsyth, "Geometricis et Arithmeticis Instrumentis" (*Archeology*, III, 1950). For the interesting suggestion that "instrumentis" may, as in Boethius, *De musica*, V, 2 (*PL*, LXIII, 1288), have to be translated as "rule" rather than "instrument," see Beseler and Roggenkamp, *Die Michaeliskirche in Hildesheim*. Thierry of Chartres also uses the term in this sense. See above, ch. 2, n. 13.

campaign almost at once. Work on the transept, the new nave, and once again the towers of the façade certainly was in progress in 1149.[36] But whether it was that Suger, with his mind on the proposed Crusade that he was to direct, did not wish to commit his funds to the extent required by the architectural enterprise or that the other project now absorbed his attention, the nave progressed but slowly and haltingly. In fact, little had been accomplished when Suger died. The south wall was not even begun until more than a decade after his death.

It is possible, however, to say something about what Suger's nave was to have looked like.[37] It was to be as luminous as the choir; and in accordance with the builder's predilection for homogeneity, the whole edifice was planned to appear as a unit. The elevations of choir, transept, and nave were, in all probability, to be identical. The transept, moreover, was nonprojecting, and two side aisles were, on either side of the nave, to continue the double ambulatory of the choir. The supports of the nave arcade were cylindrical and as slim in proportion to the intervals between them as were those in the sanctuary proper. Crosby considers it unlikely, therefore, that there were galleries above the side aisles. The cross-ribbed vault was to have reigned throughout.

Suger's design, though never completed, was impressive enough to be adapted in many essential aspects of its disposition in the cathedrals of Noyon and Senlis and, above all, in Notre Dame of Paris. In these early Gothic cathedrals we can grasp at least a shadow of the masterpiece that served as their model.

The singularity of the artistic achievement is the principal reason for the place that Suger's St.-Denis occupies in the history of art. But it is not the only reason. In the case of this monument, it can, I think, for once be shown how the artistic design was inspired by a definite metaphysical system, how and in what manner an intellectual experience impinged upon the creative process within the artist's mind. What renders this interpretation possible is the fact that we know for certain the author who had most influence upon Suger's thought, and in whose work the abbot found the source for his own philosophy of art.

36. De admin., XXVIII, XXIX, 191. See Crosby, Abbaye, pp. 48 f.
37. Aubert, Suger. Cf. Crosby, "Excavations, 1948" and "New Excavations," p. 119; Brière and Vitry, L'Abbaye de St.-Denis; and

Aubert, "Le Portail du croisillon sud de l'église abbatiale de Saint-Denis" (Revue archéologique, 6th series, XXIX [Mélanges Charles Picard], 1948).

The Abbey of St.-Denis, it will be recalled, owed its ecclesiastical position to the fact that it preserved the relics of the saint and martyr who, in the third century, had converted France to Christianity and was hence revered as the patron of the royal house and of the realm. But this St. Denis was held to be identical with an Eastern theologian who was one of the great mystical writers of the early Christian era and, in fact, of the Christian tradition. With this second Denis, the Pseudo-Areopagite, we are already familiar: his work is the main source of the medieval metaphysics of light discussed in Chapter 2. We know next to nothing about his identity. Almost certainly he was a Syrian of the late fifth century.[38] Oddly enough, at least to our minds, he combined with his profound mystical insight an irrepressible tendency to mystify his readers. In his work he dropped allusions and hints that readers understood to indicate he had witnessed the eclipse of the sun that accompanied Christ's death, had been present at the dormition of the Virgin, had known St. John the Evangelist, and that, in short, he was none other than that Denis who, according to the Acts of the Apostles, was a distinguished Athenian who "clave unto [St. Paul], and believed." To every one of these spurious claims the Middle Ages gave credence, and it is hardly possible not to suspect that the author deliberately created a confusion that, long after his death, was to have momentous consequences indeed. The Dionysian writings were soon considered to date from Apostolic times; they were studied with the respect reserved for the most venerable and authoritative expositions of Christian doctrine; indeed, one degree only seemed to separate them from the inspired Biblical writings themselves. "Among ecclesiastical writers," wrote John Sarracenus in dedicating his translation of the Areopagite to Odo, Suger's successor as abbot of St.-Denis, "Dionysius is believed to hold the first rank after the Apostles." [39]

*Plate 17*

38. See Bardenhewer, *Geschichte der altkirchlichen Literatur*, IV, 282 ff.; Bollandus (ed.), *Acta sanctorum*, Oct. IV, 696 ff.; also de Gandillac's Introduction in his edition of *Oeuvres complètes du Pseudo-Denys*, pp. 7 ff. On the legend and cult of St. Denis in France, see also Crosby, *Abbey of St.-Denis*, pp. 24 ff. The recent attempt to identify the Pseudo-Areopagite with Ammonios Sakkas appears unconvincing. See Elorduy, "¿Es Ammonio Sakkas el Pseudo-Areopagita?" (*Estudios eclesiásticos*,

XVIII, 1944).

39. "Inter scriptores ecclesiasticos primum locum post apostolicos Areopagita Dionysius sicut tempore ita etiam theologiae sapientie doctrina et auctoritate possidere creditur. Quippe qui ab eisdem apostolis eorumque auditoribus uberius edoctus. . . ." See Grabmann, "Die mittelalterlichen Übersetzungen der Schriften des Pseudo-Dionysius Areopagita" (*Mittelalterliches Geistesleben*, I, 459).

One error led to another. If the great Syrian had been guilty of the first mistaken identification, he was altogether innocent of the second. About the middle of the eighth century, Pope Paul sent the Greek manuscript of the *Corpus areopagiticum* to Pepin the Short.[40] It is possible that the pontiff himself believed the author of this work to be identical with the Apostle of France. Less than a century later this had become the accepted belief in France. Emperor Louis the Pious charged Hilduin, abbot of St.-Denis, to collect all available material concerning "our special protector" that he might be able to find in the Greek historians and elsewhere.[41] Hilduin responded with enthusiasm. He produced a biography in which the disciple of St. Paul, the Apostle of France, and the author of the *Corpus areopagiticum* were shown to be one and the same person.[42]

The Dionysian writings hardly required such false credentials to command attention. They represent a consummate synthesis of Neoplatonic and Christian mysticism, propounded with the eloquence of ecstatic vision. Yet, however great the admiration Plato the *philosopher* enjoyed during the Middle Ages and whatever the debt even Christian theology may actually owe him, Christian theologians have never approached his work without a certain hesitation. The same fate might have befallen the Pseudo-Areopagite. But his alleged discipleship of St. Paul enabled his work to pass into medieval thought unscrutinized. And his presumed identity with the Apostle of France assured his ascendancy over the entire intellectual culture of this country.

In the twelfth century, the veneration of saints was so powerful a factor in public life that it impinged even upon the course of politics. The veneration of saints impinged no less upon the life of ideas. The tribute paid to the supposed philosophical achievements of the Apostle of France is understandable enough at a time when the country was experiencing the first flowering of scholasticism. A generation enamored of philosophical speculation but still firmly rooted in faith demanded a patron who was at once a great saint and a great thinker. However that may be, the veneration of Denis the Saint had an

---

40. See Loenertz, "La Légende parisienne de St. Denys l'Aréopagite" (*Analecta Bollandiana* LXIX, 1951).
41. *PL*, CVI, 1326. Cf. Théry, *Études*

*Dionysiennes*, I, 15. On the source of this legend, see the important paper by Father Loenertz.
42. *Areopagitica sive sancti Dionysii vita* (*PL*, CVI, 13 ff.).

incalculable influence on the development of French thought during the twelfth and thirteenth centuries.

A translation of the Dionysian writings had already been made, with indifferent success, under the supervision and direction of his biographer, Hilduin.[43] A generation later, Emperor Charles the Bald persuaded an Irishman, Johannes Scotus Erigena, who was living at his court, to undertake a new translation. Erigena was a man of genius, perhaps the greatest mind of his age. He accomplished not only the translation but added a commentary and eventually developed, upon the basis of the Pseudo-Areopagite, a metaphysical system of his own. It was mainly due to Erigena, and as seen through his eyes, that the subsequent renaissance of Dionysian thought occurred.[44]

As the fortunes of the Capetian monarchy flourished, so did Dionysian theology in France. It became the source of the metaphysics of light and of "analogy"—both, as we have seen, of such consequence for the history of art. Upon the basis of that work, Hugh of St.-Victor, of the abbey founded in Paris by King Louis VI of France,[45] developed the first philosophy of beauty since Augustine. In 1137 Hugh dedicated his commentary on the *Celestial Hierarchy*, the most famous of the Dionysian writings, to Louis VII.[46] The idea of the French monarchy gradually became inseparable from the vision expounded in the *Corpus areopagiticum*. French thought was looked upon as a renaissance of Greek philosophy that St. Denis was supposed to have transplanted from Athens to Paris. Along with faith and military valor, this "treasure of wisdom" appeared as one of the three glories of French culture.[47] No wonder that the

43. According to Théry, I, 134, the translation is the work of Greeks working *c.* 835 at St.-Denis under Hilduin's direction. Hilduin's translation of Dionysius has been published by Théry, II.

44. Erigena's works are in *PL*, CXXII; cf. below, p. 125.

45. The royal charters on behalf of St.-Victor are in Luchaire, *Louis VI le Gros*, Nos. 160, 363, 534–35, 541, 561, 591.

46. *PL*, CLXXV, 923 ff. On the aesthetics of the School of St.-Victor, see especially de Bruyne, *Études d'esthétique médiévale*, II.

47. "Si enim tam pretiosissimus thesaurus sapientiae salutaris, quod olim de Graecia sequendo Dionysium Areopagitam Parisius ad partes Gallicanas devenerat, cum fide et militiae titulo, de regno Franciae tolleretur, maneret utique liliatum signum regis Franciae, quod trini floris folio depictum est, in una parte sui mirabiliter deformatum." William of Nangis, *Gesta Sancti Ludovici*, in *Recueil des historiens*, XX, 320. See the miniature representing St. Denis's journey from Athens to Paris in the life of the saint (Bibl. Nat. MS. fr. nouv. acq. 1098); cf. Delisle, "Notice sur un livre à peintures exécuté en 1250 dans l'abbaye de Saint-Denis" (*BEC*, XXXVIII, 1877). See also Thomas of Ireland, *De tribus sensibus sacrae scripturae* (shortly after 1300): "Le Bienheureux

irrepressible Abelard narrowly escaped a trial for treason against the crown itself when, as a monk at St.-Denis, he dared to suggest that the Apostle of France was not the same person as the Areopagite.[48]

It is curious to reflect that without that dual falsification of identity the entire history of ideas might have taken a different course; that perhaps even French culture during the twelfth century might not have acquired that sublime spiritual flavor which prompted John of Salisbury to call France the most civilized country of his time.[49] And it is even more curious to think that without the forged credentials of an anonymous Syrian writer who lived six hundred years earlier, Gothic architecture might not have come into existence.[50] Yet this is very likely the case. As we have seen, the prestige that, thanks to Suger, his abbey had acquired depended upon the renown of its title saint. Had St. Denis merely been a miracle worker, or one of those warrior saints after the heart of the age, his deeds could have been retold at St.-Denis in one of the conventional paintings or sculptures. The patron of France, however, though the king himself styled him his "duke" and "lord," carried his banner as his liege man, and expected his protection in battle,[51] was thought of primarily as a great theologian and visionary. If in his sanctuary art was to pay tribute to this great spiritual contribution, it could do so only by conveying something of the Areopagitical vision. This is what Suger attempted to do.

But what precisely is the link between that vision and the design of St.-Denis? The close analogy between Dionysian light metaphysics and Gothic luminosity is evident. But such analogy does not yet reveal the creative process leading from the one to the other. Still less is Gothic the only possible monumental "illustration" of that metaphysics. This much, however, we can say with some assurance: we can trace the influence of Dionysian thought in that

Denys vint . . . à Paris pour faire de cette ville la mère des études à l'instar d'Athènes. . . ." Quoted by Théry, "Existe-t-il un commentaire de J. Sarrazin sur la 'Hiérarchie céleste' du Pseudo-Denys?" (*Revue des sciences philosophiques et théologiques*, XI, 1922).

48. Félibien, pp. 147 ff.; *HLF*, XII, 94.

49. "Francia, omnium mitissima et civilissima nationum." Quoted in Heer, *Aufgang Europas*, p. 358.

50. For the influence of Dionysian thought on Suger's aesthetic views, see Panofsky, *Abbot Suger*, pp. 18 ff.; also Friend, "Carolingian Art in the Abbey of St.-Denis" (*Art Studies*, 1923, I, 75), who remarks that "the art of Capetian France rests solidly on the achievements of the great period of the abbey of the Patron Saint of France, the reputed author of the Celestial Hierarchy." Cf. Friend, "Two Manuscripts of the School of St.-Denis" (*Sp*, I, 1926).

51. See Crosby, *Abbey of St. Denis*, p. 50, and Loomis, "The Passion Lance Relic and the War Cry Monjoie in the *Chanson de Roland*" (*Romanic Review*, 1950, XLI, 241 ff.).

particular transformation of Romanesque models by which Suger and his assistants created a new style.

In developing the design of St.-Denis, Suger took up formal themes that occurred in the architectural masterpieces of the preceding epoch. He had studied, as we would expect, the art of Normandy and Burgundy. Suger knew Normandy well. Berneval, one of the possessions of his house, in the administration of which he had distinguished himself while still young, was actually situated in Norman territory.[52] The duchy was at that time among the most cultured provinces of Europe. In its monastic schools many of the luminaries of early scholasticism—Yves of Chartres among them—had been educated. Norman and Anglo-Norman ecclesiastical architecture combined a singular grandeur of design with a structural perfection that anticipated the elements of Gothic construction. This is strikingly true for the cross-ribbed vault. Only a few years before Suger started work on St.-Denis, the Cathedral of Durham had been entirely covered in this fashion.[53]

It is, therefore, perfectly natural that the abbot should have adapted aspects of Norman architecture to his own design. There may have been a political reason as well. Suger had been a particular admirer of Henry I Beauclerc, who since 1106 had governed Normandy as well as England. Although the king's policy was nearly always inimical to France, Suger speaks of him with unfailing respect.[54] The position of St.-Denis as well as Suger's own inclinations disposed him to mediate between the two powers. The French Vexin itself had at one time been annexed by Henry, and the monastery owned large revenues and estates on English soil.[55] Having gained the friendship and confidence of Henry I as much as that of Louis VI, Suger was able to establish that peace between them which brought Suger the well-deserved title from his biographer of *vinculum pacis*, bond of peace.[56] If this aim was uppermost in the mind of Suger the statesman, if his abbey was actually a link between the two powers[57]—

52. Suger, *De admin.*, XXIII, 184 f.
53. See Bilson, "The Beginnings of Gothic Architecture: Norman Vaulting in England" (*RIBA Journal*, VI, 1899; IX, 1902), and "Les Voûtes d'ogives de Morienval" (*BM*, LXXII, 1908); Bony, "Gloucester et l'origine des voûtes d'hémicycle gothique" (*BM*, XCVII, 1938); Cook, *Portrait of Durham Cathedral*.
54. *Vie de Louis* (Molinier, ed.), especially XV, 45 ff.
55. D'Ayzac, I, 359 ff.; Doublet, *Histoire de l'abbaye de S. Denys en France*, pp. 237, 411.
56. *Sugerii vita* (*Oeuvres*, p. 384); cf. Panofsky, *Abbot Suger*, p. 4.
57. "Between the French and the English, the Abbot of St.-Denis appears to have taken the attitude of a neutral power, on friendly terms with both, saddened to see them in con-

Henry II Plantagenet was to visit St.-Denis on several occasions for political as well as religious purposes [58]—the new church became a monument to this role of reconciliation. At the consecration ceremony for the choir Suger assigned to the archbishops of Canterbury and Rouen the places of honor immediately after the archbishop of Reims and ahead of the sixteen French archbishops and bishops present.[59]

To the visitors from Normandy and England, St.-Denis must at first sight have appeared like one of the great Norman abbeys. The west façade with its twin towers, as well as the arrangement of narthex and tribune, is without doubt Norman in inspiration. As we shall see in the next chapter, more than one element in the style and motifs of its sculpture connects it with the "Channel style" of the mid-twelfth century; and it has recently been pointed out, plausibly, I think, that at least one of Suger's windows shows close affinities with a celebrated work of English book illumination.[60] Yet if we compare the

*Plate 18* façade of St.-Denis with a possible Norman model, William the Conqueror's great abbey at Caen, we are struck by the differences between them. In St.-Étienne the façade is merely the base for the towers. It appears sober and subdued; the windows hardly interrupt the vertical rhythm of the buttresses,

*Plate 19* which anticipates that of the towers. In St.-Denis, on the other hand, the towers no longer dominate the façade. It is significant that as soon as the great square of the façade up to the crenelations was finished, Suger interrupted work on the upper part of the towers to begin on the choir; he never lived to see both towers completed. What concerned Suger was the façade as the entrance to his sanctuary, entrance in the physical but also in the symbolic sense. St.-Denis is the

flict and always ready to reconcile them." Luchaire, in Lavisse, *Histoire de France*, pp. 6 ff. It is not without interest in this connection that at St.-Denis passages from the history of the dukes of Normandy by William of Jumièges were incorporated, between 1135 and 1150, in a compilation of sources that eventually became part of the official and authoritative history of the French realm. See Walpole, "Philip Mouskés and the Pseudo-Turpin Chronicle" (*University of California Publications in Modern Philology*, XXVI, 1947).

58. See Halphen, "Les Entrevues des Rois Louis VII et Henri II" (*Mélanges d'histoire*

offerts à Ch. Bémont).

59. *De consecr.*, VI, 236 ff.

60. For the Norman derivation of the architecture of St.-Denis, see Anfray, pp. 231 ff.; for possible sources of the sculpture, see below, ch. 5. Mrs. Loomis, "The Oriflamme of France and the War-cry 'Monjoie' in the Twelfth Century" (*Studies in Art and Literature for Belle da Costa Greene*), suggests that Suger's crusade window may be influenced by the battle scene in the Book of St. Edmund, written c. 1130–50 at Bury St. Edmunds (Morgan Library MS. 736).

*Fig. 5. Cologne. Reconstruction of Roman north gate*

first church where the façade is designed to evoke the idea that the sanctuary is, in the words of the liturgy, the gate of heaven. It is the motif that the cathedrals were to take up thereafter. Here in St.-Denis, as we know from Suger's own testimony, it is inspired by the idea that Christian art must be "anagogical" in the Dionysian sense, a gateway leading the mind on to ineffable truths.

If we compare St.-Denis with St.-Étienne at Caen, the extent to which the symbolic purpose has effected the transformation of the model is strikingly

*Fig. 5*    apparent. The French façade is a gate, one might almost say the adaptation
of a Roman city gate.[61] It is more ornate by far than the façade at Caen, more
ornate also than the towers above it. Suger was the first to introduce a rose
window over the main entrance; but above all it is the three great portals with
their rich sculptured ornamentation that dominate everything else and express
the symbolic theme.[62]

*Plate 20a*    Of this composition only the central tympanum remains sufficiently intact
to allow some conclusions regarding composition and style. We can discuss it
in our present context only inasmuch as it elucidates the theme of the façade as
a portal of heaven. But it is worth mentioning that, while one source of this
sculpture may be Burgundian—a country that Suger knew well—the style
of St.-Denis is characteristically novel. A comparison will show what is
peculiar to this style.

*Plate 20b*    Only a few years earlier than Suger's work, probably in the early 1130's,
the tympanum of the great Cluniac abbey of Beaulieu (Corrèze) in the Languedoc had been completed. The iconographic similarity between this composition
and that in St.-Denis has not escaped the attention of scholars.[63] In both works
the scene represented is the Last Judgment. Christ appears as the Divine Judge
in the center, surrounded by Apostles and angels, while the dead rise from their
tombs. Such close iconographic correspondences make the difference of treatment all the more conspicuous. There is turmoil, a turmoil of awe and fear,
in the tympanum of Beaulieu. Innumerable figures seem to be crowded into a
narrow space; the Apostles and angels, the smaller figures of people rising from
their graves, are in wild agitation. By contrast, the composition at St.-Denis
appears serene and calm. Christ's figure is not separated from the Cross, as in
Beaulieu; he is seated in front of it, his erect body, his outstretched arms,
resuming, without unnatural stiffness, the simple axiality of the Cross that becomes the ordering pattern of the entire composition. The angels with the
instruments of the Passion are arranged symmetrically on either side of Christ's
head. The emphasis with which they display the instruments is accounted for

61. Bandmann, *Mittelalterliche Architektur als
Bedeutungsträger*, p. 158. See also Sedlmayer,
*Die Entstehung*, p. 233.

62. On these sculptures and what remains of
them, see below, p. 149.

63. See the comparison of the two works in
Mâle, *L'Art religieux du XII⁰ siècle en France*,
pp. 176 ff.; and Focillon, *L'Art des sculpteurs
romans*, pp. 268 ff.

by the fact that these were the relics of the Lendit.[64] But the trend toward clarity and simplification is noticeable throughout. Instead of the confusion that reigns at Beaulieu, six Apostles have been placed on either side of Christ, the line of their heads rigidly parallel to the horizontals of Christ's arms. Moreover, the artist has relegated the squirming figures of the dead emerging from their tombs to a different place: this scene now appears below the feet of Christ and the Disciples. Confined to a separate zone, the small figures arising from their graves no longer intrude upon the calm of the celestial vision. One might say that Christ appears all the more majestic by not mingling with the crowd as he does at Beaulieu.

Was there ever a relief below the resurrection scene with such monstrous figures as appear in the Languedoc tympanum? It is impossible to say for certain, since this part of Suger's portal is no longer in its original state. What renders such a representation unlikely, however, is the style as well as the interpretation of the general theme at St.-Denis. The style, austere in its subordination of the human figure to architectural order, is the first monumental manifestation in sculpture of the *art nouveau* emerging in the 1130's. This style, and the religious message of which it is the mouthpiece, are the very antithesis of Cluniac design, of which the monsters that still appear in Beaulieu were, to St. Bernard, the most offensive embodiment. Some grotesques appear, along with other survivals of Romanesque ornamentation, in several capitals of the façade and narthex; but the fact that the abbot of Clairvaux had singled out the representation of monsters for special criticism makes their employment in the lintel appear unlikely.[65] Suger's church, it will be recalled, postdates his reform of the monastery, undertaken at the insistence of St. Bernard. This fact and the increasingly cordial relations between the two men suggest that the art of St.-Denis may reflect Bernard's ideas.

Different as were the personalities of the two abbots, their responsibilities and inclinations, there is no doubt regarding the sincere admiration of the two

---

64. Two angels support the Cross, a third the Crown of Thorns, and the fourth what may have been—according to Guilhermy, *Notes historiques et descriptives sur . . . St.-Denis*, I, 63 ff.; and Crosby, *Abbaye*, p. 37—a cushion with the Three Nails. It is of interest to note that a nail also figured in the coat of arms of the abbot of St.-Denis (Doublet, p. 409), doubtless an allusion to the relic of the Lendit.

65. On Romanesque grotesques represented in St.-Denis, see Crosby, *Abbaye*, pp. 38, 47. The lintel seems to have been framed by a vegetative ornament. See Guilhermy, I, 61.

men for each other and the warm friendship that connected them in their later years. St. Bernard, so impatient of worldly prelates, notes with admiration in a letter to Pope Eugenius III how Suger, even in the midst of the most trying secular preoccupations, never neglects his spiritual duties but succeeds in reconciling them with worldly matters.[66] The temper of their friendship appears at the end of Suger's life when he requests, from his sickbed, a last visit from St. Bernard in order to be able "to pass more confidently out of this life." In his reply, Bernard addresses Suger as his "dearest and most intimate friend"; and unable to visit him, he requests the dying man's blessing.[67]

Bernard's influence upon Suger in matters of politics and ethics is certain. That this influence may have extended to the sphere of art was first suggested, I believe, by the late Arthur Kingsley Porter.[68] Porter thought that Suger deliberately set out to create "an art which should be national," that is, representative of the French domain, and indeed even contemporaries seem to have felt that the new church was built as an architectural example for the entire realm.[69] In doing so, Suger, according to Porter, realized that Cluniac art "was already discredited," and he "could not have failed to be influenced by the [Cistercian] current running so strongly in his time." Porter concluded that "the element of Cistercian austerity" looms powerfully in the new style—the first Gothic—that Suger created.

In view of what was said earlier in the present study, this thesis appears eminently likely. It is all the more noteworthy in that Porter proposed it, although he was at the same time convinced of the profound personal and ideological differences between Suger and the "art-hating" Bernard. In point of fact, there are more points of affinity even in their artistic views than is generally admitted. Bernard probably would have conceded that the art of a great pilgrimage center like St.-Denis had to make the same concessions to the sensuous experience of a lay public that he himself admitted for the cathedrals.[70]

66. *Ep.* CCCIX, Suger, *Oeuvres*, p. 419; Félibien, p. 161.

67. Suger's letter in *Oeuvres*, p. 282; Bernard's reply in *Ep.* CCLXIV (*PL*, CLXXXII, 470 f.).

68. *Romanesque Sculptures of the Pilgrimage Roads*, pp. 222 f. [*But see Add. for p. 58.*]

69. "Innovat inventum pater a fundamine templum ut sit in exemplum Dionysii monu-

mentum," we read in a eulogy to Suger. *Oeuvres*, p. 423.

70. This is also suggested by Félibien, p. 175. See in this connection the valuable observations of Petit on the aesthetic views of the Premonstratensians, "Le Puritanisme des premiers Prémontrés" (*BRA*). The author remarks that while the canons of Prémontré took their rule from Cîteaux, they were priests and clerics

And as such a pilgrimage center St.-Denis was, as we have seen, meant to rival the great Cluniac sanctuaries on the roads to Compostela; that their art should be eclipsed by the style of his church was surely Suger's ambition. At this time Bernard was as close to the French throne, and almost as identified with France, as was Suger himself. Obviously the art of St.-Denis had to be attuned to the religious experience of which St. Bernard was the irresistible spokesman, and it had to be at least compatible with the latter's aesthetic views. Moreover, Bernard's insistence that religious art be admitted only inasmuch as it was able to guide the beholder to the transcendental source of all beauty appealed profoundly to Suger, with whose Neoplatonic views on art we shall presently become acquainted. His west façade, where the Cluniac composition of Beaulieu is welded, as it were, into an entirely new design, is a monumental attempt to make that ultimate purpose of his art apparent to every observer.

The very motif of the *porta caeli* suggested the idea. The façade was to be understood as a threshold leading from the life in this world to the eternity that lies beyond it. It is remarkable to what extent the iconographic program of the sculpture underscores this idea. In the corners of the Last Judgment

rather than monks, and their concept of poverty, therefore, did not exclude the cult of beauty.

The thesis of an artistic antagonism between Suger and St. Bernard has again been proposed recently by Grodecki, "Suger et l'architecture monastique" (*BRA*). The author bases his argument mainly on analysis of the eight beautiful grisaille windows adorned with griffins in the ambulatory of Suger's choir, and concludes: "Their ideas differed to such an extent that it does not appear exaggerated to see in the abbey built by Suger a sort of reaction, of opposition, to Cistercian austerity." I hope to have shown that Bernard's artistic views offered no ground for such opposition. He never demanded that other religious communities should consider as binding aesthetic postulates that he had formulated in response to the ascetic ideals of his own order. And what he had written in the heated polemical style of the *Apologia* has been taken far more literally by modern scholars than by Bernard's own contemporaries. As to Suger's grisaille windows, are they not just as likely a concession to Cistercian art rather than a "reaction" to it? Is the griffin really a purely

ornamental motif, a grotesque? Dante introduced the griffin as an awesome allegory of Christ, and it is generally thought that the poet borrowed the image from Isidore of Seville, where the Saviour is likened to the lion "pro regno et fortitudine" and to the eagle "propter quod post resurrectionem . . . ad astra remeavit" (*Etymologiae*, VII, 2). Elsewhere Isidore describes the griffin as part lion and part eagle (*Etymologiae*, XII, 2). I see no reason why Suger, like Dante, should not have borrowed from the Spanish encyclopedist both the description (Suger's griffins look exactly like those in Latin twelfth-century bestiaries illustrating the descriptive passage from Isidore) and the allegorical interpretation of the griffin.

But, assuming even that the griffins are taken merely as remnants of "Romanesque" grotesques, as I have pointed out above (p. 47), such "monstrosities" occur even in the great Bible that was executed for St. Bernard. Finally, all we know about Suger makes a deliberate antagonism to St. Bernard extremely unlikely, especially at a time when the two men had become close allies in political as well as ecclesiastical matters.

there are two small female figures. They are, as it were, the leaders of the wise and foolish virgins, respectively, represented on the door jambs immediately below. To the left of Christ, the foolish virgin, her lamp reversed, has arrived at the door to paradise to find it locked (Matt. 25:10). Kneeling in a posture of imprecation and despair, she grasps the door ring, vainly praying that the door be opened. On the other side, on Christ's right, the leader of the wise virgins appears in a crenelated edifice—obviously the Celestial City, into which she has already been admitted. Here again Suger has made an invention that was to be of great consequence for the iconography and symbolism of Gothic cathedral sculpture. The Parable of the Wise and Foolish Virgins had already appeared in the sculpture of Poitou, but on the archivolts rather than along the jambs of the church portal. Suger inserted the figures of the virgins in the frame of his portal and connected the theme, as we have seen, with the Last Judgment in the tympanum. He thus blended the eschatological parable into the symbolism of the Gate to Eternity that constitutes the grandiose theme of the entire façade.[71]

The symbol of the door recurs on yet another level. The visitor to Suger's sanctuary—itself the mystical image of heaven—was reminded by him that he must leave behind the experience of his senses, or rather that he must perceive the shadowy image of an ultimate reality in whatever his senses beheld. Suger makes it very plain that this is the only interpretation in which his art has any meaning. In two inscriptions placed above the door—one on the lintel, immediately under the Last Judgment, where Suger had himself represented at the feet of the Divine Judge—he expressed the hope that through God's mercy and the intercession of St. Denis he might be received in paradise.[72] But the motif of the "threshold" is impressed upon us with even greater insistence in the inscription that Suger placed on the gilded bronze door itself. Here the visitor was admonished not to stop at the admiration of the preciosity and sumptuousness of the work, but to let its luminous brightness illuminate the mind so that it might ascend "to the true light to which Christ is the door." "How?" is explained by the golden door: the dull mind rises to the truth with

71. See Guilhermy, I, 64. On the history of the theme, see Lehmann, *Die Parabel von den klugen und törichten Jungfrauen*, especially pp. 36 ff. The example of St.-Denis was followed in Paris, Amiens, Sens, Auxerre, and Châlons-sur-Marne. Behling, "Die klugen und törich-ten Jungfrauen zu Magdeburg" (*ZK*, VIII, 1954), erroneously asserts that only eight virgins are represented at St.-Denis.

72. "Suscipe vota tui, judex districte, Sugeri;/Inter oves proprias fac me clementer haberi." *De admin.*, XXVII, 189.

the help of material things. In beholding this light the intellect is resurrected from its submersion in matter.[73]

The last words make it clear that the representation of the resurrection of the dead in the tympanum above did not only have its usual eschatological meaning but was also to convey the illumination of the mind that passes from this world to the vision of God. Suger has tried to define as clearly as possible the "analogical" nature of beauty (its partaking of a mystical prototype) and the "anagogical" purpose of art (its ability to raise the mind to the perception of ultimate truth). The idea, happy, naïve, ingenious, of choosing the portal for this initiation into the meaning of his art was typical of Suger. The inner disposition of those who entered his church was to change as they crossed the threshold. And at the same time Suger wished to prepare their minds for the design of his sanctuary and for the manner in which it was to be understood.

The simultaneous presence of Norman and Burgundian influences is equally apparent in Suger's choir. St.-Martin-des-Champs in near-by Paris, in its time one of the most powerful houses of the Order of Cluny, has a disposition, not unlike St.-Denis, of five radiating chapels around a double ambulatory. The church, which has not unjustly been called the "final expression of the Cluniac Romanesque," appears to be somewhat earlier than Suger's choir and may thus have influenced the latter.[74] Yet the relationship between the two is

73. "Portarum quisquis attollere quaeris
   honorem,
   Aurum nec sumptus, operis mirare
   laborem.
   Nobile claret opus, sed opus quod nobile
   claret
   Clarificet mentes ut eant per lumina vera.
   Quale sit intus in his determinat aurea
   porta.
   Mens hebes ad verum per materialia
   surgit,
   Et demersa prius hac visa luce resurgit."
   De admin., XXVII, 189.
For comment on this passage, see Panofsky, Abbot Suger, pp. 18 ff., 164 ff.; and "Note on a Controversial Passage in Suger's De Consecratione Ecclesiae Sancti Dionysii (GBA, 6th series, XXVI, 1944). Panofsky has rightly stressed Erigena's influence on Suger, but paid attention only to the metaphysics of light. As I shall show presently, Erigena's musical specula-

tions impressed Suger with equal force. And the latter's light mysticism, as we shall see, is indebted not only to Erigena, but even more so to Suger's great friend and contemporary—and Erigena's pupil—Hugh of St.-Victor. Suger could also find in Erigena the distinction between a proper (anagogical) and an improper enjoyment of a work of art. See De divisione naturae IV, 6 (PL, CXXII, 828).

74. Evans, The Romanesque Architecture of the Order of Cluny, pp. 14, 74, 116, dates St.-Martin 1130–1142 and stresses its influence upon St.-Denis; Bony, "French Influences," likewise considers St.-Martin earlier than St.-Denis; Gall, Die Gotische Baukunst in Frankreich und Deutschland, pp. 52 f., dates the edifice 1150–1160, but stresses the coarse and technically inadequate execution. Several scholars have noted the presence of Cluniac or Burgundian elements in Suger's choir. See Lambert, L'Art gothique en Espagne, p. 36; Crosby, "Early Gothic."

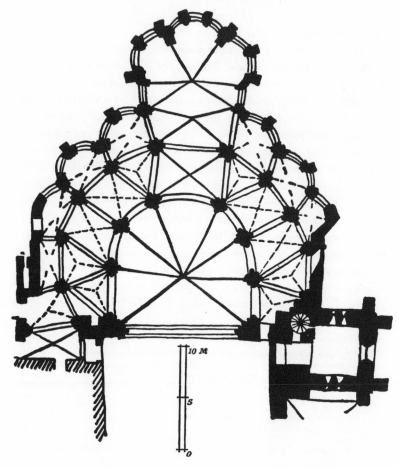

*Fig. 6. Church of St.-Martin-des-Champs. Ground plan of sanctuary*

like that between a first, awkward sketch and a consummate, definitive rendering of the same theme. In St.-Martin there still prevails the additive principle of
*Figs. 4, 6*  Romanesque architecture. The axial chapel, much larger than the other four,
juts forth and forms an almost independent unit, its roof set much lower than
the main roof line. If one compares the two ground plans, one is struck by the

"untidiness" of the older work, with its irregular bays, and the narrow, un-
even, and tortuous course of the outer ambulatory (if this term is applicable
at all).

The builder of this choir was obviously plagued by the difficulties that
confront the pioneer; it is characteristic that he uses both the groined and the
ribbed vault, as if unable to make up his mind which system is preferable. A
few years later at most, the master of St.-Denis achieved an almost flawless
perfection in his vaults. The technical shortcomings of the system of St.-
Martin have important aesthetic consequences. Although the individual chapels
receive as much light as do those of St.-Denis, the ambulatory and choir remain
relatively dark. The reason is apparent if, once again, we look at the ground
plans. In St.-Denis all supports lie on axes radiating from the center of the
choir; the light from the chapel windows thus penetrates unobstructed into the
choir. Owing to the irregularity with which the supports are placed in St.-
Martin, they interfere with the flow of the light no matter where one stands.
There is yet another reason for the relative darkness of this church: its supports
are large in proportion to the intervals between them. The columns in Suger's
ambulatory, on the other hand, are extraordinarily slim and graceful. They, as
well as the outer walls of the chapel, realize for the first time the principle of
reduced surface and bulk for the benefit of luminosity that is the great accomplishment of the Gothic.

The exact appearance of Suger's choir is unknown, even though Professor
Crosby's excavations—the complete results of which have not yet been published—have shed light on important essentials. Whether or not a gallery
existed above the ambulatory is uncertain in view of the slimness of the supports.[75] Suger's own description makes it plain that the entire choir, including
the chevet, was covered with a cross-ribbed vault.[76] This fact is of great importance not only structurally but artistically. We have seen that the Norman
builders had already used cross-ribbed vaults over large bays. Since these vaults
gathered the main thrusts along the ridges of the groins and supported them by
the ribs, the webs or vault compartments between these could be made much
lighter in the twofold sense of the word. More precisely, it was possible to
heighten the clerestory windows considerably. By the use of the pointed arch,

75. See above, n. 32.                    76. *De consecr.*, V, 227 ff.

introduced apparently from Burgundy,[77] and by "pinching back" the vaults at their springing, "plowshare" vaults could be built that enlarged the translucent area still further.[78]

It is all the more remarkable that the Norman builders hardly availed themselves of the advantages that these devices offered for the creation of Gothic luminosity. Clerestory windows remained small, and the light was still further obstructed by passageways running inside of the window area. The consistent application of the pointed arch is resorted to relatively late, only a few years earlier than St.-Denis. And it is in the Norman apse that the "Gothic opportunity" appears to have been overlooked most strikingly. Such great Norman apses as are still existent—Lessay, the Trinité at Caen, Cérisy-la-Forêt—reveal a taste for light that must have delighted Suger.[79] The treatment of the vault, however, would have offended his predilection for complete transparency as well as for homogeneity among all parts of the edifice. These large Norman apses are vaulted not by a groined or ribbed vault but by a *cul-de-four* or half dome. As a result, the upper part of the apse remains dark and also, since it lacks a clerestory, its elevation differs from that of the rest of the choir. By adopting the ribbed vault for the chevet of his choir, Suger created in the clerestory that same zone of "continuous light" which, by the disposition of his chapels, he had also achieved to his immense satisfaction in the ambulatory. The Norman builders had well known this type of apse vaulting with multiple supports without making use of them, it would seem, on a large scale.[80]

Now this failure on their part to take advantage—from a Gothic viewpoint—of their own technical invention was, to some extent at least, imposed by the shortcomings of available building materials. Norman vaults are usually executed in rubble. The superb geological resources of the Île-de-France made possible construction of vaults in ashlar or dressed stone, thereby reducing the weight and thickness of the vault by more than one half.[81] Such technical ad-

77. Bony, "French Influences."
78. See Bond, *An Introduction to English Church Architecture*, I, 295 ff.
79. Bilson, "Voûtes d'ogives de Morienval"; Gall, *Niederrheinische und normännische Architektur im Zeitalter der Frühgotik*, pp. 32 f.
80. Cf. Bony, "La Technique normande du mur épais" (*BM*, XCVIII, 1939), and

"Gloucester"; Sedlmayr, *Die Entstehung der Kathedrale*, p. 197; Anfray, p. 330; Gall, *Gotische Baukunst*, p. 136; Lasteyrie, *L'Architecture religieuse en France à l'époque gothique*, I, 24; Focillon, *Art d'Occident, le moyen-âge, roman et gothique*, p. 156.
81. See Bond, *Introduction*, pp. 318 ff.; Gall, *Niederrheinische und normännische Architektur*,

vantages, however, do not explain the style. Gothic structural devices were not ends but means judiciously and ingeniously employed for the attainment of an artistic goal that existed in the mind of the first Gothic builders.

Suger was undoubtedly assisted by a builder of genius who had an almost effortless command of the great structural inventions of Norman architecture. But in St.-Denis all these devices were—all of a sudden, as far as we know— employed for the realization of a single and powerful aesthetic vision. We cannot doubt that this vision was Suger's, that he stood as the *spiritus rector* behind his builder, and that the vision is the cause behind the transformation of Norman into Gothic.

Suger, one might almost say, was infatuated with light. The inscription on the door of his new abbey called attention to the surpassing beauty of the luminous and to its theological significance. Inside the sanctuary, this experience was reinforced by his magnificent liturgical vessels and furniture, resplendent with gold and precious stones,[82] but above all by the architecture of the choir itself. Again, Suger used an inscription to call attention to the significance of his creation. Anticipating the completion of the nave in the same translucent style that he had given to the choir, he says: "Once the new rear part is joined to the part in front, the [whole] church shines with its middle part [the nave] brightened. For bright is that which is brightly coupled with the bright. And bright is the noble edifice that is pervaded by the new light." [83] The last sentence is ambivalent, inasmuch as *lux nova* also refers to Christ and thus to the symbolic or "anagogical" significance of the physical light.

Suger's inscription is interesting for three reasons: it permits the conclusion that the elevation of the nave was to be similar to, or even identical with, that of the choir; it shows to what extent the luminosity of his church eclipsed, in Suger's mind, all other aspects of his achievement; and it also makes clear

---

p. 56; Lefèvre-Pontalis, *L'Architecture religieuse dans l'ancien diocèse de Soissons au XI<sup>e</sup> et au XII<sup>e</sup> siècle*, pp. 68 ff.; Choisy, *Histoire de l'architecture*, p. 259.

82. See *De admin.*, XXXI ff., 193 ff.; Panofsky, *Abbot Suger*, pp. 168 ff.; Aubert, *Suger*, pp. 144 ff.

83. "Pars nova posterior dum jungitur anteriori,

Aula micat medio clarificata suo.
Claret enim claris quod clare copulatur,
Et quod perfundit lux nova, claret opus
Nobile, quod constat auctum sub tempore nostro . . ."
*De admin.*, XXVIII, 190; cf. Panofsky's comment, *Abbot Suger*, pp. 152 ff.

that this mystical and aesthetic appreciation of light originated in Suger's studies of the *Corpus areopagiticum.*

To what extent this theological work actually influenced the architectural design of Suger's church is best shown by his windows. From the fragments that survive we know their beauty; their impact upon the art of the stained-glass window in general attests to the profound impression they made upon contemporaries. Suger himself has called these windows "most sacred," the light they admitted "miraculous." [84] He determined their subjects and interpreted their meaning by accompanying inscriptions.[85] Most of these subjects are taken from the Old Testament; two represent allegories that occur in the Book of Revelation and in the Epistles of St. Paul, respectively. Every one of these images suggests the theology and exegesis of the Dionysian tradition. God has revealed himself, directly in the Incarnation, obscurely in nature and the metaphors of the Bible. We must seek to grasp Him in and through these; we must perceive the divine light that illuminates them.

Suger was not the first to realize that the stained-glass window is an incomparable illustration of this "anagogical" theology. Hugh of St.-Victor had made masterful use of this metaphor in his commentary on the *Celestial Hierarchy* (1137).[86] The treatise, significantly addressed to the king, contains a magnificent theology of beauty based on the work of the supposed Apostle of France. One of the most renowned theologians of his age, Hugh was also Suger's friend. The aesthetic views of the latter and his novel idea of using the stained-glass window as a visual "demonstration" of Dionysian theology are very likely inspired by the canon of St.-Victor.[87] But the idea of such direct

---

84. See above, n. 31.

85. Suger records the inscriptions in *De admin.*, XXXIV, 205 f. See the important recent studies of the windows by Grodecki, "A Stained Glass Atelier of the Thirteenth Century" (*JWCI*, X, 1947), and "Suger et l'architecture monastique"; also "Fragments de vitraux provenant de St.-Denis" (*BM*, CX, 1952), and his Introduction to the *Catalogue* of the Exposition Vitraux de France, pp. 38 ff. Also Panofsky, *Abbot Suger*, pp. 195 f. It ought to be pointed out that only six of Suger's ambulatory windows were historiated, the others being the grisailles mentioned above.

86. See following note; also *Sermones* (PL,

CLXXVII, 902 f.); Durandus, *Rationale divinorum officiorum*, Venice, 1594, I, 1, 24, p. 4.

87. In commenting on the Dionysian passage "Etenim neque possibile est aliter nobis lucere divinum radium, nisi varietate sacrorum vel animum anagogice circumvelatum . . ." Hugh remarks: "Sacra velamina, in quibus nobis radius divinus lucet, sunt mysticae in sacro eloquio descriptiones, quae visibiles adducunt formas et similitudines invisibilium ad declarationem. Quibus videlicet velaminibus ipse radius divinus anagogice circumvelatur. Anagoge enim, sicut dictum est, ascensio mentis, sive elevatio vocatur in contemplationem supernorum. Anagogice igitur circum-

translation of a mystical image into the language of art is characteristic of Suger; the representation of the *porta caeli* on the façade of St.-Denis is another translation of this kind, but in Suger's windows the exposition of Dionysian theology by means of art is singularly impressive. These translucent panels, "vested," as he put it, with sacred symbols, are to him like veils at once shrouding and revealing the ineffable. What they meant to him, what they were to mean to others, is best shown in Suger's selection of the scene of Moses appearing veiled before the Israelites. St. Paul had used the image to elucidate the distinction between the "veiled" truth of the Old Testament and the "unveiled" truth of the New.[88] In Suger's interpretation it epitomized his very world view, to which, in the footsteps of the Pseudo-Areopagite, the entire cosmos appeared

velatur, quia ad hoc velatur ut amplius clarescat; ob hoc tegitur ut magis appareat. Ejus igitur obumbratio nostri est illuminatio; et ejus circumvelatio, nostri elevatio. Quemadmodum infirmi oculi solem nube tectum libere conspiciunt, qui coruscum ejus lumen intueri non possunt: sic et divinum radium lippientibus mentis oculis lucere impossibile est, nisi varietate sacrorum velaminum circumvelatum et praeparatum providentia paterna connaturaliter et proprie iis, quae secundum nos sunt." *Expositio in hierarchiam caelestem*, II (*PL*, CLXXV, 946). See also the following passages: "Mens etenim hominis tenebri ignorantiae suae obvoluta ad lumen veritatis exire non potest, nisi dirigatur, et quasi caecus manuductione utens, quo non videt, incedat. Ipse autem manuductiones et directiones, quibus mens ad invisibilia tendens utitur, a visibilibus sumuntur signis, et demonstrationibus secundum visibilia formatis. . . . Est tamen aliqua similitudo visibilis pulchritudinis ad invisibilem pulchritudinem, secundum aemulationem, quam invisibilis artifex ad utramque constituit, in qua quasi speculamina quaedam diversorum proportionum unam imaginem effingunt. . . . Et similiter immaterialis luculentiae, hoc est spiritualis lucis imaginem esse materialia, id est corporalia lumina." Ibid., pp. 948 ff.

88. Panofsky, *Abbot Suger*, p. 198, seems to have misunderstood Suger's exegesis of the passage in Exodus 34:33–35. Suger (*De admin.* XXXIV, 205) obviously leans on St. Paul (II Cor. 3:12–18), who interprets the Moses episode as follows: "Seeing then that we have such hope, we use great plainness of speech: And not as Moses, which put a vail over his face, that the children of Israel could not stedfastly look to the end of that which is abolished: But their minds were blinded: for until this day remaineth the same vail untaken away in the reading of the old testament; which vail is done away in Christ. But even unto this day, when Moses is read, the vail is upon their heart. [The frequent medieval references to the "blindness" of the Jews—and the iconography of the blindfolded synagogue—are based on this passage; see St. Bernard, *PL*, CLXXXII, 570; also Valois, *Guillaume d'Auvergne*, p. 131.] Nevertheless when it shall turn to the Lord, the vail shall be taken away. Now the Lord is that Spirit: and where the Spirit of the Lord is, there is liberty. But we all, with open face beholding as in a glass the glory of the Lord, are changed into the same image . . ."

The inference, obviously, is not that "Moses must remain veiled in the presence of human beings, and those who would presume to uncover *him* would commit an offense." For St. Paul, as for Suger, the veil of Moses denotes the dullness of the senses of those not yet illuminated by grace; and the "denuding" of Moses, far from being an offense, signifies that the "veiled" truth of the Old Testament has been replaced by the revelation of the New, a substitution that replaces the law (*lex*) by "freedom" (*libertas*). According to this exegesis, the Biblical image epitomizes the metaphysics and epistemology of illumination. [*See Add.*]

like a veil illuminated by the divine light. Such a world view was peculiarly that of his century. The image he had found for it in the stained-glass window was so obvious, so irresistible, that it was bound to impress itself upon everyone's mind. We cannot be surprised that the image was powerful enough to induce Suger to transform the entire sanctuary into a transparent cosmos.

Here again there should be no misunderstanding. Suger did not invent the stained-glass window. On the contrary, he used an artistic medium that was peculiarly French in that it had long been practiced in France.[89] In England this art never flourished to the same extent; in fact, as late as the fifteenth century greased linen or paper was occasionally used there in lieu of glazed windows, even in churches.[90] Would the development of Norman architecture have taken a different course had the glass painter's art been developed there as it was in France? And what would Suger have done had his abbey been situated in England? Such questions are, of course, idle. The "Dionysian" renaissance is as characteristically French as are the calcareous deposits of the Île-de-France and the art and use of the stained-glass window in the twelfth century. All these elements were needed for the creation of Gothic, and only in France could this style have come into existence. In the use he made of the stained-glass window Suger did no more and no less than to give compelling significance to an image that was known to all. That is precisely what every great artist or poet does. Suger was the first to conceive the architectural system as but a frame for his windows, and to conceive his windows not as wall openings but as translucent surfaces to be adorned with sacred paintings. This dual "invention" distinguished Suger's style from Romanesque and is indeed the basic novelty of Gothic architecture. The "Dionysian" source of this artistic revolution can no longer be in doubt. [See Add.]

Fortunately, the proof for this statement does not rest on circumstantial evidence alone, but on Suger's own explicit testimony. We are already acquainted with some of his inscriptions. Their purpose was probably twofold.

89. Theophilus Presbyter, in his *Schedula diversarum artium*, I, Praefatio (Ilg, ed., pp. 9 ff.; Theobald, ed., p. 10), obviously considers the art peculiarly French: "quicquid in fenestrarum pretiose varietate diligit Francia." (The *Schedula* is a work of the tenth or eleventh century; cf. Degering, "Theophilus Presbiter" [*Westfälische Studien . . . Alois Boemer*, pp. 250 ff.]; and *MJ*, 1952.) See also Hubert, *L'Art pré-roman*, p. 127: "Il est . . . un art qui appartient en propre à la Gaule: celui de la peinture sur verre."

90. Salzman, pp. 173 f.

Suger may have wished, as has been suggested, to avoid possible misunder-
standings on the part of St. Bernard and his followers. Bernard had generally
disparaged religious art by pointing to its distracting effect upon the beholder.
Suger provided visitors to his abbey with a singular kind of guide that told them
exactly how to look at his art in order to derive from it that spiritual benefit for
which it had been created. St. Bernard, to be sure, had censured even the
pleasure that might be derived from contemplation of luminous objects.[91] But
as a child of his age and of France he was himself deeply sensitive to the experience of light. In one of his most moving passages he describes the mystical
union of the soul with God as the "immersion in the infinite ocean of eternal
light and luminous eternity." And he can think of but one image to convey this
vision: illumination of the air by sunlight.[92] Thus it would seem that Bernard
considered light, as well as harmony, a medium capable of conveying something
of the nature of transcendental reality to the senses. They are quite similarly
singled out by Suger. But in emphasizing them, a "defense" of his art against
Bernard's asceticism was hardly uppermost in his mind. Eternal light and
harmony had their inspired witness in the Pseudo-Areopagite. His vision Suger
sought to convey by means of his art, seeking to elucidate by words what the
language of form might be unable to reveal.

   Not only inscriptions were to fulfill that purpose. Suger has described and
interpreted his church and its art treasures in two separate treatises. Nearly one
half of his account of his administration as abbot is devoted to that subject.[93]
A second and earlier work, the *Booklet on the Consecration of the Church of St.-
Denis*, deals entirely with it. The two works are intimately related. The
relevant chapters in the *Report on the Administration*, which describe the completed monument and contain the inscriptions already mentioned, also expound
the rudiments of what we may call the Sugerian aesthetics of light. The *Booklet
on the Consecration*, on the other hand, recalls the actual building of the church
and stresses the aesthetic value of harmony. This work, however, hardly deals
with the concrete, professional aspects of the undertaking; and for the technical

91. *Apologia ad Guillelmum*, XII, 28 (PL,
CLXXXII, 95); see Heckscher, "Relics of
Pagan Antiquity in Medieval Settings" (*JWCI*,
I, 1937/38).
   92. *Liber de diligendo Deo*, X, 28 (PL,
CLXXXII, 991). It is not without interest in

this connection that Rose, *Die Frühgotik im
Orden von Cîteaux*, p. 137, and Sedlmayr,
*Entstehung*, p. 408, stress the luminosity of
Cistercian church interiors.
   93. The following is based on my paper,
"The Birth of the Gothic" (*Measure*, I, 1950).

accomplishment Suger has no interest. For him, as for his contemporaries, structural problems were disheartening obstacles or occasions for miraculous interventions from above. Their practical solution was not yet an object of admiration as in the Renaissance and perhaps even in the thirteenth century. Instead, Suger represents the building of his abbey, from the germinal idea to the completed structure, as a spiritual process.

At first sight this kind of report appears disappointing to the historian of architecture. Building is not, after all, an esoteric affair but a very concrete one. However, Suger's intention clearly was not that of writing an edifying treatise. Whatever he wrote was directly related to the main purpose of his career. If in the midst of pressing responsibilities he took the time to write at such length on the building of his church—or at least on that aspect of it which concerned him most—this must be of real concern to us who try to understand his art.

The *Booklet* begins as follows: "The admirable power of one unique and supreme reason equalizes by proper composition the disparity between things human and divine; and what seems mutually to conflict by inferiority of origin and contrariety of nature is conjoined by the single, delightful concordance of one superior, well-tempered harmony."

What the author seeks to unfold before us is a vision of the cosmos, created and maintained by the One who transcends and reconciles the many. Suger's language is emphatically musical. Like his contemporaries, the Platonists of the School of Chartres, he conceives the universe as a symphonic composition. In fact, Alan of Lille, in a passage that I have quoted earlier,[94] was to use almost the same terms in describing the divine architect who builds the edifice of the world according to the laws of musical consonance. Suger, however, understands this vision as the mystical prototype of the sanctuary he is about to erect:

Those who seek to be glorified by a participation in this supreme and eternal reason, as if their penetrating mind were seated in a kind of judgment seat, strive continuously to accord the similar with the dissimilar and to render justice between conflicting things. With the aid of charity they draw from the source of eternal reason the means by which they may withstand internal strife and inner sedition: preferring the spiritual to the corporeal and the eternal to the perishable. They set aside the vexations and grievous

94. See above, p. 31.

anxieties caused by sensuality and the exterior senses; emancipating themselves from their oppression and focusing the undivided vision of their minds upon the hope of eternal reward, they seek jealously only that which is enduring. They forget carnal desires rapt in the admiration of other sights; and they rejoice to be united one day, through the merit of a glorious consciousness, to supreme reason and everlasting bliss.[95]

At first glance, the relation of the two quoted passages to one another and to Suger's main theme is quite obscure. Professor Panofsky thinks that they constitute but "an organ prelude filling the room with magnificent sound before the appearance of a discernible theme." [96] Suger's theme, however, was entirely discernible to his contemporaries. It becomes equally intelligible to us as soon as we look into the work of the theologian on whom Suger relied as the translator and interpreter of the *Corpus areopagiticum*, that is, Johannes Scotus Erigena.[97] The Irish Platonist dwells repeatedly and at length on the law of harmonic proportion, by which, he says, the contrariety and dissonance among the different parts of the universe are reconciled. This musical law is for Erigena, as for Augustine and Plato, the source of all beauty. It is here that the

95. *De consecr.*, I, 213. My translation deviates here somewhat from Panofsky's *Abbot Suger*, p. 83.

96. *Abbot Suger*, p. 26.

97. In fact, Suger's musical aesthetics is almost certainly a reminiscence of the following passage of Erigena: "Nam quae in partibus universitatis opposita sibimet videntur atque contraria et a se invicem dissona, dum in generalissima ipsius universitatis harmonia considerantur, convenientia consonaque sunt." *De divisione naturae*, I, 72 (*PL*, CXXII, 517). Note also the following passages: "Omnibus namque recte philosophantibus perspicue patet, ex uno genere multas formas nasci; ex monade multos numeros; ex puncto multas lineas . . . Numeri ex monade procedentes diversarum proportionum causae sunt; proportiones vero proportionalitatum, proportionalitates harmoniarum." II, 31 (c. 602). "Et quemadmodum in proportionibus numerorum proportionalitates sunt, hoc est, proportionum similes rationes, eodem modo in naturalium ordinationum participationibus mirabiles atque ineffabiles harmonias constituit creatrix omnium sapientia, quibus omnia in unam quandam concordiam, seu amicitiam, seu pacem, seu amorem, seu quocumque modo rerum omnium adunatio significari possit, conveniunt. Sicut enim numerorum concordia, proportionis; proportionum vero collatio, proportionalitatis: sic ordinum naturalium distributio, participationis nomen, distributionum vero copulatio, amoris generalis accepit, qui omnia ineffabili quadem amicitia in unum colligit." III, 6 (cc. 630 f.). "Proinde pulchritudo totius universitatis conditae, similium et dissimilium, mirabili quadam harmonia constituta est ex diversis generibus variisque formis, differentibus quoque substantiarum et accidentium ordinibus, in unitatem quandam ineffabilem compacta. Ut enim organicum melos ex diversis vocum qualitatibus et quantitatibus conficitur, dum viritim separatimque sentiuntur, longe a se discrepantibus intentionis et remissionis proportionibus segregatae, dum vero sibi invicem coaptantur secundum certas rationabilesque artis musicae regulas per singulos tropos, naturalem quandam dulcedinem reddentibus: ita universitatis concordia, ex diversis naturae unius subdivisionibus a se invicem, dum singulariter inspiciuntur, dissonantibus, juxta conditoris uniformem voluntatem coadunata est." III, 6 (cc. 637 f.). Cf. also V, 12 (cc. 883 f.). For the Dionysian source of this idea, see *De divinis nominibus*, III, 10; cf. Théry, *Études*, II, 207.

supreme will of the Creator is revealed.[98] In placing this thought at the head of his treatise on the building and consecration of his church, Suger wished to underscore the anagogical significance of the architectural harmony of the sanctuary, as he stressed elsewhere the anagogical significance of its luminosity. It is not as a restatement of the musical aesthetics of the Platonic tradition that the opening passage is significant. Its interest lies in the fact that, owing to the context in which it occurs, we can actually grasp the connection between that aesthetics and the architectural design of a great medieval builder, the author of the first Gothic sanctuary. For Suger, in short, this design reflected the vision of cosmic harmony and was so to be understood.

The validity of this interpretation is confirmed by a document that represents something like a link between the *Corpus areopagiticum* and Suger's work. This document, the *Mystagogia* by Maximus the Confessor (d. 662), is of considerable interest to the art historian in that it is the first known treatise to contain a specific application of Dionysian mysticism to the interpretation of the church edifice. According to Maximus, the Christian sanctuary is first of all an image of God, who through His infinite power creates everything, embracing and chaining together the physical and intelligible realms; and by the single power of His reason God conjoins and brings into one harmony even what is most diversified and mutually conflicting. Since the same principle of concord is reflected in the created universe, Maximus continues, the church edifice is also an image of the cosmos. This opening passage of the *Mystagogia* is strikingly similar to that of Suger's treatise. It contains, moreover, the explicit reference of the vision of cosmic harmony to the Christian basilica that, if my interpretation is valid, is implied in the first sentences of Suger's *Booklet*.

98. "Aliud est enim considerare singulas universitatis partes, aliud totum. Hinc conficitur, ut, quod in parte contrarium esse putatur, in toto non solum non contrarium, verum etiam pulchritudinis augmentum reperitus." *De divisione naturae*, V, 35 (c. 954). "Nulla enim pulchritudo efficitur, nisi ex compaginatione similium et dissimilium, contrariorum et oppositorum." V, 36 (c. 982). The musical experience behind this aesthetics is obvious: ". . . libero mentis contuitu clare perspicerem universae naturae adunationem ex diversis sibique oppositis copulari, musicis rationibus admonitus, in quibus conspicor, nil aliud animo placere pulchritudinem efficere, nisi diversarum vocum rationabilia intervalla, quae inter se invicem collata musici modulaminis efficiunt dulcedinem. Ubi mirabile quiddam datur intelligi, et solo mentis contuitu vix comprehensibile quod non soni diversi . . . harmonicam efficiunt suavitatem, sed proportiones sonorum . . ." V, 36 (cc. 965 f.). See above, p. 28.

Suger is almost certain to have known the *Mystagogia*. The Confessor was the greatest exponent of Dionysian theology; a treatise of his had been translated by Erigena. Excerpts and a summary of the *Mystagogia*, moreover, had been translated into Latin and sent to Charles the Bald by Anastasius the Librarian, an eminent scholar as well as an influential dignitary of the see of Rome. In his dedicatory epistle Anastasius had called the emperor's special attention to the fact that Maximus, in his preface, had himself stressed his close dependence upon Dionysius, "whom you love [Anastasius adds] and who loves you." Of the Anastasian text, two copies, of the ninth or tenth century, survive even today. But the *Mystagogia* may have existed, both in the original Greek and in yet another translation, at St.-Denis, which, during the twelfth century, as Léopold Delisle has shown, was one of the most important Western centers of Hellenic studies.

The probability of Suger's acquaintance with Maximus is of great interest. To what he called "symbolic contemplation" Maximus assigned the function of grasping invisible reality behind the world of visual phenomena. He preceded Suger in choosing the church edifice as the noblest subject for such contemplation, and may thus have encouraged the abbot of St.-Denis to envisage and actually to design his basilica as a paradigm of the "anagogical" world view. Suger may even have found the symbolism of door and threshold in Maximus, who interpreted the closing of the church doors in the rite of his Church as signifying the passing away of all earthly things and the entry of the elect, upon the day of judgment, into the kingdom of Christ.[99]

Suger wished to express yet another thought at the beginning of his *Booklet:* the great enterprise that is about to be undertaken requires an inner disposition, a state of grace, on the part of the builder. The mystical vision of harmony can become a model for the artist only if it has first taken possession of his soul and become the ordering principle of all its faculties and aspirations.

That Suger wished to convey this thought—a typically medieval one—is also the opinion of the Benedictine scholar, Dom Jean Leclercq, who has trans-

99. The *Mystagogia* is in *PG*, XCI; see especially cc. 664 ff., 688 f., 693. For the translation by Anastasius, see Pétridès, "Traités liturgiques de Saint Maxime et de Saint Germain" (*Revue de l'Orient chrétien*, X, 1905). On the Hellenic studies at St.-Denis during the twelfth century, see Delisle, "Traductions de textes grecs faites par des religieux de Saint-Denis au XII⁰ siècle" (*Journal des Savants*, 1900, p. 725).

lated Suger's *De consecratione* into French.[100] With reference to the introductory passage, Leclercq in his Preface points to the synthesis of the lives of contemplation and action in the ascetic ideal of his (and Suger's) order. The goal of monastic life is sanctification. The monk's daily work in the service of this ideal may be described as "edification." Ascetic writers like to dwell on the ancient image of the soul as a temple, and to describe the work of sanctification as an act of building. Recalling the ancient architectural overtones of the word "edification," Leclercq suggests that the Benedictine concept of labor as a process of edification may find its perfect realization in sacred architecture, designed and constructed as an image of the Celestial City, and thus requiring the vision of divine glory for its design but physical labor for its material construction. Hence the church cannot be completed without the assistance of grace, which illuminates the builder's intellect as well as his moral and artistic powers. Suger experienced this supernatural assistance even in the purely technical phases of his undertaking.

To a large extent all this is typically medieval. The Middle Ages thought of art as resulting from and reflecting the subjective perfection of the artist and the spiritual power that enables him to partake of absolute reality. According to this view, there are two modes of aesthetic insight: that of the artist and that of the contemplator of the artist's work. The insight of the artist alone is pure since only he beholds both the reality and the image of it that he creates. The contemplator who sees merely the image has but a dim and indirect impression of that reality. For the religious artist or poet this creates a peculiar problem: the sole concern and justification of his work are to mirror ultimate reality. But for this very reason he cannot leave the onlooker alone with his work but will seek to reveal to him the state of soul, the act of divine illumination, that enenabled the artist or poet to create his work and that is of so much greater significance than the work—mere image of that illumination—can ever be. St. Augustine had been the first to direct the eyes of the faithful from the visible beauty of a new church to the "beauty of the inner man from which it had proceeded." The invocations with which so many medieval poems open or close

100. *Comment fut construit Saint-Denis*, p. 20. See also *Tractatus de interiori domo seu de conscientia aedificanda* (PL, CLXXXIV, 507): "studeamus ergo templum Deo aedificare in nobis . . ."

have the similar purpose of directing the reader's attention to the divine assistance that the author experienced in composing his work.[101] And Dante's main concern in the *Divine Comedy* is not the unfolding of a tremendous eschatological panorama, but rather the account of his own gradual illumination, which we are to relive as we read his poem.

Something very similar is true for Suger's account of the building of St.-Denis. What he describes in the treatise on the *Consecration* is less, as the title seems to indicate, the final dedication of the completed edifice than the process by which it is brought to completion. We are to relive this process step by step in order to understand the finished work whose true significance is revealed in the liturgical act of consecration. To Suger, as to his master, St. Augustine, this process is not so much the physical labor as it is the gradual "edification" of those who take part in the building, the illumination of their souls by the vision of the divine harmony that is then reflected in the material work of art.

The medieval reader could not have misunderstood this meaning. What Suger seeks to point out about the mental and moral disposition of those who build the sanctuary is but a paraphrase of certain passages from St. Augustine that were familiar to most of Suger's readers; their subject being precisely the dedication of the church, these passages form part of the canonical office for the ceremony. St. Augustine describes here the basilica as an image of heaven and goes on to relate the manual labor of its construction to the spiritual process of edification.[102] For Augustine, as for Suger, the two are inseparable.

101. For the aesthetic views summarized above, see de Bruyne, III, 115. The Augustinian passage is in *Sermo* 337 (*PL*, XXXVIII, 1475 f.): "Neque enim occupata est fides inspicere, quam pulchra sint membra hujus habitationis; sed de quanta interioris hominis pulchritudine procedant haec opera dilectionis." For the invocations in medieval poetry and their significance, see the important paper by Schwietering, "The Origins of the Medieval Humility Formula" (*Publications of the Modern Language Association of America*, LXIX, 1954). 102. See *Sermones*, CCLII (*PL*, XXXVIII, 1171 ff.) and CCLVI (*PL*, XXXVIII, 1190), where Augustine remarks "quodhic factum corporaliter videmus in parietibus, spiritaliter fiat in mentibus; et quod hic perfectum cernimus in lapidibus et lignis, hoc, aedificante gratia Dei, perficiatur in corporibus vestris." See also the following, likewise inserted in the Office of the Day of Dedication, and referring to "Jerusalem quae aedificatur ut civitas [Ps. 122:3]. Si autem fundamentum nostrum in caelo est, ad caelum aedificemur. Corpora aedificaverunt istam structuram, quam videtis amplam surrexisse hujus basilicae; et, quia corpora aedificaverunt, fundamentum in imo posuerunt. Quia vero spiritaliter aedificamur, fundamentum nostrum in summo positum est." Augustine adds: "Et quia aedificium spirituale similitudinem quandam habet aedificii corporalis, ideo aedificatur ut civitas." *Enarrat. super Psalmos* (*PL*, XXXVII, 1620 ff.). The comparison of the basilica with the Celestial City, ibid., 1620: "sed ista Jerusalem umbra est illius." See also *Sermones*, CCCLXII (*PL*, XXXIX, 1615).

The spiritual and mystical significance that the abbot of St.-Denis thus ascribes to building is made even more explicit in subsequent chapters of his *Booklet*. In Chapter V he recalls the completion of the Gothic choir, "the City of the great King," as he calls it, in terms that evoke the image of Christ the Cornerstone "which joins one wall to the other; *in whom all the building—* whether spiritual or material—*groweth unto an holy temple in the Lord. In whom ye also* are taught to be *builded together for an habitation of God through the* Holy *Spirit* by ourselves in a spiritual way, the more loftily and aptly we strive to build in a material way." [103] The italicized words of this quotation, and only these, are taken from Paul's Epistle to the Ephesians (2:19 ff.); but whereas the architectural imagery is a mere metaphor for St. Paul, Suger directly relates it to his building. His own additions to the Biblical text—the little phrase "whether spiritual or material"—so adroitly inserted that they have escaped the attention of all his editors except Panofsky,[104] impart to the act of building an almost sacred significance; we, that is, all who have had any part in this great work, shall be builded together for an habitation of God in the measure in which we strive to make His material temple worthy of Him. Again, however, Suger's exegesis is sanctioned by an almost identical thought expressed in one of St. Augustine's early sermons for the dedication of a church: "How will God reward those who build for Him with so much piety, joy, and devotion? He will build them, as living stones, into his spiritual edifice toward which those direct themselves who are informed by faith, solidified by hope, and united by charity."

With the same theme the treatise is brought to an end. In the two final chapters Suger describes the consecration of the choir. To Suger the symphony of voices chanting the liturgy sounded like "an angelic rather than a human melody." [105] And the visible hierarchy of prelates in attendance seemed like the image of the celestial hierarchy of angels as the Areopagite had described it. The enactment of the eucharistic sacrifice is described, in conclusion, as "the

---

103. *De consecr.*, V, 227 f. Cf. Augustine, *Sermo* 337 (*PL*, XXXVIII, 1476): "Retribuet ergo Dominus fidelibus suis tam pie, tam hilariter, tam devote ista operantibus, ut eos quoque ipsos fabricae constructione componat, quo currunt lapides vivi, fide formati, spe solidati, charitate compacti." The same idea is alluded to in the metrical *Life of St. Hugh, Bishop of Lincoln*, vv. 946 ff.

104. *Abbot Suger*, pp. 223 f.

105. *De consecr.*, VII, 238.

joining together of the material with the immaterial, the human with the divine, by which God transfers the present kingdom into the celestial one." [106]

The content of Suger's *Booklet on the Consecration* may thus be summed up as follows. It opens with the intellectual vision of divine harmony that reconciles the discord among conflicting things and infuses in those who behold that concord the desire to establish it also within the moral order. The construction of the church is the subsequent realization of that vision both in the work of art and in those who have undertaken it from a desire "to be glorified by participation in the Eternal Reason." The work of "edification" is consummated in the consecration of the completed sanctuary, the rite that enacts the sacrament of union between God and man to which the church itself is dedicated.

Suger's aesthetics, or rather his theology of beauty, is in all its main aspects that of the twelfth century. His Platonizing tendencies and their main sources, Augustine and, above all, the Pseudo-Areopagite, his feeling that sense experience is meaningful only inasmuch as it reveals that which lies beyond—"de materialibus ad immaterialia"—all this Suger shares with his contemporaries.[107]

His work neither as theologian nor even as writer is equal to the best among them. Compared with, say, Hugh of St.-Victor's magnificent exposition of Dionysian theology, Suger's own writings are at best sketchy annotations to the thought of the mystic whom he considered his patron saint. But then, they were not meant to be more than clues to the work in which he had actually undertaken to paraphrase, and indeed to render palpable, the vision of Dionysius Areopagita. This paraphrase, the most magnificent illustration ever bestowed upon a system of thought, is the architecture of St.-Denis.

It is this reference to existing works of art that renders the fragments of

106. "Materialia immaterialibus, corporalia spiritualibus, humana divinis uniformiter concopulas, sacramentaliter reformas ad suum puriores principium; his et hujusmodi benedictionibus visibilibus invisibiliter restauras, etiam praesentem in regnum coeleste mirabiliter transformas, ut, *cum tradideris regnum Deo et Patri*, nos et angelicam creaturam, coelum et terram, unam rempublicam potenter et misericorditer efficias; *qui vivis et regnas* Deus *per omnia* saecula saeculorum. Amen." *De consecr.*, VII, 238.

107. Otto of Freising, *Chronica*, IV, Prologus: "Nullum iam esse sapientem puto, qui

Dei facta non considerat, considerata non stupeat ac per visibilia ad invisibilia non mittatur" (*MGH SS*, 1912, p. 180). See Hofmeister, "Otto von Freising als Geschichtsphilosoph und Kirchenpolitiker" (*Leipziger Studien aus dem Gebiet der Geschichte*, VI, 2, 1900, p. 34), who suggests that Otto too may have received this notion from Hugh's commentary. Hofmeister also recalls the frequent occurrence of the notion in the sacramentology of the Latin Fathers, Augustine and Gregory. See, e.g., Augustine (*PL*, XXXVII, 1413): "per quod visibile sacramentum ad invisibilem gratiam regnumque coelorum duceret . . ."

Sugerian aesthetics more vivid and probably more important to our under-standing of art and artistic experience in the Middle Ages than any other literary work of its time. As a sort of guide, at least for the clerical visitors to his sanctuary, Suger's *Booklet*—not unlike the contemporary *Pilgrim's Guide to Santiago de Compostela*—seeks to explain the treasures of St.-Denis in order to kindle devotion to the titular saint. How successful are Suger's writings in their attempt to link aesthetic and religious experience? To put it more simply, How much sense does the text make in the presence of the work of art? Does it really describe what is to be seen?

To a considerable extent, yes. In the *Booklet on the Consecration* it is the musical theme that imparts unity to the entire argument. At the beginning of the treatise, the ultimate peace in God is divined through the experience of a cosmic symphony. At the end, it is the symphony of the liturgical chant in which the same idea is realized. It is a sublime and ancient thought, voiced by St. Ambrose and in the eleventh century by Fulbert of Chartres, that all crea-tion is a symphonic praise of the Creator, in which the roaring waves of the ocean and the twitter of birds join with the voices of angels and the liturgical hymnody of the Church.[108] According to Suger, this cosmic music conjoins not only the universe with the liturgy; the design of his sanctuary is the visual equivalent of this music. As we have seen in Chapter 2, the affinity between architecture and music was more obvious to medieval man than it is to us. The *Pilgrim's Guide to Santiago de Compostela*, which devotes an entire chapter to the "measure" of the church, similarly calls attention to the harmony that pre-vails among the well-proportioned dimensions of width, length, and height.[109] The care that Suger, according to the *Booklet*, took to equalize, "by means of geometrical and arithmetical rules," the new parts of his church with the old one probably aimed at the same aesthetic effect.[110] His desire to achieve

108. Ambrose, *Hexaemeron*, III, 5 (*PL*, XIV, 178). Fulbert, *Philomela* (*PL*, CXLI, 348), a work that recently has again been vindi-cated for Fulbert of Chartres: see Raby, "Philomela praevia temporis amorem" (*Mé-langes Jos. de Ghellinck*, I, 438). Biblical sources of this idea are Ps. 93:3 ("The floods have lifted up . . . their voice") and 98:8 ("Let the floods clap their hands: let the hills be joy-ful together"). Cf. also Ps. 148, Isaiah 55:12, Daniel 3:5, and Rev. 5:13. For the classical

tradition of the idea of a cosmic symphony, see Spitzer, "Classical and Christian Ideas of World Harmony" (*Traditio*, II, 1944, pp. 424 ff.).

109. IX, 2: "latitudine, longitudine et alti-tudine congruenti." Whitehill, *Liber Sancti Jacobi Codex Calixtinus*, pp. 377 f.; Vielliard, *Le Guide du pèlerin de Saint-Jacques de Compo-stelle*, p. 90.

110. See above, n. 35.

concord and homogeneity among all parts of the church is mentioned repeatedly in the work, and we have seen to what extent it actually determined its design. The "continued light" created by the merging of ambulatory and chapels, the "tub-shaped" ground plan with its nonprotruding transept, and the similar, if not identical, elevations of choir and nave—all these attest a taste for unity as novel as was the craving for luminous transparency. Suger's contemporaries may well have recognized in it the realization of that celestial harmony which he had invoked in his treatise.

In his writings, then, Suger appears, and wished to be understood, as an architect who *built* theology. But this thought had not occurred to him only after the church had been completed. Nor did he state it merely for the pious edification of visitors or pilgrims. The *Booklet on the Consecration* is actually as much confession as it is didactic exposition; Suger had experienced the vision that he describes. It was, moreover, not only Suger's fancy that the new style, which in a sense he had really invented, owed its inspiration to Dionysian thought. As we have seen, the transformation of Norman and Burgundian models in the design of St.-Denis can really be explained as the artistic realization of ideas actually taken over from the Pseudo-Areopagite. Thus, by recording the building of his church, Suger has, as it were, rendered transparent the creative process that translated the theology of light and music into the Gothic style.

It is hardly necessary to insist on the importance of this insight with which Suger has provided us for our entire understanding of medieval art and its message. When we inquire into the relationship between medieval art and medieval thought, we usually overlook that basic aspect of the thought which distinguishes it radically from our own. That aspect is what we may perhaps call the archetypal orientation of medieval thinking. Ideas, and ideas alone, were real. Facts and things were real only insofar as they partook of the reality of ideas.[111] This means that we must not—as with our modern mentality we are apt to do— look upon medieval interpretations of the world as gratuitous allegories embellishing "real" facts or events. Quite the contrary, such interpretations were

111. Adler, "The *Pèlerinage de Charlemagne* in New Light on Saint-Denis" (*Sp*, XXII, 1947), offers some valuable remarks on this orientation of medieval thought, even though his particular interpretation does not seem to me in all parts convincing. See also Gilson, *The Spirit of Medieval Philosophy*, pp. 84 f., and *La Philosophie de Saint Bonaventure*, pp. 196 ff.

to establish the sense in which a fact or event was "real." Thus, if a medieval writer describes the cathedral as an "image" of the Celestial City, the art historian has every reason to take such a statement seriously. The vision that Suger related at the beginning of his treatise, his comparison of his church with the Temple of Solomon, of his choir with the Heavenly City of the divine King, are never mere allegories, but, on the contrary, recall the archetype that Suger, as builder, had sought to approximate. How literal this relation between image and archetype was occasionally understood appears from Suger's account of the foundation ceremony for his new church. While chanting the liturgical "Lapides preciosi omnes muri tui"—which, of course, refers to the walls of the Celestial City—some persons actually deposited gems and precious stones in the foundation walls.[112] Even a correspondence that at first sight appears to be purely allegorical, as that between Suger's church and the Ecclesia as the communion of saints, does not seem to have remained without effect upon the design of St.-Denis. The selection of twelve supporting columns each for ambulatory and choir may well have been prompted by the Biblical metaphor, mentioned by Suger himself, of "building spiritually . . . upon the foundation of Apostles and Prophets, Jesus Christ being the keystone that joins one wall to the other." [113] The Gothic ribbed vault, with its ribs continuing the surging movements of supports and converging in a prominent keystone, made Suger's use of the Biblical image a description of his church. Has not that image even had some influence upon the design of the cross-ribbed vault? The ribs are not absolutely indispensable structurally. The aesthetic prominence they receive in Gothic architecture, and even more the consistent correlation of ribs and supporting shafts, correspond to the taste for unity and unification.[114] But this taste found its theological justification, as it were, in the Biblical metaphor. Such influence of theological notions upon ecclesiastical builders is well documented by literary sources.[115] It certainly finds expression in the actual repre-

112. *De consecr.*, IV, 226.
113. Ibid., V, 227 f.
114. Though not a "Gothic" invention (the first consistent co-ordination of vault ribs and responds in existence is that of S. Ambrogio, Milan [c. 1125]), only the Gothic conceived the baldachin as the aesthetically and structurally decisive principle of its architecture. See Sedlmayr, *Die Entstehung*, pp. 208 ff.

115. In Carolingian times, St. Angilbert had the cloister of the famous abbey of Centula constructed on a triangular ground plan: "Quia igitur omnis plebs fidelium sanctissimam atque inseparabilem Trinitatem confiteri . . . firmiterque credere debet." Mortet and Deschamps, *Recueil*, I, 284. Number symbolism may well have influenced the design of the cloister of the Cathedral of Vaison-la-Romaine

sentation of Christ to be found in the keystone of many Gothic vaults.[116]

Suger's own testimony enables us to answer the question, In what sense was he—and in what sense was he not—the father of Gothic architecture? Certainly he did not "invent" the forms of the new style as illustrations of his ideas. But he did perceive what we may call the symbolic possibilities lying dormant in the architecture of Burgundy and above all Normandy. And it was in accordance with that singular insight that he set out to transform these Romanesque models so as to render them vehicles of his theological experience: the twin-tower façade became the *porta caeli*—it is hardly a coincidence that the crenelations of Suger's façade recall a Roman city gate; the design of his sanctuary and ambulatory was certainly inspired by the Dionysian metaphysics of light; and it is not even impossible that the co-ordination of vault ribs and supporting shafts, the emphasis given to these architectural members in the Gothic system, may owe something to the architectural symbolism of the New Testament, which impressed Suger as much as it had St. Augustine. In other words, the technical achievements that distinguish the first Gothic from Romanesque seem to have obeyed rather than preceded Suger's symbolic demands upon architecture, and it was his overriding desire to align the system of an ecclesiastical building with a transcendental vision that ultimately accounted for the transformation of Romanesque into Gothic. The instant and irresistible success of the new style in France was owing to its power as a symbol. In a language too lucid and too moving to be misunderstood, Suger's Gothic evoked an ideological message that was of passionate concern to every educated Frenchman.

(second half of the twelfth century), as the inscription on the wall of the northern side aisle suggests. See Rambaud, "Le Quatrain mystique de Vaison-la-Romaine" (*BM*, CIX, 1951). And as regards the fascinating allegorical description of St. Michel at Cuxa, which the monk Garsia, around 1040, sent to its builder, Bishop Oliva, it seems probable that he did not invent his interpretations but described what had actually been in the builder's mind. See Petrus de Marca, *Marca Hispanica sive Limes Hispanicus*, App. 222, cc. 1072 ff.

116. See, e.g., Seymour, *Notre Dame of Noyon in the Twelfth Century*, fig. 6. Cf. Bandmann, p. 74. In the more general context of the anthropomorphic symbolism of the medieval church—so well attested by the architectural terminology that names the different parts of the edifice after the different parts of the human body—belongs the enigmatic representation that once adorned the vault of the famous jube of Mainz Cathedral: a nude man, resembling medieval representations of the microcosmos, whose outstretched limbs, attached to the diagonal vault ribs, held the symbols of the cardinal virtues. For a possible interpretation of the figure, see Schmitt, "Zur Deutung der Gewölbefigur am ehemaligen Westlettner des Mainzer Doms" (*Festschrift für Heinrich Schrohe*).

Only now that we know the archetype that Suger's church was designed to resemble can we also see the relation of this great project to the abbot's political vision. St.-Denis was to be the capital of the realm, the place where the different and antagonistic factions within France were to be reconciled and where they would rally around the patron saint and the king as they had in 1124. Suger used the consecration of the new church, twenty years later, for a most impressive demonstration of this destination of his abbey.

It was customary to use religious feasts, such as the consecration of an important sanctuary, as the occasion for the convocation of a royal assembly.[117] Such an assembly was held in connection with the consecration of Suger's church. After long and painful negotiations, the most redoubtable of the king's enemies, Thibault the Great of Chartres-Champagne, had finally declared his willingness to make peace. The chief mediators were St. Bernard, who had long defended the count as a champion of the reform, and Suger, to whose church Thibault had generously contributed.[118] It is probable that the final reconciliation, which occurred in 1144, was actually effected at the time of the consecration of the abbey. St. Bernard wrote to Suger's close friend, Bishop Jocelin of Soissons, requesting the bishop's assistance in bringing about peace between the two princes. In closing he expressed the hope of seeing Jocelin "during the feast of the Lendit at St.-Denis." [119] The consecration of Suger's church took place only three days before this festival began, the date having been fixed after prior consultation with the king or, rather, at the latter's request.[120] The two events could not but reflect upon one another, and the unprecedented gathering of dignitaries for the consecration may be at least partly accounted for by the political assembly that also called for their presence at St.-Denis.

117. Luchaire, *Histoire des institutions monarchiques de la France sous les premiers Capétiens*, I, 254 ff. See the royal charter of 1144 granting further donations to the abbey and confirming Suger's account of the assembly: Félibien, p. cvi; Tardif, *Monuments historiques*, No. 496, p. 255.

118. *Ep.* CCXXII (*PL*, CLXXXII, 387); *Recueil des historiens*, XIII, 273, 331, 421; XV, 588. See also Aubert, *Suger*, p. 97.

119. *Recueil des historiens*, XV, 593. To Jocelin, who may have been his teacher, Suger dedicated his *Life of Louis VI*. The bishop is known to have attended the consecration of St.-Denis.

120. "Regiae majestatis serenissimi regis Francorum Ludovici placido favore (desiderabat enim sanctos Martyres suos protectores ardentissime videre) . . ." *De consecr.*, VI, 232. The Lendit began on the second Wednesday in June; the consecration of the abbey took place on June 11, 1144.

In the Middle Ages the dedication of a church could be an act of considerable political importance, depending on the dignitaries present.[121] The dedication of St.-Denis took place in the presence of Louis VII and his consort, Eleanor of Aquitaine, of the Queen Mother, and of the great nobility of the kingdom.[122] The nineteen prelates consecrating the altars of the new sanctuary included five archbishops and, with one exception,[123] all ecclesiastical peers of the realm. Suger had taken extraordinary care to arrange this solemn ceremony in such a way as to make the homage paid to St. Denis the occasion for a similar homage to the king of France.[124] Louis VII himself received the silver chasse of "our special patron," St. Denis, from the hands of the archbishops of Reims and Sens and carried it to the altar. "All the ceremonies," writes Panofsky, "were calculated to stress the prerogatives of the patron saints who, from the point of view of St. Denis, were to all other saints, however worthy, as the king of France was to all his subjects, however great." [125] The ceremony was not only designed to stress the special bond between the sovereign and the patron saint of France; the procession of the relics, in which the "most Christian king," as Suger significantly calls him,[126] outranked even the ecclesiastical dignitaries, evoked before the abbot's eyes a supernatural spectacle. At the legendary consecration of the original church of St.-Denis, Christ himself, in pontifical robes, was said to have led the celestial hierarchy of angels and saints to the dedication of the sanctuary.[127] Suger likens this wonderful procession to the splendid assembly of prelates and nobles in the ceremony that he took to be the second consecration of St.-Denis.

Such a comparison is typical of twelfth-century France and it is typically

121. See Crozet, "Étude sur les consécrations pontificales" (BM, CIV, 1946).
122. De consecr., VI, 232 f.
123. The Bishop of Laon, temporarily suspended since 1142 (cf. GC, IX, c. 531).
124. De consecr., VII, 236.
125. Abbot Suger, p. 230.
126. De consecr., VII, 235. When did the celebrated title originate? Abbot Hilduin of St.-Denis, in addressing Louis the Pious, speaks of the "christianissimus animus vester" (PL, CVI, 14).
127. See Doublet pp. 165 ff.; C. J. Liebmann, "La Consécration légendaire de la basilique de Saint-Denis" (Le Moyen Âge, 3rd series, VI, 1935). Following Levillain, Liebmann believes that the legend was circulated for the purpose of attracting crowds to St.-Denis for the feast commemorating the dedication. This feast, too, provided the occasion for a fair, which, however, never attained real importance. Suger himself insists that in reconstructing his church he left untouched those parts that Christ had touched with his own hands. De admin., XXIX, 191, and De consecr. IV, 225. See also Crosby, Abbey of St.-Denis, pp. 43 ff., 197; and Dom Leclercq, "La Consécration légendaire de la basilique de Saint-Denis et la question des indulgences" (RM, XXXIII, 1943).

Dionysian. The king was, indeed, a likeness of Christ. The coronation rite transformed him sacramentally into a *Christus Domini*, that is, not only into a person of episcopal rank, but into an image of Christ himself.[128] By this rite, Professor Kantorowicz writes, "the new government was linked with the divine government and with that of Christ, the true governor of the world; and the images of King and Christ [were] brought together as nearly as possible." [129] Such dramatic representations of the meaning of the monarchy were not confined to the king's coronation. On the great religious feasts of the year, "the king's day of exaltation was made to coincide with the . . . exaltation of the Lord" in order to make "terrestrial kingship all the more transparent against the background of the kingship of Christ." [130] In Capetian France as elsewhere, such religious feasts often were made the occasion for the king's festive coronation; and, as the political assemblies of the realm were likewise held on these feasts, the interweaving of the two spheres was underscored by liturgical pageants that stressed the sacerdotal dignity of kingship.

What appears to us as no more than festive pageantry was, in point of fact, an act of sacramental as well as constitutional significance. It was precisely his anointment as *Christus Domini* that raised the king above even the most powerful dukes.[131] In the political controversies of the early twelfth century this fact is adduced again and again.[132]

Suger understood the full significance of these ideas. In his *Life of Louis VI* he puts into the mouths of French bishops requesting the king's protection the

128. See Bloch, *Les Rois thaumaturges*, pp. 41, 54, 194 ff.; Schramm, *Der König von Frankreich*, pp. 23 ff., 50 ff.; Kern, *Kingship and Law in the Middle Ages*, pp. 51 f.; de Pange, *Le Roi très-chrétien*, especially pp. 93 ff.; Williams, "The Norman Anonymous of 1100 A.D." (*Harvard Theological Studies*, XVIII, 1951, pp. 76 ff., 131 ff., 157 ff., 187 ff.); Kantorowicz, "Deus per naturam, Deus per gratiam" (*Harvard Theological Review*, XLV, 1952).

129. *Laudes Regiae. A Study in Liturgical Acclamations and Medieval Ruler Worship*, p. 81.

130. Kantorowicz, *Laudes Regiae*, pp. 92 ff.

131. Besides the works quoted in the preceding notes, see also Lemosse, "La lèse-majesté dans la monarchie franque" (*Revue du Moyen Âge Latin*, II, 1946). Numerous anecdotes show how literally the Christlike dignity of the king was often understood. See, e.g., the enactment of the Last Supper by Philip Augustus and twelve knights before the battle of Bouvines (de Pange, p. 369), or the gentle rebuke Lanfranc had to administer to a cleric who, upon beholding the splendor of King William I, exclaimed, "Ecce Deum video." Williams, p. 161.

132. See above all the polemical writings of the Norman Anonymous (tentatively identified by Williams with William Bona Anima, Archbishop of Rouen), who bases his claim that the Christian *regnum* is superior to the *sacerdotium* precisely on the king's anointment as *Christus domini*.

conviction that the king "bears in his person the living image of God."[133] Suger discovered the vision that lent colorful reality to this idea in the Dionysian writings.

The Pseudo-Areopagite explicitly paralleled the "celestial hierarchy" of angels with the "ecclesiastical hierarchy" that governs the City of God on earth. In Capetian France, in the France of Suger, the ecclesiastical and political hierarchies were not distinct. Louis VII himself on occasion emphasized his episcopal rank.[134] In his commentary on the *Celestial Hierarchy*, Hugh of St.-Victor describes the "human hierarchy" by which "society, in its temporal course," is governed as an image of the angelic hierarchy so that from the visible order of men the invisible order of angels may be learned.[135] It is no wonder that early in the thirteenth century another prelate, who was adviser to his king and a student of the Areopagite, William of Auvergne, Bishop of Paris, gave a description of the State of Angels that is in every detail patterned upon the composition of the royal court and the different functions of its dignitaries.[136] We learn from such writings to what an extent even the theory and justification of royal government in Capetian France was inspired by the alleged writings imputed to the patron saint.

The consecration ceremony of St.-Denis was conceived by Suger as the liturgical enactment of this royal ideology. In the account of it that he gives in the *Booklet*, he stresses time and again the analogies between the rite and the celestial liturgy.[137] The two hemicycles of bishops, nine surrounding the Archbishop of Reims in the choir, and nine officiating in the crypt, were undoubtedly meant to represent the nine tiers of angels as described in the *Celestial Hierarchy*.

133. ". . . Dei, cujus ad vivificandum portat rex imaginem, vicarius ejus . . ." *Vie de Louis*, XVIII, 62.

134. Luchaire, *Études sur les actes de Louis VII*, No. 119; see the discussion of this passage in Bloch, p. 191.

135. "Ut ex visibili dispositione hominum, invisibilis innotescat dispositio angelorum" *Commentaria in Hierarchiam caelestem* II (*PL*, CLXXV, 946).

136. *De universo*, II, 2 (*Opera*, Orléans, 1674, II, 987 ff.). Cf. Valois, *passim*; also Vallentin, "Der Engelstaat" (*Grundrisse und Bausteine zur Staats- und zur Geschichtslehre zusammengetragen zu den Ehren Gustav Schmollers*, pp. 56 ff.); Berges, *Die Fürstenspiegel des hohen und späten Mittelalters*, pp. 32, 79.

137. See *De consecr.*, VI, 234; VII, 236, 238. Here again Suger appears to be influenced not only by Dionysius but more specifically by Maximus the Confessor. See the latter's idea of all the different estates of human society being united in their common participation in the liturgy of the Church, and the emphasis on the liturgical chant as a "symbol" of the symphony in which the elect join with the angels in the eternal praise of God (*PG*, XIC, cc. 665 f., 696).

And the king, as the center of the procession, represented Christ in the midst of the heavenly hosts. It is likely that the very disposition of nine chapels around Suger's choir was inspired by Dionysius.

The consecration of the church was but the first liturgical ceremony in which the monarchical and the theological spheres were to converge—one might say, to the glory of both. Suger certainly had this politico-religious function of his church in mind when he designed his sanctuary as a *typos* of the Dionysian vision of heaven. We cannot bypass this political significance of the new style, not only because its builder himself did not want it to be overlooked but because that significance accounts for the eventual adoption of Suger's design for the ecclesiastical architecture of the French monarchy. The reader of the *Booklet on the Consecration* becomes aware of a curious and bewildering ambivalence, a "shuttling back and forth" between the moral and aesthetic spheres and between moral and aesthetic values. Cosmic harmony inspires the beholder with the desire to establish a similar harmony within himself, and this desire in turn leads to the building of the sanctuary. This great undertaking is described as a "spiritual building" that conjoins all who take a part in it as "fellow citizens with the saints and of the household of God." St.-Denis had been raised from contributions not only of the king but also of his enemy, Thibault of Champagne. The consecration rite, the solemn order it imposed upon the entire assembly of dignitaries, ecclesiastical and secular, the harmony into which the liturgical chant blended their voices, was, for Suger, not merely an image of the celestial order but a promise of its realization on earth. He concluded the treatise with a fervent prayer that God, who "invisibly restorest and miraculously transformest the present [state] into the Heavenly Kingdom . . . mayest Thou powerfully and mercifully make us and the nature of the angels, heaven and earth, into one republic."

The political overtones of such language are not chosen accidentally. At once a mystic and a realist, Suger hoped that the building of his church and the ceremony of its dedication, in both of which the entire kingdom had taken part, would actually contribute to the consolidation of France under the crown. That Suger should have expected such an effect may appear incredible to us. For us the aesthetic and moral spheres no longer intersect; we cannot imagine that a great sanctuary might exert an influence affecting the order of the commonweal. But it was quite otherwise in the twelfth century, owing to what I have called the archetypal orientation of medieval thought. The Dionysian picture of the celestial hierarchy presented not just an idealization of government, but laid down the design to whose realization the Christian ruler was committed. Even to St. Thomas Aquinas it appeared necessary that royal government be modeled after the divine rule of the universe.[138] And the astonishing figure of Louis IX, at once king and saint, shows how seriously that demand was taken. Suger's St.-Denis, the moral values he attributed to its design, attest the public significance of architecture and aesthetic experience generally even more than its artistic achievement.

It is this significance, beyond the purely artistic achievement, that accounts for the extraordinary impression caused by Suger's church. Contemporaries felt immediately that it was designed as an architectural prototype,[139] and seem to have understood likewise that correspondence between the style and decoration of the sanctuary and Dionysian theology which the builder had intended. Precisely because it evoked the mystical archetype of the political order of the French monarchy, the style of St.-Denis was adopted for all the cathedrals of France and became the monumental expression of the Capetian idea of kingship. It is not surprising, therefore, that in the cathedrals of Paris and Chartres, of Reims and Amiens, the royal theme, evoked not only in the Galleries of Kings but also in the selection of certain Biblical scenes and figures, is completely merged into the Christological one.[140]

138. *Summa Theologiae*, Ia IIae 93, a3; cf. *De regimine principum*, I, 2.

139. See above, p. 112, n. 69.

140. See Bréhier's important study, "L'Histoire de la France à la cathédrale de Reims" (*RH*, XXII, 1916). In Chartres, the name *Portail royal* can be traced back as far as the first part of the thirteenth century. Cf. Houvet, *Cathédrale de Chartres, Portail occidental*, p. 2, n. 1; Sablon, *Histoire de l'auguste et vénérable Église de Chartres*, p. 30, who seems to deduce the name from the statues of "kings." It may be asked whether the predilection noticeable in the monumental sculpture of the Île-de-France, for the group of Solomon and the Queen of Sheba, does not originate in the royal ideology. If the king was conceived as another Solomon, the building of Christian temples was among his loftiest obligations. According to Williams, p. 104, a passage in one of the tractates of the Anonymous of Rouen that emphasizes how Solomon built and dedicated the House of God may refer to William the Conqueror's patronage of St. Stephen at Caen. It would have been similarly fitting to commemorate the royal benefactors of the churches of the French domain under the image of Solomon. On this theme in French early Gothic sculpture, see Chastel, "La Rencontre de Salomon et de la Reine de Saba dans l'iconographie médiévale" (*GBA*, 6th series, XXXV, 1949). [*See Add.*]

# 5. SENS AND CHARTRES WEST

Plate 21

THE Cathedral of Sens is the first Gothic cathedral. Its plan may even ante-date Suger's St.-Denis. Begun under Archbishop Henry (d. 1142), surnamed the Boar, the foundations seem to have been laid shortly after 1130. Cross-ribbed vaults and that logical integration of the entire tectonic system which is typical of Gothic were provided for even in the original plan:[1] in the nave the bases of the shafts supporting the diagonal ribs are placed obliquely, proof that the shafts were designed for that purpose from the beginning.[2] The system of Sens, more-over, shows the clear distinction between the tectonic "skeleton," ribs and responds, and the wall segments between them—the latter, as mere "fillings," reduced to a minimum—that we have come to identify as Gothic. Single ele-ments, such as the articulation of individual shafts in the bundle of supports or the sexpartite vault, are probably imports from Normandy. But the oblique arrangement of the shaft bases under the diagonal ribs goes beyond the known models in that region. None of the surviving examples of Norman architecture employ diagonally placed responds consistently in the entire system; in fact, the earliest known examples of this feature anywhere occur no more than a decade before its appearance in Sens.[3] Aesthetically this seemingly insignifi-cant detail is of great importance. It induces the eye, as Professor Sedlmayr has pointed out, to see the entire edifice, vaults and supports, as a unit: the ribs

---

1. "Suger adopta hardiment le style nouveau pour la construction du choeur de l'abbaye de Saint-Denis (1140–1144). Mais, avant lui, l'architecte qui, dès 1130 environ, avait tracé le plan et appareillé les premières assises de la cathédrale de Sens, avait resolu de couvrir l'immense édifice d'une voûte sur croisée d'ogives." Chartraire, *La Cathédrale de Sens*, p. 12. Gall, *Die Gotische Baukunst in Frankreich und Deutschland*, p. 182, dates the beginning of the church *c.* 1140.

2. See Gall, *Die Gotische Baukunst*, Pl. 35.

3. Cf. Sedlmayr, *Die Entstehung der Kathedrale*, pp. 208 ff., and Gall, "Neue Beiträge zur Geschichte vom 'Werden der Gotik'" (*MKW*, IV, 1911).

springing from the diagonal responds can be understood as rising directly from the floor level.[4]

Another important feature of Sens Cathedral is the vault of its apse. As in St.-Denis, it is a genuine rib vault, its distinct webs supported by ribs that converge in a common keystone.[5] Only a few years earlier, the master of the great Norman abbey of St.-Georges-de-Boscherville had sought to overcome the discrepancy between the rib vault covering nave and forechoir and the half dome over the chevet by placing "false ribs" under the half dome.[6] We cannot say for certain whether the far more satisfactory "Gothic" solution was achieved earlier in Sens or St.-Denis. The choir of Sens was probably completed much later than that of St.-Denis, but the original design may predate that of Suger.

In other respects, however, Sens Cathedral is much more conservative. Luminosity was evidently not a primary consideration. If one compares Sens and St.-Denis in this respect, one realizes all the more clearly the singularity of Suger's aspirations. The clerestory windows at Sens were small. One century later, when the general craving for light also prompted the enlargement of the windows of Notre Dame of Paris, it was decided to undertake the same step in Sens. The windows of the cathedral were heightened despite the fact that this measure required the rather difficult task of changing the curvature of the vaults.[7]

Not the least important aspect of the Cathedral of Sens with regard to the future development of Gothic architecture is its tripartite elevation. Instead of the quadripartite plan adopted by all the French cathedrals during the second part of the twelfth century—a gallery and triforium placed between the nave arcades and clerestory—the architect of Sens constructed merely a "false triforium," that is, openings onto the loft over the side aisles, not a passageway. The tripartite elevation he borrowed not from Normandy but from Burgundy

4. Sedlmayr, *Die Entstehung*, p. 209. Strangely enough, Sedlmayr does not mention Sens.

5. Van der Meer, *Keerpunt der Middeleeuwen*, p. 85.

6. Cf. Sedlmayr, *Die Entstehung*, p. 197; Anfray, *L'Architecture normande. Son influence dans le nord de France*, p. 80; and Michon (*CA, Rouen*, 1926, p. 531). See above, p. 118. For an evaluation of the functional and aesthetic aspects of the *cul-de-four nervé*, see Gall, *Niederrheinische und normännische Architektur im Zeitalter der Frühgotik*, pp. 30 ff.

7. The windows in the choir were enlarged around 1230, those in the nave around 1310 See Chartraire, p. 44; Gall, *Die Gotische Baukunst*, p. 176.

(Autun, Langres).[8] Its aesthetic consequences are twofold: it greatly reduced the zone that lies between the openings of the arcades and windows and thus enhanced still further the importance of the supports at the expense of the walls between them. Secondly, the tripartite elevation had a profound effect on the proportions of the edifice. It obviously reduces its height; but this "moderation" —in St. Bernard's sense—also makes possible a harmony of proportions that is Burgundian in the more specific sense of Cistercian architecture: the ground plan of Sens being designed *ad quadratum*, the square bays of the nave are twice as wide as those of the side aisles; owing to the tripartite elevation, it was possible to give the same proportion to the relative heights of nave and aisles. The elevation of the nave to the springing of the vaults, moreover, is subdivided, at the level of the arcade imposts, into two equal parts: the octave ratio of $1:2$ permeates the entire edifice.

We can hardly doubt that this pointedly unostentatious cathedral, the austerity of its forms softened by the harmony of its proportions, bears the imprint of the artistic views of St. Bernard. The builder of the cathedral, Archbishop Henry, was perhaps the most forceful exponent, among the prelates of the French domain, of the Bernardian ideas of reform. After his early worldly conduct had elicited Bernard's criticism, he submitted, in 1126, to the ecclesiastical and ascetic ideas of the abbot of Clairvaux to such an extent that he, as well as his suffragan, the Bishop of Paris, momentarily incurred the wrath and, it would seem, even the persecution of Louis VI, which even Suger was unable to prevent.[9] It is characteristic that in this emergency Henry appealed to the general chapter of the Cistercians, which was just then being held at Cîteaux, requesting the intervention of the order, since, as he put it, ties of brotherly affection connected it with the king as well as with himself. Ever since his conversion, the archbishop could count on Bernard of Clairvaux as his friend and ally. The abbot appealed directly to Louis VI, and, rebuked by the king, he had recourse to Rome. In his letter to Pope Honorius, in which he associated the signatures of the abbots of Cîteaux and Pontigny with his own, Bernard calls the king another Herod bent on destroying the recently reformed bishops, whom he compares to the Innocents of Bethlehem since they are "reborn" to a new life.[10]

8. Van der Meer, p. 83     9. On Henry's life, see *GC*, XII, 44.     10. *PL*, CLXXXII, 157.

There can be no doubt about the sincerity of Bernard's esteem for Henry. Toward the end of his career (1137) the archbishop's inflexible and tempestuous character brought him into serious difficulties with his hierarchy and eventually with the pope. Even in the angry reproach that Bernard addressed to Henry on that occasion, one senses real concern for a friend who furnishes his enemies with weapons of attack that leave his supporters helpless to defend him.[11]

We learn more about the relation between the two men from the treatise *On the Conduct and Office of a Bishop*, composed by Bernard at Henry's request, soon after the latter's "conversion," which is mentioned with high praise in the preamble. In the treatise Bernard outlines what he considers the exemplary conduct of a bishop, surely with an eye on the special character and obligations of the Archbishop of Sens.[12]

Among the points that Bernard specifically enjoins upon the prelate is moderation in building.[13] One is reminded of this fact in looking at Sens Cathedral. Begun but a few years after Henry's "conversion" and the completion of the treatise, the sanctuary was bound to reflect the architectural postulates of the reform party.[14] It is a tempting thought—though no more than a bare possibility—that the synod which, in 1140, Henry convoked at Sens may have met in the newly completed choir of the cathedral.[15] The synod resulted in the complete defeat of Abelard and the greatest theological triumph of Bernard of Clairvaux. On that occasion Bernard may have seen at least part of the first Gothic cathedral completed that bore witness, in the very language of its style, to the astonishing ascendancy over the entire hierarchy of France achieved by the abbot of Clairvaux in that hour.

That the first Gothic cathedral should have been built at Sens was sig-

11. *PL*, CLXXXII, 314 f. After Henry's death Bernard refers to him as "benedictus" (ibid., c. 522).

12. *De moribus et officio Episcoporum tractatus* (*PL*, CLXXXII, 809 ff.). The treatise was composed in 1126. Henry's "conversion" is mentioned on cc. 810 f.

13. *PL*, CLXXXII, 812: "Honorificabitis . . . non amplis aedificiis."

14. Sens may not be the only example of Bernard's influence upon cathedral building. Rolland, "Chronologie de la Cathédrale de Tournai" (*Revue belge d'archéologie et d'histoire*

de l'art, IV, 1934), has sought to connect the style of the transept of Tournai Cathedral with the visit Bernard paid to that city in 1140: "Il est impossible de ne pas rapprocher de l'opposition de Saint Bernard à toute décoration luxuriante, la simplicité ornamentale du transept." On that visit and its ecclesiastical background and consequences, see Canivez, "Les Voyages et les fondations monastiques de St. Bernard en Belgique" (*ABSS*, I, 29 ff.).

15. Chartraire, "Le séjour de St. Bernard à Sens" (*ABSS*, II), denies the possibility that the council could have met in the cathedral, which was not completed until 1163.

nificant, and undoubtedly it was important for the fortunes of the new style. The see of Sens had not been able to maintain its lofty claims to the primate-ship "of all Gaul and Germany," but within the French domain proper it was beyond question the first.[16] At the insistence of Louis VI, who considered it in-sufferable that the foremost archdiocese of his realm should be subject to the "foreign" metropolitan of Lyons, Pope Calixtus II had consented to the sever-ing of this tie.[17] The province of Sens included among its suffragans the bishops of Paris and Chartres. It was a fact of great consequence that the Archbishop of Sens, along with the bishops of Paris and Chartres, should have been won over to Bernard's idea of ecclesiastical reform. The Gothic style of Henry's ca-thedral pays tribute not only to the spirituality of Clairvaux, however; the monarchy itself, as we have seen, had submitted to that spirituality. The archi-tecture of Sens Cathedral is like a symbol of the concept of the "conduct and office of a bishop," which became exemplary for the French episcopate during the greatest phase of Capetian rule.

The third member of the triumvirate of Gothic builders was one of Arch-bishop Henry's suffragans, the Bishop of Chartres. Geoffrey of Lèves, scion of an ancient and powerful house of the Beauce, is one of those rare personalities that seem to encompass the important movements of his generation.[18] He was at once the friend of Henry of Sens, whom he actually converted to the ideas of St. Bernard, and of Suger of St.-Denis. Even more intimate, however, were his relations with the abbot of Clairvaux; to contemporaries the two seemed in-separable.[19] At Geoffrey's request Bernard came to Chartres in 1146 in order to preach the Crusade; on that occasion the great Cistercian moved the chivalry of the region so deeply that they implored him, in vain, to assume the leader-ship in the Holy War.[20] Bernard mentions the Bishop of Chartres, whom he oc-casionally accompanied on his missions, with admiration in his own writings.[21]

Geoffrey was above all else a statesman; for fifteen years papal legate, he

16. GC, XII, 1.

17. See Recueil des historiens, XV, 339 f.; Fliche and Martin, Histoire de l'Église, VIII, 402.

18. On Geoffrey, see Fisquet, La France pontificale. Chartres, p. 88; Clerval, Les Écoles de Chartres au moyen-âge, pp. 153 ff.; HLF,

XIII, 83 ff.; and Poole, Illustrations of the History of Medieval Thought and Learning, p. 131, who calls the bishop "the most respected among the prelates of Gaul."

19. Fisquet.

20. Lépinois, Histoire de Chartres, I, 99 f.

21. Clerval, pp. 153 ff.

was present at no less than ten councils.[22] And, as a member of the king's intimate circle, it was probably he, next to Suger, who was responsible for the *rapprochement* between Louis VI and St. Bernard that was to have such important consequences.[23]

At the same time, however, the bishop was a distinguished theologian in his own right, with a profound and extremely broad interest in the intellectual currents of his age. Geoffrey found friendship and respect for St. Bernard not incompatible with his admiration for the genius of Abelard.[24] His chief claim to immortality rests, perhaps, on the fact that it was under his episcopate and owing to his initiative that the School of Chartres passed through the most splendid period in its history, the period "most fertile in literary productions and richest in outstanding scholars." [25] Geoffrey appointed the three great chancellors of the Cathedral School, Bernard, Gilbert, and Thierry.[26] In 1137, when John of Salisbury journeyed to Chartres, the faculty included Thierry, William of Conches, and Richard l'Évêque.[27] But even these names give no more than a partial picture of the number of eminent theologians associated with the School of Chartres during Geoffrey's episcopate. Its teachers and students exerted, during the twelfth century, an influence that extended from England to Sicily and possibly to the Moslem world as well. Without the

22. ". . . legatione sedis apostolice . . . per annos circiter XVcim sancte et religiose functus, multa in ipsa legatione a scismaticorum infestatione quos ad sinum matris ecclesie revocavit pericula passus, symoniace pestis egregius extirpator, excutiens manus a munere, florens et firma suo tempore ecclesie Dei, tam in sacerdotii dignitate quam in honore regni, columna . . ." The passage, from Geoffrey's necrologue, is in *CC*, III, 28; cf. I, 18. Cf. Merlet, *Dignitaires de l'église Notre-Dame de Chartres*, p. 233.

23. Louis VI refers to him as "fidelis noster" and "amicus noster karissimus" (*CC*, I, 135, 143). On Thibault's initial opposition to Geoffrey's appointment, whom he considered too much of a "royalist," see Lépinois, I, 87.

24. Clerval believes that Geoffrey was actually Abelard's student. Geoffrey defended Abelard at the Council of Soissons (1121) and seems to have dropped him only in 1131, when

William of St.-Thierry addressed both to him and to St. Bernard his scathing accusation of Abelard as a heretic. Cf. Clerval, and Poole, "The Masters of the School of Paris and Chartres in John of Salisbury's Time" (*EHR*, XXV, 1920).

25. "Assurément la plus belle époque des écoles de Chartres, la plus féconde en écrits, la plus riche en écolâtres fameux, pendant le XIIe siècle." Clerval, pp. 153 ff.

26. One catches a glimpse of Geoffrey's personal relations with Thierry in the famous episode at the Council of Soissons, as reported by no less a witness than Abelard, *Historia calamitatum mearum*, X (Cousin, ed., I, 22). Clerval remarks that Geoffrey secured splendid material positions for his chancellors. Thierry was made Archdeacon of Dreux. See Clerval, pp. 208 ff.; Merlet, *Dignitaires*, p. 104.

27. See below, p. 190.

encouragement and protection of St. Bernard's enlightened friend, the daring cosmological system outlined in Chapter 2 could not have been developed.

It was under Geoffrey that the west façade of Chartres Cathedral, even in its present composite shape the most beautiful of all medieval facades, was built.

*Plate 25* Its completion, along with the construction of the two great flanking towers, kindled in the entire population an enthusiasm unheard of until that time.[28] The entire façade was developed in successive steps. The northern tower, still isolated from the rest of the edifice, was begun after a fire in 1134 that had caused considerable damage to the Romanesque cathedral of Bishop Fulbert.

*Plate 27* The magnificent Royal Portal, along with the southern tower, was started somewhat later. Around 1145 work was in progress on both towers. It is possible that the program of sculptures of the *Portail royal* was developed gradually rather than at one stroke.[29]

These labors show the importance of religious art at this time; they suggest a surprising concern with problems of design and composition over and above all practical considerations. The architectural parts mentioned were unnecessary from a practical point of view. Their function was primarily symbolic. It is of considerable interest that very large resources and a singular accumulation of artistic talent were employed—and by a friend of St. Bernard's—on an architectural undertaking of this kind.

The west facade of Chartres has for Gothic sculpture the same significance that the Cathedral of Sens and the choir of St.-Denis have for Gothic architecture. It is, moreover, closely related to the west façade of St.-Denis. The Bishop of Chartres was a close friend of Suger and a frequent visitor to St.-Denis. Suger

28. See the famous account by Robert of Torrigni in *MGH SS*, VI, 496.

29. Lefèvre-Pontalis, "Les Façades successives de la Cathédrale de Chartres au XIe et au XIIe siècles" (*SAELM*, XIII, 1904; *CA, Chartres*, 1900); Aubert, "Le Portail Royal et la façade occidentale de la Cathédrale de Chartres" (*BM*, C, 1941), and *La Sculpture française au moyen-âge*, pp. 176 ff. Lefèvre-Pontalis' theory, according to which the figure portals were originally erected farther to the east but subsequently taken apart and reassembled at their present location, has become untenable in the light of the excavations conducted by Fels. See his report "Die Grabung an der Fassade der Kathedrale von Chartres" (*Kunstchronik*, VIII, May, 1955). The chronology of the sculptures of Chartres West remains unsettled. Besides the works just listed, see also Voege, *Die Anfänge des monumentalen Stiles im Mittelalter*, pp. 135 ff. (with splendid analyses, even though the author's chronological conclusions were erroneous); Giesau, "Stand der Forschung über das Figurenportal des Mittelalters" (*Beiträge zur Kunst des Mittelalters. Vorträge der Ersten Deutschen Kunsthistoriker-Tagung auf Schloss Brühl*); and Stoddard, *The West Portals of Saint Denis and Chartres*, pp. 14 ff.

mentions a mass that Geoffrey celebrated in the hardly completed choir, and also his presence at the final consecration.[30] The stylistic affinities between the two facades reflect the personal relations between the two prelates and basic affinities in their convictions and tastes. The St.-Denis façade precedes that of Chartres and may, in some respects, even have served as its model. Craftsmen seem to have been exchanged between the two workshops. But details regarding the relationship between the facades have so far defied satisfactory clarification. Since the jamb figures of Suger's portal are not mentioned in his description of it, they may not have been executed until after the abbot's death in 1151.[31] In that event, they might be later than the corresponding statues from the Royal Portal at Chartres. The drawings after the St.-Denis statues, on the other hand, published by Montfaucon (the statues were destroyed in 1771), as well as three heads, now in American museums, that may be assigned to these jamb statues, suggest a more primitive style than that of Chartres West, at least more than that of the figures attributed to the master sculptor.[32] The same impression is confirmed by W. S. Stoddard's recent analysis of ornamental details of both façades. Definitely archaic and of inferior quality is a group of small heads, now in the Louvre, that seem to have belonged to the statues in the tympanum and archivolts of St.-Denis.

*Plates 24, 19*

The comparison of the two façades underscores the singular achievement of Chartres. It is here that the new style, under the guidance of a great sculptor, seems to come all of a sudden into its own, realizing the aesthetic vision of the first Gothic with definitive clarity and grandeur. No other work of medieval sculpture produced an equal impression upon contemporaries; even today we can trace its influence far beyond the boundaries of the French domain or even of France. And no other work similarly outdistances its possible prototypes or models. Inasmuch as the statuary of Chartres West is essentially a part of the

*Plate 28*

---

30. *Oeuvres complètes de Suger*, pp. 230, 233, 235.

31. Cf. Aubert, "Têtes des statues-colonnes du portail occidental de Saint-Denis" (*BM*, CIV, 1945); *Sculpture*, pp. 182 ff.; and Suger, p. 141. Crosby, *L'Abbaye royale de Saint-Denis*, p. 38, maintains that the statues were completed before Suger's death and hence before those of Chartres. This thesis seems the more convincing to me.

32. Montfaucon, *Les Monumens de la monarchie française*, I, 16, 17, 18; Ross, "Monumental Sculptures from St.-Denis" (*Journal of the Walters Art Gallery*, III, 1940); Crosby, "Early Gothic Architecture—New Problems as a Result of the St. Denis Excavations" (*JSAH*, VII, 1948) (on the recently discovered relief, which he rightly dates earlier than Chartres); an illuminating comparison of the styles of the two façades is in Voege, p. 223.

architecture and dramatically underscores the stylistic impulse that produced the first Gothic art, a word must be said about its significance as well as its possible sources.

According to one thesis that has gained wide acceptance among scholars, the *statue colonne* was actually inspired by Cistercian book illumination, where a human figure is occasionally attached to the initial I in a manner that suggests indeed the association of column and statue in the cathedral sculpture of the Île-de-France.[33] Burgundian influences upon this sculpture are likely since, in ornamental detail at least, several correspondences have been found in works of both regions.[34] But to derive the *statue colonne* from the Cistercian initials seems to me quite a different matter, and this for two reasons. For one thing, what matters in a work of art is not the iconographic "what" but the stylistic "how": to attach the human figure to a column, painted or carved, is one thing; to co-ordinate the two in such a way that the rhythm of the one also permeates the other is something quite different. Even if we disregard the difference of size and medium that separates the statues of St.-Denis and Chartres from the Cistercian miniatures, the latter fall entirely short in the co-ordination of statue and stem. Second, even the motif as such is not confined to the Burgundian illuminations (even though it may possibly appear here for the first time); it occurs, from the middle of the twelfth century onward, in a number of manuscripts produced in regions as widely apart as northern France and England, on the one hand, and Alsace or southwest Germany, on the other. In particular, it seems to have been in works of the "Channel style"—produced within the Norman orbit on either side of the Channel—that a truly monumental integration of figure and initial (or frame) was first achieved that invites comparison with the *statue*

*Plate 22a*

---

33. Oursel, *La Miniature du XII*ᵉ *siècle à l'Abbaye de Cîteaux d'après les manuscrits de la Bibliothèque de Dijon;* and, following him, Giesau; Goldscheider's dissertation, *Les Origines du portail à statues colonnes;* and Stoddard, pp. 49 ff.

34. See Stoddard, p. 48. It ought to be pointed out, however, that other ornamental details have striking parallels in northern French and English book illumination. (See following note.) Ornament, moreover, is so easily diffused and imitated that it is often

hazardous to attempt the determination of origins and sources. Stoddard singles out the "four-leaf-clover pattern" as occurring both in Chartres and in the Burgundian Paray-le-Monial. The motif, however, the *hémicycles adossés*, occurs in nearly every phase and medium of medieval art and can be traced back to antiquity. On the style and possible derivation of the St.-Denis and Chartres statues, see Mâle, *Notre-Dame de Chartres*, p. 30, and Aubert, *Sculpture*, p. 186.

*colonne.*[35] Such possible ties with the North deserve our attention all the more in view of the remarkable evidence for Norman sources of the first Gothic art, especially that of Suger, to which I have pointed in the preceding chapter.

It should not be forgotten, however, that the affinities between the first Gothic sculpture and contemporary book illumination are perhaps owing less to an influence of the one upon the other than to a general stylistic trend that underlies both. And those affinities do not really explain what is so novel and striking about the statues of St.-Denis and, even more so, of Chartres West: we can describe it only as the idea of an icon in stone. The closest formal parallel of this extraordinary idea occurs, characteristically enough, in the truly statuesque figures of saints in certain mosaics of Norman Sicily, for example, the images in the two lower zones of the side walls of the presbytery of Cefalù, and above all those of the Greek Fathers on the northern transept wall of the Palatine Chapel at Palermo and eight other saints on the faces of the pillars of the nave in the same sanctuary.[36] These works were created shortly after 1150 and are

*Plate 22b*

*Plate 23*

35. Examples from the northern French group, so impressively represented at the recent exhibit of illuminated manuscripts at the Bibliothèque Nationale (see the catalogue *Les Manuscrits à peintures en France du VIIe au XIIe siècle*), include the St. Augustine from St.-Amand (Valenciennes MS. 80), opening page; and the Life of St. Amand, from the same abbey (Valenciennes MS. 501), fol. 59, r. and v. As regards English illumination, see Boase, *English Art 1100–1216*, p. 243 and Pls. 29 and 76b ("column statues" in initials I in the Bodleian MS., Auct. E infra 1, and in the Puiset Bible, respectively). Cf. also the important paper by Wormald, "The Development of English Illumination in the Twelfth Century" (*Journal of the British Archaeological Association*, 3rd series, VII, 1942). In the Bodleian MS. just mentioned there also occurs a striking example of the motif of the human figure climbing in vines that we find in both St.-Denis and Chartres West (Boase, Pl. 29). The motif is so frequent in English art that I am not sure whether its occurrence at Lincoln Cathedral really points to the influence of St.-Denis. For a fine example of the same motif in northern French illumination, see the Concordance of the Gospels from Anchin (Douai MS. 42), fol. 101. [*See Add.*]

As to the second group of manuscripts mentioned, see the large miniatures of the Codex Guta-Sintram (dated 1154) from the Augustinian monastery at Marbach-Schwarzenthann in Alsace (Strasbourg, Grand-Séminaire, MS. 78), also the superb evangelistary (now Laon MS. 550), not necessarily of Alsatian origin, though at the beginning of the thirteenth century in the possession of the same monastery (see the Bibliothèque Nationale catalogue just mentioned, p. 95); here (fol. 19) a veritable *statue colonne* has been placed against the initial I. See Walter, "L'Évangeliaire de Marbach-Schwarzenthann de la fin du XIIe siècle" (*AHA*, IX, 1930), and "Les Miniatures du Codex Guta-Sintram de Marbach-Schwarzenthann (1154)" (*AHA*, IV, 1925). See also the initial (fol. 422 v) in the Great Bible at Clermont-Ferrand (MS. 7), a work that is closely related to the "Channel style." For an antecedent, see the figure of St. James in the initial I in the famous Bible of Stavelot, A.D. 1097 (Brit. Mus. Add. 28107, fol. 197 v), reproduced in Swarzenski, *Monuments of Romanesque Art*, fig. 414.

36. Demus, *The Mosaics of Norman Sicily*, pp. 14 ff., 46 ff.; Pls. 7A and B, 23B, 33, 34. "The contribution of Byzantine art to the formation of the new style which manifests itself in the great west portals of St.-Denis and

thus exactly contemporary with the most mature sculptures of Chartres West.[37] Given the close political and cultural ties that just then existed between Capetian France and Norman Sicily, a common source of inspiration for both mosaics and sculptures appears entirely plausible.[38] Byzantine influence is present in the three great windows above the Royal Portal. It is noticeable even in the illuminated manuscripts from Cîteaux.[39] There can be no doubt that the spell which the art of the Greek Church exerted upon the age of St. Bernard is also reflected in the first Gothic art.

Such stylistic considerations apart, we may ask if anything tangible can be ascertained regarding the relationship between the art of Chartres West and the intellectual and spiritual currents of the time that we have discussed. Is it merely a coincidence that a work of such singular importance was executed at the very moment when both the influence of St. Bernard and the prestige of the Cathedral School of Chartres stood at their zenith? Bishop Geoffrey was intimately connected with both movements; it is unlikely that their aesthetic views should not be reflected in the great—and, even to contemporaries, memorable—artistic enterprise for which he was responsible. But it is much easier to assume the existence of such influences than to say specifically of what nature these were.

A relatively easy approach is the iconographic one. Thus the northern tower, which was begun ten years before the remainder of the facade and apparently without any thought of a comprehensive program (its donors were two

Chartres" has already been suggested by Koehler, "Byzantine Art and the West" (*Dumbarton Oaks Papers*, I, 1941). We should not exclude the possibility of yet another Byzantine source for the composition of Chartres West: mid-Byzantine ivories of the so-called Romanos group, like the famous Harbaville triptych (Louvre), show a similar co-ordination of the enthroned figure of Christ with groups of saints standing motionless on either side of his throne below. Byzantine ivories had long been treasured in the West. And the close political ties with Byzantium that prevailed at the beginning of the twelfth century render it more than likely that the first Gothic artists were acquainted with ivories of the type mentioned.

37. On the dates of these mosaics, see Demus, pp. 375 ff., 404 ff.; also Kitzinger, "The Mosaics of the Cappella Palatina in Palermo" (*AB*, XXXI, 1949).

38. Kitzinger stresses the relations between France and Sicily and shows the presence of "French" elements in the iconography of the Palatine Chapel. Such influence by no means excludes the possibility of a stylistic impact that the Sicilian mosaics, by means of model books, may have exerted upon French art. Such influence is well attested elsewhere. See, e.g., Demus, pp. 443 ff.

39. The best example is the beautiful *hodegetria* in Jerome's commentary on Isaiah in the Dijon Library (MS. 129).

dignitaries of the chapter),[40] still has some of those "monstrous" mythological capitals that were condemned by St. Bernard. In the southern tower, however, the capitals are reduced to austerely stylized vegetative forms that correspond to the postulates of the reform.[41] The composition of the three portals, more-over, is much farther removed from Cluniac influences or models than is even that of St.-Denis. And the benign Saviour in the central tympanum, so different from the awesome judge of Romanesque sculpture, is like a monumental illustra-tion of the "amor vincit timorem" that epitomizes the new, more lyrical piety of St. Bernard.

The right-hand portal of the Chartres façade reflects, in its iconography, the ideas of the School of Chartres. In the tympanum there appears the Mother of God enthroned, surrounded, in the archivolts, by the personifications of the liberal arts, which are accompanied by the great classical masters of each of these disciplines; the rendering of this theme is the first in monumental sculp-ture. Its appearance at this portal has been very plausibly connected with the fact that the cultivation of the liberal arts, especially of the quadrivium, was the particular concern of the School of Chartres and at that time its chief title to fame.[42] The felicitous thought of co-ordinating this theme with the figure of Mary as the Seat of Wisdom bespeaks the ultimate goal and purpose of liberal studies at the Cathedral School. In a sequence on the Incarnation, Alan of Lille depicts the *artes liberales* as being confounded by this mystery.[43] As a student he may well have stood before the Chartres portal. The Incarnation is the general theme to which its program is dedicated, and it was here that the celebrated school acknowledged that act of faith in which its knowledge and wisdom originated and ended.

But has the Christian Platonism of Chartres also exerted an influence upon the style, the formal design, of the west façade? There can, of course, be no question of ascribing to the abstract thought of theologians or philosophers the

*Plate 29*

40. Gauterius, archdeacon of Chartres (d. after 1132), and Ansgerius, archdeacon of Blois (d. after 1139). GC, III, 124, 131; cf. Merlet and Clerval, *Un Manuscrit chartrain du XI^e siècle*, pp. 86 f.; Merlet, *Dignitaires*, pp. 128, 178.

41. Aubert, "Le Portail Royal," and the reproductions in Lassus, *Monographie de la Cathédrale de Chartres*.

42. See Mâle, *Notre-Dame de Chartres*, p. 24, and *L'Art religieux du XII^e siècle en France*, pp. 104 ff.

43. *De Incarnatione Christi* (PL, CCX, 517 ff.). [*See Add.*]

achievement of a very great artist. On the other hand, chapter as well as bishop normally would assume an important role in the planning and supervision of cathedral art. And we are apt to underestimate the extent to which the ideas and wishes of his ecclesiastical patrons guided the work of the medieval artist. It is precisely the singularity and novelty of the style achieved at Chartres West that leads one to ask if this style was not created in response to the wishes and ideas expressed by the cathedral chapter.

The striking and unique aspect of this style is the complete integration of architecture and sculpture. The human figure seems to merge into the rigid pattern of columns and archivolts; perhaps it is more adequate to say that this pattern has come to life in the serene and noble order of the statues. And the concordance of architecture and sculpture renders apparent the geometrical element that is at the root of the entire composition. As was remarked earlier, geometrical formulae have also been employed in Romanesque sculpture, but as technical devices that aided the artist and in the completed work remain largely unnoticed. The master of Chartres renders his composition transparent, as it were, in order to reveal the geometrical principle as the law that has guided his artistic inspiration.

This is no mere impression. Whoever designed the façade was a master of empirical geometry. Around 1150, Chartres, in light of the speculations of its Cathedral School, would seem to have been the likeliest place where such knowledge could have been gained, as well as applied to architecture.

*Plate 26*
As regards the west façade, the total width of the three portals was prescribed, or at least limited, by the two flanking towers, but an upper frame for the composition is provided by the horizontal stringcourse. The resulting rectangle in which the portals are inscribed is proportioned "according to true measure," since its sides are related as are the sides of two squares whose areas have the ratio of $1:2$. The square and the equilateral triangle prevail in each of the three portals and their tympana; but of even greater interest is the use of the "golden section." This proportion—one of the "two true treasures" and the "precious jewel of geometry," as Kepler called it [44]—occurs

---

44. In his *Mysterium cosmographicum* (1596), quoted by Ghyka, *Le Nombre d'or*, I, 50. On the harmonical equivalents of the golden sec-tion, see Fischer, *Zwei Vorträge über Proportionen*, pp. 72 f.

both in the most accomplished statues in the jambs and in the groups of the *artes* and their corresponding philosophers in the archivolts of the Incarnation portal. Moessel's measurements are so exact and the use of the golden section so obvious—it divides the jamb figures at the bent elbow, the most notable     *Plate 22b* horizontal division of the figures—that no doubt appears possible in this instance.

The School of Chartres knew the mathematical importance of the golden section from Euclid; [45] Thierry possessed the *Elements* in the Latin translation by Adelard of Bath.[46] Moreover, how to construct the *sectio aurea* geometrically could be learned from Ptolemy's *Almagest*.[47] It is not without interest that a Latin translation of this work, attributed to the same Adelard of Bath, seems to have been completed around 1150 and to have been dedicated either to Thierry of Chartres or to his successor as chancellor of the school, Bernard (Silvestris?).[48] [*See Add.*]

In conclusion, I should venture the following suggestion. The geometrical system used on the west façade of Chartres was furnished to its master or masters by the Cathedral School. The school wished to underscore the theological significance of the four mathematical disciplines by having them represented, in the allegories of the quadrivium, on the portal of the Incarnation. And to the members of that Platonic academy, geometry appeared as the principle of order that alone could convey to the senses the vision of ultimate glory to which the entire facade is dedicated. The façade evokes more perfectly even than that of St.-Denis the mystical character of the sanctuary as "the house of God and the gate of heaven." Surrounding the majesty of Christ depicted in the central tympanum there appear the choirs of angels and saints in the "concert" of the heavenly hierarchy. In "measure and number and weight" Thierry of Chartres sought to seize the primordial principle of the Creation. The great

---

45. With regard to the place of the golden section in Euclid's *Elements*, see Lund, *Ad Quadratum*, p. 134: "[it is] the only one of all geometrical proportions which enters constantly into a multitude of proofs"; and Heath, *The Thirteen Books of Euclid's Elements*, II, 97 ff.

46. Clerval, p. 190 ff. On the tradition of Euclid in the Middle Ages, see Lund, pp.

143 ff.; Cantor, *Vorlesungen zur Geschichte der Mathematik*, II, 91 f.; and Heath, I, 92 f.

47. *Almagest* (ed., Halma and Delambre, Paris, 1813), p. 26; cf. Cantor, I, 907 and II, 7; and Funck-Hellet, "L'Équerre des maîtres d'oeuvres et la proportion" (*Les Cahiers techniques de l'art*, II, 1949).

48. See Bliemetzrieder, *Adelhard von Bath*, pp. 149 ff.

schoolman may have lived to see the unforgettable tribute paid to the same
principle by the master craftsman who created the cathedral façade.[49]

49. *Postscript* (1956). This book was in press
before the appearance of Ernst Gall's review
(*AB*, XXXVII, 1955) of Crosby, *L'Abbaye
royale de Saint-Denis*. Gall seeks to refute the
view that Suger's St.-Denis represents the
original creation of Gothic church architecture,
basing his criticism on the following arguments.
Since Suger's church was completed only in its
western and eastern parts, it cannot have influenced the Gothic cathedrals "since their
decisive characteristics are found in the shape
of the nave." Moreover, St.-Denis preserves
many Romanesque elements, not only in its
sculptured decoration but also in its tendency
toward a unified ground plan and the fusion of
spatial units. In support of this view, Gall claims
that such unification marks the late phase of
both Romanesque and Gothic, whereas clarity
of articulation is characteristic of the "flowering" of both styles. The latter argument seems
to me dubious not only on grounds of logic but
on the basis of the evidence. Gall attributes the
ground plan of Notre Dame, Paris, to its peculiar location but fails to mention its sister church,
the cathedral of Bourges; nor does he mention
Chartres. As to the Romanesque elements in
St.-Denis, no one has ever denied their existence. The question is whether the survival of
such details outweighs the novelty of the design
as a whole. If we compare Suger's façade with
that of St.-Étienne at Caen or his choir with that
of St.-Martin-des Champs, can we really do
justice to St.-Denis by describing it as a mere

continuation of those Romanesque antecedents?
Again, if we compare Suger's façade with that
of Chartres West, Noyon, or even Paris, and
his choir with that of Chartres (which Gall
himself will hardly call "late" Romanesque or
"late" Gothic), can we seriously deny that the
stylistic principles underlying these Gothic
buildings were first formulated in St.-Denis?

According to Gall, Gothic "may be said to
begin with the conscious effort to permeate the
elevation with a distinct vertical tendency, embodied in the dynamic power of slender rising
shafts . . . a symbol of transcendental forces
which are to fill the soul of worshipers with
deep longing for the celestial kingdom of God."
I am far from sure that such verticalism was
altogether absent from Suger's choir; but verticalism is neither the exclusive property of
Gothic nor even its most prominent feature.
Gall says nothing of the diaphanous character
of Gothic. Yet, while I know of no historical
evidence for the romantic assumption that the
Gothic architect employed verticalism in order
to fill the soul with longing for the kingdom of
God, we know from Suger himself that luminosity was the esthetic principle he strove to
realize in St.-Denis. How well he succeeded is
attested even today by his ambulatory and
chapels; how well he was understood is attested
by the triumph of luminosity in the Gothic
cathedrals. These facts alone, it seems to me,
warrant the claim that Suger's St.-Denis is indeed the first Gothic church.

PART

3

THE CONSUMMATION

# 6. THE PALACE OF THE VIRGIN

WE CANNOT be certain about the exact date on which the Royal Portal of Chartres Cathedral was completed. However, since the statuary has influenced the figures of the southern portal of Le Mans Cathedral, executed prior to 1158, some, at least, of the sculptures of Chartres West can hardly be later than 1155.[1] But work on the façade as a whole, including the three magnificent windows above the Royal Portal, may have continued through the entire third quarter of the century, if not longer. The great southern tower—somewhat misleadingly named *vieux clocher*, since it was actually begun after its northern counterpart—was not completed until around 1164.[2] And individual donations "ad opus ecclesiae" made in subsequent years by individual members of the cathedral chapter suggest that perhaps plans were under way, or work had even been started, for the completion of the northern tower when the catastrophe occurred that must have altered all existing plans.[3]

*Plate 26*

During the night of June 10 to 11, 1194, a general conflagration, the causes of which are unknown, destroyed a large part of the town of Chartres, the splendid episcopal palace built by Bishop Yves, and the entire cathedral, except for the west façade. The impression the disaster left upon contemporaries was tremendous. Guillaume le Breton, the historian and court poet of Philip Augustus, mentions it both in his *Philippid* and in his history of the king;[4] the author of the Chronicle of Auxerre also recorded the event, and it passed from this source into the celebrated *Speculum historiale* of Vincentius of Beauvais.

1. See above, ch. 5, n. 29.
2. Lefèvre-Pontalis, "Les Architectes et la construction des cathédrales de Chartres" (*SNAFM*, 7th series, IV, 1905).
3. Lefèvre-Pontalis; cf. Lecocq, "La Ca-

thédrale de Chartres et ses maîtres d'oeuvre" (*SAELM*, VI, 1873; *CC*, III, 80).
4. *Philippid*, IV, 598, and *Gesta Philippi Augusti*, LXXIII (Delaborde, ed., II, 121; I, 169; cf. ibid., 128). See *HLF*, XVI, 191 ff.; XVII, 336 ff.

Beyond the Channel, the English reader found a record of the great fire in the Chronicle of William of Newbridge.[5]

That the calamity that had befallen Chartres, above all the destruction of its cathedral, should arouse such prolonged and distant echoes is not surprising. The sanctuary was one of the most revered shrines of the Occident. Its chief relic, the tunic or shirt that the Virgin Mary was said to have worn at the birth of Christ, had for centuries attracted large numbers of pilgrims.[6] Early in the twelfth century, Guibert of Nogent noted that the relic, as well as the name of the Virgin of Chartres, were venerated "by almost the entire Latin world." [7] The abbot of Nogent did not regard without skepticism the cult of relics as he encountered it among many contemporaries. Yet he looked with the most reverent affection upon the Sacred Tunic of Chartres.

The cathedral owed its association with the cult of Mary not only to this relic, however. In presenting it to the basilica in 876, Emperor Charles the Bald may either have wished to establish this sanctuary as a great pilgrimage center or he may merely have acknowledged the existence of a much older tradition. Divine Providence, it was believed, had called Chartres as the first of the churches of Gaul to the knowledge of the mystery of the Incarnation. Indeed, the sanctuary itself was said to have been built more than a century before the birth of Mary, in response to the oracles of prophets and sibyls about the *Virgo paritura*. The See of Chartres made itself the mouthpiece of such beliefs. Before the end of the Middle Ages they had been embodied even in the authoritative and solemn language of its liturgy.[8]

The basilica of Chartres was thus the center of the cult of Mary in France, if not in western Europe. No wonder that its devastation kindled the deepest

5. On the fire and the literary sources mentioned, see Bulteau, *Monographie de la Cathédrale de Chartres*, I, 97 ff.

6. Delaporte, art. "Chartres," in Baudrillard, *Dictionnaire d'histoire et de géographie ecclésiastique*, XII, 544 ff.

7. "Domina Carnotensis . . . cujus nomen et pignora ibidem totius pene Latini orbis veneratione coluntur." *De vita sua*, I, 16 (*PL*, CLVI, 871). On Guibert's attitude toward the cult of relics, see Lefranc, "Le Traité des reliques de Guibert de Nogent" (*Études . . . Monod*).

8. See the famous *Vieille Chronique* of 1389 (*CC*, I, 2, pp. 1 ff., especially 54 ff.). About this work and its influence, see ibid., 1 f., and below, pp. 225 f. The author certainly did not invent his fabrications. In 1367 Charles V declared the cathedral to be "in antiquissimo tempore fundata videlicet adhuc vivente beata Maria." See also the prayer in the Missal of Chartres of 1482: "Domine, civitatem istam Carnotensem . . . quam primam apud Gallos de mysterio tuae incarnationis instruere voluisti." Bulteau, *Monographie*, I, 9; and below, p. 226.

human emotions. The historian has every reason to take such emotions seriously. They provide the impulse without which great collective efforts are impossible and unintelligible. In Chartres, the grief over the destruction of the ancient shrine prompted, soon after the calamity had occurred, the resolution to rebuild it more splendidly than it had ever been before. The general mood during those days can perhaps alone explain the almost incredible effort that produced, within the brief span of one generation, the cathedral that we admire today as the loftiest example of medieval art.

We are fairly well informed about the mood that prevailed in Chartres after the fire, thanks to a curious document written by a cleric, perhaps a canon of the cathedral, who, if he was not an eyewitness of the conflagration, was certainly well acquainted with the events and sentiments he describes. The treatise, *Miracles of the Blessed Virgin Mary in the Church of Chartres*, dates from around 1210, that is, from the years when the construction of the new cathedral was under way, and was probably written to help raise funds for this enterprise. Half a century later, and after the building had been completed, the little work was still considered sufficiently meritorious by a member of the cathedral chapter who had literary inclinations—a certain Jehan le Marchand—to be translated into French verse.[9]

The treatise opens with a vivid description of the enormous damage caused by the great fire. The author dwells on the distress of those whose houses and personal property had been destroyed, but maintains that such grief was entirely overshadowed by the consternation felt by everyone at the devastation of the cathedral, in the ashes of which had also perished, or so it was believed, the Sacred Tunic.

The people of Chartres had long looked upon this relic as their shield against all perils. In 911, when the Norman Rollo besieged Chartres, Bishop Gaucelinus had mounted the city gate; and displaying the *sancta camisia* like a standard in front of them, he had thrown the terrible Norman warriors into panic and flight.[10] Two centuries later, in 1119, the relic, carried in solemn procession by clergy and people, had moved Louis VI, then at war with

9. *Miracula B. Mariae Virginis in Carnotensi ecclesia facta*, p. 33; cf. Bulteau, *Monographie*, I, 97 f.

10. Lépinois, *Histoire de Chartres*, I, 38 ff.; Bulteau, *Monographie*, I, 33.

Thibault of Chartres, to spare the city.[11] The disaster of 1194, which seemed to have destroyed the relic as well as the sanctuary, was generally looked upon as a sign of divine wrath. Because of the sins of the people, the Virgin had abandoned her shrine, which had been "the glory of the city, the pride of the country, an incomparable house of worship." [12] Its disappearance made everyone forget his own personal losses momentarily. The first reaction, significantly enough, was that it would be futile to rebuild either the basilica or the town. With the destruction of the cathedral, the numinous power to which Chartres owed its prosperity, its security, and indeed its existence seemed to have departed.

At this time Cardinal Melior of Pisa happened to be sojourning in the city. A renowned canonist, he seems to have united great gifts as a teacher and orator with unusual diplomatic skill. Celestine III had appointed him papal legate in France.[13] According to the *Miracles of the Blessed Virgin*, it was to a considerable extent this man who was responsible for changing the mood of the cathedral chapter as well as of the people of Chartres from despair to enthusiasm.

The cardinal was well acquainted with the chapter. He had assisted the bishop, Renaud of Mouçon, in the recently completed reform of the chapter's administrative setup (see below, p. 176). Now, immediately after the fire, Melior undertook two steps. He convened with the bishop and prebendaries, and at this conference he pointed out with great force of argument that the only adequate answer to the calamity that had befallen Notre Dame was to rebuild the cathedral. The impression of his words was such that bishop and chapter decided to commit the greater part of their revenues for the next three years, excepting only what was necessary to their subsistence, to the rebuilding of the church.[14]

---

11. Suger, *Vie de Louis le Gros* (Molinier, ed.), pp. 92 ff.

12. "Specialem urbis gloriam, tocius regionis speculum, domum orationis incomparabilem . . ." *Mirac.*, pp. 509 f.

13. *Mirac.*, pp. 509 f. On Melior, see Bulteau, *Monographie*, I, 103, and *HLF*, XV, 316, where, however, Bulteau's contention that Melior occupied a chair in Paris is declared to be unfounded.

14. "Convocatis ad se episcopo et canonicis divine animadversionis vindictam et a quanta cedissent gloria plenius ostenderet, et eos postmodum ad penitenciam provocans eorumdem animos suis sermociniationibus emolliret. Episcopus igitur et canonici partem redditum suorum non modicam per triennium conferendam ad reparationem ejus ecclesie absque ulla contradictione concesserunt." Cf. *Mirac.*, pp. 513 ff.; also Stein, *Les Architectes des cathédrales gothiques*, p. 37; Bulteau, I, 104.

*Christ in the Heavenly City*
From the Bible historiée of Jean de Papeleu, 1317

1

*Abbey of St.-Étienne, Caen. Nave (1064–1120)*

2

*Abbey of St.-Étienne, Caen. Choir* (c. *1200*)

Note in the Gothic choir the tendency to screen and "dissolve" the actual thickness of walls and piers by the multiplication of shafts and arches and by tympana over slender columns placed in the gallery openings.

*Noyon Cathedral*
4

*Cathedral of Notre Dame, Paris*

a. *God as architect of the universe*
From a Bible moralisée, Vienna

b. *Reims Cathedral. Tomb of Hugh*
*Libergier (d. 1263)*

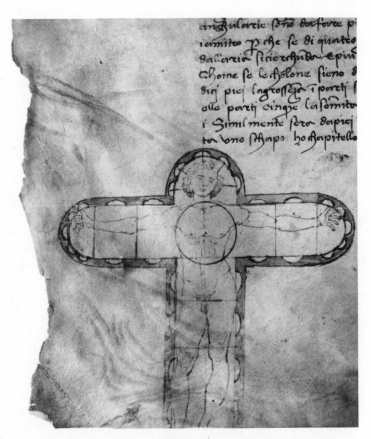

*Francesco di Giorgio. Ground plan of a church corresponding to the proportions of the human figure*
Biblioteca Laurenziana, Florence

7

*The mystical Paradise of church doctrine in analogy to that of the Old Testament*
From a German manuscript, first half of twelfth century

8

*The mystical Paradise of church doctrine in analogy to that of the Old Testament*
From a German manuscript, 1170–85

9

*The air as an element of cosmic harmony*
Pen drawing, *c.* 1200

10

*Fontenay Abbey. North aisle and nave*

11

IN
PRIN
CIPIO.
CREA
UIT
DE
US.
CE
LVM
ET
TER
RAM

Terra autem erat inanis
& uacua:? & tenebre erant
sup faciem abyssi: & sps di
ferebatur sup aquas. Dix
q deus. Fiat lux. Et facta
est lux. Et uidit ds lucem
qd eet bona: & diuisit luce
ac tenebras. Appellauitcq
luce diem: & tenebras no
ctem. Factumcq est uespe
& mane: dies unus. II.
Dixit quocq ds. Fiat fir
mamtum in medio a
quaru: & diuidat aquas ab
aquis. Et fecit ds firmam
tum. Diuisitcq aquas. que
erant sub firmanto: ab his
que erant sup firmamentu.
Et factum est ita. Vocauitcq
ds firmamtum. celu. Et factu
est uespt & mane: dies sccds.
Dixit uero deus. III.
Congregentur aque
que sub celo sunt. in locum
unu: & appareat arida. Fa
ctumcq est ita. Et uocauit
deus aridam. terram: con
gregationescq aquaru. appel
lauit maria. Et uidit ds

*Initial letter of the book of Genesis*
From the Bible of Clairvaux, mid twelfth century

12

a. *Benediction of the Fair of the Lendit by the
Bishop of Paris*
From a pontifical, fourteenth century

b. *Initial letter of the book of Leviticus, with
entwined serpents*
From the Bible of Clairvaux, mid twelfth century

13

*Abbey of St.-Denis. West façade*

*Abbey of St.-Denis. Vault of Suger's narthex*

15

*Abbey of St.-Denis. Suger's ambulatory*

16

*Scenes from the life of St. Denis: his consecration as bishop and (below) his work as theologian*
From a manuscript written at St.-Denis, thirteenth century

*Abbey of St.-Étienne, Caen*

*Abbey of St.-Denis. Reconstruction of Suger's façade*

a. *Abbey of St.-Denis. Central tympanum*

b. *Beaulieu Abbey. Tympanum*

*Sens Cathedral. Nave*

a. *St. Augustine: initial letter
from an Alsatian (?) evangelistary*

b. *Chartres Cathedral. Statue from
the Royal Portal*

*Palatine Chapel, Palermo. Mosaic: St. Gregory
of Nazianzus*

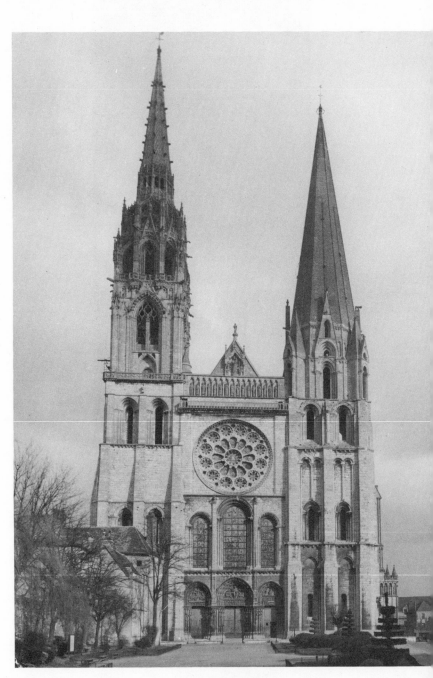

*Chartres Cathedral*

24

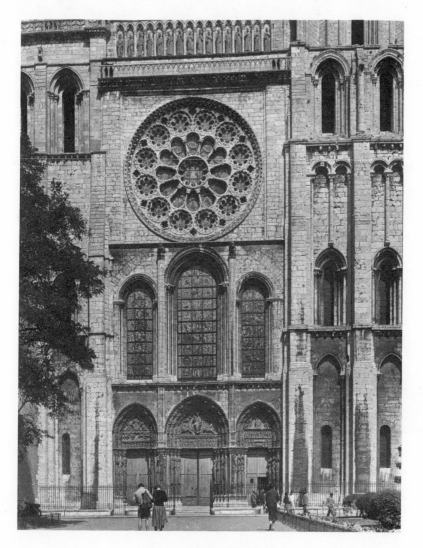

*Chartres Cathedral. West façade*

*Chartres Cathedral. West façade, showing parts completed by* c. *1175*

*Chartres Cathedral. Royal Portal*

27

*Chartres Cathedral. Royal Portal, central door*

*Chartres Cathedral. Royal Portal, right-hand door, archivolts: the liberal arts, philosophers, angels*

*Chartres. Fulbert's cathedral*
Reconstruction by Merlet after the eleventh-century miniature by Andrew of Mici

*Abbey of St.-Remi, Reims. Peter of Celle's double bay (left) and Romanesque nave with later Gothic modifications*

Note the vault ribs over slender colonnettes and the tympana with pointed arches over gallery openings of the Romanesque nave.

31

Chartres Cathedral. System of buttresses and horizontal sections of nave

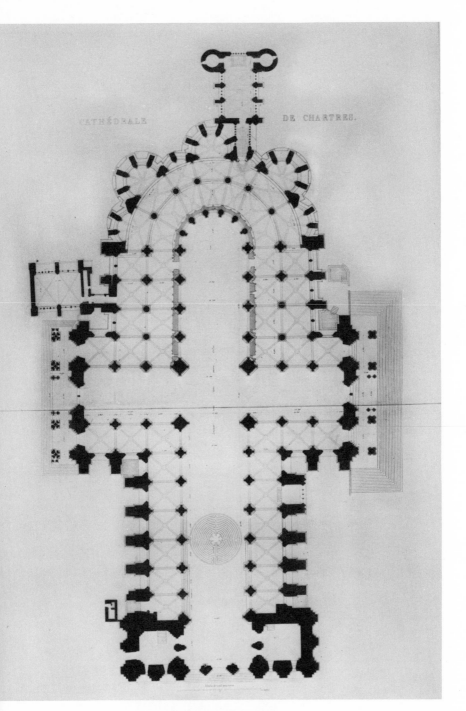

CATHÉDRALE          DE CHARTRES.

*Chartres Cathedral. Ground plan*

33

*Chartres Cathearal. Transverse section of choir*

34

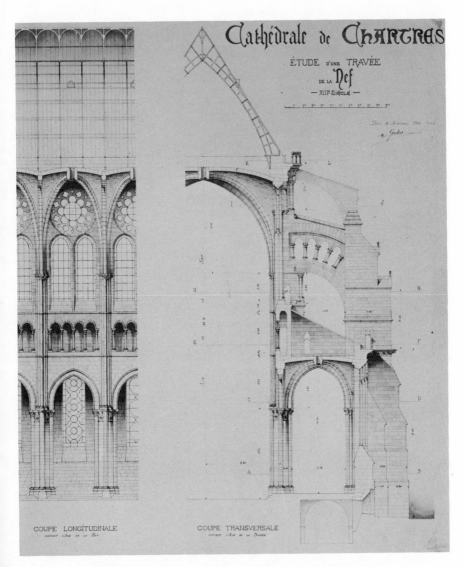

Chartres Cathedral. Longitudinal and transverse sections of nave

*Chartres Cathedral. Section of buttressing system of nave at clerestory level*

*Chartres Cathedral. Northern transept, middle portal, left jamb*

37

*Chartres Cathedral. Flying buttresses of nave*

*Chartres Cathedral. Flying buttresses of nave*

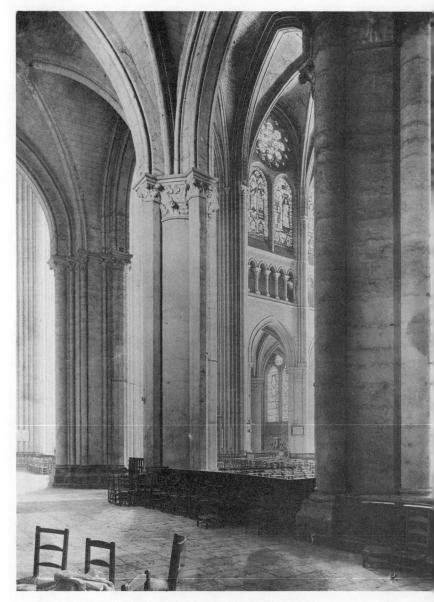

*Chartres Cathedral. View into nave and south transept*

*Chartres Cathedral. North transept portal, center door: John the Baptist*

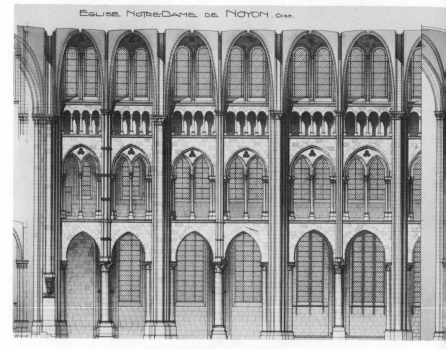

*Noyon Cathedral. Longitudinal section*

42

*Chartres Cathedral. Choir seen from the south*

43

*Chartres Cathedral. Flying buttresses of choir*

44

*Laon Cathedral. Northern transept, rose window*

*Villard de Honnecourt. Rose window*

46

*Chartres Cathedral. Southern transept, rose window*

47

*Chartres Cathedral. Northern transept, rose window*

*Jericho. Hisham Palace*

49

*Lausanne Cathedral. Southern transept*

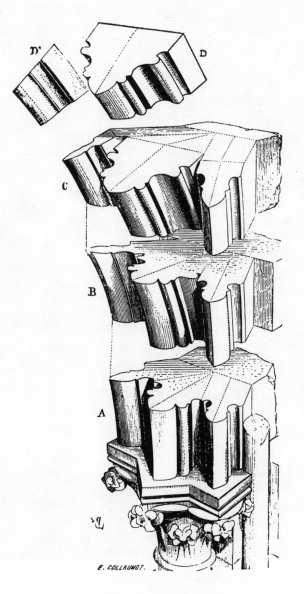

*Construction of a tas-de-charge*

*Chartres Cathedral. Northern transept, rose window*

The Cardinal of Pisa next chose a feast day to call an assembly of the townspeople of Chartres. Before this crowd he repeated his plea with an eloquence that brought tears to the eyes of his audience. And, by what seemed to be a happy coincidence, at this very moment the bishop and chapter appeared carrying in solemn procession the Sacred Tunic, which contrary to general belief had, safe in the cathedral crypt, survived the conflagration undamaged. The wonderful occurrence caused an incredible impression. Everyone pledged the possessions he had salvaged to the reconstruction of the sanctuary. The medieval temper, as we can often observe, was given to sudden changes from despair to joy. In Chartres it was now suddenly believed that the Virgin herself had permitted the destruction of the old basilica "because she wanted a new and more beautiful church to be built in her honor."[15]

Guillaume le Breton echoes this sentiment. "At this time," he writes in his great Latin poem in honor of Philip Augustus, "the Virgin and Mother of God, who is called and indeed shown to be the Lady of Chartres, wanted the sanctuary that is so specially hers to be more worthy of her. She therefore permitted the old and inadequate church to become the victim of the flames, thus making room for the present basilica, which has no equal throughout the entire world." [16] The first to voice this conviction may actually have been the Cardinal of Pisa. Not unlike Suger of St.-Denis, he represented the building of a magnificent sanctuary as an act of spiritual edification, a work of true penitence that demands that every endeavor be placed in the service of Christ and his mother.

The emotions of those who were about to undertake the great architectural project are noteworthy in both aspects I have described. There is first of all the intensity of grief at the loss of the sanctuary. It would be a mistake o see in the description of this grief a pious or poetical commonplace or simply an exaggeration by the author of the *Miracles of the Blessed Virgin*. The religion of medieval man was a communication with a sacred reality that was invisible,

15. "Beata Dei genetrix novam et incomparabilem ecclesiam sibi colens fabricari . . ." *Mirac.*, p. 510.

16. ". . . Virgo Dei mater, que verbo se docet et re Carnoti dominam, laudabiliore paratu, Ecclesiam reparare volens specialiter ipsi Quam dicat ipsa sibi, mirando provida casu Vulcano furere ad libitum permisit in illam, Ut medicina foret presens exustio morbi Quo Domini domus illa situ languebat inerti, Et causam fabrice daret illa ruina future, Cui toto par nulla hodie splendescit in orbe." IV, 598 (Delaborde, II, 121).

yet immediately and continuously present. The veneration of saints and their relics, the repercussions that this cult exerted upon nearly every phase of medieval life—Suger and St.-Denis have furnished us an example—are unintelligible unless the immediacy of this relationship with the supernatural is properly understood. The life of the city depended upon the divine power and, more directly, upon the protection and intercession of the city's patron saint. This sentiment, as the *Miracles of the Blessed Virgin* make quite plain, prevailed among the population of Chartres. The cathedral was referred to as the "celestial court of the Mother of God," selected by the Virgin as her "special residence on earth," and preferred by her to all other sanctuaries dedicated to Notre Dame.[17] Heaven and earth were close to one another in those days. They were as one in the sanctuary. It was here that Our Lady dwelt among her people. Can we marvel that the assumed destruction of the Sacred Tunic—probably the most venerable relic of Mary possessed by Christianity—seemed to spell the city's doom; that it was generally considered an ominous indication that the Virgin had departed from Chartres?

Conversely, the miraculous recovery of the relic seemed to be a token of her continued affection for her city. And the destruction of the cathedral was now viewed not as a calamity but, almost paradoxically, as a sign that Mary had indeed destined Chartres to be her special residence, and that she expected the faithful to bend every effort for the erection of a sanctuary worthy of this exalted destination. Hence the sudden change from despair to joyful confidence.

But in urging that the task of reconstruction be undertaken at once, the Cardinal of Pisa did not only express the religious sentiment of the community; he also made himself the spokesman for its economic and political interests. The prestige and prosperity of the city depended upon the religious element to such an extent that to rebuild the celebrated church was a necessity if the city's survival was to be assured.

We do not easily realize to what extent the religious and economic spheres interlocked in those days. The age of the towering pilgrimage churches and cathedrals was, economically speaking, the age of the great fairs. It is well

17. See Charles V's letter of 1367, where the cathedral is called "quam quidem ecclesiam ipsa Virgo gloriosa elegit pro sua camera speciali," and quite similarly the *Vieille Chronique* of 1389 (*CC*, I, 2, 56).

known how powerfully these recurrent markets—spasmodic concentrations
of the economic life of entire regions—stimulated the development of the
medieval city. The fairs, however, are inseparable from the religious life of
the Middle Ages; indeed they originate in it. "Religious festivals," the historian of the medieval fairs has written, "by their solemnity, by the number of
people they attract, by their regular recurrence, and by the security that divine
protection extends to all gatherings taking place under the auspices of such
festivals necessarily provide opportunities for commercial transactions. The
temple has always attracted the merchant just because it attracts the faithful.
. . . There is no great feast without its fair, no fair without its feast: one calls
for the other." [18]

Fairs were naturally held on those feast days that drew the largest crowds
of worshipers to a given sanctuary. On these occasions, the merging of economic and religious concerns became strikingly apparent. Merchants often
found it convenient to adopt the guise of pious travelers in order to avail themselves of the many benefits accorded pilgrims. As a rule, though, this expedient
was unnecessary. The church herself had every interest in protecting, as valuable sources of revenue, the markets and fairs held under its patronage. Some
of the most important fairs of the time were actually established by monasteries
and cathedrals. In that event, the religious element remained a decisive factor
in the development of these fairs. As we have seen, the Lendit originated in
the feast established in honor of the relics preserved at St.-Denis. The abbey's
jurisdictional claims over the fair rested on this fact; so did the vast income that
the house derived from the fairs.

This curious interrelationship is but another aspect of the religious
"personalism" of the age. Every concession granted to a religious institution,
every economic activity from which it derived material benefits, were considered personal tributes to the holy patron. Their infringement was an outrage
committed against him. Charles the Bald occasionally directed his officials to
protect the possessions of a monastery "as if they were things offered and
consecrated to God." [19] The abbot of St.-Denis threatened with excommunica-

18. Huvelin, *Essai historique sur le droit des
marchés et des foires*, pp. 37 ff.
19. Fournier, *Nouvelles recherches sur les
curies, chapitres et universités de l'ancienne église*
de France, p. 83; cf. Lesne, "Histoire de la
propriété ecclésiastique en France" (*Mémoires
et travaux publiés par des professeurs des Facultés
Catholiques de Lille*, fasc. VI).

tion whoever dared to molest in any way the merchants attending the Lendit.[20]
The security and even the commercial benefits of all those attending the fair
were thought to be jealously guarded by the patron saint of the abbey. Indeed,
so directly was he understood to interfere in these commercial gatherings that
a sudden decline of prices that occurred at one of the Lendits was interpreted
as a miraculous intervention of St. Denis in favor of the consumers! [21]

All this is equally true for Chartres. Here the economic life of the entire
city centered primarily in four great fairs, which, by the end of the twelfth
century, had acquired nearly the reputation of the fairs of Brie and Champagne.[22] The major fairs of Chartres coincided with the four feasts of the
Virgin (Purification, Annunciation, Assumption, and Nativity), which drew
innumerable pilgrims to the cathedral. As the fairs, in all probability established
by the cathedral chapter, had originated in these festivals, so they remained
dependent upon them. Religious souvenirs and devotional objects were purchased by pilgrims in very considerable quantities. At the fair of the Nativity
(called the Septembresce, as the birth of the Virgin was celebrated on Septem-
ber 8), such articles seem to have comprised the bulk of all goods sold.[23] These
devotional objects were most often small leaden images of Our Lady or of the
Sacred Tunic, but the more well-to-do pilgrims liked to take home real chemisettes, which, when blessed by a priest, were thought to be beneficial to the
expectant mother and even to protect the knight who wore them under his
armor in battle.[24]

Thus, even the manufacture and sale of textiles—the most famous product
of the region—profited directly as well as indirectly from the cult of the Sacred
Tunic. This is even truer for the producers of victuals—the bakers, butchers,
fishmongers—and the merchants of Beauce wine, the quality of which was once
famous.[25] During the festivals of the Virgin, business throve for all these trades-

20. Cf. Roussel, "La Bénédiction du Lendit
au XIV⁰ siècle" (*Bulletin de la Société de l'histoire
de Paris*, XXIV, 1897).

21. Levillain, "Essai sur les origines du
Lendit" (*RH*, CLV, 1927).

22. Lecocq, "Histoire du cloître Notre-
Dame de Chartres" (*SAELM*, 1858, I, 82 ff.;
*CC*, I, lxxviii); Lépinois, I, 378 f.; Levasseur,
*Histoire du commerce de la France*, I, 82 ff. On
the other fairs held at Chartres, see Aclocque,

*Les Corporations, l'industrie et le commerce à
Chartres du XI⁰ siècle à la révolution*, pp. 172 ff.
The symposium volume *La Foire* (*Recueils de
la Société Bodin*, V) appeared too late for consideration.

23. Lecocq, "Histoire," p. 147.

24. Lecocq, "Recherches sur les enseignes
de pèlerinages et les chemisettes de Notre-
Dame de Chartres" (*SAELM*, VI, 1873).

25. *CC*, I, ccxxviii ff.; Lépinois, I, 509.

men. Their professional organizations, the guilds, figure very conspicuously, as the modern visitor notices with astonishment, among the donors of the stained-glass windows of the reconstructed sanctuary. In fact, the five great windows in the chevet that honor the Virgin and are in a sense the most important of all were the gifts of merchants, principally the butchers and bakers.[26] These translucent compositions thus seem to have retained something of the emotions, of the sense of attachment to their cathedral, that animated the merchants and craftsmen of Chartres in 1194.

Without the great basilica their professional life would indeed have been hardly imaginable. The fairs of the Virgin were held in the *cloître* of Notre Dame, that is, in the immediately adjoining streets and squares that constituted the property of the chapter and stood under its jurisdiction. The dean guarded the peace and security of the fairs. Merchants erected their stands in front of the canons' houses. The three squares just outside the cathedral were the scenes of the most lively activity. Fuel, vegetables, and meat were sold by the southern portal of the basilica, textiles near the northern one.[27] At night strangers slept under the cathedral portals or in certain parts of the crypt.[28] Masons, carpenters, and other craftsmen gathered in the church itself, waiting for an employer to hire them. Even the selling of food in the basilica was not considered improper if carried on in an orderly fashion.[29] At one time the chapter had to forbid the wine merchants to sell their product in the nave of the church, but assigned part of the crypt for that purpose, thus enabling the merchants to avoid the imposts levied by the Count of Chartres on sales transacted outside.[30] The many ordinances passed by the chapter to prevent the loud, lusty life of the market place from spilling over into the sanctuary only show how inseparable the two worlds were in reality.

Even more revealing than these facts is the intimate interconnection between religious and economic elements in the corporate life of artisans and merchants. It was usual for medieval guilds to place themselves under the protection of a patron saint and to join in the regular observation of certain devotional practices. Elsewhere, however, these were entrusted to confraterni-

---

26. Delaporte and Houvet, *Les Vitraux de la cathédrale de Chartres*, pp. 464 ff.

27. Lépinois, I, 186 f.; Lecocq, "Histoire,"

p. 149; *CC*, I, lxxviii; Acloque, pp. 172 ff.

28. Acloque, p. 34.

29. Acloque, p. 253.

30. Bulteau, *Monographie*, I, 118.

ties that, although formed within and recruited from the membership of a given guild, maintained an independent existence.[31] In Chartres, however, guild and confraternity tended to merge. The heads of the guild also headed the confraternity. One treasury served both organizations, and it seems to have been impossible to join one without the other. It is of great interest that in Chartres several professions were originally organized as religious confraternities long before they received their statutes as guilds. In one of the windows in the chevet of the cathedral we see a banner with a red stocking, certainly the emblem of the hosiers, who became a sworn community only three centuries later.[32] Again, in the second chapel of the northern part of the ambulatory, a window is dedicated to St. Vincent by the linen weavers, who did not receive their first statutes until 1487. In the dedicatory inscription of the window they identify themselves as "confrères de St. Vincent," the patron saint of their profession.[33] Even the corporate life of the artisans of Chartres was thus rooted in a religious reality whose mainstay was the cathedral. Without the sanctuary, the corporate existence of Chartres was inconceivable.

This aspect of medieval life is foreign to our own outlook. We concede and appreciate the sincerity of religious convictions. But the penetration of such convictions into the world of business and politics is quite another matter. It has been suspected that invoking religious sanctions on behalf of such activities was hypocritical. And the expenditure of vast public effort and the resources of an entire community on a religious project seems equally incomprehensible. Compare the snail's pace at which, in our own large and opulent country, work progresses on the cathedrals at Washington, D. C., and Morningside Heights in New York with the building of Notre Dame of Chartres by a small community of less than 10,000 inhabitants within less than a generation; or compare our church-building ventures in their entirety with the incredible figure of eighty cathedrals and nearly five hundred abbeys that the Abbé Bulteau, usually a cautious historian, insists were built in France between 1180 and 1270. But then, we do not perceive the Virgin, as did the people of Chartres, invisibly yet radiantly enthroned in our midst. "If you are to get the full enjoyment of

---

31. For the following, see Acloque, pp. 54 ff.

32. The window was donated by a certain Gaufridus and his family; he may have occu-pied an important office in the confraternity of his profession. See Delaporte and Houvet, p. 469.

33. Delaporte and Houvet, pp. 319 ff.

Chartres," Henry Adams has written, "you must, for the time, believe in Mary as Bernard . . . did, and feel her presence as the architects did in every stone they placed, and every touch they chiseled."

This rapport with the supernatural explains the mood and the public effort that created the Cathedral of Chartres. The peculiar pattern of medieval life makes it quite likely that the community might not have survived the destruction of the relic of the Virgin; and the reconstruction of a sanctuary worthy of the Sacred Tunic was a task as inescapable as is the rebuilding of its hive for a colony of bees.

But the religious sentiment that demanded so great an undertaking also provided the means for its realization. It has recently been suggested that ecclesiastical building, from the viewpoint of economic history, was the most destructive undertaking of the Middle Ages; that the cathedrals ruined the economic health of the epoch.[34] As if the economic and spiritual forces of the time were antagonistic or could be conceived as independent of one another! In point of fact, ecclesiastical building opened up new natural resources, developed technical skills and insights, provided work for large numbers of people, and even created new professions.

In the cases of both St.-Denis and Chartres, the magnificent dressed stone of which these churches were built was yielded by quarries whose very existence had remained unknown until the determination to build had led to their discovery. In the technological sphere, the thirteenth century has been called an age of "great ideas rather than great deeds." [35] Yet the vaulting and buttressing of the great Gothic churches represented achievements that may well have given a fresh impulse to the science of statics (which begins its prodigious development at this very time) [36] and greatly widened the scope of the mason's

34. Lopez, "Économie et architecture médiévales, celà aurait-il tué ceci?" (A, VII, 1952). The criticism of sumptuous church building by Petrus Cantor—who died a Cistercian—is based primarily on ascetic considerations. The economic argument is incidental. The passage is printed in Coulton, Life in the Middle Ages, II, 26.

35. Feldhaus, Die Technik der Antike und des Mittelalters, p. 277.

36. The key figure in the history of medieval statics is Jordanus Nemorarius, about whose

identity almost nothing is known. Duhem, Les Origines de la statique, I, 97 ff., assigns the earliest treatise attributed to Jordanus to the twelfth century "at the latest." Straub, Geschichte der Bauingenieur-Kunst, pp. 59 ff., and Sarton, Introduction to the History of Science, III, 2, p. 613, both incline to place Jordanus' life—and the beginnings of medieval statics along with it—in the thirteenth century. According to Moody and Clagett, The Medieval Science of Weights, p. 14, Jordanus taught mathematics on the faculty of arts at Paris in

craft. This is even truer for the profession of the glazier. This craft might have honored the Apostle of France as its patron saint, inasmuch as the metaphysics of light produced translucent churches whose large glazed surfaces gave a sudden boost to the art and techniques of windowmaking.

Religious impulse was so all-pervading an element of medieval life that even the entire economic structure depended upon it. Almost static otherwise, the economy received from religious customs and experiences the impulse it needed for its growth. "At Chartres, the building of the cathedral attracted numerous artisans. Work on this enterprise . . . undoubtedly transformed the upper part of the town into one immense building site that occupied, directly or indirectly, an entire population of workers." [37]

But how were projects of such magnitude financed? A celebrated relic was a valuable object, even in financial terms. Emperor Baldwin II of Constantinople did not hesitate to offer the Crown of Thorns as security for a large loan; it was promptly accepted by the Venetians, who cannot be reproached for lack of business acumen.[38] The acquisition of a famed relic and the subsequent building of a sanctuary permitting its solemn exposition before large numbers of pilgrims represented, financially speaking, not a waste but a wise investment. Although this aspect of the cult of relics was not the most important one in the minds of those responsible, it certainly could not be ignored. The fantastic auction (no other term seems quite adequate) of the great booty of relics seized in 1204 by the crusaders in Constantinople, and the subsequent transfer of these relics to the religious centers of the West, offer a good example.[39] One of the relics was sent to Châlons-sur-Marne. It was expected that it would attract a great number of pilgrims and that these would leave substantial offerings in the sanctuary. This mere expectation was considered so sound as to be judged acceptable as collateral for a large loan, part of which was applied to the completion of the Cathedral of Châlons, part to the construction of the city bridge. Notre Dame of Chartres likewise received a gift

the early part of the thirteenth century. The authors call the *Liber de ratione ponderis*, which Duhem believed to be the work of a "gifted pupil," Jordanus' chef-d'oeuvre. They print it, along with the *Elementa super demonstrationem ponderum*, on pp. 127 ff., 174 ff.

37. Acloque, p. 10.

38. Cf. Rohault de Fleury, *Mémoire sur les instruments de la Passion de N.-S. J.-C.*, pp. 213 and 357 ff.

39. Cf. de Riant, "Des dépouillées religieuses enlevées à Constantinople au XIII⁰ siècle et des documents historiques nés de leur transport en Occident" (*SNAFM*, 4th series, VI, 1895).

out of the sacred hoard of Constantinople. Louis, Count of Chartres, purchased and sent to the cathedral the head of St. Anne, a relic that undoubtedly proved an incentive for additional donations to the building fund.[40]

What was the actual amount of these pious donations? Suger, as we have seen, obtained from this source the greater part of the resources required for the building of his new choir.[41] Another example is provided by the Abbey of St.-Trond in Belgium.[42] During the second half of the eleventh century the miracles that occurred at the tomb of the titular saint produced a flood of pilgrims. The donations they offered "exceeded by far," according to a later abbot of the house, "all the revenue then or now collected by the abbey." Contributions to the shrine of St. Thomas of Canterbury amounted in 1220, on the occasion of the translation of his relics, to nearly £1075, roughly the equivalent of the purchasing power of £43,000 in the early 1930's, according to Professor Coulton's rule of thumb.[43] Over a number of years the shrine of St. Thomas produced one fourth of the cathedral's annual revenues.

It was an added advantage that such income yielded by a popular relic hardly strained local resources but was mostly contributed by pilgrims from "abroad." And if an extraordinary event, such as the necessity or desire to rebuild the sanctuary sheltering the relic, called for extraordinary expenditure, the area to be drawn on for donations could be increased still further by sending the relics abroad on a fund-raising campaign. Early in the twelfth century the canons of Laon sent their relics as far as England in order to solicit building funds.[44] The relics of Chartres were taken abroad for the same purpose, in the

40. CC, I, 60.

41. See above, p. 91; Suger spent no more than 650 livres (roughly the equivalent of $208,000 [see below, n. 43]), not counting unnamed special donations by individuals, on the construction of his choir and crypt. See Aubert, Suger, p. 142.

42. For the following, see Cheney, "Church Building in the Middle Ages" (BJRL, XXXIV, 1951/52). On medieval building costs, see also Graham, "An Essay on English Monasteries" (Historical Association Pamphlet, CXII, 1939).

43. Coulton, "The Meaning of Medieval Moneys" (HAL, XCV, 1934). Needless to say, all such computations, as Coulton stresses, are at best but rough approximations. Other computations yield quite different figures. My

friend William Letwin and I have based our calculations on the average daily wage of an unskilled worker in early thirteenth-century France and present-day America. The former drew 6 d. (med.), the latter $8. (See d'Avenel, Histoire économique de la propriété . . . , III, 491.) On this basis, the dollar today would be the equivalent of $\frac{1}{320}$ livres tournois. I have assumed this rate wherever I have tried to give approximate modern equivalents of monetary values in medieval France. On some of the problems involved, however, see Blanchet and Dieudonné, Manuel de numismatique française, II, 95 ff., and Bloch, "L'Histoire des prix: quelques remarques critiques" (A, I, 1939).

44. Guibert of Nogent, De vita sua, III, 12 (PL, CLVI, 1113).

eleventh century when the Romanesque basilica was being built,[45] and again, as we shall presently see, after its destruction in 1194. If the relics worked miracles, their appeal was, of course, all the more effective. Early in the thirteenth century, after work on the west front of St. Albans had to be interrupted for lack of funds, the abbot organized a preaching tour through many dioceses. "He sent relics and also a cleric named Amphibalus whom the Lord had raised from the dead after four days, by the merits of St. Alban and St. Amphibalus, so that he might bear ocular evidence for the miracles of these saints." [46] We are told that a great deal of money was raised by this appeal.

From the thirteenth century the practice of indulgences provided additional possibilities for financing the reconstruction of a famous church with the help of contributions from abroad. In 1272, the Bishop of Regensburg took advantage of his presence at the Council of Lyons to persuade twenty-two of his fellow bishops, including those of distant Toledo and Compostela, to proclaim indulgences in their dioceses for those who gave money for the building of Regensburg Cathedral.[47] In representing the reconstruction of Notre Dame of Chartres as an act of penance that would earn spiritual rewards for all participants, the Cardinal of Pisa in 1194 may well have proclaimed what was in fact, if not in name, an indulgence in behalf of that project.[48]

As regards this cathedral, a relic as universally revered throughout Europe as was the Sacred Tunic not only demanded the speedy reconstruction of the destroyed sanctuary but was also bound to attract funds adequate for the execution of even the most grandiose plan. The age was indeed the age of the Virgin. Its most noble aspirations were directed to the cult of the Queen of Heaven. And the Cathedral of Chartres was her palace. No other town or diocese, it seems in retrospect, was at that or any other time better prepared, spiritually, politically, or economically, than was Chartres to erect a sanctuary that would have, as Guillaume le Breton wrote, no equal in Christendom.

Politically speaking, the See of Chartres was one of the "royal episco-

45. Bulteau, "Saint Fulbert et sa cathédrale" (SAELM, 1882, VII, 300).
46. Cheney.
47. See Janner, Die Bauhütten des deutschen Mittelalters, p. 180.

48. "The practice of indulgences began to expand during the thirteenth century." Leclercq, "La Consécration légendaire de la basilique de Saint-Denis et la question des indulgences" (RM, XXXIII, 1943).

pates" that had helped the kings of the Capetian dynasty so greatly to increase their ascendancy over France.[49] The counts of Chartres were certainly in a position to jeopardize that ascendancy. Thibault the Great was the ruler of Champagne as well as Chartres and Blois. A grandson of William the Conqueror, he was allied to England and Normandy, and we have seen how formidable an enemy of Louis VI and Louis VII he continued to be for many years. Under such conditions it was all the more important for the king to be able to nominate the bishop who was spiritual ruler of the count's capital and exerted as much political control over the town of Chartres as did the count himself.[50] The bishops appointed were, of course, loyal supporters of the king. Bishop Geoffrey, the builder of the west façade of Notre Dame, was so close a friend of Louis VI that Thibault the Great for some time prevented him from taking possession of his see.[51] Upon Geoffrey's death in 1149, Suger reminded the chapter of the loyalty that every bishop of Chartres owed to the king of France.[52]

The See of Chartres thus being in their hands, the Capetian rulers used it as a wedge to establish their power in hostile territory. Even when their relations with the counts of Chartres were strained, the kings held the *curia regis*, the Royal Assembly, not infrequently in this town.[53] And in 1150, when Suger convoked the assembly that was to decide on his plan for a Crusade, he chose Chartres as the site of the gathering that he had every reason to make as impressive and representative as possible.[54] It is a revealing fact that, at least since the mid-twelfth century, the popular epic names Chartres in one breath with Paris as one of the royal capitals and residences.[55]

49. See Newman, *Le Domaine Royal sous les premiers Capétiens*, p. 21; Imbart de la Tour, *Les Élections épiscopales dans l'église de France*, p. 424; Fawtier, *Les Capétiens et la France*, p. 71; Schwarz, "Der Investiturstreit in Frankreich" (*Zeitschrift für Kirchengeschichte*, XLII, 1923).

50. *CC*, I, xxiv; and for an interesting reflection of episcopal claims, see the *Vieille Chronique*, I, 2, 52.

51. Lépinois, I, 90.

52. *Oeuvres complètes de Suger*, pp. 256 f.

53. Luchaire, *Histoire des institutions monarchiques de la France sous les premiers Capétiens*, I. 254 ff.

54. *Recueils des historiens*, XV, 614, 523, 648. Cf. Luchaire, *Études sur les actes de Louis VII*, pp. 178 f., 247 f.

55. To give but a few examples: "Voist s'en en France, a Paris o a Chartres" (Langlois, ed., *Couronnement de Louis*, v. 2378); "Paris ne Chartres ne le cit d'Orellois" (*Le Chevalrie Ogier de Danemarche*, v. 11,185); "Que vos fussiés en France, a Paris u a Chartres" (Normand and Raynaud, eds., *Aiol*, v. 459). In the *Élie de Saint-Gilles* (Raynaud, ed., 45 ff.), Count Julian of St.-Gilles reproaches his son for not having departed as yet "pour Paris ou pour Chartres au service du roi Louis, fils de Charlemagne." See also "Si'st costume en

This political role of the town demanded the demonstration and symbolic display of royal authority. The Cathedral of Chartres, as its liturgy proves, was destined for the solemn enactment of those festive *curiae coronatae* in which the sovereign, to the exultant accompaniment of the *Laudes regiae*, appeared invested with the insignia of his royal power, the living embodiment of the Christlike dignity that his office bestowed upon him.[56] The munificence of the Capetian kings toward Notre Dame of Chartres was designed to underscore and enhance the importance of the basilica as a royal cathedral.

During the second half of the twelfth century, the relations between the houses of France and Chartres-Champagne gradually underwent a complete change. Louis VII appointed Thibault the Great's son, Thibault V, Grand Master and Seneschal of France. A few years later (1160) the king married the count's sister, Alix; and the subsequent birth of the future Philip Augustus united the two illustrious houses forever. In 1164 a brother of Thibault V, William, Cardinal of Champagne, was appointed to the episcopal see of Chartres. At the same time, the count married Adèle, a daughter of Louis VII by his previous marriage to Eleanor of Aquitaine. It was a significant implementation of the new alliance that in 1167 the troops of the count as well as those of his brother, the Bishop of Chartres, joined forces with Louis VII in his campaign against the King of England. The house of Chartres-Champagne, as its blood and fortunes merged with those of the French dynasty, reached the zenith of its power. When Philip Augustus, in 1188, departed for the Holy Land, he appointed a regency council composed of his mother, Alix of Champagne, Cardinal William, and his half-sister, Adèle, Countess of Chartres. France, it might be said, was momentarily ruled by the house of Chartres-Champagne.[57]

---

France a Paris et a Chartres" (Koschwitz, ed., *Charlemagne, Voyage à Jérusalem et à Constantinople*, p. 654). In the *chanson de geste* the king usually is called, not *roi de France*, "mais il est qualifié par les noms de lieux où il fait sa résidence" (Mayer, tr., *Girart de Roussillon*, p. lix). The frequent pairing of Paris and Chartres is significant. For further information concerning Chartres in the *chansons de geste*, see Langlois, *Table des noms propres . . . dans les chansons de geste.*

56. On the *curiae coronatae* and their significance, see Luchaire, *Manuel des institutions françaises*, p. 460; Schramm, *Der König von Frankreich*, p. 122; Kantorowicz, *Laudes Regiae*, pp. 92 ff. On the *Laudes* of Chartres, see Kantorowicz, *Laudes*, p. 100, and Prost, "Caractère et signification des quatre pièces liturgiques composées à Metz" (*SNAFM*, 4th series, V, 1874), p. 185.

57. Lépinois, I, 103 ff.

The prestige and prosperity of the See of Chartres could only profit from such close alliance of the king, the bishop, and the count. It was fortunate that this political constellation coincided with the reconstruction of the cathedral. The great sanctuary, as we shall see, bears eloquent testimony to the fact that the rulers of France and Chartres vied with one another in embellishing it. The particular interest and support the project received from Philip Augustus may be accounted for by the fact that the blood of both houses flowed in his veins. The bishop under whom the work on the new cathedral was begun was Renaud of Mouçon (1182–1217) of the family of the dukes of Bar. But he was also a nephew of the Queen of France and of the Cardinal of Champagne, since his mother had been a daughter of Thibault the Great.[58] Renaud's family connections as well as his skill as an administrator were of decisive importance in rendering the building of the basilica possible and in aligning his chapter in support of the undertaking. A word must be said of this body.

The chapter of Notre Dame was one of the most illustrious of the Middle Ages. "Li clerc nostre Dame de Chartres" became a synonym for a chapter equally distinguished by the birth of its prebendaries and their cultural achievements, by the splendor with which they enacted the liturgy, and by their possessions.[59] The ecclesiastical province of Chartres was at that time possibly the largest and wealthiest of France; even Rome referred to it simply as the "great diocese." Encompassing an area of 100 by 130 miles—911 parish churches, not counting those in the town of Chartres—its grain harvests and silver alone yielded the bishop the immense income of nearly $1,500,000 in modern money annually.[60] The total revenues of his chapter exceeded those of the bishop by far. The dean alone drew an income that would today be over $700,000 a year.[61]

58. GC, VIII, 1152.

59. Lépinois, I, 543; CC, I, xi.

60. CC, I, xiv, lxviii f., and Luchaire, La Société française au temps de Philippe Auguste, p. 156. The editors of CC base their estimate on an annual grain harvest of 796 muids (although the measure of the muid varies from province to province, it may be said to be roughly the equivalent of 35 hectoliters) and income from silver amounting to 1711 livres of Chartres. They calculate the bishop's income

from these two sources of revenue as amounting to 463,917f. 28c. (value of 1862); the ratio of the franc to the livre is given as 100 to 1. For the (more than tentative) method of computation I have used, see above, ch. 6, n. 43.

61. CC, I, lxxvii f., xcix ff.; Amiet, Essai sur l'organisation du Chapitre Cathédrale de Chartres, p. 43, where the dean's income is given as 2300 livres annually. It may be noted that the annual income of Louis VII is given as 228,000 livres; see Fawtier, p. 99.

If the treatise on the *Miracles of the Blessed Virgin* is to be believed, and in view of its authorship we have no reason to assume the opposite, the greater part of this enormous wealth was, in 1194 and for a period of three years, committed to the reconstruction of the cathedral. This far-reaching decision on the part of the chapter must have been greatly facilitated by the fact that, only a year before, the administration of its revenues had been taken out of the hands of the provosts (whose malfeasance had long provided both chapter and population with ample ground for complaint) to be placed directly under the authority of the chapter.[62] The measure is said to have nearly doubled the revenues of the prebendaries.[63] The reform had been initiated by the Cardinal of Champagne; it was completed by his nephew and successor, Renaud of Mouçon, whose relations with his chapter seem to have been generally excellent, and by the Cardinal of Pisa in his capacity as papal legate.[64] It is no wonder that both prelates met with sympathetic response on the part of the chapter when, after the great fire, they pleaded for extraordinary sacrifices for the sake of a new cathedral. But, of course, the canons themselves had a very palpable stake in this project. The cathedral was their property. They derived a sizable income from its altars.[65] This income could only be expected to increase as the fame of the sanctuary and its relics spread throughout the Christian world. The chapter's decision, in 1194, was thus, in budgetary terms, sound and even inevitable. The preceding administrative reform made it possible to raise a large sum almost at once. Even so, that decision must have involved grave deliberations.

How regrettable it is that we know nothing about their exact nature. What amount did the canons retain for their subsistence? The responsibilities of the medieval bishop and his chapter resemble in many respects those of a modern government. Revenues must be balanced against budgetary commitments that cannot be canceled from one day to the next, no matter what emergency may occur. By accident the record of a payment of something over 307 livres has survived, apparently but one installment of a regular obligation

62. *CC*, I, xxix ff.; I, 2, 188 ff., 225; II, 283 ff. The Chartres settlement was often used as a model. Cf. Fournier, p. 181 ff.

63. This assertion is made in the obituary of the Cardinal of Champagne (*CC*, III, 169).

64. *CC*, I, 2, 226.

65. *CC*, I, cvi f., lxxviii ff.

that the Bishop of Chartres paid, in 1202, to Philip Augustus' bailiff at Étampes.[66] At that time work on the cathedral was in full progress. The amount paid, nearly $100,000 in modern currency, compares very favorably with the sum of 200 livres that the same king offered a few years later to Notre Dame "for the building of the sanctuary." [67] Such regular obligations made it impossible for the bishop and chapter to shoulder the immense burden they assumed in 1194 for more than a few years.

But the chapter could count on the co-operation of the town, which had never been more prosperous than it was just then. "La vile esteit mult bone, de grant antiquité, Burgeis i aveit riches et d'aveir grant plente" ("The town was very good and of great antiquity, and there was a rich and opulent citizenry"), wrote Wace about Chartres in his Roman de Rou around 1160.[68] Textiles from Chartres were sold at the fairs of Fréjus in distant Provence.[69] In the same province harnesses and weapons from the city's famed armories competed with those of Edessa.[70] The wealth accruing from such transactions was never likely to evade the needs and admonitions of the medieval Church. Bishop Maurice of Sully, under whose administration Notre Dame of Paris was begun, in his famous sermons was wont to depict the devil as a merchant and to thunder against the rich that were unwilling to make charitable gifts.[71] Such admonitions were hardly needed in Chartres. We have seen how intimately the economic prosperity of the city was tied to the fame of Notre Dame. But just before the great fire an event occurred that highlighted the significance of the alliance between town and cathedral.

For many generations the canons had claimed and exerted the right of admitting into their domestic family any burgher of Chartres they chose. Those

66. See Lot, Le Premier budget de la monarchie française, le compte générale de 1202/3, p. 65.

67. Lépinois, I, 120: "ad opus edificationis ecclesiae." See the obituary of this king in the necrology of Notre Dame, where it is said that the deceased "istam precipue sanctam ecclesiam, speciali favoris gratia et quasi quodam amoris privilegio, fovit propensius et protegit, et quem habebat erga ipsam dilectionis affectum, multociens affectu operis comprobavit." CC, III, 138.

68. Andresen (ed.), Maistre Wace's Roman de Rou et des ducs de Normandie . . . , I, 6, vv. 818 f.

69. Laurent, Un Grand commerce d'exportation au moyen-âge: La draperie des Pays-Bas en France et dans les Pays Méditerranéens, pp. 67 ff.

70. Lépinois, I, 399. On other activities of the merchants of Chartres, see Acloque, pp. 184 ff.

71. Robson, Maurice of Sully and the Medieval Vernacular Homily, pp. 105, 136.

who thus became *avoués* of Notre Dame partook of the liberties of the *cloître;* that is, they enjoyed the valuable privilege of exemption from the jurisdiction as well as taxation of the count. The latter, of course, looked with hostility upon this custom which reduced his authority as well as his income and often led to close alliances between the canons and influential burghers anxious to evade the count's jurisdiction. Armed skirmishes, even invasions of the *cloître,* resulted. In each such case the chapter resorted to its spiritual weapons, interdict and excommunication, which proved invincible.[72]

In 1192, however, the dangerous situation developed into an acute crisis. Thibault V having been killed the previous year on crusade, the government of Chartres passed into the hands of his widow, Adèle, while her son, Louis, resided at Blois. This princess, the daughter of Louis VII, resolved to let the quarrel come to a head. There were acts of violence on both sides. The issue was appealed to Pope Urban III, who appointed the Queen Mother and the Cardinal of Champagne as arbiters. Their efforts were of no avail. But a new arbitration committee, appointed by the next pope, Celestine III, finally reached a decision that completely upheld the chapter and formally recognized its privileges in the matter of the *avoués.* The main parties to this struggle, the Dowager Countess Adèle and Bishop Renaud, were relatives, and the close alliance between the houses of France and Chartres prevented any more serious political issues being raised. While this fact may have facilitated acquiescence in the settlement on the part of the countess, it did not diminish the significance of the victory for the chapter, as well as for the town. The town was not recognized as a commune until a century later. The verdict in the matter of the *avoués,* as has been justly observed, opened for the town of Chartres the door that eventually led to municipal liberty. The verdict also proved the cathedral chapter to be the champion of that liberty.[73]

Pope Celestine appointed the arbitration committee four days before the great fire. The disaster that struck the cathedral found town and chapter in close alliance. Notre Dame had proved to be the source and mainstay of the town's freedom as well as of her prosperity. The townspeople had every reason to make the rebuilding of the cathedral their own cause.

But the contributions of the royal house, the count, the people, and the

72. *CC,* I, cxxix f.; Lépinois, I, 125 ff.          73. *CC,* I, 2, 227 ff.; Lépinois, I, 116 ff.

bishop and chapter of Chartres did not yet suffice to bring the great edifice to completion. Additional funds were raised with the help of the cathedral's relics. The procedure is again reflected in the treatise of the *Miracles of the Blessed Virgin.* At the end of the three-year period during which bishop and chapter had underwritten most of the building expenditures, a financial crisis developed, so acute that it was not even possible to pay the wages of the workers currently engaged on the building. According to the author of the treatise, the emergency subsided when a new wave of enthusiasm was kindled by a series of miracles through which Our Lady made manifest "that she had indeed chosen Chartres as her special residence" and "wanted her church to be rebuilt with incomparable magnificence." [74] This time contributions for the basilica were solicited and received far away from Chartres. The chapter sent relics accompanied by preachers abroad in an attempt to raise additional funds. The *Miracles of the Blessed Virgin* was probably written for the same purpose. Devotion to the Virgin of Chartres spread all over France and even beyond it. We hear of a knight from Aquitaine whom she protected in battle; [75] of a young scholar from London, who, upon returning home after completing his studies in France, happened to enter a church where a preacher was just delivering a sermon on behalf of the new sanctuary of Chartres. The youth was so moved that after an inner struggle he parted with the only valuable he possessed, a golden necklace he had meant to take home for the girl he loved; he gave it instead to Our Lady.

Even Richard the Lionhearted heard of this episode and of the vision of the Virgin the young man was said to have had after he had offered his donation. The king too was touched. "Although then at war with the King of

74. *Mirac.*, pp. 510 f. "Verum ad tanti structuram operis laicorum munera vel auxilia nequaquam sufficerent nisi [ut] episcopus et canonici tantam, et supra dictum est, ex propriis redditibus tribus annis pecuniam contulissent; quod siquidem, transa[u]cto eodem triennio, omnibus manifestum apparuit, cum omnis subito pecunia defecisset, ita ut qui preerant operi quod daretur operariis non haberent, aut quid dari posset de cetera non viderent . . . humano penitus deficiente auxilio, cum necessarium esset adesse divinum, beata Dei genetrix novam et incomparabilem

ecclesiam sibi colens fabricari ad facienda ibidem miracula, ejusdem filii sui potentiam meritis suis et precibus incitavit . . ."

75. *Mirac.*, pp. 526 f. Even the cult of relics apart, there was nothing unusual in thus soliciting contributions abroad for church building. Bishop Geoffrey I of Coutances (1049–93) sent his emissaries as far as Apulia and Calabria in order to approach Robert Guiscard and other Norman notables in this region. See Mortet and Deschamps, *Recueil de textes relatifs à l'histoire de l'architecture et à la condition des architectes en France au moyen-âge,* I, 73.

France," he received the emissaries from Chartres with great kindness, insisted "like another David" that he himself carry the chasse containing the sacred relic that the clerics had brought along, and granted them safe conduct throughout his kingdom.[76] The material success of this journey may be attested by a window of the cathedral donated by Stephen Langton, Archbishop of Canterbury.[77]

As a whole, however, Notre Dame of Chartres is a national monument. Bishop Fulbert had obtained contributions for the Romanesque basilica from Knut, King of England and Denmark, from the dukes of Normandy and Aquitaine.[78] Later a tower had been donated by William the Conqueror. And early in the twelfth century, at a time when his relations with King Philip of France were strained, Yves of Chartres secured substantial contributions from Henry I of England and his queen for the "preservation and embellishment" of the basilica.[79] Again, the Abbey of St.-Denis, according to Suger, was built with the donations of princes and prelates. He has not found it necessary to mention the innumerable lesser benefactors whose offerings on the feasts of St.-Denis helped to raise his church. But a century later, the nave and façade of Strassburg Cathedral were built by the burghers only, who were hostile to the bishop and chapter and allowed them no share in the project.

The Gothic Cathedral of Chartres was the work of France and of all France, as no other great sanctuary had been before. The cathedral windows bear magnificent testimony to the national effort.[80] I have mentioned those contributed by the guilds. Along with them appear the ancient feudal houses of the Île-de-France as donors: Courtenay, Montfort, Beaumont, Montmorency.[81] The counts of Chartres, but especially the royal house, made great con-

76. *Mirac.*, pp. 528 ff.
77. Bulteau, *Monographie*, I, 121.
78. Bulteau, "Saint Fulbert," pp. 294 ff.
79. Bulteau, *Monographie*, I, 66 ff.
80. This general sense of attachment to Notre Dame of Chartres is attested elsewhere. On the cover of the cathedral necrology (Bibliothèque de Chartres, No. 1032), which was begun in 1124, there were represented "on one hand, choirs of angels, apostles, martyrs, confessors, and virgins; on the other hand, the image of the blessed Virgin with

pontiffs, clerks, knights, burghers, and peasants on her left, and kings, queens, burghers, and peasants on her right." The inscription on the left read: "Pontifes, clerus, cum militibus dare proni, Undique dona ferunt burgenses atque coloni"; and on the right: "Reges, regine pariter sua munera donant, Dant et matrone, que burgi, que quoque ruris." Merlet and Clerval, *Un Manuscrit chartrain du XIᵉ siècle*, p. 141.
81. Delaporte and Houvet, pp. 439 ff.

tributions.[82] The entire composition in the northern façade, consisting of the rose and lancet windows and exalting Mary and her Biblical ancestors, was given by Queen Blanche, the mother of St. Louis. All corresponding windows in the opposite transept were donated by Peter of Dreux, Duke of Brittany.[83]

The splendor and ostentation of this contribution have always aroused a good deal of speculation. What prompted this gift which seems almost designed to surpass that of the French queen? The house of Dreux was a side branch of the Capetian dynasty, Peter a great-grandson of Louis VI. Having acquired Brittany by his marriage to the heiress, Alix of Thouars, he set out to raise the power of the duchy at the very time when the other great feudal dynasties— the duchies of Aquitaine and Normandy (the duke of which had once been the suzerain of the ruler of Brittany), the counties of Toulouse, Champagne, and Flanders—were succumbing one by one to the irresistible progress of Capetian power. Peter owed his dukedom to Philip Augustus; his schemes do not seem to have disturbed the king, and until the monarch's death in 1223 Peter remained generally loyal to the monarchy.[84]

No other French prince of his time could have entertained the idea of appearing, along with the royal house, as the main benefactor of Notre Dame of Chartres. It was, in any event, excellent political propaganda, as we would call it, not the less, perhaps, because there existed in Chartres an influential and prosperous colony of Bretons, whose members lent enthusiastic support to the reconstruction of the cathedral.[85] Prior to his donation of the transept windows, where his portrait, along with those of his wife and children, appeared below the figures of prophets and evangelists, Peter had also given the statuary of the great southern portal: his image and that of Alix of Thouars appear under the feet of the statue of Christ in the central *trumeau*.[86] The decision to enrich each end of the transept by three sculptured portals and porches did not form part of the original design for the cathedral. It was reached so late that it became necessary to cut back the already completed

82. Delaporte and Houvet, pp. 475 ff., 493 ff.

83. Delaporte and Houvet, pp. 431 ff.

84. See Painter, *The Scourge of the Clergy, Peter of Dreux, Duke of Brittany*.

85. *Mirac.*, p. 522; Bulteau, *Monographie*, I, 125 f.

86. Not "over the head of the central Christ," as Painter, p. 31, erroneously states. Bulteau, II, 292.

buttresses of the façades.[87] To what extent was this change of plan made possible by the munificence of Peter of Dreux? He had only acquired his duchy in 1212, and his great donation to Notre Dame of Chartres seems to have been among the first acts of his government. Philip Augustus, to whom he owed his sudden ascendancy, had the sanctuary much at heart; by the contribution he made to its embellishment, Peter may have wished to express his loyalty to the sovereign, as well as his loyalty to the Queen of Heaven.

For this public demonstration of his piety and prestige Peter may well have chosen the most imposing place the cathedral offered. Erler has proved that the southern transept and portal of the Cathedral of Strassburg served, during the thirteenth century, as the setting and backdrop for courts of law convoked and presided over by the bishop in his capacity as spiritual and secular lord of the town; here and elsewhere, representations of the Last Judgment were designed to remind judge, defendants, and witnesses of the eternal source of the bishop's judicial power and of the eternal principles of justice to which the verdict of the human judge must be attuned.[88] The spacious southern porch of Chartres Cathedral may well have served the same purpose, and the Judgment scene in the tympanum, donated by Peter of Dreux, may have addressed itself to man's concern with justice as well as to his hope for redemption. According to a medieval legal text, quoted by Erler, a representation of the Last Judgment is to be placed in the courtroom because "wherever the judge sits in judgment, there, and in the same hour, God is sitting in his divine judgment above the judge and the jury."

87. Cf. Grodecki, "The Transept Portals of Chartres Cathedral: The Date of Their Construction According to Archeological Data" (*AB*, XXIII, 1951).

88. See Erler, *Das Strassburger Münster im Rechtsleben des Mittelalters*, and Gall's review in *Kunstchronik*, VII, 1954, pp. 315 f.

# 7. THE CATHEDRAL OF CHARTRES

A LARGE part of the preceding chapter has been devoted to the economic aspects of cathedral building, especially to the economic aspects of the building of Chartres Cathedral. The material effort does not explain the artistic achievement. But it does reflect the significance of the great project for all those whose contributions made its realization possible. Our willingness to part with material possessions for the sake of values other than material provides something like a crude yardstick by which we can measure the relevance of spiritual matters for our life and our experience. The building of a cathedral like Notre Dame of Chartres required an economic effort far greater than that demanded by any other public project of the Middle Ages. In our own time, no work of art, religious or otherwise, has an importance that is even remotely comparable to that which compelled an entire generation to pour its energies and resources into the construction of the cosmos of stone that, between 1194 and 1220, rose gradually and breathtakingly above the town of Chartres.[1]

The mood, the expectation, the suspense of the audience before the curtain rises represent the specific challenge that confronts the artist. They set the standard that his work has to meet. Our own indifference and lack of expectation are to be blamed for the boredom, interrupted by attempts to arouse the public's attention with the help of cheap visual tricks, that characterizes most monumental architecture today. We no longer expect, and are not prepared for, the overwhelming experience of a consummate work of architecture. Consider, on the other hand, the responsibility of the master builder of Chartres.

1. It is generally assumed that the construction proceeded from west to east and was in the main completed by 1220. See Mâle, *Notre-Dame de Chartres*, p. 34; and Grodecki, "The Transept Portals of Chartres Cathedral: The Date of Their Construction According to Archeological Data" (*AB*, XXIII, 1951), p. 157, who refutes Bulteau's contention (*Monographie de la Cathédrale de Chartres*, I, 112) that the choir was completed in 1198. The question, however, remains unsettled.

The emotions that the great fire of 1194 had kindled, the sacrifices of the entire community, the demand for a new sanctuary of incomparable splendor—all these had to be satisfied by the architect's achievement. The cathedral had to surpass all others not only in the eyes of human beings; the Queen of Heaven herself demanded that its beauty be commensurate with the rank she had bestowed upon Chartres Cathedral as her "special chamber."

The task would appear staggering, or rather preposterous, to a modern architect. Not so for the medieval builder. The expectations of his public, its notions of what the new church was to be like, were probably vague and even inarticulate. They nevertheless limited the alternatives of his design and indeed provided him with something like a general outline for it. In some respects, the vision of the medieval cathedral resembles a great popular myth. The architect, like the Greek or even the Elizabethan dramatists, did not have to invent the "myth" but to give it concrete expression. "All art," the Irish dramatist John Synge has written, "is a collaboration." That applies to the cathedral as well. Its architect had to give expression to an image that he shared with his generation and that the long religious tradition of his people had gradually shaped.

That tradition the master of Chartres accepted quite literally as the basis for his design. His own work rose upon the foundations of the destroyed cathedral. That earlier church, built by Bishop Fulbert in the first third of the eleventh century, we know relatively well. The crypt, which is as large as the church above it, and excavations conducted during the last century, enable us to determine the ground plan of the eleventh-century edifice.[2] But we know even its elevation, thanks to the singular good fortune by which a "portrait" of Fulbert's church, painted soon after its completion, has survived. The municipal library of St.-Étienne (Loire) has long possessed an eleventh-century manuscript written for the Cathedral Chapter of Chartres, containing the obituary of this church.[3] The names of its deceased members and benefactors have been inscribed in a calendar under the dates of their deaths. In the case of more important personages, brief obituary notices follow the entries. These obit-

2. Cf. Lefèvre-Pontalis, "Le Puits des Saints-Forts et les cryptes de la Cathédrale de Chartres" (*BM*, LXVII, 1903).

3. For the following, see Merlet and Clerval, *Un Manuscrit chartrain du XIᵉ siècle*, pp. 47 ff. The manuscript has recently been returned to Chartres.

uaries were read during the canonical office of prime in the place where the liturgy calls first for the recital of the names of the saints who are commemorated on that particular day, and second for a prayer on behalf of deceased members and benefactors of the community. Our manuscript, therefore, contains not only the obituaries of these persons but also a martyrology or list of the saints commemorated by the church of Chartres in the course of the liturgical year. And it is here, after the date of April 10, the date of Bishop Fulbert's death, that a disciple of his, a certain Sigon, has ordered a *tumulus*, a kind of illustrated eulogy of the dead, to be inserted.

This *tumulus* seems to have contained originally the obituary, in which Fulbert is hailed as the builder of the cathedral, as well as three large miniatures, of which only one has survived. It is this one, however, representing the bishop as he addresses his flock in the cathedral, that contains the portrait of the Romanesque church. We know the author of this miniature as well as its date. The inscription mentions that Andrew of Mici, probably a monk at St.-Mesmin at Mici, near Orléans, has painted the picture. He undoubtedly started the *tumulus* immediately after Fulbert's death in 1028; and, since his miniature shows the cathedral without the transept that was added after a fire that occurred in 1030, his work must have been completed before then.[4]

Andrew of Mici has given us a remarkably accurate picture of the Romanesque cathedral despite the fact—or perhaps because of it—that he tried to represent at the same time both its external and internal appearances. His "portrait" of Notre Dame and the archaeological evidence complement each other perfectly. Fulbert's church was a three-aisled basilica, the clerestory as well as the side aisles amply illuminated by rows of windows. It had no transept; an ambulatory with three radiating chapels surrounded the apse. These as well as the apse were covered by a half dome and illuminated by windows (although Andrew's painting is not entirely clear on this point). In addition to this information furnished by the miniature, we know through documentary evidence that the nave was not vaulted but covered with a trussed wooden roof destroyed by the fire of 1030. Of the two towers represented in Andrew's painting, the one to the north of the sanctuary may have

*Plate 30*

4. "Ultimus in clero Fulberti nomine Sigo/Andree manibus hec pinxit Miciacensis." Merlet and Clerval, p. 51.

been a remainder of the Carolingian building. However, the recent excavations conducted by Étienne Fels have yielded evidence that the basilica of the eleventh century was equipped with a monumental western porch and tower not unlike that of St.-Benoit-sur-Loire.

The fire of 1030 destroyed only the upper portions of Fulbert's church and does not seem to have touched its eastern parts. But in the course of the repairs that had become necessary, Bishop Thierry added two slightly protruding transepts.[5] During the latter part of the eleventh century and in the course of the twelfth, the cathedral underwent a number of slight modifications. Three porches were added to the west façade and to the northern and southern façades. We have seen in the preceding chapter how the present west façade was constructed after 1134. To join it with Fulbert's church, the side aisles of the latter were prolonged westward and a narthex, consisting of three vaulted aisles and as wide as the nave, was erected in front of the nave and behind the three sculptured portals of the west façade. The upper floor of this narthex was lighted by three stained-glass windows that are still among the most beautiful of the cathedral.[6]

Only these western parts of the cathedral escaped the great fire of 1194. All the rest seems to have perished in that disaster. But the old sanctuary was still to live on in the design of the new. Despite the delight that medieval builders took in rejuvenating, enlarging, or even reconstructing their churches, a sentiment of reverent awe prevented them from obliterating all vestiges of the old sanctuary. Suger hesitated to demolish the walls of the Carolingian church, which were said to have been consecrated by Christ himself. Crypts, especially those parts that were hallowed by the remains of martyrs or other relics deposited there, were particularly sacrosanct. The architect of Chartres Cathedral has taken extraordinary care to preserve the dimensions of the Romanesque church and to adapt his own edifice to the contours of Fulbert's crypt, even though it proved most difficult, as we shall see, to reconcile the old structure with the new Gothic vision of what a great sanctuary should look

5. Merlet and Clerval, pp. 65 f. and 80 f.

6. See Lefèvre-Pontalis, "Les Façades successives de la Cathédrale de Chartres au XIᵉ et au XIIᵉ siècles" (*SAELM*, XIII, 1904; *CA*, *Chartres*, 1900), and "Les Architectes et la construction des cathédrales de Chartres" (*SNAFM*, 7th series, IV, 1905); Aubert, "Le Portail Royal et la façade occidentale de la Cathédrale de Chartres" (*BM*, C, 1941). See above, p. 148, n.29.

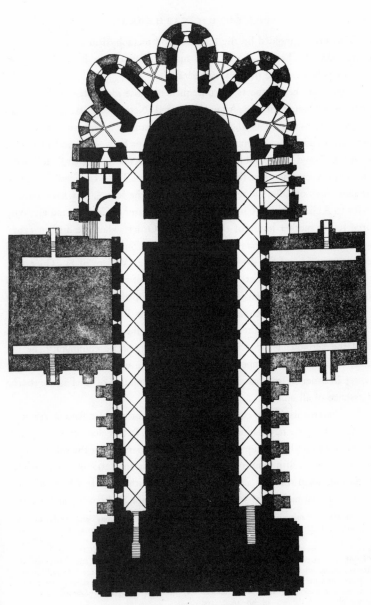

*Fig. 7. Chartres Cathedral. Ground plan*

Romanesque cathedral in black, Gothic edifice in light gray,
twelfth-century additions in dark gray

like. This vision, molded by the religious and metaphysical ideas of the age, the architect of Chartres shared with his contemporaries; it "collaborated" with him as he designed the new cathedral.

In their aesthetic aspects or consequences those ideas presented the consistent development of the Augustinian and Neoplatonic trends that had emerged so powerfully in the mid-twelfth century. In subsequent decades these trends had gradually converged. The affinities between them had always been marked, and innumerable personal ties connected St. Bernard's followers with the main exponents of the School of Chartres. Thus, to mention but two examples, Alan of Lille, the renowned disciple of the school, may have acted as adviser to Abbot Peter of Cîteaux at the Third Lateran Council, and certainly retired to the mother house of the Cistercian Order, where he died in 1202.[7] Isaac, abbot of the Cistercian monastery of Stella, on the other hand, who had been a companion of St. Bernard and the austere William of St.-Thierry at Cîteaux and Pontigny, where he absorbed much of their mysticism, was also imbued with Neoplatonism. His sermons contain allusions to the *Timaeus;* he shows himself to be strongly influenced by the Pseudo-Areopagite and at the same time by the mathematizing method of the School of Chartres.[8] In one of the sermons Isaac delivered before his monastic community, he expounds "measure and number and weight" as the unifying principles of the universe in order to lead his monks to the contemplation of God as the source and essence of all unity.[9]

In Chartres itself, we can trace the survival of the Neoplatonic tradition to the time when the new cathedral was being built. In this element of continuity the school was perhaps unique. The intellectual character of the other French schools of the twelfth century depended upon the interests and personalities of their individual teachers and usually changed with them. In Chartres it was the tradition that molded its scholars.[10] This tradition, Platonizing and focusing

---

7. On Alan, see above, p. 32, n. 28

8. Isaac was abbot of Stella from 1147; his successor is not mentioned until 1169; see *HLF*, XXII. Bliemetzrieder, "Isaac de Stella" (*RTAM*, IV, 1932), traces the influences of Plato's *Timaeus*, the Pseudo-Areopagite, and the School of Chartres in Isaac's work. For a not altogether convincing attempt to connect his thought with the art of his time, see Grinnell, "Iconography and Philosophy in the Crucifixion Window at Poitiers" (*AB*, XXVIII, 1946).

9. *Sermo* XXI (*PL*, CXCIV, 1760).

10. See Paré, Brunet, and Tremblay, *La Renaissance du XIIe siècle. Les écoles et l'enseignement*, p. 30; Poole, *Illustrations of the History of Medieval Thought and Learning*, pp. 95 ff.

around mathematical and musical studies, had been established as early as the eleventh century by Bishop Fulbert, whom his disciples compared with Socrates and Pythagoras.[11] It reached its fullest efflorescence, as we have seen, in the twelfth century. True, with the death of Thierry the time of the great chancellors of the Cathedral School was over. But the bishops who governed the see and the school during the second half of the century were, as Clerval remarks, among the most erudite Chartres had ever had.[12] Let us take a brief glance at these men.

Bishop Geoffrey's immediate successor was his nephew, Gosselin of Musy (1148–55). A man of scholarly and artistic inclinations, he was possibly responsible for the completion of the west façade of Notre Dame.[13] The next bishop, Robert le Breton (d. 1164) may have lived to see the *vieux clocher* completed. He took an active interest in the embellishment of his cathedral and cultivated the ancient musical tradition of his see.[14] With his follower, William, Cardinal of Champagne, we are already acquainted. John of Salisbury describes him as the most magnificent French prelate of his day. A brilliant pupil of Peter the Lombard, William employed his almost unlimited wealth and influence to support and encourage many eminent men of letters.[15] Among these was Walter of Châtillon, one of the great poets of his century and equally renowned as a teacher. Walter paid eloquent tribute to the mathematical aesthetics of his time:

> Creatori serviunt omnia subjecta,
> sub mensura, numero, pondere perfecta.
> Ad invisibilia, per haec intellecta,
> sursum trahit hominem ratio directa.[16]

11. Clerval, *Les Écoles de Chartres au moyen-âge*, pp. 29 ff.; Haskins, *The Renaissance of the Twelfth Century*, pp. 15 f.

12. Clerval, pp. 274 f.; Haskins, *Renaissance*, p. 276.

13. *CC*, III, 32 f.; Clerval, pp. 153 ff. That his name was Gosselin of Musy, rather than of Lèves, was established by Merlet, *Dignitaires de l'église Notre-Dame de Chartres*, pp. xv, 230.

14. His obituary (*CC*, III, 180) mentions several architectural undertakings and artistic donations by Robert. In the cathedral he had the pavement at the entrance to the choir

"mirifice" repaired. See also Fisquet, *La France pontificale. Chartres*, p. 92; Clerval, pp. 274 ff.

15. See *HLF*, XV, 505 ff.; above, p. 174; Clerval, pp. 274 ff. The austere William of St.-Thierry and the humanist Walter of Châtillon, Peter of Poitiers, and Peter of Blois all dedicated works to the cardinal.

16. Wright (ed.), *The Latin Poems Commonly Attributed to Walter Mapes*, p. 32; on the attribution to Walter of Châtillon, see Wilmart, "Poèmes de Gautier de Châtillon" (*RB*, XLIX, 1937), and Curtius, *European Literature and*

William was succeeded by John of Salisbury (1176–78), the most famous of all the bishops of Chartres. John did more than any of them to keep alive the great tradition of the first half of the century. He was familiar with the teachings of Thierry of Chartres and, through his own teacher, William of Conches, with those of Thierry's older brother and predecessor, Bernard, whom John calls "the most perfect Platonist" of his century.[17] But the broad and cultured humanism of John of Salisbury—he made no secret of his respect for Abelard [18] —did not preclude his admiration for the more austere religious trend that emanated from Cîteaux and Clairvaux. In describing the momentous encounter between St. Bernard and Gilbert de la Porrée at the Synod of Reims, John characterizes the antagonists with an almost Homeric impartiality: the grave Bishop of Poitiers, the most learned man of his time; and the abbot of Clairvaux, whose eloquence, John thinks, had been unequaled since Gregory the Great.[19]

We have no record of John's views on religious art. In musical matters he was, as Webb observes, in sympathy with the Cistercian movement.[20] But

the Latin Middle Ages, pp. 501 ff. Walter was born in 1135 at the latest, studied in Paris and Reims, and subsequently headed the School of Laon; later he was made a canon of Reims Cathedral and went from there to the court of Henry II Plantagenet. As the king's emissary, he journeyed to England in 1166. Later we find Walter as a teacher in Châtillon and in Bologna and Rome. The Cardinal of Champagne appointed him his notary and public orator, and later secured for him a canonry at Amiens. According to his epitaph, "perstrepuit modulis Gallia tota." Walter's poems have been edited by Strecker, Die Gedichte Walters von Châtillon, and Moralisch-Satirische Gedichte Walters von Châtillon. See Manitius, Geschichte der lateinischen Literatur des Mittelalters, III, 920 ff.; Raby, History of Secular Latin Poetry in the Middle Ages, II, 190 ff. On Walter's influence upon, and relations to, Alan of Lille, see Huizinga, "Über die Verknüpfung des Poetischen mit dem Theologischen bei Alanus de Insulis" (Mededeelingen der Akademie van Weetenschappen, Afdeeling Letterkunde, LXXIV, 1932). For interesting evidence of the esteem in which Walter's works were held by the Cistercians at the end of the twelfth century, see Wilmart,

Gautier de Châtillon; and, on the anonymous English Cisterican of the late twelfth century who quotes from Walter's Alexandreis, Pitra, Spicilegium Solesmense, II, xxv ff.; III, 467.

17. Metalogicus, IV, 35 (PL, CIC, 938). On John's education, see Clerval, pp. 317 ff.; Paré, Brunet, and Tremblay, p. 30; Poole, "The Masters of the School of Paris and Chartres in John of Salisbury's Time" (EHR, XXV, 1920), and Illustrations, pp. 101, 176 ff. He was a friend of John Sarracenus, the translator of the Pseudo-Areopagite, who dedicated to him one of his translations. Cf. PL, CIC, 143, 161 ff., 259. On John's library, see CC, III, 201.

18. "Clarus doctor et admirabilis omnibus praesidebat" he calls Abelard, under whom he had once studied. Metalogicus, II, 10 (PL, CIC, 867); Poole, "Masters."

19. Historia Pontificalis (ed., R. L. Poole, Oxford, 1927), ch. 12, p. 27.

20. Webb, John of Salisbury, p. 26. Liebeschuetz, Medieval Humanism in the Life and Writings of John of Salisbury, p. 27, stresses the Platonic element in John's attitude toward music. In insisting on the ethical value of music John shows himself a pupil of Boethius; see De musica I, 1 (PL, LXIII, 1169 f.).

his criticism of an overelaborate church music springs from a Platonic interpretation of the nature and power of music. Music, he observes, embraces the universe, reconciling the dissident and dissonant multitude of beings by the law of proportion: "by this law the heavenly spheres are harmonized, the cosmos as well as man governed." It is the Boethian notion of a triple music, cosmic, human, and instrumental. With the traditional reference to David playing before Saul (which we also encounter in St. Bernard), John of Salisbury invokes the authority of Plato, "the prince of philosophy," for the theory that "the soul is said to be composed of musical consonances." Nothing therefore is more apt than music, the proper kind of music, to educate and elevate the soul, and to direct it toward the worship of God. Even the Church triumphant, in the choirs of angels and saints, renders symphonic praise to the Lord.[21]

To the reader all these thoughts will sound familiar. They resume the musical metaphysics of Plato and Augustine. And they do not represent the ideas of a philosopher only. The impact of metaphysics and theology upon the actual practice and theory of music is evident throughout the twelfth and thirteenth centuries and accounts for the dominant role assigned to the three Pythagorean consonances.[22] John of Grocheo (c. 1280) explains their preeminence with a reference to the Trinity. Since, moreover, musical writers of the Gothic age explicitly compare music and architecture because of the cosmic applicability of the laws of harmony,[23] we may assume that the Platonizing

21. "Disciplina quidem liberalis est . . . virtutis suae potentiae, specierumque varietate, et sibi famulantibus numeris, universa complectitur, omnium quae sunt et quae dicuntur, dissidentem et dissonam multitudinem proportionum suarum, id est inaequali quaedam aequitatis lege concilians. Hac etenim coelestia temperantur mundana sive humana reguntur . . ." Policraticus, I, 6 (PL, CIC, 401).
22. For the decisive role of the three perfect consonances in medieval music, to the end of the thirteenth century, see Coussemaker, Histoire de l'harmonie au moyen-âge, pp. 8 f. and 36 ff.; Wolf, "Die Musiklehre des Johannes de Grocheo" (Sammelbände der Internationalen Musikgesellschaft, I, pp. 69 ff.); Reese, Music in the Middle Ages, pp. 294 ff., 446. For the metaphysical background of this preference for the perfect consonances, see Spitzer, "Classical and Christian Ideas of World Harmony"

(Traditio, II, 1944; III, 1945), and Bukofzer, "Speculative Thinking in Medieval Music" (Speculum, XVII, 1942).
23. Professor Gerstenberg, of the University of Tübingen, calls my attention to the two following passages, where music is compared to architecture: John of Grocheo (c. 1280), Theoria (Wolf, ed.), p. 108; and Speculum musicae by Jacobus of Liége (see above, ch. 2, n. 53), SSM, II, 386: "Quis enim sine tenore discantat, quis sine fundamento edificat? Et sicut edificium debet proportionari fundamento [an interesting reflection of the architectural practice of "taking the elevation from the ground plan"!] ut fiat edificium non ad libitum operatoris, sed secundum exigentiam fundamenti, sic nec discantans ad libitum suum notas proferre debet . . ." For twelfth-century references to the affinity between architecture and music, see above, p. 125.

views John of Salisbury expresses about music applied equally to architecture, attesting the vitality of a tradition that we have traced earlier. Its survival, at the end of the twelfth century, in the School of Chartres is further confirmed by John's pupil, Peter of Blois.[24]

John's immediate successor as Bishop of Chartres was Peter, abbot of Celle, and subsequently of St.-Remi at Reims.[25] He was, like Suger, a Benedictine abbot with a passionate interest in architecture. Between 1170 and 1180 he rebuilt the choir and western part of St.-Remi and seems, again like Suger, to have intended eventually to rebuild the entire church.[26] Unlike the abbot of St.-Denis, however, he was not concerned with political affairs and unlike John of Salisbury, his intimate friend, he was no humanist. A famed preacher, he was a man of ascetic and mystical leanings who considered himself a disciple of St. Bernard. He so calls himself in a letter soliciting the continued friendship and advice of the Cistercian community after he had been

24. John of Salisbury has on occasion administered a gentle rebuke to the geometrical speculations of the older theologians of Chartres: "Opinor ideo cum qui illam veram unitatem considerare desiderat, mathematica consideratione praetermissa, necesse est ad intelligentiae simplicitatem animus sese erigat." *De Sept. Septenis*, VII (*PL*, CIC, 961). Such criticism has close parallels in the writings of Alan of Lille (see above, ch. 5, n. 43), and in those of John's friend, Peter of Celle (see below, p. 194). A similar criticism of the exaggerated study of the quadrivium, from the pen of John's pupil, Peter of Blois (*PL*, CCVII, 231, 311 ff.), is, according to Clerval, pp. 294 ff., 317 ff., an indication of the intellectual situation that prevailed in the Cathedral School of Chartres even around 1200. Peter of Blois and his younger namesake are both figures of singular interest. The older Peter, who became preceptor of William the Good of Sicily, and later chancellor of this realm, never ceased dreaming of a return to Chartres. But John of Salisbury as well as Renaud of Mouçon bitterly disappointed him by refusing him a canonry. He finally passed into the service of Henry II and became Archdeacon of Bath. It is through men of his type that the thought and culture of Chartres were diffused throughout Europe. The younger Peter, who was master of the School and Canon

of Chartres, embodied the enlightened humanism of his time: "un lettré si passionné pour l'antiquité profane et qui professait un dédain si singulier pour les lettres sacrées." Hauréau, *Mémoire sur quelques chanceliers de l'école de Chartres*, 31, 2. It is significant that such a man could be a canon of Notre Dame. As for John of Salisbury, the extent of his Platonism appears in *Policraticus*, VII (*PL*, CIC, 645 f.), where the thought of Plato, entirely in the spirit of the older masters of Chartres, is found to be in accord with the Biblical account of the Creation.

25. See *HLF*, XIV, 236 ff.; Fisquet, p. 105 f.; Clerval, pp. 274 ff.; and above all Leclercq, *La Spiritualité de Pierre de Celle*. Peter belonged to one of the most distinguished families of Champagne; his cousin, Agnes of Braine, married in second marriage Robert of France, Count of Dreux, a brother of Louis VII and grandfather of the Peter of Dreux of whom I have spoken earlier. Peter of Celle received his education at St.-Martin-des-Champs. The Archbishop of Canterbury and the Bishop of Paris invited Peter to preach in their cathedrals.

26. On St.-Remi, see the article by Demaison (*CA, Reims*, 1911, I, 57 ff.); Gall, *Die Gotische Baukunst in Frankreich und Deutschland*, pp. 110 ff.; Anfray, *L'Architecture normande. Son influence dans le nord de France*, p. 60; and *BM*, 1937.

raised to the See of Chartres (1180).[27] It is all the more noteworthy that such inclinations did not quench Peter's passion for building. On the contrary, it was precisely in architecture, more particularly in Gothic architecture, that he sought and found the means to communicate his religious experience.[28]

The relatively few writings of Peter of Celle include a mystical and moral exegesis of the Tabernacle of Moses.[29] The work, needless to say, is not concerned with Gothic architecture. Yet it is of considerable interest for our understanding of the meaning of Gothic in the eyes of a man like the abbot of Celle. He declares at the beginning that the tabernacle that concerns him is not built with human hands or earthly materials but belongs to the celestial, spiritual, and eternal world. Even so, Peter continues, let us visualize the historical Tabernacle that Moses built, as a means of guiding our attention from things visible to things invisible. Moses himself meant to direct the minds of the initiated, by means of the work he was building, to the spiritual vision that lay behind it. He, whose true tabernacle is in heaven, has nevertheless commanded the building of His sanctuary here on earth, so that the eye, illuminated by faith and reason, might perceive, "as in a mirror and an enigma, the glory that lies beyond. Hence where should we treat of the tabernacle, if not in the tabernacle itself?"

For Peter and his contemporaries the tabernacle was a synonym as well as the mystical archetype of the Christian sanctuary.[30] Although a curious state of

---

27. *Ep.* CLXXIV (*PL*, CCII, 632 f.). Peter's friendship for both the Cardinal of Champagne and John of Salisbury appears in his letters. Cf. *PL*, CCII, 567.

28. See the references to the rebuilding of St.-Remi, *Epp.* CLIV (*PL*, CCII, 598), CLVIII (ibid., 602), CLXVI (ibid., 610). In the last letter is the moving passage: ". . . spes excitat vota mea mortem non timere, sed amare, non fugare sed patienter exspectare. Interim neque dormitare neque dormire volo, sed juxta sapientis consilium quaecumque possim instanter operari. Hinc est quod nobilem ecclesiam nostram tam in fronte quam in ventre, cui caput secundum se deerat, fabricandam suscepimus, et, ut speramus, cum Dei adjutorio perficiemus." As Bishop of Chartres he won the extraordinary affection of his flock by his charities. According to his obituary (*CC*, III, 46, erroneously identified by the editors as that of Bishop Peter of Mincy), Peter paved the city's streets and built a considerable part of its walls out of his own funds. These were large-scale projects; they may not be without significance for the history of the cathedral: the suggestion has been made that part of the great dressed stones of which the church is built were originally destined for, or even employed in, the city's walls.

29. *Mosaici Tabernaculi mystica et moralis expositio* (*PL*, CCII, 1047 ff.). A second, slightly different treatise on the same subject is published (from Troyes MS. 253) by Leclercq, *Spiritualité*, pp. 147 ff.

30. See, e.g., the *Rationale div. offic.* by Peter's contemporary John Beleth (*PL*, CCII, 15 f.); Peter of Poitiers (ed., Moore and Corbett), *Allegoriae super Tabernaculum Moysi*, pp. 69, 110; or the *Speculum ecclesiae* by Peter of Roissy, Chancellor of the School of Chartres, a

suspense and uncertainty pervades the abbot's exegesis, and to him the visible, in all its beauty and splendor, is as nothing compared with transcendental reality, yet he knows that the visible mirrors that invisible reality and is in fact our only guide toward it.[31]

Peter's treatise complements the writings of Suger. The abbot of St.-Denis interprets the church he has actually built in spiritual terms; the abbot of St.-Remi conveys his mystical vision by means of architectural metaphor. Both take for granted the "anagogical" function of Christian architecture. And both see in Gothic design the appropriate expression of theological reality. Peter's choir of St.-Remi is a masterpiece of early Gothic, perhaps the most perfect choir of the period between St.-Denis and Chartres; its ground plan served as a model for the Cathedral of Reims. Of almost equal interest are the alterations Peter undertook in the nave of his abbey. Not all of these were demanded by the ribbed vault that replaced the wooden ceiling. The pointed arches over the gallery openings, the elimination of wall surfaces by the triforium and enlarged clerestory windows, are indications of a preference for the new style that is based not on structural but on aesthetic considerations, or rather, we should conclude, in view of Peter's metaphorical use of architecture, on spiritual considerations.[32] It is significant that after Peter had been appointed Bishop of Chartres, his successor at St.-Remi completed the vaulting of the nave but contented himself with a most superficial "modernization" of

*Plate 31*

work to which I shall return later. The comparison between church and tabernacle, moreover, occurs in the liturgy for the dedication of a church. See Andrieu, *Le Pontifical de la curie romaine au XIII* siècle*, p. 436 (xxiii, 66); also, in the Breviary, the office *In octava dedicationis ecclesiae*, in which Pope Felix IV's first letter, with its lengthy reference to the Tabernacle of Moses, has been inserted.

31. Peter explains the anagogical meaning of the sanctuary in terms that recall those of Suger: "sed ubi agendum de tabernaculo, nisi in tabernaculo? Tabernaculum vero de quo tractare proposuimus est non manufactum, id est non hujus creationis, sed admirabile, sed coeleste, sed spiritale, sed angelicum, sed perpetuum. Prae oculis tamen illud terrenum Moysi, opere terreno fabricatum ponamus, et a visibilibus ad

invisibilia intentionem transferentes . . ." Peter, too, introduces the cosmic edifice of the *Timaeus* into his architectural allegory; but, significantly, he has no use for it in his present context. In the *Timaeus*, he writes disparagingly, the reader will find a description of the "visible palace of the creation" so complicated that he will struggle with the subtleties of the author instead of being moved with admiration for the Creator.

32. Further proof that the Gothic system was introduced for its aesthetic rather than presumed functional qualities is evident in the choir. To make room for the stalls, six of the slender shafts under the vault ribs were cut off, as it were, well above the floor level and rest, as they often do elsewhere, on consoles.

the older parts of the building that Peter had left untouched. Perhaps he did not share his predecessor's spiritual vision and thus did not feel compelled to attune the design of the church to it.

The last of the twelfth-century bishops of Chartres was Renaud of Mouçon. His reforms, as we have seen, had much improved the organization of the chapter, and he was largely responsible for the prompt decision to rebuild the cathedral after the great fire. But he was not only an ecclesiastical statesman but also a soldier. He joined with his uncle, Thibault of Chartres-Champagne, in the ill-fated Crusade of 1188, and in 1210 led his own troops in the Albigensian "crusade" to bring relief to the hard-pressed Simon of Montfort.[33] Renaud's arms appear in one of the cathedral windows, but we know nothing about his intellectual or artistic inclinations. Contemporaries may not have accused him unjustly of avarice and neglect toward the Cathedral School.[34]

A word ought to be said, however, about the chancellor of his Cathedral School, Peter of Roissy, who occupied this position between c. 1200 and 1213. His obituary praises him as a distinguished theologian, philosopher, and orator; he bequeathed to the cathedral an important library (which included the sermons of St. Bernard and Seneca's *De naturalibus quaestionibus*) and in addition a sizable amount of money for the reconstruction of Notre Dame.[35] This donation is not the only reflection of his interest in the great church, which he saw rise above Chartres during his term in office. Peter composed a *Manual on the Mysteries of the Church*, of which the first part is devoted to an allegorical interpretation of the Christian basilica.[36] Such an approach to architecture is, of course, customary in the Middle Ages. And while it strikes us as somewhat dry and unreal, we must admit that in a theological context this is the only way

33. Delaporte and Houvet, *Les Vitraux de la cathédrale de Chartres*, p. 484.

34. Clerval, pp. 274 ff., 307 ff.; Hauréau, *Mémoire*; Merlet, *Dignitaires*, p. 105.

35. *CC*, III, 171 f. On Peter and his work, see Kennedy, "The Handbook of Master Peter, Chancellor of Chartres" (*Mediaeval Studies*, V, 1943); Kuttner, "Pierre de Roissy and Robert of Flamborough" (*Traditio*, II, 1944); and Kennedy's answer to a criticism of Kuttner's in *Mediaeval Studies*, VII, 1945, p. 291.

36. The Bibliothèque Nationale possesses the following manuscripts of the work: Lat. 14500, fol. 126 ff.; Lat. 14859, fol. 288 ff.; Lat. 14923, fol. 144 ff.; Nouv. acq. lat. 232, fol. 4 ff. Mortet and Deschamps, *Recueil de textes relatifs à l'histoire de l'architecture et à la condition des architectes en France au moyen-âge*, II, 183 ff., have published the relevant passages from the last MS. mentioned, the title of which is *Manuale Magistri Petri Cancellarii Carnotensis de misteriis ecclesie*. I have used Lat. 14923 (early saec. XIII).

in which architecture can be introduced at all. There are two specific reasons that make Peter of Roissy's treatise interesting reading for the student of Chartres Cathedral.

His allegory, to begin with, is closer to the actual architecture of his time than are similar works of its kind. It was doubtless intended as an "anagogical" interpretation of existing buildings. Peter speaks of churches of two or three "stories"—apparently he means churches with what we call tripartite or quadripartite elevations.[37] Such consideration of two alternatives is interesting. In Peter of Roissy's time the more sumptuous churches had quadripartite elevations; in his own cathedral, however, the architect had gone back to the simpler theme of Sens and had given it its classical solution. Again, Peter speaks of a church that has "major" and "minor" columns for supports.[38] May we see here an allusion to the *pilier cantonné*, the large column surrounded by smaller ones, which was one of the finest inventions of the master of Chartres? Peter also gives an elaborate allegorical interpretation of the church windows.[39] Finally, he dwells repeatedly on the symbolic significance of the square: the church and its towers (in both cases Peter seems to be referring to their design *ad quadratum*), the lower parts of the windows, even the dressed stones of which the church is built, are of this shape. The square thus recalls for Peter the moral perfection of man (it is the ancient notion of the "square" man) and the "unity" of the Ecclesia, which was mystically prefigured in Noah's ark and Solomon's Temple.[40]

Peter of Roissy's architectural allegory may thus have been patterned on

---

37. "Et sicut in Templo erant tria tabulata et in archa Noe secundum quosdam, ita in ecclesia quandoque sunt duo tabulata que significant contemplativam vitam et activam. Vel tria tabulata significant tria hominum genera, in ecclesia conjugatos, continentes et virgines."

38. "Columne quae sunt in ecclesia maiores vel minores . . ." See Suger, *De consecratione ecclesiae sancti Dionysii*, V (*Oeuvres complètes*, p. 227), where there is a similar allegory regarding the columns, though no distinction between major and minor columns. Cf. Sauer, *Die Symbolik des Kirchengebäudes*, p. 134.

39. This allegory follows a conventional pattern. Cf. Sauer, pp. 120 ff.

40. "De forma ecclesie . . . ecclesia quadrata est a fundo [Lat. 14923 has "quadrata est in fronte"] et tendit in conum, per quos figuratur unitas ecclesie, sicut in archa Noe, que consummata est in uno cubito." "Sunt autem fenestre quadrate in inferiori, quia prelati debent quadrari virtutibus." "Lapides quadrati significant quadratura virtutum in sanctis que sunt: temperancia, justicia, fortitudo, prudentia." "Turres . . . sunt etiam quadrate que designant quadraturam virtutum . . ." On allegorical interpretations of arithmetical or geometrical aspects of architecture, see Rambaud, "Le Quatrain mystique de Vaison-la-Romaine" (*BM*, CIX, 1951).

the Cathedral of Chartres.[41] But there is yet another reason why it ought to be mentioned in the present context. His interpretation may reflect ideas that the architect may well have wished to convey in his design. We have seen to what extent ecclesiastical builders were concerned with the symbolic significance of the sanctuary.[42] Suger is not alone in insisting that such ideas have actually shaped the pattern of his edifice. His design was to make this relation clear to the beholder. Even at the end of the Middle Ages, the architects of Milan Cathedral, not clerics but professionals, propose four towers at the corners of the crossing tower "after the model" of the apocalyptic vision of Christ surrounded by the four evangelists.[43] [*See Add.*]

Our own skepticism about the architectural relevance of such comparisons springs from a nominalistic attitude that has little application to the Middle Ages. As was suggested earlier, the architectural visions of the Bible were considered archetypes to which the religious edifice must conform. Even a Renaissance architect like Philibert Delorme regretted having deviated from the "divine proportions" that God himself had revealed to the inspired builders of the Old Testament.[44] The architect of Chartres worked in the intellectual and religious milieu of the cathedral. He would certainly heed the views and wishes of the chapter to which his plans had to be submitted. It is therefore quite likely that the theological ideas of the chapter impinged upon his design. After all, the "anagogical" interpretation to which the church might lend itself was a function of the edifice as legitimate and nearly as important as the liturgical one. The beauty of the basilica was experienced in terms of such anagogical significance. Man's thinking and experience are never divided into airtight compartments. Just as our own art and taste are related to our view of the world, so the design of the medieval cathedral builder and its impression upon contemporaries were colored, and indeed inspired, by the metaphysical vision that dominated medieval life. We must assume therefore that the aesthetic traditions of Platonism and also the allegorical theology that Peter of Roissy expounded were factors that affected the architect's imagination and "collaborated" (in Synge's sense) with him in his design.

41. See the comparable reference to Paris—"apud Lutetiam Nostram"—in John Beleth's *Rationale*, to which I have referred earlier, which was probably composed around 1165

(*PL*, CCII, 16; cf. *HLF*, XIV, 218).
42. See above, p. 134.
43. *Annali*, I, 209 f.
44. See below, p. 228, n. 108.

How closely Gothic architecture and the metaphysics of the thirteenth century are interconnected is shown by the only theoretical work by a Gothic architect that has come down to us. I have already mentioned the famous model book of the Picard architect, Villard de Honnecourt. A younger contemporary of the master of Chartres Cathedral—under whom he may even have worked in his youth—he saw, completed or in the process of completion, nearly every one of the classical cathedrals of the Île-de-France.[45] A distinguished architect in his own right, he composed his model book in order to set forth what he considered the principles that underlie all artistic composition, not only building but sculpture and painting as well. These principles are geometrical. On nearly every page of his work Villard pays tribute to this discipline; every one of his models, whether human figures or architectural designs, is based upon or derived from simple geometrical figures. The artistic procedure he describes was the practice actually followed by the artists of the high Middle Ages.[46] And it is but the application of the metaphysical and cosmological views of the time.

Focillon has pointed to the astonishing similarity between the aesthetics of Villard and the natural philosophy of his contemporary, Robert Grosseteste (1175–1253), who declares that without geometry it is impossible to understand nature, since all forms of natural bodies are in essence geometrical and can be reduced to lines, angles, and regular figures.[47] One may add that Grosseteste also offers the metaphysical confirmation of the Gothic tendency to blend the aesthetics of harmony and "musical" proportions with that of light. The beauty of light, he maintains, is due to its simplicity, by which light is,

45. See above, p. 16, n. 34. The model book reproduces details from the cathedrals of Laon, Reims, and Chartres; cf. Hahnloser, *Villard de Honnecourt*, Pls. 18; 19; 20B; 30B, C; 60–64; 6; 17. [*See Add.*]

46. The correspondence between Villard's drawing of a head "according to true measure" (cf. Hahnloser, Pl. 38E) and the head of Christ in a window in the choir of Reims Cathedral was first pointed out by Panofsky, "Die Entwicklung der Proportionslehre als Abbild der Stilentwicklung" (*MKW*, XIV, 1921). On the use of such geometrical aids, see Ueberwasser, *Von Maasz und Macht der alten Kunst*, p. 48; also Thibout, "À propos de peintures murales de la Chapelle Ste.-Catherine de Montbellet" (*BM*, CVIII, 1950).

47. Focillon, *L'Art des sculpteurs romans*, pp. 219 ff., quoting from *De lineis, angulis et figuris* (*BGPM*, 1912, IX, 59 f.). "Utilitas considerationis linearum, angulorum, et figurarum est maxima, quoniam impossibile est sciri naturalem philosophiam sine illis." These geometrical forms "valent in toto universo et partibus ejus absolute"; "omnes enim causae effectuum naturalium habent dari per lineas, angulos et figuras."

like unison in music, "ad se per aequalitatem concordissime proportionata" ("most harmoniously related to itself by the ratio of equality").[48]

Villard's model book expounds not only the geometrical canons of Gothic architecture but also the Augustinian aesthetics of "musical" proportions, proportions that correspond to the intervals of the perfect musical consonances. He is our earliest theoretical witness to the proportion "according to true measure"; even more interesting, however, is one of his designs representing the ground plan of a Cistercian church drawn *ad quadratum*, i.e., the square bay of the side aisles is the basic unit or module from which all proportions of the plan are derived. And these proportions, as Professor de Bruyne observes, correspond in each case to the ratios of the musical consonances, the same ratios that, as we have seen, were actually employed by the Cistercian builders. Thus the length of the church is related to the transept in the ratio of the fifth (2:3). The octave ratio (1:2) determines the relations between side aisle and nave, length and width of the transept, and, we may assume on the basis of Cistercian practice, of the interior elevation as well. The 3:4 ratio of the choir evokes the musical fourth; the 4:5 ratio of nave and side aisles taken as a unit corresponds to the third; while the crossing, liturgically and aesthetically the center of the church, is based on the 1:1 ratio of unison, most perfect of consonances.[49]

Villard's testimony is of great significance. He may have received his architectural training at the Cistercian monastery of Vaucelles, and was certainly employed as an architect by the order. His design, probably intended as the ideal plan of a Cistercian church, undoubtedly embodied the aesthetic tradition of the Cistercians that was alive in his time, and thus bears testimony to the ties that connected this tradition with Gothic art.[50] Indeed, the musical ratios occur in some of the most perfect architectural compositions of the thirteenth century. In the southern transept of Lausanne Cathedral (before 1235) the magnificent disposition of the inner wall "conveys an overwhelming

48. See Baur, "Das Licht in der Naturphilosophie des Robert Grosseteste," and de Bruyne, Études d'esthétique médiévale, III,131 ff.

49. Hahnloser, Villard, Pl. 28, p. 250; de Bruyne, I, 22. This ground plan may not be the only example of the "musical" motivation of Villard's proportions. With regard to his

human figure (Hahnloser, Villard, p. 37), see the interesting "harmonical" interpretation of Kayser, Ein harmonikaler Teilungs-Kanon.

50. See Enlart, "Villard de Honnecourt et les Cisterciens" (BEC, LVI, 1895); Hahnloser, Villard, pp. 79, 179, 233 f., 250; Dimier, Recueil de plans d'églises cisterciennes, p. 41.

experience of harmony" with the 1:2:3 ratio of its horizontal division.[51] The consonance of the fifth is "sounded" in the façades of Paris, Strassburg, and York. We shall presently find in Chartres itself the realization of the Augustinian aesthetics of measure and number.

The ideas expounded by Villard and Grosseteste, by John of Salisbury and Peter of Roissy, suggest something of the intellectual climate in which the master of Chartres created his cathedral. These ideas were in the minds of those who commissioned the church and saw it completed, and the master's design responded to them. We, too, should recall these concepts as we turn to the study of this monument.

Among the great works of architecture none conceals as successfully as does Notre Dame of Chartres the masterful solution of all technical problems behind a seemingly conservative rendering of a traditional theme. The Parthenon, the Hagia Sophia at Constantinople, Brunelleschi's dome of Florence Cathedral, Michelangelo's dome of St. Peter's are not only novel and unique in fact; the novel and unique nature of the achievement strikes us at a glance as it did contemporaries. The same is true for some of the Gothic sanctuaries of the thirteenth century. There is an element of the virtuoso in Peter of Montreuil, the builder of the Sainte-Chapelle at Paris (and of the St.-Denis that replaced Suger's), and in Robert of Luzarches, the architect of Amiens Cathedral. Compared with them, the master of Chartres seems restrained and austere, the enemy of everything that is emotional, ostentatious, novel. "In der Beschränkung zeigt sich der Meister"—Goethe's dictum is eminently true for the architect of Chartres Cathedral. The hallmark of his genius is the way in which he turned to advantage the restrictions that tradition imposed upon his design.

We have already seen that the ambulatory and choir of the old church, the contours and foundations of which survived in the crypt, were also to determine the outline of the new choir. The elevation of the latter, however, was to be not Romanesque but Gothic. Indeed, the master decided to base his design on the model of St.-Denis. The decision is not surprising. As one of the royal cathedrals, Notre Dame was likely to take up the theme that Suger had first

51. Beer, *Die Rose der Kathedrale von Lausanne*, p. 11. For another example of the use of such "musical" proportions, see Webb, "The Sources of the Design of the West Front of Peterborough Cathedral" (*Archaeological Journal*, LVI, suppl. 1952).

sounded in his great church. "Dionysian" motifs, incidentally, are generally conspicuous in the Cathedral of Chartres. On the southern portal, above the Last Judgment, the sculptured choirs of angels are arranged in the hierarchical order described by the Pseudo-Areopagite.[52] In the southern transept, St. Denis is represented, in one of the most beautiful of all the windows, as an abbot of his monastery presenting the oriflamme to the donor, who was marshal of France.[53] Another window, apparently a gift of King Louis VIII, depicted the life of St. Denis.[54] As regards architectural disposition, the task of placing a "Dionysian" choir upon the foundations of Fulbert's apse presented problems that at first may have seemed insurmountable.[55]

The three deep chapels that jutted forth from the old ambulatory admitted little if any light into the latter. The old plan made no concession to the Gothic taste for either luminosity or that unbroken continuity of outline which Suger's perimeter of shallow chapels provided. The walls of the Romanesque chapels did not converge in a common center, nor did they divide the circumference of the ambulatory into equal intervals.

A comparison of the two ground plans will show how the Gothic master solved all resulting difficulties. After the model of St.-Denis, he replaced the single by a double ambulatory, ingeniously using for this purpose the transepts that Bishop Thierry had built in the mid-eleventh century. The second ambulatory reduced the depth of the old chapels by nearly one half. Their number, moreover, was increased from three to seven. The additional four flank each of the three chapels that rose in the place of their Romanesque predecessors and unify the external contour still further. Shallower than the old chapels, these smaller chapels appear as a gentle outward swelling or expanding of the ambulatory. Throughout, solid walls have been replaced by transparent walls of windows between buttresses: each of the three main chapels has five large windows; the smaller chapels have two and three windows, respectively. Cylindrical piers support the cross-ribbed vaults over the ambulatories.

The same happy synthesis between the traditional and the novel—or rather the will to conceal the novel behind the traditional—is apparent in the

---

52. Mâle, *Notre-Dame de Chartres*, p. 50.
53. Delaporte and Houvet, pp. 439 ff.
54. Delaporte and Houvet, pp. 475 f.
55. Merlet, *La Cathédrale de Chartres*, pp. 37 f.; Mâle, *Notre-Dame de Chartres*, p. 35.

general elevation of choir and nave. Here again, the old building imposed its dimensions. But the Romanesque edifice, of very large dimensions for its time, had not been vaulted; the Gothic cathedral was to receive a cross-ribbed vault. The span that the master covered in this fashion was wider than that of any of the Gothic cathedrals—Sens, Noyon, Paris, Laon—that had just been completed. And the vault of Chartres was sprung at a much greater height.[56] In praising the new cathedral, which he thought to be without equal anywhere in the world, the poet Guillaume le Breton singled out two features: the vault, which he thought would last to the end of time; and the magnificent dressed stone of which the church was built, which had been, contemporaries thought, miraculously discovered in a quarry on the episcopal fief of Berchères-l'Évêque,[57] only about five miles from Chartres. As in the case of St.-Denis, the very soil came to the assistance of the architect: without these resources, his technical and artistic achievement would not have been possible.

For, despite the weight of its great vault, the cathedral was to be luminous as no other church had been before. To render this possible the master abandoned the quadripartite elevation, more specifically, the gallery that the most renowned among his immediate predecessors had adopted in the cathedrals of Paris, Noyon, and Laon. From the viewpoint of the requirements of congregational worship, these galleries were unnecessary, especially in a church as large as Chartres, which offered ample space for large congregations in its nave and side aisles. But the galleries fulfilled an important static purpose inasmuch as they buttressed the thrusts of the nave vaults. The abandoning of the quadripartite elevation in Chartres shows, as clearly as we can wish, the integration of aesthetic and structural considerations, more specifically, the influence of the aesthetics of light upon the development of architecture. By omitting the gallery the master was able to realize with perfect consistency the principle

*Plates 32, 35*

of translucent walls in all parts of the building. He could now give greater height to the side aisles as well as to the clerestory windows, and it was also possible to render the side aisles much shallower, since their width was no

56. The heights of the four cathedrals mentioned are 24.40, 22.70, 32.50, and 24 meters, respectively. Their naves are 15.25, 10.50, 13.14, and 12 meters wide (measures as given by Seymour, *Notre Dame of Noyon in the Twelfth Century*, p. 101). [*See*

*Add.*]

57. "Que, lapide exciso surgens nova, corpore toto Sub testudineo, jam consummata decore, Judicii nihil usque diem timet igne noceri." *Philippid*, IV, 598.

longer determined by that of a gallery above (which in turn was limited by the curvature of the vault thrusts). The side aisles of Chartres, illuminated by large windows, thus became a luminous foil enveloping the nave.

All that remained between nave arcades and clerestory was the narrow triforium zone, its wall surface dissolved by the openings of the pointed triforium arcades, four in each bay of the nave, five in the transepts, and two in the apse. The entire wall surface above the triforium was replaced by windows: a double lancet in each bay divided by a slim mullion laid in horizontal courses and surmounted by a rose.

The tripartite elevation as such was no innovation: as we have seen, even the elevation of Suger's St.-Denis may have been of this type; the abbey of St.-Vincent (1175–1205) at Laon, a town whose monuments the master of Chartres seems to have known well, may have provided another model,[58] or, and perhaps more likely, he may have been influenced by the Cathedral of Sens, the mother church of the metropolitan province to which Chartres belonged. Yet neither the aesthetic nor technical aspects of this church invited adoption. Its vault, the section of which approachès a hemicycle, seems to be hunched above its supports. And in order not to weaken the clerestory walls at the critical junctures with the vault thrusts, the master of Sens kept the windows small. The architect of Chartres gave his vault a much steeper section. And he relieved the walls of their function as supports by the great row of buttresses that he placed perpendicularly to the course of the walls. These buttresses are far more nearly perfect than those which the master of the nave of Notre Dame of Paris had employed a decade or so earlier.[59] Each of the great supports meets the thrust of the vault by means of two arches. The third may have been added early in the fourteenth century after a group of consulting architects had discovered a number of structural weaknesses that time had caused in the cathedral fabric. But it is doubtful whether the additional arches fulfill a necessary or useful function, and far from probable that the great architect of Notre Dame can be blamed for any of the flaws uncovered.[60] At any

*Plate 36*

*Plate 38*

*Plate 39*

58. Lambert, "L'Ancienne abbaye de St.-Vincent de Laon" (*AIBLM*, 1939).

59. Aubert, *Notre-Dame de Paris*, pp. 86 ff.

60. The experts' report nowhere blames the builder for the damage found. With reference to the buttressing·arches, it merely speaks of the need of filling the joints with mortar. See Mortet, "L'Expertise de la Cathédrale de Chartres en 1316" (*CA*, LXVII, 1900). It is an exaggeration if Colombier (*Les Chantiers des cathédrales*, p. 72) calls the report "devastating" and evidence for the imperfection of Gothic

rate, the flying buttresses of Chartres are the first to have been conceived, not only structurally but also aesthetically, as integral parts of the over-all design. They seem to have made a profound impression upon contemporaries.[60a] Built in huge blocks of stone from Berchères, their shape is admirably attuned to the quality of this material; it bespeaks no less that virile, somewhat coarse-grained genius which characterizes the work of the master of Chartres throughout. Obviously, both the master and his stone were natives of the same soil.

Inside, the system presents itself as a series of "canopies," each composed of four piers supporting the vault over each bay.[61] It is an architecture designed for the windows, developed from the magnificent conception of transparent walls. This appears with particular clarity in the design of the apse. Its contour is no longer hemispherical but polygonal. This device became necessary as soon as the windows were no longer openings in the walls but walls themselves; their flat surfaces required the transformation of the spherical apse into a polygon. Here again the architect has not invented his solution; in the Cathedral of Laon, the apses of the transepts, and originally the main apse itself,

---

building. Such imperfections are not infrequent in Gothic architecture, but I know no evidence of it in Chartres Cathedral. See also Viollet-le-Duc's analysis of the Chartres buttresses, *Dictionnaire raisonné de l'architecture française,* I, 65, fig. 54. [*See Add.*]

60a. Kunze, *Das Fassadenproblem der französischen Früh- und Hochgotik,* p. 63, seems to have first suggested that the buttressing arches of Chartres are represented in the aedicula enframing the image of the Virgin in the northern transept of Reims Cathedral. Recently Panofsky, in *Early Netherlandish Painting,* p. 146, has interpreted the architecture of the famous relief as an abridged representation of Notre Dame of Chartres. Both theses, appealing though they are, present some difficulties. If Kunze is right, we would not only have to date the sculpture considerably later than French scholarship, at least, is still inclined to do; we would also have to ask, as the author himself admits, why should Sancta Maria Remensis have been depicted within a model of the Cathedral of Chartres? The only alternative, which Panofsky does not seem to exclude, would be that the relief was actually meant to be a representation of Our Lady of Chartres. Granting that Chartres, as we have seen, had become something like the na-

tional shrine of the Virgin in France, it is not altogether easy to imagine that such pre-eminence should have been so emphatically acknowledged in the great rival sanctuary at Reims.

61. The term canopy (*Baldachin*) was first introduced into the analysis and history of architecture by Sedlmayr, "Das erste mittelalterliche Architektursystem" (*Kunstwissenschaftliche Forschungen,* II, 1933), and subsequently further developed in his *Die Entstehung der Kathedrale,* passim. In the symbolic and aesthetic emphasis that he gives to the "canopy" as the decisive element in Gothic architecture, Sedlmayr surely goes too far, even though his insight is a valuable one. The Latin equivalent for the term canopy, *ciborium,* was actually used by medieval writers to denote the crossing or the tower over the crossing. See Lambert, *L'Art gothique en Espagne,* pp. 60 ff., and *Annali,* I, 209 f. Sedlmayr has shown that the monk Gervase, in his chronicle of the building of Canterbury Cathedral, also calls the bays of the nave *ciboria.* "Ein zeitgenössischer Fachausdruck für die Raumform 'Baldachin'" (*Österreichische Akademie der Wissenschaften, phil.-hist. Klasse,* 1949, p. 23).

closed as polygons, at least at the level of the windows.[62] But in Chartres, and not in Laon, the device appears as the consistent application of the concept of transparency that pervades every part of the edifice.[63]

The comparison of the elevations of Chartres and Laon is generally illuminating, all the more so since the master of Chartres certainly knew the Cathedral of Laon: in the façades of his transepts he combined the lower part of the west façade of Laon with the upper parts of the transept façades of this cathedral. Its famous towers likewise seem to have given him the idea (never realized) of surmounting the eastern parts of his edifice with a monumental group of towers.[64] Yet he remained indifferent to the interior elevation of Laon. Its design, though not yet complete when work on Notre Dame of Chartres was begun, dated back to the 1170's or 1180's. To the master of Chartres that design appeared altogether obsolete. It combined sexpartite vaults with an alternating system of supports that had also been employed in Sens and Noyon but was already abandoned in Notre Dame of Paris and eventually in Laon itself, that is, in the more recent parts of the nave. The master of Chartres dropped these features along with the gallery. He adopted instead the quadripartite vault, sprung over rectangular rather than square bays. And he also adopted a new type of pier.

The earlier cathedral churches of France had employed either a uniform type of heavy cylindrical pier or compound piers that rose to the springing of the diagonal vault ribs and alternated with single or double columns. Wherever columns are employed, slender shafts that correspond to the vault ribs rise above the abaci of the columns. These older systems of support introduce strongly marked contrasts: in the alternating system, a horizontal contrast between compound piers and columns; in the uniform system, a vertical contrast between the bulky cylinders of the columns below and the slender shafts of the

*Plate 21*

62. See Frankl, "The 'Crazy' Vaults of Lincoln Cathedral" (*AB*, XXXV, 1953), and Adenauer, *Die Kathedrale von Laon*, pp. 19 ff. According to Crosby, *L'Abbaye royale de Saint-Denis*, pp. 13, 15, both apses of the Carolingian St.-Denis were already polygonal, as was that of St.-Maurice at Agaune (751). Sedlmayr is thus factually mistaken in suggesting (*Die Entstehung*, p. 257) that the polygonal apse appears first in Chartres; yet this cathedral is indeed the first where this design is the logical realization of the distinction between supports and translucent "membranes"—the windows—between them.

63. Cf. Frankl, "'Crazy' Vaults"; Grodecki, "Le Vitrail et l'architecture au XIIe et au XIIIe siècle" (*GBA*, series 6, XXXVI, 1939), and *Vitraux des églises de France*, p. 5.

64. See Lambert, "La Cathédrale de Laon" (*GBA*, XIII, XIV, 1926).

colonnettes above. To the master of Chartres such lack of homogeneity constituted an aesthetic flaw, which he overcame by the design of his piers.

These piers—so far as we know, the first *piliers cantonnés*— [65] are composed of four slender colonnettes that surround a powerful central core. The sense for unity could not have been satisfied by a more felicitous invention. It eliminates the contrast between the heavy monolithic shape of the column and the soaring bundle of shafts above it. In Chartres, the vertical rhythm begins at the base, owing to the deeply shaded zones between the colonnettes, which seem to dissolve the total bulk of the support into four vertical lines. On the other hand, the *pilier cantonné* of Chartres reduces the contrast between the colonnettes that merely support the nave arcades and the shafts that rise all the way to the springing of the vault: even these shafts are articulated by a profile that continues the abacus over the capitals of the rest of the pier. Again, the capitals of the colonnettes under the nave arcades are only half as high as those of the main supports [66]—another detail that the architect may have borrowed from the Cathedral of Laon. They thus mediate between the earthbound heaviness of the main piers and the soaring verticalism of the shafts under the vault ribs. Articulation rather than contrast, articulation that does not disrupt unity, is the aesthetic principle that appears as clearly in these *piliers cantonnés* as in the entire system of Chartres.

This principle is shown in yet another aspect of the piers. The master has employed alternation without sacrificing the principle of homogeneity. His piers consist, alternatively, of a cylindrical core surrounded by octagonal colonnettes, and an octagonal core surrounded by cylindrical colonnettes. It is worth noting that William of Sens had already alternated cylindrical and octagonal supports in the choir of Canterbury Cathedral (1175–78); [67] in the crossing, he had even used the motif of slender colonnettes surrounding a cylindrical core. Relations between the sees of Chartres and Canterbury were close. The appointment of John of Salisbury to the See of Chartres was, we are told, meant to be an act of homage to St. Thomas of Canterbury, to whom

*Plate 40*

65. Mâle, *Notre-Dame de Chartres*, p. 36; Panofsky, *Gothic Architecture and Scholasticism*, p. 79. The support flanked by four colonnettes seems to appear for the first time in Jumièges (c. 1067); see Lefèvre-Pontalis, "Les Influences normandes dans le nord de la France" (*BM*, LXX, 1906).

66. See Viollet-le-Duc, *Dictionnaire*, VII, 165.

67. The same alternation is employed in the nave of Oxford Cathedral. [*See Add.*]

John had been close and whose martyrdom he had witnessed.[68] It would not be surprising, therefore, if the architect of Chartres Cathedral had studied the magnificent shrine of St. Thomas that his countryman, master William, had begun less than a generation earlier. Yet, here again, the master of Chartres gave to the elements he borrowed an aesthetic significance they had not before possessed. The slight variation of the supports is just sufficient to induce the eye to perceive not one bay but two as a unit. The reason cannot be doubted: the ground plan of two consecutive bays comprises a square. Although the architect had adopted rectangular bays for his vaults, he did not want the square, which he had also employed in the side aisles, to be entirely lost in the nave. This fact calls our attention to the proportions employed in Chartres Cathedral; they constitute its most significant aesthetic aspect.

In the choice of his proportions, as in so many other respects, the architect was not entirely free. He had to consider the proportions that his predecessors had employed in the Romanesque cathedral. Professor Ernst Levy's measurements of the *vieux clocher* [see above, my preface to the 2nd edition] have thrown much light not only on the proportions used in the south tower but also on the conservatism with which these proportions were re-employed by the Gothic architect and even by his sixteenth-century successor, Jean of Beauce.

The ground plan of the *vieux clocher* is developed "according to true measure." The basic square has a side length of 16.44 m., or, we may assume, of 50 feet of 0.329 m. each, a measuring unit that comes close to others known to have been in use at the time.[69] The same dimension of 16.44 m. determines the width of the crossing, as it had also determined that of its Romanesque predecessor. Its length, however, measures 13.99 m. The present ground plan of the crossing, in other words, does not form a square, if distances are measured from the centers of the piers. Now this is peculiar. What calculation led the architect to determine the length of the crossing—and of the bays of the nave and choir—in this fashion?

We know that the medieval architect determined all dimensions of his

68. Gervase of Canterbury, *Opera historica*, pp. 259 f.

69. See, e.g., Arens, *Das Werkmass in der Baukunst des Mittelalters*; also Berriman, *Historical Metrology*, p. 136. A *pied* of 324.839 mm. was, according to Viollet-le-Duc (*Dictionnaire*, s.v. "échelle"), used in the cathedrals of Reims, Amiens, and Semur. The module used by Peter of Montreuil in St.-Denis was 0.325 m., according to Crosby, *Abbaye*, p. 61.

edifice by mathematical, i.e., geometrical means. More specifically, starting from a basic unit—in our case 16.44 m.—he developed all other dimensions
with the help of geometrical figures set out, on the building site, by means of
cords and pegs.[70] What geometrical method yielded the length of 13.99 m.;
or, rather, in what geometrical figure does the ratio of 16.44 : 13.99 occur? The
answer, according to Professor Levy's calculations, is the pentagon. Let 16.44
be the side of the pentagon; the radius of the circle circumscribing it is 13.984.
The correspondence between this figure and 13.99 is far too close to be accidental, but not too close to prohibit our conclusion: despite the seemingly crude
methods of "setting out," we have ample evidence for the surprising exactness
of results obtained.[71]

   The use of the pentagon by the master of Chartres is of great interest.
The Gothic artist knew the golden section, most perfect of all proportions, as
the matrix from which he could develop the pentagon.[72] As we have seen in
an earlier chapter, the *sectio aurea* occurs in the figures of the west façade of
Chartres. In the Gothic church it determines the ground plan, as Dehio was
the first to observe; [73] it is also present in the esthetically relevant parts of the
elevation.

70. See Harvey, *The Gothic World*, p. 16;
Salzman, *Building in England*, pp. 17 ff. See also
Kletzl, *Plan-Fragmente aus der deutschen Dombauhütte von Prag*, pp. 18 f. A curious illustration of this method occurs in a miniature of a
twelfth-century Life of St. Hugh (Paris, Bibl.
Nat. lat. 17716, fol. 43); Colombier, Pl. IV, 6.
It ought to be added that the architect did not
merely compose his design in his workshop, but
executed the design of all important details, in
actual size or on a very large scale, on the
building site itself. Thus, on the granite slabs
covering the side aisles of Limoges Cathedral,
the architect sketched the outline of the piers,
the curve of the ribs, and other details. The
same practice can be observed in Narbonne,
Clermont, and elsewhere. See de Verneilh,
"Construction des monuments ogivaux" (*AA*,
VI, 1847); Kletzl, p. 9; Harvey, p. 31;
Colombier, p. 66; and Anfray, "Les Architectes des cathédrales" (*Les Cahiers techniques
de l'art*, 1947, I, 11).
   71. See the observations of Gall, "Über die

Maasze der Trierer Liebfrauenkirche."
   72. See above, p. 155. The *Geometria deutsch*
(1472) treats of the significance and application
of the pentagon (see Heideloff, *Die Bauhütte
des Mittelalters in Deutschland*, pp. 95 ff.): "So
einer ein fünffort reisse will mit unveruckte
zirkel . . ." The employment of the golden
section by medieval builders is no longer open to
question, even though not all analyses offered
by Lund, *Ad Quadratum*, especially ch. XIII,
and Moessel, *Vom Geheimnis der Form und der
Urform des Seins*, are convincing. See Texier,
*Géométrie de l'architecture*, especially p. 59, for
an interesting analysis of the church of Taverny
(Île-de-France); and Maillard, "Recherches
sur l'emploi du Nombre d'or par les architectes
du moyen-âge" (*Congrès d'esthétique et de science
de l'art*, II, n.d.). Of some interest in this connection is the star-pentagon on the seal of Simon
de Beron, canon of Chartres (1209); see Merlet,
*Dignitaires*, p. xxxiv.
   73. Dehio and Bezold, *Kirchliche Baukunst
des Abendlandes*, II, 562 ff.

The dimensions and proportions obtained by the setting out of the ground plan were also employed for the elevation. At my request, Frédéric Hébrard, Surveyor of the Department of Eure-et-Loir, has measured the main parts of Plate 35 the elevation of Chartres Cathedral, with the following results. The height of the piers (taken from above the plinth and to the springing of the nave arcades) is 8.61 m. The height of the shafts above (excluding their capitals) is 13.85 m. The distance between the base of the shafts and the lower stringcourse is 5.35 m. The three ratios, 5.35:8.61:13.85, are very close approximations indeed to the ratios of the golden section. If, starting from the smallest figure, 5.35, we calculate the sequence of the golden section by arithmetical means, we obtain 8.656 and 13.880. Again, the actual measures taken are too close to these figures to have been accidental.

How are the dimensions of the elevation related to those of the ground plan? If we assume the master to have chosen the pentagon as his basic figure, he may also have developed from it the dimension of his elevation. The side of a regular decagon inscribed in the same circle as the pentagon already mentioned is 8.64 m. The height of the piers (to the capitals under the nave arcade) is, as we have seen, 8.61 m. The difference between the two figures is only 3 cm., a very slight inaccuracy if we consider the difficulties of taking vertical measurements by means of cords or rods. Again, Bulteau gives 13.85 m. as the width of the nave between columns (and also as the height of the vault of the side aisles).[74] As we have seen, 13.85 is also the length of the shafts under the main vault.

The heights of piers and shafts do not represent the only horizontal articulations of the elevation. Two stringcourses, below and above the triforium, mark the level of the horizontal slabs that serve as floor and ceiling, respectively, for the triforium passage. The lower stringcourse intersects with the vertical shafts at a level that divides these, if we include their capitals, with great exactness according to the golden section (14.19 m.:8.78 m.). The neatness of these proportions is remarkable. We have seen that the medieval Platonists ascribed a technical function to perfect proportion, conceiving it as the ratio that bestows cohesion upon an aggregate of units. One wonders if

74. Bulteau, *Monographie*, II, 10.

considerations such as these did not determine the levels at which the string-courses were set. These stringcourses, which are the facings of the top and bottom courses of masonry of the inner triforium wall,[75] have a structural function with regard to the tall vertical shafts: they hold in place those sections of the shafts that are not engaged with the masonry of the walls or piers by chaining them to the triforium wall.[76] The stringcourses therefore mark structurally the interconnection of the horizontal and vertical members of the elevation. Thus even these simple horizontal moldings were not installed for purposes of decoration. But the beautifully proportioned divisions of the elevation that these stringcourses establish are largely responsible for the singularly harmonious effect that the system of Chartres produces.

It should be added that the level of the lower stringcourse is determined not only by the height of the shafts but also by that of the total elevation. The architect, as we have seen, by the alternating forms of his *piliers cantonnés*, induced the eye to see not one bay but two as a unit. The length of two bays is equal to the width of the nave between the piers, each double bay thus forming a square.[77] As we look upward, the same square occurs in the elevation, the lower stringcourse being placed at a height exactly equal to the width of the nave. The height of the window sills of the clerestory, moreover, is exactly equal to the diagonal of that square; in other words, it is related to it "according to true measure." According to Ernst Levy's recent measurements, moreover, the cathedral's exact height, from *clef-de-voûte* to top of plinth, is 32.90 meters. Colonel Cox (see my preface to the 2nd edition of this book) kindly

---

75. "These slabs," Jean Maunoury, Chief Architect of the Department of Eure-et-Loir and of the cathedral, writes me, with reference to the stringcourse slabs, "do not run beyond the arcaded face of the triforium. They are functional, however, as being foot, and cap, layers of this arcade."

76. A curiously composite technique seems to have been used in building the responds, as can still be observed on the southern wall of the first bay from the entrance. The five shafts of the responds were built in segments that are alternatingly constructed *en délit* and engaged with the wall. I owe this information to M. Maunoury. In Reims, according to Viollet-

le-Duc, *Dictionnaire*, VII, 165, the middle shaft is engaged with the wall while the four remaining colonnettes are built *en délit*. On the construction of these composite shafts and the function of the cornice in general, see ibid., II, 108 f.; Choisy, *Histoire de l'architecture*, pp. 264, 350; and Villard de Honnecourt's interesting drawing of the ground plan of the Reims piers (Hahnloser, *Villard*, Pls. 30B, 63C).

77. The bays of the nave are of unequal length. The Gothic piers and the intervals between them had to correspond to those of the Romanesque nave, except for the two bays to the west where the architect had to take account of the existence of the façade and the towers.

informs me that according to his geometrical study of Chartres Cathedral this height is exactly equal to the inner width, the design of the edifice being *ad quadratum*.

The proportions of Chartres Cathedral tell us much about the method by which its design was produced; they reveal even more about the artistic conviction that stands behind it. Medieval metaphysics conceived beauty as the *splendor veritatis*, as the radiant manifestation of objectively valid laws. The elevation of Chartres Cathedral is the supreme vindication of this philosophy of beauty. The perfection of this great architectural system is the perfection of its proportions, proportions that the master developed not according to his personal intuition but by exact geometrical determination. He certainly knew the great attraction of these proportions to the human eye; Platonic insistence upon the correspondence between visual proportion and musical harmony can only have sharpened awareness of the aesthetic qualities of proportions that were "right." (It is worth noting in this connection that the golden section has its musical equivalents too, the third and sixth, consonances that, though considered "imperfect," were since the twelfth century allowed by medieval musicians in order to relieve the monotony of the perfect consonances.) [78] Even so, the beauty of proportions was understood as a by-product, a function of those laws which secured the stability and order of the church edifice. The

See Lefèvre-Pontalis, "Influences normandes." The measurements of the central bays, from east to west, as given by Lassus, *Monographie de la Cathédrale de Chartres*, are as follows: 7.215, 7.070, 7.070, 7.040, 6.875, 6.312, 6.278 meters. Lassus' measurements are generally very exact, far more so than his drawings of the cathedral. His measurements are taken between centers of piers. There is ample evidence to suggest, however, that the architect, in using the geometrical method of setting out, used as his lines of direction not only the center line of the wall (or the line connecting the centers of his piers) but also the lines representing the inner width of the edifice. See above, p. 49, n. 69. In Chartres the rectangle of the crossing is indeed determined by the intervals between the centers of the piers. The square of the double bays of the nave, however, is determined by the visible distances between piers, i.e., by the inner width of the nave.

78. Note the terms used by the thirteenth-century mathematician, Campanus of Novara, in his description of the golden section: "Mirabilis itaque est potentia lineae secundum proportionem habentem medium duoque extrema divisae. Cui cum plurima philosophantium admiratione digna conveniant, hoc principium vel praecipuum ex superiorum principiorum invariabili procedit natura, ut tam diversa solida tum magnitudine tum basium numero, tum etiam figura, irrationali quadam symphonia rationaliter conciliet." Lib. XIV prop. 10, quoted from the Basel edition of 1537 by Chasles, *Aperçu historique sur l'origine et le développement des méthodes en géométrie*, p. 512. See Lund, p. 140, and Ghyka, *Le Nombre d'or* I, 50, 64. Campanus was chaplain of Pope Urban VII and a canon of Paris Cathedral.

architect's abiding concern with that order, his disregard for mere decoration and effect, are what render the Cathedral of Chartres so imposing. It is not the use of mathematical proportions as such, or even the exactness with which they are realized in Chartres, that is noteworthy. Few ecclesiastical builders, even in pre-Gothic times, seem to have disregarded the authority of Augustine and Boethius, and, as was noted earlier, mathematical formulae underlie nearly all medieval architecture and indeed most medieval art. What distinguishes Gothic from Romanesque in this respect is what might be called the aesthetic and structural relevance of proportion. A comparison will elucidate this difference.

The eleventh-century abbey of St. Michael's, at Hildesheim, one of the grandest of Romanesque basilicas, may here represent the older style. The mathematical element is so conspicuous in its design that a recent student, H. Roggenkamp, has sought to connect it with the mathematical writings of Boethius, with which the builder, St. Bernward, was well acquainted.

St. Michael's is designed *ad quadratum*. The nave as well as the two transepts describe three large squares, each of which is in turn composed of three units of nine feet. (The trinitarian symbolism underlying the choice of these measurements seems to me quite obvious.) The height of the nave is twice that of the side aisles, which in turn is equal to the side of the basic square of the ground plan. Thus even a perfunctory glance at ground plan and elevation reveals the presence of the "perfect" ratios 1:1, 1:2, 2:3. It is to be noted, however, that these proportions constitute the principle according to which the church was designed but appear far less clearly in the completed building. This is because the architect—following what seems to have been general pre-Gothic practice—did not choose the intervals between axes, the centers of walls and piers, as his lines of direction, but alternated instead between their inner and outer surfaces. As a result, the squares do not appear as regular squares, because they either include the width of the wall and piers or "overlap" one another. Moreover, since the squares that determine the proportions of St. Michael's do not coincide with the structural axes of the edifice, they do not articulate structure and are thus not relevant to it. The architect seems to have used mathematical proportion as an operational device rather than for its effect upon structure or appearance.

Elsewhere in St. Michael's proportion appears with greater aesthetic

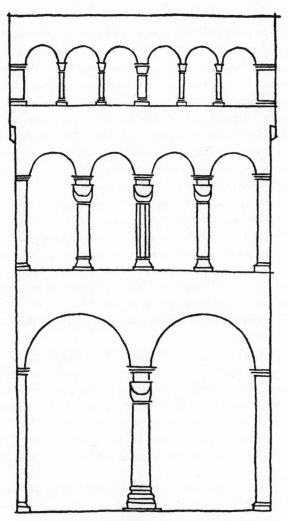

*Fig. 8. Abbey of St. Michael, Hildesheim. Northwest transept, Galleries of Angels*

emphasis. The north and south arms of both transepts terminated originally in the magnificent Galleries of Angels, of which the composition in the north-

*Fig. 8*

west arm, even after the heavy damage of the second World War, preserves its original form. Two galleries, superimposed upon the double arcade on the ground level, open with four and six arcades, respectively, into the transept. The "musical" ratios 1:2:3 are thus immediately apparent; they also determine the relative sizes of the supporting columns. The entire elevation, tripartite like that of Chartres, and almost equally exact in the application of the proportion chosen, thus invites comparison with the Gothic cathedral. This comparison, however, reveals a profound contrast.

In Chartres, proportion is experienced as the harmonious articulation of a comprehensive whole; it determines the ground plan as well as the elevation; and it "chains," by the single ratio of the golden section, the individual parts not only to one another but also to the whole that encompasses them all. The same desire for unification that induced the architect to treat piers and superimposed shafts not as independent units but rather as articulations of a continuous vertical rhythm suggested to him the choice of the proportion that might indeed be called the mathematical equivalent of that unifying design.

In St. Michael's, on the other hand, the characteristic tendency of treating the different parts of the edifice as autonomous units is also apparent in the role of proportion. The three types of columns in the transept endings are perfectly proportioned to one another. Yet they are separated by broad strips of wall surface so that we experience their proportion not as a "chord" of simultaneously "sounded" harmonious units, but rather consecutively, by proceeding from the first horizontal level to the second and from the second level to the third.

This, however, is not the most important difference. No visitor to St. Michael's is likely to remain unaware of the proportion used in the Galleries of Angels or, for that matter, of the mathematical law that has determined its over-all design. Yet, as an aesthetic factor, proportion does not play a primary role in the elevation and appears, as we have seen, somewhat "stunted" in the ground plan. In the Galleries of Angels, wall paintings, remnants of which have been found, must have further increased the divisive effect of the wall segments between the arcaded stories, thus diverting attention from the proportion of the columns. This proportion, moreover, seems to be confined to the columns and unrelated to the design or structure of the elevation as a whole. Owing to this fact, proportion in the elevation of St. Michael's, as in the ground plan, fails fully to assert itself aesthetically.

In Chartres, on the other hand, the architect has used as his lines of direction either the axes of the system or the inner width; proportion thus coincides with and articulates the "joints" of the structural anatomy, and subjects even the compositions of the stained-glass windows to the magnificent geometry of its law. It is when we compare Chartres with St. Michael's that we realize the full significance of proportion for the "geometrical functionalism" of early Gothic architecture.[79]

Notre Dame of Chartres is an edifice without architectural ornament. The architect designed his system with an eye to the great stained-glass windows whose color and light would counterbalance the simplicity of his architecture. Even so, this architecture is extraordinarily austere. If we glance at the most famous contemporary churches with which the Cathedral of Chartres had to stand comparison, and which were before the architect's eyes as he developed his own plan, it seems that the master created the first classical cathedral by reducing the design of those earlier churches to a new simplicity. I have already mentioned the Cathedral of Laon. We may also compare Chartres with the choir of St.-Remi at Reims and the southern transept of Soissons

79. For the above, see Beseler and Roggenkamp, *Die Michaeliskirche in Hildesheim*, pp. 100 (autonomy of individual parts), 84 (wall paintings), and 127 ff., for Roggenkamp's study of proportions. I have accepted in my own analysis his measurements, including the valuable determination of the foot used at St. Michael's, without being convinced of all his conclusions. Is it really possible or necessary to connect the sequence of 20, 35, 84, 35, and 56 feet, which, according to Roggenkamp, composes the main axis of the church, with Boethius' sequence of *numeri solidi* corresponding to the tetrahedron? Such a connection is all the less likely in that, as the author does not seem to realize, the builder could not have known with the passage in the *Timaeus* that deals with the cosmological function of the triangle and tetrahedron. Again, I am uncertain whether the 3:2:1 ratio between the columns in the northwest galleries is realized by means of a module of five feet. Roggenkamp's measurements include, not too plausibly, bases as well as capitals and imposts. Since the shafts of the largest columns measure exactly nine feet, I wonder if the ratios, consistent with the trinitarian symbolism noted elsewhere, are not based on a module of three feet. Be this as it may, the author's thesis regarding Boethius' possible influence upon the builder seems to me of great interest; I think the *De musica* may have played a role at least as important as the *De arithmetica*. For the question of lines of direction used by medieval architects, see above, n. 77, and p. 49, n. 69.

Cathedral, both masterpieces of the immediately preceding period and perhaps creations of the same artist. The design of these works is much more varied and rich. Their style is at once fiery and delicate, dramatic and graceful, attributes that we would not apply to Chartres. The quadripartite elevation imparts to those churches a certain restlessness. The light penetrating through the gallery windows tends to render shafts and colonnettes even slenderer than they actually are, and seems to suffuse the forms of the edifice with a luminosity that dissolves their contours. By comparison, Notre Dame of Chartres appears severe and restrained.

The contrast between the two styles is particularly striking if we compare the capitals. The most characteristic capitals of the 1180's—we might say, of the period before Chartres—are rich and leafy; their majestic foliage seems to rustle in a strong breeze; deep undercuttings produce contrasts of light and shadow. Such work required the skillful use of the chisel rather than the stone ax. In his description of Canterbury Cathedral, as rebuilt after the fire of 1172, Gervase specifically points out that in the new edifice capitals were carved with the chisel, whereas in the much simpler older church they had been cut with the stone ax.[80] The style of these years demanded the general use of the chisel. Such capitals as those of Laon, St.-Remi at Reims, and the ambulatory of Notre Dame of Poissy are truly monumental creations that remind us that the last quarter of the twelfth century was the age of that tempestuous genius, Nicolaus of Verdun—or that it would be, were it not overshadowed by the Cathedral of Chartres.[81]

Plate 40

Throughout the nave the master of Chartres has employed the crocket capital, a volute corresponding to each angle of the abacus above, as an almost functionally efficient means of linking the shape of the supports with the springing of the vault ribs or arches above them. Floral motifs are more developed in the capitals of the ambulatory, but still very simple by comparison with the capitals of the great sanctuaries of the preceding period. The crocket capital

80. Gervase of Canterbury, p. 27. Salzman, *Building*, p. 333, remarks that "the most momentous change in the working of stone was the introduction of the use of the chisel not only for carving but, to a rapidly increasing extent, for dressing stones, which occurred in the second half of the twelfth century." See also Colombier, p. 23.

81. The same fiery monumentality characterizes book illustrations of this period. See, e.g., the great Bible in the Bodleian Library, Oxford (MS. Auct. E. infra 2 [S.C. 2427], especially fols. 67 v, 77 r, 90 r).

has its forerunners in Norman architecture of the eleventh century.[82] It was subsequently adopted by the Cistercian Order. Around the mid-twelfth century it appears in the western ensemble of Suger's St.-Denis and on the southern tower of Chartres Cathedral. Its consistent employment in the Gothic Notre Dame is well attuned to the spirit of conservatism and restraint that pervades the edifice throughout. There were surely material reasons for such restraint. The need for economy may have been one reason, and for economy of time even more than of money. The architect did not employ the time of his masons on the carving of ornate and elaborate capitals. No one can have seriously planned to rebuild the cathedral before the fire of 1194; the architect cannot have sketched his first design before that date. Yet, barely twenty-five years later, in 1220, Guillaume le Breton saw the great vault complete.

There was yet another reason for the great simplicity of design. Choisy was the first to observe how admirably the master of Chartres turned to advantage the very limitations of his building material.[83] The coarse limestone he had to use precluded the possibility of basing the effect of his design upon refinement of detail. He decided to let the stones speak their own truly "lapidary" language: the very simplicity of his design brings into play the imposing amplitude of the masses and the harmony of proportions that holds these masses together.

Finally, the architect's restraint attests his desire to harmonize his own design with the spirit of the older building, above all, with the west façade that the fire had spared.

It was decided to retain this masterpiece and, indeed, to concede to it the aesthetic prominence it deserved. The decision posed yet another problem. In place of the old narthex and the chapel above it, the new Gothic nave was extended westward as far as the façade. But the height of this nave was to be far loftier than the façade. To equalize their dimensions the master superimposed upon the Royal Portal and the three windows the rose that is a grandiose

82. Such as in Lessay, Caen, St.-Étienne (cf. Gall, *Die Gotische Baukunst*, pp. 316 ff.), St.-Nicolas, and Mont-St.-Michel. See also Lapeyre, "Les Chapiteaux historiés de l'église de Deuil" (*BM*, 1938, XCVII, 401). For early antecedents in the Île-de-France, see Deshoulières, "L'Église Saint-Pierre de Mont-martre" (*BM*, 1913, LXXVII, especially p. 17); and for the entire development, Lasteyrie, *L'Architecture religieuse en France à l'époque gothique*, II, 322 ff.; Jalabert, "La Flore gothique" (*BM*, XCI, 1932); and Seymour, pp. 167 ff.

83. Choisy, p. 438.

Plate 25

development of the theme first employed at St.-Denis and yet beautifully attuned to the older composition beneath it. Both the choice of the rose theme and the way the master has developed it in Chartres are as characteristic of him as they were to be portentous of cathedral architecture in France. There are, to be sure, traditional or conservative aspects that we have already encountered with

Plate 19

the master of Chartres. Suger's round window as the center of a twin-towered west façade had been followed, in similarly modest proportions, at the Cathedral of Senlis. It is at Chartres, however, that the motif that was to be the glory of the royal cathedrals of France appears for the first time—radiating, magnificent, dominating the entire façade.

In the design of his rose, the master of Chartres may have at once followed and improved upon the probably somewhat earlier rose of the northern transept of Laon, the cathedral he knew so well. Both roses are developed around an innermost circle containing short columns under round arches. Radiating from that circle there are again columns with pronounced bases and capitals. In Laon,

Plate 45

however, these columns meet arches rising from the outer periphery of the rose. This solution was not adopted by the architect of Chartres. Maybe he disliked the somewhat "thorny" pattern of Laon; at any rate, he eliminated the peripheral arches and obtained a design resembling the petals of a flower by placing round arches above sturdy columns and surrounding these with twelve rosettes. Round forms prevail throughout in the western rose of Chartres. We also note that in order to obtain the largest glazed surface possible, the architect at Laon uses slender, somewhat brittle forms, whereas the master of Chartres leaves much more of the solid surface intact. In this regard his rose is less advanced than that at Laon. It is curious to note that the design of the flying buttresses of the nave may indicate a certain caution on the part of their architect, inasmuch as their splendidly vigorous forms may reflect his wish to supply too much rather than too little material support for the thrust of the great vault and roof. Similarly, the design of the western rose may have been influenced by statical considerations, since its surface, as we shall presently see, had to brace the horizontal wind pressure as well as the load above. Comparison of the rose and the flying buttresses reveals yet another trait characteristic of the master's artistic handwriting—his leitmotiflike repetition of certain elements: the round arches over sturdy columns that form the "petals" of his rose are repeated between the two main arches of the nave buttresses (see below, p. 240).

A generation later, Villard de Honnecourt copied the Chartres rose in his model book, but, as was his habit, he made certain changes so as to adapt it to *Plate 46* the taste of his time. In his drawing forms are more slender, and openings have been enlarged or even added where in Chartres they do not exist. Thus the round windows along the periphery have become larger in comparison with the central rosette, and so have the trefoils between them that replace the small quatrefoils of the Chartres façade; and whereas the master of Chartres left solid wall segments between his "petals" and the surrounding rosettes, Villard perforates the surface with quatrefoils.

In this regard, although Villard explicitly states that his design represents the rose at Chartres, it is a critique rather than a copy of the western rose and thus anticipates the second great rose at Chartres, that of the southern façade. *Plate 47* Here the architect, in accordance with the general principle of increasing luminosity in the transept and choir, which governed the design of the windows as well as that of the buttresses, developed his southern rose from its western predecessor: he moved the circle of twelve rosettes inward, taking up at the same time the motif of the twelve arches rising from the periphery that we have seen at Laon. And he placed quatrefoils between these arches and the rosettes while giving more slender and elongated forms to the columns radiating from the center and placed under trefoil arches. Thus, despite certain similarities, the two roses are essentially different: while the western rose appears as a surface perforated by a rich and beautiful pattern, the transept rose, much like its sister in Laon, appears as an essentially linear configuration laid over a single glazed surface.

At Chartres a last stage seems to have been reached in the design of the rose that illuminates the northern transept. A vast stylistic difference separates it *Plate 48* from the western rose not so much because angular shapes—triangles and squares—have replaced round ones but because these shapes seem to interpenetrate, merge into, and envelop one another: thus the triangles over the colonnettes are also sides of the squares above them, and the eye is induced to perceive each pair of triangles and the square they support as parts of a larger, petallike form that envelops all three of them. So different is this northern rose from the two others that it is difficult to recognize here the artistic hand of the same master (see below, pp. 238 ff.). But we cannot approach this problem by viewing the design of the three great roses from the outside only, disregarding the fact that this design, however splendid, was conceived as the frame for the compositions of stained glass visible only from within. We must assume that these compositions, if they did not determine the design of their architectural frames, certainly exerted an influence upon them.

In Chartres the compositions of the three great roses have been preserved. In the western rose there occurs—for the first time, for all we know—one of those "cosmic" themes that were to be taken up in the two later roses. The west end of a church building (as in Torcello or in Giotto's Arena Chapel) was reserved for representations of the Last Judgment, and the western rose at Chartres is dedicated to the same theme—its earliest monumental representation in stained glass and in the pattern of a great rose.

In medieval thought the rose pattern had long been fraught with symbolic significance. No invention of Christian art, the rose window occurs in Islamic architecture long before its adaptation in the West. Probably the earliest example, and certainly by far the largest, occurs in the palace erected at Jericho

*Plate 49*    by the Omayyad Caliph Hisham in 724 A.D. Unfortunately the palace was destroyed by an earthquake soon after its completion. We cannot be certain, therefore, exactly where this rose was originally placed, or even whether it actually served as a window opening. No other function, however, appears plausible, even though the voids in that beautiful pattern surely were not glazed.

As a symbol, however, the Gothic rose window is rooted in a different tradition. Isidore of Seville in his work *On the Nature of Things* seems to have been the first Christian writer to employ the circular pattern as an image of the cosmos. As such it appears (as B. Tessèdre in *GBA*, LVI, 1960; Beer; and others have shown) in medieval illuminations of Isidore's work. Its iconography is taken over and translated into monumental proportions in the great rose window

*Plate 50*    of the southern transept of Lausanne Cathedral. At the same time, however, the

*Plates 8, 9*   circular image was used as a symbol for the spiritual cosmos in a way that curiously anticipates the pattern of the Gothic roses. And even though according to modern thinking the physical and the spiritual universe are quite distinct, we

*Plate 10*    must not be surprised if in medieval imagery the two are merged, as they still are for Dante (see above, p. 37). Hence one cannot imagine a more adequate symbol of the medieval cosmos than the rose window. Etymologically the word *kosmos*, we noted, signifies at once order and ornament. The architecture of Chartres Cathedral is the perfect evocation of the "geometrical" cosmology of the School of Chartres precisely because, as we saw, it is a sanctuary devoid of decoration, its beauty residing in the pure harmony of its geometrical proportions. Nowhere is what Werner Gross has called the Gothic tendency to merge the mathematical with the ornamental—we might add, the transfiguration of the one into the other—more apparent than in Chartres Cathedral, and nowhere in Chartres Cathedral is it more apparent than in the three great roses.

Abbot Suger, we recall, had attempted by means of the sculptural program of his façade to make us aware that as we cross its threshold, we pass "anagogically" and mystically from this world into eternity, with the Last Judgment standing between the two. At Chartres the same theme is depicted in the western rose. Both in the Gospel of St. Matthew and in the Book of Revelation the Last Judgment is evoked as immediately preceding the creation of a "new heaven and a new earth," in other words, of that Heavenly Jerusalem of which the church is the image. In Chartres this is made quite clear by the "cosmic" symbolism of the rose and even more so by the "Dionysian" medium of stained glass. Let us recall once more the sentence in which Dante sums up the entire metaphysics of light: "the divine light penetrates the universe according to its dignity" (see above, p. 52). As we enter Chartres Cathedral and look up at the Judgment scene above us we realize how superbly its translucency as well as its architectural pattern is attuned to the theme—the creation of a new cosmos.

The message is conveyed even more perfectly by the southern rose. Its subject is the second Epiphany of Christ, again according to St. John's Book of Revelation. The Lord appears seated, surrounded by the four beasts symbolizing the evangelists, by angels, and by the twenty-four elders. Again Dante may be recalled: "In forma dunque di candida rosa / mi si mostrava la milizia Santa" (*Paradiso*, 31:1), "The hosts of saints appeared to me in the shape of a luminous rose."

The northern rose is dedicated to the Virgin Mary, who is depicted in the center, enthroned, with the Christ child in her lap. Four doves above her—possibly allusions to his having been conceived by the Holy Ghost—and eight angels surround her, while the twelve squares are occupied by the kings of Juda, Christ's ancestors. Along the periphery are placed the twelve minor prophets. The four lancets on either side between the lower circle of the rose and its square frame are filled, in alternation, with the royal lilies of France (which also occupy the twelve quatrefoils of the rose) and the castles of Castille, indicating that the donor of this great composition was, as we noted earlier, Queen Blanche, mother of St. Louis. The queen's patronage was certainly not unconnected with the selection of the theme of mother and son. But transcending it seems to be another theological interpretation of Christ's birth. According to the Fourth

*Plate 52*

Gospel the Incarnation is the divine light shining into darkness. The three great roses are thus inspired by St. John.

Most visitors to Chartres Cathedral will have noticed that the programs of the west, south, and north portals and of the stained glass inside are largely identical, except that those of the southern and western façades have been "reversed": the second Epiphany depicted in the sculptures of the west façade appears in the southern rose, while the Last Judgment, the theme of the western rose window, has been taken up again in the sculptures of the central portal of the southern transept. The reason for this—the statuary of the west façade was preserved from the earlier church, while the Last Judgment, as we saw, was the appropriate theme for the west end of a church—need not detain us. Far more important is the fact that the identity of subject matter conveys all the more forcefully the vast "anagogical" difference between sculpture and stained glass, a difference of which the master architect and even more those who commissioned the entire work must have intended to make us aware. Statues are tangible; they belong to this world. But as we enter the sanctuary we behold, as in a vision, the Incarnation and the world to come, suffused by light and revealing their theological meaning to our eyes according to the "Dionysian" theology of royal France. Electric light has dulled our sense experience. We must try to relive the full contrast that medieval man experienced as he entered from the accustomed daylight outside into the mysterious and overwhelming splendor within.

But as we admire this artistic achievement, we must not overlook the immense technical problems involved in designing the three great roses in such a way that their beautiful architectural patterns also carried the grand message of their programs.

Some years ago a German architect, the late Werner Thiedke, calculated the horizontal wind pressures to which the rose of the southern transept of Paris Cathedral is exposed. Thiedke concluded that since its diameter measures 12.90 m., the surface of the rose must resist wind pressure corresponding to the enormous weight of 13,100 kg. Thiedke's calculation, which he kindly made available to me, may be inexact, inasmuch as he does not tell us on what data regarding wind velocity it is based. Even so, his study is by no means without interest. He concludes that the architect took as his model a cartwheel, in which rings of arcades or similar concentric elements brace the radiating spokes. The architect of Chartres Cathedral, with no scientific knowledge of statics at his disposal, had to rely on experience. He had to bear in mind that the design of his three roses had to be adequate to the grandiose theme they were to convey but also able to withstand the pressure of the proverbial "great winds" of the Beauce region. No wonder the master was cautious in designing his first rose window, that of the west façade, keeping glazed surfaces relatively small. The two transept roses he placed under discharging arches, thus diverting the thrust of the dead load above the roses. As regards the southern rose the master may have profited from his experience with the west façade. Just as the buttresses of his choir are more slender than those of the nave, so the solid surfaces of this rose are, by comparison with its western predecessor, greatly reduced. The greater translucency thus gained was no end in itself. It responded both to the iconographic program for this rose and to that "Dionysian" worship of light so notable in the entire architectural system of Chartres.

Looking at the northern rose both from without and from within, we realize that the outside and inside patterns differ significantly from one another. The inside appears as pure surface, all tactile values having been suppressed in order not to impede the great geometrical vision transfigured by the superbly chosen coloring of the stained glass. And we now perceive elements, such as the quatrefoils with the lilies of France, that are invisible from the outside. The inside pattern is altogether much richer. Compare, for instance, the triangular arches surrounding the center outside with their counterparts within. Those arches now appear as nothing but frames. Within them are inscribed, with the help of the iron armatures of the stained glass, much richer configurations called for by the iconographic program. In short, the rose that we see from the outside was designed for a dual purpose: it not only provides a frame for the stained glass but also braces the large glazed surface against the pressure of the wind. That outside pattern, then, must be understood as a function of the luminous composition of the rose that we see inside the church. That composition therefore was conceived and designed first. The great web of the bar tracery outside must be regarded as having been designed primarily to protect that composition. That the pattern of that web is also a work of art is well worth noting.

What I have earlier called the master's predilection for the leitmotif is particularly true for the rose. The rose motif does not only dominate the three façades. In the clerestory of the nave the roses that appear again above the pair of lancet windows in each bay have the obvious purpose of increasing the translucent surface. If one compares the clerestory of Chartres with that of the contemporary St.-Yved at Braine, which is similar as regards the elevation, the in-        *Plate 40* tention of the master of Chartres becomes very clear. Whereas at St.-Yved there is but a single, relatively small window, framed on either side by wide wall surfaces, at Chartres the lancets and rose occupy the entire clerestory, which, moreover, is now as tall as the nave arcade. And the master has not allowed the vaults to obscure this luminous foil. Whereas at St.-Yved the vault is sprung from capitals only slightly below the window sills, "the clerestory windows at Chartres descend far below the springing line of the ribs and of the whole curvature of the vault" (Bony). One must add that both vaults and ribs were designed so as not to impede the expanse of the windows between them. The vaults are "pinched back," giving way to the roses, while the ribs above their springing are constructed according to the system that has come to be called *tas-de-charge*.

*Plate 51*  The *tas-de-charge* collects, as it were, crossribs and diagonal ribs above the capitals in horizontal beds; these "bundles" are actually part of the wall, now reduced to a mere pier between the window openings, which continues upward "so that its stability [is] assured in supporting the superstructure" (Fitchen). The *tas-de-charge* also occurs at St.-Yved, a church that—for reasons I find by no means convincing—has been claimed to be a few years earlier than Chartres. At any rate only at Chartres has the *tas-de-charge* been used for a purpose, magnificent in its artistic consistency: to render possible the translucency of the entire clerestory. If St.-Yved really is earlier, its architect used the *tas-de-charge* in complete ignorance of its possibilities or its purpose. It is in Chartres that this device—and the entire design of the cathedral—is first employed in the service of the aesthetics of light.

The roses of Chartres call our attention to the range of the architect's responsibilities, unimaginable to his modern equivalent. When he was commissioned to design the roses, to translate their program into artistic form, his task was no less than that of pitting a transcendental vision against the laws of nature, laws which he knew from experience only. But he also was at least generally responsible for the design of both stained glass and sculptures. At Chartres this seems to be proven by the fact that certain figures in the stained glass and the sculptures appear to be identical. Thus a horseman stumbling from his mount appears as an allegory of pride in the southern porch, while under the figure of Aaron in the lancet window on the right of the northern transept façade Pharaoh is represented in exactly the same way (Villard de Honnecourt has drawn this figure in his model book, possibly as a copy of what he had seen at Chartres). Again, the donor Clément in the southern transept is almost identical with the chivalrous saint in the southern porch. Moreover, stylistic affinities between certain transept sculptures and stained glass figures have also been noted (L. Grodecki, *Chartres* [Paris, 1963], p. 125; K. M. Swoboda, *Festschrift H. R. Hahnloser* [Basel, 1961]).

The sculptures are so essentially a part of the architecture that a few observations are indispensable. The two transept façades have not been preserved as originally designed. The master had not originally provided for them.[84] The munificence of the houses of Dreux and France may have suggested the idea. The three entrances that lead from the north and south into the cathedral, as well as the porches sheltering them, were adorned with a profusion of sculptures such as had never been seen before. In the present context I must again refrain from an analysis of this statuary, which influenced the monumental style of the thirteenth century as decisively as did the architecture itself, and as the sculpture of the west façade influenced the art of the second half of the twelfth century.

The statues in the jambs, especially those which flank the two central portals and were probably executed first, differ significantly from the style that monumental sculpture had developed but a few years before, notably at the façade of Senlis.[85] The difference is all the more remarkable since the stone of the Chartres figures comes from the neighborhood of Senlis,[86] and the tympanum of the central portal of Chartres North repeats the theme of the triumph of the Virgin that had been previously represented over the main portal of the Cathedral of Senlis. The style of the Chartres figures, however, can only be understood as a deliberate revival of the style of the west façade. I do not know any other masterpiece that is similarly attuned to a composition fifty years older, an adaptation prompted not by lack of originality but by an almost reverent esteem for the earlier work.

The statues of the Chartres transepts move us not so much by their inventiveness or originality as by an austerity and reserve imposed by tradition. At first sight they appear stiff, even monotonous. They recall the statues of the west façade not only in their attitudes and the motifs of their delicately pleated garments but also by the rigid order of their arrangement, which conforms completely to the simple geometry of the architectural setting. Yet their posture and expression are neither forced nor lifeless. Theirs is the same quality of soul

84. See above, p. 181.
85. See Aubert, *La Sculpture française au moyen-âge*, pp. 219 ff.

86. See Lefèvre-Pontalis, "Comment doit-on rédiger la monographie d'une église?" (*BM*, 1906, LXX, 462).

that moves us in the statues of the Royal Portal. The master of Senlis has portrayed his Old Testament figures in forceful, even violent, movement. The
*Plate 37*     same figures are represented on the northern transept of Chartres with the utmost restraint, as if neither the dramatic nor the lyrical mood had been considered appropriate for the great forerunners of Christ. Yet this very restraint
*Plate 41*     and simplicity render the figures unforgettable. The David is truly regal, Moses a lawgiver divinely inspired; John the Baptist is perhaps the most moving image of this saint in Christian art.

The sculpture of the Chartres transepts is as essentially fresh and original as the architecture is novel and even daring. Both, however, contain these qualities within, or even conceal them behind, a seemingly conservative and retrospective form. This fact is hardly surprising. The fame and eminence of the cathedral rested, as we have seen, on the cult of the Virgin, claimed to have been practiced here since immemorial times. The chapter may well have felt that this venerable continuity of religious tradition also demanded, so far as the new cathedral was concerned, a design that combined the resplendent with the conservative. And even such understandable considerations apart, we have every reason to believe that the ecclesiastical body with which the master of Chartres Cathedral had to deal was unlikely to be susceptible to novelty and invention. The speculative impulse that characterized the Cathedral School two generations earlier had abandoned it before the turn of the century. The mood was now retrospective, if not timid. Peter of Roissy, though neither the least learned nor the least literate of the chancellors of Chartres, was as an author certainly the most derivative of them all. And it is with men of this type that the architect of the new cathedral had to deal. Their tastes and wishes had to be taken into account as he began to develop his design.

None of them was able to stifle the extraordinary forcefulness of his genius. The sculptures of the transept portals partake of the "noble simplicity and calm grandeur" that truly characterize the architecture as a whole—so much so that we cannot doubt that sculpture and architecture are essentially the work of the same artist. What this affinity of style suggests is confirmed by our knowledge of medieval practice. The master who directed the building of the cathedral was also in charge of its entire sculptural decoration. And he was fully qualified to assume such vast responsibilities. The medieval builder had passed through the same school as did the stonecutter and the sculptor.[87] The apprenticeship of all began in the quarry. The quarryman and stonecutter became a "freemason" if he was able to work "freestone," i.e., fine-grained sandstone or limestone, carving moldings, capitals, ornamental figures, after models that had previously been designed by the master.[88] The best freemasons created the statues of the façades; the best among these rose to be master of the fabric and leader of all.

This is the career we must envisage for the architect of Chartres. Even as he directed and carried the tremendous responsibility for the great work as a whole, it was still customary for the master to take an active hand in its execution.[89] He might carve the figures, or at least the heads, of the main statues and he certainly supervised the design of the entire program.

This task of guidance and supervision, with the indispensable blend of authority and tolerance that is required in artistic matters, must have been the most difficult of all. The statuary of the transepts is the work of many artists; we can venture a rough guess as to their number. We know that fifteen *imagiers*, of whom at least three were assisted by an apprentice each, worked on the main portal of the Cathedral of Rouen, creating, during fifteen years, thirty-four large statues as well as the tympanum and numerous smaller figures on the bases and archivolts. This work dates from the early sixteenth century only. But Mme. Lefrançois-Pillion, who has studied the Rouen documents, in-

87. See Aubert, "Building Yards and Master Builders in the Middle Ages" (*Liturgical Arts*, XIX, 1951); Mortet, "La Maîtrise d'oeuvre dans les grandes constructions du XIIIᵉ siècle et la profession d'appareilleur" (*BM*, LXX, 1906); Colombier, p. 85; and *RDK*, art. "Baumeister."

88. Knoop and Jones, *The Medieval Mason*, pp. 86 f. For a different interpretation of the term freemason, see Frankl, "The Secret of the Medieval Masons" (*AB*, XXVII, 1945). Cf. Colombier, p. 41.

89. This situation gradually changed, however, owing to the increasing theoretical responsibilities as well as the social prestige that devolved upon the builders of the great cathedrals. The often-quoted passage from a sermon of Nicolas of Briard, "Magistri cementariorum

virgam et cyrothecas in manibus habentes, aliis dicunt: Par ci le me taille, et nihil laborant; et tamen majorem mercedem accipiunt . . ." suggests that at this time (1261) at least the architect's abstention from manual work was not yet considered either normal or satisfactory. It is to be noted that Gisbergus, the master of St.-Victor at Xanten, carved himself "formas ad sculpendum lapides," and Konrad Roriczer, the architect of Regensburg Cathedral, executed several statues himself. See Juettner, *Ein Beitrag zur Geschichte der Bauhütte und des Bauwesens im Mittelalter*, pp. 41 ff. For similar examples, see Colombier, pp. 58, 74. See also Mortet, "Maîtrise d'oeuvre," and Pevsner, "The Term 'Architect' in the Middle Ages" (*Sp*, XVII, 1942).

sists with good reason that Rouen may be used as an example for building practices in medieval France generally.[90]

The program of the Chartres façade was much vaster than that of Rouen. We must therefore assume that nearly twice as many sculptors were employed in its execution. Several were artists of genius. The statues of St. Anne and, in the southern portal, John the Baptist, the Christ, St. Martin, and St. Gregory the Great (not to mention some figures, such as the Theodore and Modeste, that were executed somewhat later), as well as many others, are masterpieces of the first rank. Those who created them worked side by side, willing to attune their styles and techniques to a common vision. When we think of the self-centered and quarrelsome individualism of Renaissance and modern artists, the achievement seems truly astonishing.

We know, of course, of many great artists who employed numerous assistants. But the responsibilities of a cathedral builder were extraordinarily diversified. He had to be an accomplished sculptor and at the same time an engineer and mathematician. The great Gothic builders thought of themselves above all as geometricians; [91] and the master of Chartres—his knowledge of geometry proves it—had certainly studied the quadrivium. But his influence and obligations extended beyond the artistic sphere. In Chartres, the financial administration of the cathedral fabric was in the hands of two or three canons, the *canonici provisores operis ecclesiae*, or *magistri fabricae ecclesiae* as they were called at a later date. To them the master was responsible.[92] His original designs or models were submitted to them or, more likely, to the bishop and entire chapter. This body or its deputies also determined the iconographic subjects of the great program of sculptures.

At the same time, however, the master's artistic authority of necessity involved jurisdictional and social obligations of considerable scope. Since he was

90. Lefrançois-Pillion, *Maîtres d'oeuvre et tailleurs de pierre des cathédrales*, pp. 143 ff. The author estimates that at least three times as many craftsmen must have worked on the statuary at Amiens.

91. See above, p. 34.

92. See Jusselin, "La Maîtrise de l'oeuvre à Notre-Dame de Chartres" (*SAELM*, 1915–22, XV, 244, 256). For a similar arrangement elsewhere, see Edwards, *The English Secular Cathedrals in the Middle Ages*, p. 124; and Thompson, "Cathedral Builders of the Middle Ages" (*History*, X, 1925). On the entire question of the medieval architect's responsibilities and functions, see now Colombier, pp. 28 ff.

responsible for the quality of the work, he was also responsible, to a large extent at least, for the hiring, training, supervision, and, if necessary, dismissal of the very numerous workers employed on the vast undertaking. He had a similar stake in their material and moral well-being. No deputy could have entirely relieved him of these manifold concerns.

When the Cathedral of Chartres was being built, masons' lodges, with their relatively clear-cut regulations and division of functions, had almost certainly not yet come into existence. They were organized only in consequence of those vast construction projects of which Notre Dame of Chartres was one of the first, and French medieval sources are so curiously silent regarding the masons' lodges that it has been doubted whether these ever existed in France.[93] Yet the Cathedral of Chartres could not have been built without a relatively large and efficient organization. And medieval institutions were more flexible than is often believed, and a great deal depended upon the individual. Where there were no precedents or earlier experiences to be followed, a man of genius, a forceful personality, might well be able (or even compelled) to concentrate in his own hands, as did Suger half a century earlier, the responsibilities of administrator, architect, and contractor. Anyway, our sources seem to indicate that only after the second half of the thirteenth century was it found expedient, on the Continent at least, to separate the financial and economic aspects of

---

93. In England, the master mason seems to have been frequently in charge of finance and administration. At Exeter, in 1300, he was one of the two *custodes operis* and it was his duty to keep a counterroll of the building account (Knoop and Jones, *Medieval Mason*, p. 34); in Wells, around 1265, the master workman was similarly concerned with the financial side of the fabric (ibid.); on the master mason's responsibility to hire and fire his workers, see ibid., pp. 34, 175. For Germany, cf. Janner, *Die Bauhütten des deutschen Mittelalters*, p. 116, and *RDK*, art. "Baubetrieb." Conversely, however, the canons who were appointed as "masters of the fabric" were surely chosen because of their artistic and technical abilities. At Auxerre the bishop, Geoffrey of Champallement (1052–76), "Elegit etiam, cum laude et cum gratiarum capituli sui actione, quosdam,

quos gratis canonicos . . . constituit, aurifabrum mirabilem, pictorem doctum, vitrearium sagacem, alios necnon, qui singuli prout cuique erat facultas, in officio suo deservirent." Mortet and Deschamps, *Recueil*, I, 93. Here the artistic qualifications of the canons were the conditions of their appointment, and their share in the embellishment of the cathedral is beyond question. Something similar may have been true for Godefroid of Huy, the great twelfth-century goldsmith, who became a canon of Neumostier and created beautiful liturgical vessels for this church. See also Thompson, p. 140. Examples such as these show how rash it would be to define too rigidly the master's responsibilities on the basis of his position. The position and its scope varied from place to place and underwent certain changes in the course of time. See Colombier, p. 44.

cathedral building from the technical and artistic tasks, and to entrust these and only these to a professional architect.[94]

What renders an exact understanding of the functions of a medieval architect so difficult is the vagueness of medieval terminology. *Magister operis* may refer either to the administrator in charge of supplies needed on the building site, of financial matters, of labor relations, or the term may be used for the architect in our sense.[95] But such indistinct use of terminology may actually indicate an indistinctness of functions. Not only the documents we possess in regard to the cathedral fabric of Chartres—all of a much later date—but also analogous situations elsewhere [96] suggest at least the possibility that the master of Chartres Cathedral united large administrative responsibilities with his architectural tasks. And the general supervisory authority of the bishop and chapter, the more specific powers of the canons *provisores*, may often have complicated rather than facilitated the realization of the great project for whose artistic and technical aspects the master bore the responsibility alone.

Unfortunately, the thirteenth-century account books of the Cathedral of Chartres are lost. We have only some shreds of evidence on which to base our estimate of the exact nature of the master's position and authority. Early in the thirteenth century—at the time, that is, when work on Notre Dame was under way—two *magistri operis* are mentioned, one of whom is attached to the cathedral, the other to the bishop.[97] Only the first, we may assume, was in charge of the fabric. Both received revenues and privileges considered as a fief. A century later, around 1300, the so-called polyptych of Notre Dame was drawn up, which lists the prebends, revenues, and possessions of the cathedral. One entire prebend is set aside for the master of the fabric: "prebenda magistri operis que est perpetua pro quolibet magistro." [98]

At this time, then, the master was a prebendary of the cathedral. Somewhat later still, around the mid-fourteenth century, we learn that the chaplain of the Altar of the Crucifix administered the sacraments of baptism, matrimony, and penance to the family of the master of the fabric.[99] The text makes it

94. Colombier, p. 61.
95. On this much-discussed subject of terminology, see most recently Colombier, pp. 53 ff.
96. Colombier, pp. 62, 74, and above, n. 92.
97. Jusselin, pp. 253 ff.
98. *CC*, II, 2, 279. Cf. Jusselin, pp. 235 f.
99. Jusselin, pp. 247 f.

clear that the custom was considered a privilege of quite unusual significance. The prebend and this custom were certainly long-established institutions at the time they are mentioned, and very likely date back to the time when the master of the fabric was not merely the supervisor of an existent building but the famed architect who erected it.[100] We may thus treat these scanty references as faint echoes of the recognition the master received in his lifetime. To get the full measure of his achievement it is sufficient to realize that within a quarter of a century (and probably in a much shorter time, given the life span granted a man who has reached the full maturity of his talents) he designed the great edifice, and perhaps assembled and certainly trained the artists and craftsmen who were to carry it out. As likely as not he died before the cathedral was completed. But he did impress upon those who worked under him and after him his particular vision with sufficient clarity to make the architecture and sculp-true of Notre Dame of Chartres an artistic unit of unexcelled homogeneity and indeed the expression of his unique genius.

We can say no more—and no less—about him. Of his identity nothing whatever is known. His Italian contemporary, the great architect and sculptor Benedetto Antelami, is a definite historical personality for us. We know the

100. Jusselin remarks: "Le privilège dont jouissait le maître de l'Oeuvre, constaté en 1354, remontait certainement à une époque plus ancienne, et ce privilège avait, dans l'ordre moral, une valeur exceptionelle." With regard to the passage in the polyptych of 1300 he writes likewise: "Ces renseignements . . . n'auraient sans doute pas une forme aussi précise si la maîtrise de l'Oeuvre était un office de création récente." Jusselin has tried to show that the office of the *magister operis* of Chartres, a hereditary one in the fourteenth century, was purely administrative, and required neither the skills of the architect nor those of the mason. This conclusion is certainly justified with regard to the fourteenth century. But was it always like that? Jusselin himself observes that "On peut déjà penser que le jour où cesseront les grands travaux à la cathédrale, un tel office ne pourra plus rendre des services en rapport avec les privilèges dont il jouit." In other words, the privileges of the *magister operis* originated, almost without doubt, at the time of the building

of the cathedral. What was the scope of this position at that time? On the basis of analogies elsewhere, it is not impossible to maintain that the *magister operis* of Chartres Cathedral was the administrator of the cathedral fabric rather than its architect, and that he was the supervisor of the latter. But this is most unlikely in view of the fact that the chapter had appointed, as we have seen, two *supervisores*, whose functions would have overlapped with those of the lay supervisor. Moreover, we know that in the session of the chapter held at Christmas, 1300, a certain Jean des Carrières was introduced, a mason, *lathomus*, who was also *magister operis* (Lépinois, *Histoire de Chartres*, I, 179). Hence there can be no doubt that at this time the term and position of *magister operis* referred to the master mason, and that the unknown architect of the cathedral held the same title and—we may assume—enjoyed those privileges which later were enjoyed by men who had and needed no longer the qualifications of a great builder.

artist of Fulbert's cathedral,[101] and we know the celebrated builders of the thirteenth century. The names of the architects of Reims and Amiens were inscribed on the labyrinths on the floor of their cathedrals; the names of a Peter of

*Plate 6b*

Montreuil or a Hugh Libergier survive in the proud inscriptions on their tombstones.[102] We need no further proof that the age looked upon celebrated architects with an admiration reflected in their social and economic position and hardly surpassed in the Renaissance.[103] But the man, whose disciple every one of the masters just mentioned should have considered himself, is unknown. The labyrinth in Notre Dame of Chartres may have contained a metal plaque with his name; if so, it must have been lost at a relatively early date. The documents listing his revenues and privileges make it clear that he was a layman. But the obituaries extant mention no one, cleric or layman, whom we could associate in any major capacity with the great work. Some canons are listed as benefactors; none of these notices allows us to assume that they had any share in the design or execution of the cathedral. If Bishop Renaud took an artistic interest, we have no record of this fact. In short, it would be difficult to name a monument of similar importance whose maker or makers have been so completely forgotten.

Toward the end of the fourteenth century, in 1389, an anonymous writer

101. See *CC*, III, 204: "Obiit Berengarius, hujus matris ecclesie artifex bonus." Cf. Bulteau, "Saint Fulbert et sa cathédrale" (*SAELM*, 1882, VII, 306).

102. On the tomb of Peter of Montreuil, see de Mély, "Nos vieilles cathédrales et leurs maîtres d'oeuvre" (*Revue archéologique*, 5th series, 1920, XI, 311). The tomb of Hugh Libergier, the builder of St.-Nicaise at Reims, is now in the Cathedral of Reims. It was first reproduced by Didron, "Les Artistes au moyenâge" (*AA*, I, 1844); see also de Mély, p. 315.

103. Coulton's notion regarding the low esteem and humble status of the medieval architect (cf. *Social Life in Britain*, p. 468) was ably refuted by Briggs, *The Architect in History*, pp. 66 ff., and more recently by Colombier, pp. 81 f. On architects' wages, see recently Salzman, *Building*, pp. 68 ff.; Harvey, p. 41; and Colombier, pp. 75 ff. On the position of the great cathedral builders in later times, see

Kletzl, pp. 6 f., and Salzman, *Building*, p. 47, who remarks: "It is obvious that these master masons were men of good standing . . . Even the masters who were working on their own often undertook contracts running into hundreds of pounds—equivalent to more than as many thousands in modern money; and when they were employed to take charge of building operations they frequently received 7s. a week, equal to just over £18 a year, at a time when the possession of twenty pounds' worth of land entitled, or even compelled, a landed proprietor to become a knight. The great mason, Henry Yevele, in October 1389, received two Kentish manors . . . in lieu of his salary of 12d. a day; and his predecessor, Master John of Gloucester, was given the sergeantry of Bletchingdon (Oxon.) in 1256." See also Janner, pp. 35 ff., 101 ff.; and *RDK*, art. "Baumeister." There is also interesting information in Pariset, "Étude sur l'atelier de la Cathédrale de Strasbourg" (*AHA*, VIII, 1929).

compiled a history of the Cathedral and Chapter of Chartres, the so-called *Vieille Chronique*, which acquired a considerable and ill-deserved reputation among the earlier historians of Chartres.[104] It was the author's main concern to prove the venerable age of the sanctuary, which he claims to have been founded in the time of the prophets and sibyls in honor of the *Virgo paritura*.[105] The writer was equally intent upon proving the existing cathedral to be far older than it actually was. For this purpose he omitted all references to the fire of 1194 or the subsequent rebuilding of the sanctuary, insisting that the Gothic cathedral was the same that Bishop Fulbert had built in the eleventh century.[106] The chronicler's authority was considerable. The legends he told were accepted as truth, and gradually all memories of the incomparable endeavor that had produced the present cathedral were silenced. Only the scholarship of the nineteenth century yielded incontrovertible evidence of the actual date of the church.

One wonders if the oblivion into which the master of Chartres has passed is altogether unconnected with this forgery. Whoever concocted it was certainly in a position that allowed him to destroy documents that contradicted his thesis. He actually did erase the memory of the fire of 1194 from the poem *Miracles of the Blessed Virgin*.[107] Had the inscription on the labyrinth existed at that time, it would have given the lie to his fabrications.

Such conjectures apart, there is a sense in which the master of Chartres may be brought into relation with the forgery that nearly succeeded in erasing the memory of his achievement along with that of his name. As we know him through his work, might he not have smiled if he could have seen the *Vieille Chronique?* To continue unbroken the tradition of the older builders of Notre Dame had been his consuming ambition. He had revived in his own church the

---

104. Printed in *CC*, I, 2, 1 ff.
105. See above, p. 160.
106. *CC*, I, 2, p. 14. "Hujus tempore, anno . . . Domini MoXXo, civitas et ecclesia incendio totaliter devastatur; sed postquam idem Fulbertus, adhibita diligencia, sua magna industria, dictam ecclesiam, a fundamento usque ad summum ejus, in decore quo nunc est fere totaliter consummavit . . ."
107. *CC*, I, 2, pp. 14 ff. "De quibus miraculis pauca, que vix postmodum scripta reperta sunt,

[huic operi sint, et supra patent, annexa]." The editors add (n. 1), "Malgré les efforts du faussaire pour faire disparaître dans le Poème des Miracles toute trace de l'incendie de la cathédrale qui eut lieu en 1194, malgré les dates surchargées, les vers effacés ou ajoutés et autres supercheries encore évidentes aujourd'hui, il a néanmoins laissé échapper des détails qui ne permettent pas la moindre confusion entre ces deux incendies." See also Bulteau, *Monographie*, I, 97. ff.

destroyed sanctuary and summed up in his vision and achievement the great Platonic legacy of the twelfth century. The synthesis he created was not an end but a beginning. Not one of the major features of earlier architecture that he had eliminated here was to appear again, while his innovations were adopted by the master builders of the thirteenth century. They looked upon Chartres as the classical example of Gothic architecture and so have all subsequent generations. [*See Add.*]

It is not impossible to explain the classical character of Chartres Cathedral. Its design, authoritative and austere, offers nothing that one would attribute to personal invention or individual fancy. Indeed, we can no longer distinguish between structure and appearance, between the technical and the aesthetic accomplishment. The beauty of the edifice consists of the crystalline clarity of its structural anatomy. And these two aspects of the cathedral have in turn become inseparable from its symbolic character.

Notre Dame of Chartres, like every medieval church, is a symbol of heaven. It is the supreme solution of this theme, as the twelfth century defined it. But the Gothic cathedral is not, as Professor Sedlmayr suggests, an illusionistic image of the heavenly city. Illusionistic in a sense are the evocations of the eschatological theme in the mosaics and murals of Byzantine and Romanesque sanctuaries. But the term is Baroque, not medieval. It certainly does not apply to the grandiose abstraction of the Gothic system. The tie of analogy that in the Cathedral of Chartres connects the basilica with its celestial prototype is the clarity of order that number and light establish in both.

For this analogical function even of the proportions we have an unexpected witness. It is the French architect Philibert Delorme. Although he lived in the sixteenth century, he had a profound knowledge of Gothic building practice. In the Preface to his treatise on architecture, Delorme advises the reader to look in the order of the universe for the model of the proportions on which his own buildings are to be based. Too few architects, he says, observe these proportions. Yet God is the great and admirable architect, who by creating the cosmos according to measure and number and weight has also given to the human architect proportions so perfect that without such divine help he would never have been able to discover them. Delorme promises to write a work on the divine proportions in which he proposes to deal with the "sacred proportions" that God prescribed to Noah (for the building of the Ark), to Moses (for the Tabernacle), to Solomon (for the Temple), and to Ezekiel (in his description of the Celestial Temple). According to Delorme, nothing proves more clearly the dignity of the architect's profession than that God himself has instructed him about the measures and proportions to employ. With their aid the builder can design structures that, although they may not bear comparison with those mentioned in Holy Scripture, may nevertheless be infinitely more nearly perfect than anything the architects of emperors and kings have built until now. His own buildings, Delorme confesses, despite the recognition they have found, now appear worthless to him if he compares their order with that of those divinely inspired buildings. If he could build them anew, he exclaims, he would be able, with the help of those eternal proportions, to impart to them an unheard-of perfection.[108]

Delorme's statement is as revealing as it is moving. Here in the words of a great Renaissance architect we have the last acknowledgment of the conviction that, rooted in the cosmology and metaphysics of Platonism, had shaped medieval architecture. His thoughts are no different from those of the Gothic builders. In the Cathedral of Chartres the architect has realized the cosmological order of luminosity and proportion to the exclusion of all other architectural motifs and with a perfection never achieved before. Light transfigures and orders the compositions in the stained-glass windows. Number, the number of perfect proportion, harmonizes all elements of the building.

Light and harmony, it is to be noted, are not merely images of heaven, symbolic or aesthetic attributes. Medieval metaphysics conceived them as the formative and ordering principles of creation, principles, however, that only in the heavenly spheres are present with unadulterated clarity. Light and harmony have precisely this ordering function in the Gothic cathedral. The first architectural system in which these principles are completely realized is that of Chartres.

In order to appreciate this achievement let us compare Notre Dame with one of the earlier cathedrals, such as Noyon, the nave (1185–1205) of which

108. Delorme, Le Premier tome de l'archi-tecture, "Epistre aux lecteurs," pp. 3 ff. The passage is quoted by Jouven in Rhythme et architecture, pp. 20 f.

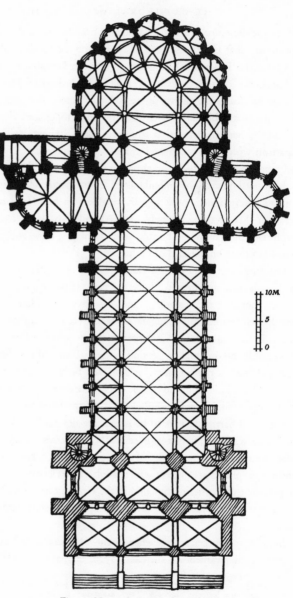

Fig. 9. Noyon Cathedral. Ground plan

was completed at the very time when work was in progress on that of Chartres. If both edifices are viewed side by side, Noyon is curiously lacking in cohesion. The ground plan is still Romanesque in that it suggests an additive process of composition: one could easily add or eliminate one or more of the rectangular bays of which it is made up. The ground plan of Chartres, on the other hand, represents the compact cohesiveness of an organism; it is a unit in which the slightest alteration of any part would destroy the whole. As we have seen, this cohesiveness is owing to the application of the golden section to the ground plan.

*Plate 42*

*Fig. 9*

We encounter the same difference if we compare the two elevations. In Noyon, as Seymour observes, we encounter "shifts of design and alternations of proportions" in almost every bay. The variation of design in Noyon may be attributed to the fact that the building of this cathedral extended over many decades. But this time lag and the concomitant change of architects do not account fully for the shifts of design. In the eyes of this earlier generation, variety was not yet a vice but rather a virtue. But to the classical age of Gothic architecture such lack of unity was intolerable. Homogeneity of interiors was demanded, and we know that architects were often obliged by contract to carry out unaltered the original plan of their predecessors. In Noyon even the individual bay shows a taste for variety of detail and relative autonomy of parts that is typical of the period of transition. It is most significant, however, that this variety and ornamental detail decrease perceptibly, as Seymour's analysis has shown, in those parts of the nave that were completed last. At the same time parts are related to one another by an increasing clarity and rigor of proportions. Only in the three western bays, which were completed last, is the relation of the width of an aisle to that of the nave brought to a ratio "of nearly exactly one to two." The elevation of Chartres, on the other hand, is a unit bonded together by exact proportion.

The master of Chartres began where the architect of the last bays of Noyon had left off. And there is an element of necessity, a grandiose objectivity, in these proportions that seems to withdraw the structure from the realm of individual invention and render it anonymous, anonymous or impersonal like the great mathematical discoveries or the classical experiments of science. And indeed Notre Dame bears some resemblance to these. We may well define it as a "model" of the cosmos as the Middle Ages perceived it. But this "model" was ontologically transparent. It reflected an ultimate reality.

May not this relation of his work to an objective truth be precisely the reason why the name and memory of the master of Chartres could so easily have passed into oblivion? Man has always craved recognition and fame, and medieval man was no exception. But an individual's achievement may be absorbed by a reality that is far more than personal. In this case his work will speak to us not as the artist's unique experience but as the expression of universal truth. The author of a sublime achievement of this kind, paradoxically enough, recedes behind his work; we are absorbed infinitely more with the objective reality to which this work bears witness than we are with the individual mind that created it. That precisely is the experience the medieval architect wanted to convey. On the portal of the Church of Pont-Hubert near Troyes the master has written

Non nobis, Domine, non nobis, sed nomini tuo da gloriam.

\*

POSTSCRIPT (1961)

Since this book was first published a number of studies have again taken up the chronology of the cathedral and more particularly the question whether the building campaign proceeded from west to east or from east to west.* While I believe with Grodecki in the greater plausibility of the first alternative,

* See especially L. Grodecki, "Chronologie de la Cathédrale de Chartres" (BM, CXVI, 1958), and P. Frankl, "Reconsiderations on the Chronology of Chartres Cathedral" (AB, XLIII, 1961).

the argument does not seem to me altogether settled. But the discussion is of
great value in that it has focussed attention on the problem of the stylistic
homogeneity of the cathedral and on the artistic personality of its creator.
These aspects call for a brief comment.

In the controversy mentioned, the marked differences between the flying
buttresses of the nave and of the choir have always played an important role.
I think both groups of buttresses are designed by the same master. To begin *Plates 34, 35,*
with, there seems to be almost general agreement today that the lighter *volume* *38, 39, 44*
of the choir buttresses must have been planned by the architect of the cathedral
from the beginning, since it was imposed by the space available between the *Plates 33, 43*
chapels of the choir and between the windows of the clerestory. Another
reason was the more luminous structure of the choir aisles as compared with
the side aisles of the nave: there are two windows to each bay in the first
instance as against one in the second. It is worth comparing, moreover, the
windows in each case: those of the side aisles of the nave leave intact enough *Plate 32*
wall surface to serve as relatively wide frames for them; but the windows of
the choir aisles are so wide that their surface consumes the available wall entirely. In short, the slender design of the choir buttresses shows that increasing *Plate 43*
reduction of volume and surface that also marks the other great inventions in
the structure of Chartres that we have studied, but was particularly called for
by that added luminosity by which the master meant to enhance the esthetic
dignity of the choir.

Is it correct, therefore, to conclude, as I have done in the preceding pages,
that Chartres Cathedral is the homogeneous work of a single master? Grodecki
does not think so. According to him, the same master who had conceived the
general plan of the nave, transept, and choir also directed the actual construction to the moment of the vaulting of the choir. At this point, however, a
second master with an artistic personality quite different from that of the
older man is supposed to have taken over. To this architect Grodecki attributes not only the two porches (which are indeed, as we have seen, an
"afterthought") but also the transept façades, the choir vaults, and, last but
not least, the design, though not the slender volume, of the flyers of the choir.

That the design of these flyers differs markedly from the design of the
flyers of the nave is evident. Is it necessary to explain this difference by as-

suming the succession of two different artistic personalities? It is in this question that the real interest of the problem resides. Let us compare, therefore,
the two groups of flyers. The two main arches of the flyers of the nave are

*Plates 34, 35* connected by short, radiating columns under round arches. The corresponding
members of the choir buttresses are slender "spokes" without bases and capitals
and supporting pointed arches. The motif is definitely more "gothic." But between these two sets of flyers, as Grodecki has shown in his remarkably acute
and sensitive analysis, an intermediary or transitory group exists on the east
side of the transepts. From the flyers of the nave this group borrows the
columns; but their proportions and the pointed arches they support point to
the flyers of the choir. The deliberately "transitional" character of this middle
group renders, to my mind, more difficult the assumption that the two types
of flyers, between which that group mediates, were designed by two different
artists. Grodecki, moreover, has pointed out that in the southeast corner of the
transept and choir a common pier supports one flyer of the "advanced"
(gothic) type and another flyer of the "intermediary" type, a fact that leads
Frankl to ask whether both of them must not have been designed as well as
built by one and the same architect. Be that as it may, there is stylistic evidence
to show that it was the master to whom we owe the main body of the cathedral
(excepting, that is, besides the west façade, possibly the porches, though not,
to my mind, the transept façades) who also designed the flyers of the choir.
The windows of the choir aisles consist of a double lancet divided by a pris-
*Plate 43* matic mullion and topped by a rose. This austere design resumes (or rather
anticipates) in large dimensions exactly the design of the "gothic" flyers that
adjoin them, even the rose corresponding with the round openings that appear
*Plate 34* in the spandrels above the prismatic "spokes." The master of Chartres liked
to repeat the same motif in different parts of the cathedral and in different
dimensions (see above, p. 206, n. 67). In the present case the stylistic harmony
produced by this device is particularly effective.

My assumption, if correct, allows an insight into the creative scope of
the master of Chartres. Art historians may be inclined to conceive this scope
of a great artist as more limited than it actually is and to assume that there
must have been as many artistic personalities as there are variations of style.
To how many different artists might we assign the oeuvre of Michelangelo

if we did not know it to be the work of a single man? The master of Chartres—
to judge him by his work—matured as the great edifice progressed. The design
of the choir seems in many respects the work of an old man; it is also the perfect
realization of the architectural vision that guided him throughout and that
posterity has come to define as classical gothic.

Also see Addenda to the List of Works Cited, p. 263

### TO P. 43, PAR. 2

"Bernard," G. Cattin rightly observes in his recent essay *Saint Bernard de Clairvaux*, 1960, p. 51, "was sensitive to all forms of beauty," and he quotes the saint's admonition, "Don't allow yourself to be ignorant of beauty if you do not want to be confounded by the ugly."

### TO P. 48, N. 67

Hahn's dissertation has subsequently been published under the title *Die frühe Kirchenbaukunst der Zisterzienser*, 1957.

### TO P. 50, N. 72

In his remarkable work, Hahn (ibid.) has further confirmed my conclusions regarding the prevalence of the "Augustinian" proportions in early Cistercian architecture and Bernard's "intimate participation" in its development (esp. pp. 66 ff.).

### TO P. 58, PAR. 1

This distinction, which seems to have eluded one reviewer of my book (see S. M. Crosby in *AB*, XIII, 1960, p. 149, and our correspondence, ibid., pp. 316 ff.), permeates Bernard's entire thought. "To you, brethren," he says in his first sermon on the Canticle of Canticles, "one has to speak of different things, or at least in a different mode, than to those living in the world" (*PL*, CLXXXIII, 785).

TO P. 90, END OF CHAPTER

Since the preceding remarks concerning the relations between the *chanson de geste* and the political and religious trends of Suger's time were written, a masterful attack by the great Spanish scholar Ramón Menéndez Pidal has seriously shaken, if not invalidated, the "individualist" thesis of Bédier and his school (*La Chanson de Roland et la tradition épique des Francs*, 2nd edn., 1960). According to Pidal the medieval French epic is not a spontaneous creation of the eleventh century but the gradual elaboration, continued and uninterrupted since Carolingian times, of the historical deeds of Charlemagne; it is, therefore, neither inspired by the Spanish "crusades" of the eleventh century nor rooted in the pious legends of sanctuaries along the pilgrimage roads to Compostela. On the contrary, these legends and their fame owe much to the *chansons de geste*, which, always according to Pidal, are the works not of clerics of genius but of generation after generation of *jongleurs*.

If this brilliantly substantiated thesis is accepted, several of its aspects are of great interest within the present context. Those epic narratives fulfilled the role of a national history, "à l'origine s'identifiaient à l'Histoire, continuaient à s'assimiler à l'Histoire, et à jouer le rôle de l'Histoire" (p. 496). And as such, as a patriotic "histoire chantée," the French epic kept alive the memory of the Carolingian past, as of an age in which the French armies, conquering and converting the Spanish infidels, had carried out a divinely ordained mission. Now Suger's view of French history was no different. He considered it his task as a statesman to revive the legacy of Charlemagne (and Charles the Bald) because he found in their reigns that intersecting of the political and the religious spheres that to him demonstrated God's particular love of the French nation. Pidal shows that these ideas and interpretations, far from being inventions of the *chansons de geste*, can be traced to chronicles and state papers of Carolingian times. As "histories," then, as part of the Carolingian revival, these epics attracted Suger, and he used their wide popular appeal, as the heads of other great monasteries did, to further his political and ecclesiastical purposes. If Pidal is right, I have unjustly suspected Suger of utilizing "fiction," of being responsible for "historical and political forgeries." Alas, the puzzle of the *Pseudo-Turpin* remains. Pidal's observations regarding this work are of particular interest. He remarks, somewhat tartly, that the

*Pseudo-Turpin* and its author, eight centuries before Bédier, incarnate all the false theories of "Bédierism": the author is indeed a cleric and his work was explicitly designed to foster devotion to Santiago and to those heroes who died for Christ in Spain as in the Orient (p. 341). But in order to achieve this purpose the *Pseudo-Turpin* has, according to Pidal, completely changed the spirit of the *Chanson de Roland*, transforming a heroic saga into a pious narrative. This transformation, this clerical attitude with its emphasis on religious motivation, has many parallels in the historical works of Suger.

### TO P. 121, N. 88

My interpretation has recently been confirmed by L. Grodecki, "Les Vitraux allégoriques de Saint-Denis," *Art de France*, I, 1961, p. 24.

### TO P. 122, PAR. 2

The best discussion of the St.-Denis windows is now offered in two articles by Grodecki: see ibid. and "Les Vitraux de Saint-Denis; L'Enfance du Christ," *Essays in Honor of Erwin Panofsky*, 1961. The author stresses the peculiarly "Sugerian" and "dionysian" character of the form as well as the content of these compositions—a welcome and convincing confirmation of the thesis expounded in these pages.

### TO P. 141, N. 140

As to the possibility of a dual—monarchical and biblical—significance of the statuary of St.-Denis and Chartres, see now Katzenellenbogen (see Add. for p. 153). Primarily, however, these statues of prophets and kings are surely to convey Christ's words: "Many prophets and kings have desired to see those things that ye see . . ." (Luke 10:24). Cf. the important observation of P. Kidson (*Sculpture at Chartres*, 1958, p. 16) regarding the horizontal division of the Chartres portal.

### TO P. 151, N. 35

Significant in this connection is the recent insistence on "a marked inner affinity" between the figure style of the famed St. Alban's Psalter and the sculptures of Chartres West in O. Pächt, C. R. Dodwell, and F. Wormald, *The St. Alban's Psalter*, 1960, p. 113.

TO P. 153, N. 43

For the probable influence of the Cathedral School upon the sculptural program of the west façade, see now A. Katzenellenbogen, *The Sculptural Programs of Chartres Cathedral*, 1959, pp. 17 ff. The author's interpretation of the group of the Virgin and Child differs somewhat from my own.

TO P. 155, PAR. 2

Since these lines were written, it has been pointed out that the *sectio aurea* occurs in only one of the jamb figures. The objection is quite valid, even though the adjoining figure offers at least a very close approximation to the same proportion. Are the proportions of the other statues created by the headmaster of the west façade perhaps based on experiments with the golden section? This seems to be still a possibility, even though I do not wish to insist on it.

TO P. 197, PAR. 1

It ought to be mentioned in this connection that Katzenellenbogen (see Add. for p. 153) believes Peter of Roissy may have had a share in formulating the program of the transept façades (p. 78).

TO P. 198, N. 45

And now P. Kidson, *Sculpture at Chartres*, 1958, pp. 55 f.

TO P. 202, N. 56

The Cathedral of Chartres, according to the recent measurements of Ernst Levy, measures 32.90 meters from plinth to *clef-de-voute;* its nave has a width of 16.44 meters.

TO P. 204, N. 60

As to the date of these third arches, cf. now L. Grodecki, "Chronologie de la Cathédrale de Chartres," *BM*, CXVI, 1958, pp. 96 ff.

TO P. 206, N. 67

This alternation, of which the Master of Chartres seems to have been particularly fond (see ibid., p. 118), seems to be of Norman origin. Besides Oxford Cathedral, it occurs in a number of other English buildings of the same period.

TO P. 227, PAR. I

See, however, J. Bony, "The Resistance to Chartres in Early Thirteenth-Century Architecture," *Journal of the British Archaeological Association*, XX–XXI, 1957/1958.

| | |
|---|---|
| *A* | *Annales; Économies, Sociétés, Civilisations* (Paris) |
| *AA* | *Annales archéologiques* (Paris) |
| *AB* | *The Art Bulletin* (New York) |
| *ABSS* | Association Bourguignonne des sociétés savantes, *St. Bernard et son temps* (Dijon, 1928) |
| *AHA* | *Archives alsaciennes d'histoire de l'art* (Strasbourg) |
| *AIBLM* | Académie des inscriptions et belles-lettres, *Mémoires* (Paris) |
| *Annali* | *Annali della Fabbrica del Duomo di Milano* (Milan, 1877–85) |
| *BEC* | *Bibliothèque de l'école des chartes* (Paris) |
| *BGAM* | *Beiträge zur Geschichte des alten Mönchtums und des Benediktinerordens* (Münster) |
| *BGPM* | *Beiträge zur Geschichte der Philosophie des Mittelalters* (Münster) |
| *BJRL* | *Bulletin of the John Rylands Library* (Manchester) |
| *BM* | *Bulletin monumental* (Paris) |
| *BRA* | *Bulletin des relations artistiques France-Allemagne* (Mainz) |
| *CA* | *Congrès archéologique* (various places) |
| *CC* | *Cartulaire de Notre-Dame de Chartres*, edited by E. Lépinois and L. Merlet (Chartres, 1862–65, 3 vols.) |
| *DVLG* | *Deutsche Vierteljahrsschrift für Literaturwissenschaft und Geistesgeschichte* (Halle) |
| *EHR* | *English Historical Review* (London) |
| *GBA* | *Gazette des beaux-arts* (Paris) |
| *GC* | *Gallia Christiana in provincias ecclesiasticas distributa* . . . (Paris, 1715–1865) |

HAL    *Historical Association Leaflet* (London)

HLF    *Histoire littéraire de la France* (Paris, new edition, 1869)

JSAH    *Journal of the Society of Architectural Historians* (Troy, N. Y.; Louisville, Ky.)

JWCI    *Journal of the Warburg and Courtauld Institutes* (London)

MD    Musée de Dijon, *Saint Bernard et l'art des Cisterciens* (Dijon, 1953)

MGH SS    *Monumenta Germaniae Historica, Scriptores* (Berlin)

MJ    *Münchner Jahrbuch der bildenden Kunst* (Munich)

MKW    *Monatshefte für Kunstwissenschaft* (Leipzig)

PG    *Patrologiae cursus completus . . . series Graeca*, edited by J. P. Migne (Paris, 1857–66)

PL    *Patrologiae cursus completus . . . series Latina*, edited by J. P. Migne (Paris, 1844–80)

RB    *Revue bénédictine* (Abbaye de Maredsous, Belgium)

RBSS    *Rerum Britannicarum Medii Aevi Scriptores*, edited by W. Stubbs (London, 1825 ff.)

RDK    *Reallexikon zur deutschen Kunstgeschichte* (Stuttgart, 1953 ff.)

RH    *Revue historique* (Paris)

RIBA    Royal Institute of British Architects, *Journal* (London)

RM    *Revue Mabillon* (Paris)

RTAM    *Recherches de théologie ancienne et médiévale* (Louvain)

SAELM    Société archéologique d'Eure-et-Loir, *Mémoires* (Chartres)

SNAFM    Société nationale des antiquaires de France, *Mémoires* (Paris)

Sp    *Speculum: A Journal of Medieval Studies* (Cambridge, Mass.)

SSM    *Scriptores de musica medii aevi*, edited by E. de Coussemaker (Paris, new series, 1867)

ZK    *Zeitschrift für Kunstgeschichte* (Leipzig)

## LIST OF WORKS CITED

For the works of medieval writers, which are not included here, see the Index.

ABRAHAM, P. *Viollet-le-Duc et le rationalisme médiéval.* Paris, 1934.

ACKERMAN, J. S. "Ars sine scientia nihil est." *AB*, XXXI (1949).

ACLOCQUE, G. *Les Corporations, l'industrie et le commerce à Chartres du XI<sup>e</sup> siècle à la révolution.* Paris, 1917.

ADENAUER, H. *Die Kathedrale von Laon.* Düsseldorf, 1934.

ADLER, A. "The *Pèlerinage de Charlemagne* in New Light on Saint-Denis." *Sp*, XXII (1947).

AHLVERS, A. *Zahl und Klang bei Plato.* Bern, 1952.

AMIET, L. *Essai sur l'organisation du Chapitre Cathédrale de Chartres.* Chartres, 1922.

*Analecta Hymnica.* Edited by G. M. Dreves and C. Blume. Leipzig, 1922. 55 vols.

ANDRESEN, H. (ed.). *Maistre Wace's Roman de Rou et des ducs de Normandie . . .* Heilbronn, 1877.

ANDRIEU, M. *Le Pontifical de la curie romaine au XIII<sup>e</sup> siècle.* (Le Pontifical romain au moyen-âge, Vol. II.) Vatican City, 1938.

―――. *Le Pontifical romain au XII<sup>e</sup> siècle.* (Le pontifical romain au moyen-âge, Vol. I.) Vatican City, 1938.

ANFRAY, M. "Les Architectes des cathédrales." *Les Cahiers techniques de l'art* (Paris), I (1947).

―――. *L'Architecture normande. Son influence dans le nord de la France.* Paris, 1939.

ARBOIS DE JUBAINVILLE, H. D'. *Etudes sur l'état intérieur des abbayes cisterciennes.* Paris, 1858.

ARENS, F. V. *Das Werkmass in der Baukunst des Mittelalters.* Würzburg, 1938.

AUBERT, M. "Building Yards and Master Builders in the Middle Ages." *Liturgical Arts* (Concord, N. H.), XIX (1951).

―――. *L'Architecture cistercienne en France.* Paris, 1943. 2 vols.

―――. *Notre-Dame de Paris.* Paris, 1928. 2 vols.

―――. "Le Portail du croisillon sud de l'église abbatiale de Saint-Denis." *Revue archéologique* (Paris), 6th series, XXIX, Mélanges Charles Picard (1948).

AUBERT, M. "Le Portail Royal et la façade occidentale de la Cathédrale de Chartres." *BM*, C (1941).

———. *La Sculpture française au moyen-âge.* Paris, 1946.

———. *Suger.* Abbaye S. Wandrille, 1950.

———. "Têtes des statues-colonnes du portail occidental de Saint-Denis." *BM*, CIV (1945).

AVENEL, G. D'. *Histoire économique de la propriété* . . . Paris, 1894.

AYZAC, F. D'. *Histoire de l'abbaye de St.-Denis en France.* Paris, 1860.

BACHMANN, E. Review in *Zeitschrift für Kunstgeschichte* (Leipzig), XV (1952).

BAEUMKER, C. "Witelo." *Beiträge zur Geschichte der Philosophie und Theologie des Mittelalters* (Münster), III, 2 (1908).

———. "Zur Frage nach Abfassungszeit und Verfasser des irrtümlich Witelo zugeschriebenen Liber de intelligentiis." In: *Miscellanea Francesco Ehrle*, Vol. 1. Rome, 1924.

BALTRUSAITIS, J. "L'Image du monde céleste du IX⁰ au XII⁰ siècle." *GBA*, series 6, XX (1938).

BANDMANN, G. *Mittelalterliche Architektur als Bedeutungsträger.* Berlin, 1951.

BARDENHEWER, O. *Geschichte der altkirchlichen Literatur.* Freiburg, 1924.

BAUMGARTNER, M. "Die Philosophie des Alanus de Insulis." *BGPM*, II (1896).

BAUR, L. "Das Licht in der Naturphilosophie des Robert Grosseteste." *Abhandlungen aus dem Gebiete der Philosophie und ihrer Geschichte. Eine Festgabe zum 70. Geburtstag Georg Frhrn. v. Hertling.* Freiburg, 1913.

BECKER, P. A. "Das Werden der Wilhelms- und der Aimerigeste." *Sächsische Akademie der Wissenschaften, Philo.-hist. Klasse* (Leipzig), XLIV, 1 (1939).

BÉDIER, J. *Les Légendes épiques: Recherches sur la formation des chansons de geste.* Paris, 1913.

BEENKEN, H. *Romanische Skulptur in Deutschland.* Leipzig, 1924.

BEER, E. J. *Die Rose der Kathedrale von Lausanne.* Bern, 1952.

BÉGULE, L. *L'Abbaye de Fontenay.* Paris, 1950.

———. *L'Abbaye de Fontenay et l'architecture cistercienne.* Lyon, 1912.

BEHLING, L. "Die klugen und törichten Jungfrauen zu Magdeburg." *ZK*, VIII (1954).

BERGER, E. "Annales de St.-Denis, généralement connues sous le titre de *Chronicon sancti Dionysii ad cyclos paschales.*" *BEC*, XL (1879).

BERGES, W. *Die Fürstenspiegel des hohen und späten Mittelalters.* Leipzig, 1938.

BERRIMAN, A. E. *Historical Metrology.* London and New York, 1953.

*Beschreibendes Verzeichnis der illuminierten Handschriften in Österreich*, VIII, 7 (Leipzig, 1935).

BESELER, H., and ROGGENKAMP, H. *Die Michaeliskirche in Hildesheim.* Berlin, 1954.

BIBLIOTHÈQUE NATIONALE. *Les Manuscrits à peintures en France du VII<sup>e</sup> au XII<sup>e</sup> siècle.* Paris, 1954.

BILSON, J. "The Beginnings of Gothic Architecture: Norman Vaulting in England." *RIBA*, VI (1899), IX (1902).

——. "Les Voûtes de la nef de la Cathédrale d'Angers." *CA Angers*, 1910.

——. "Les Voûtes d'ogives de Morienval." *BM*, LXXII (1908).

BIRKENMAJER, A. "Robert Grosseteste and Richard Fournival." *Medievalia et Humanistica* (Boulder, Colo.), V (1948).

BLANCHET, A., and DIEUDONNÉ, A. *Manuel de numismatique française.* Paris, 1912–36. 4 vols.

BLIEMETZRIEDER, F. *Adelhard von Bath.* Munich, 1935.

——. "Isaac de Stella." *RTAM*, IV (1932).

BLOCH, M. "L'Histoire des prix: quelques remarques critiques." *A*, I (1939).

——. *Les Rois thaumaturges.* Paris, 1924.

BOASE, T. S. R. *English Art 1100–1216.* Oxford, 1953.

BOECKLER, A. "Die Pariser Miniaturen-Ausstellung von 1954." *Kunstchronik* (Leipzig), VIII (1955).

——. "Die romanischen Fenster des Augsburger Domes und die Stilwende vom 11. zum 12. Jahrhundert." *Zeitschrift des deutschen Vereins für Kunstwissenschaft*, X (1943).

BOLLANDUS, J. (ed.). *Acta sanctorum.* Paris, 1863 ff.

BOND, F. *Gothic Architecture in England.* London, 1906.

——. *An Introduction to English Church Architecture.* London, 1913. 2 vols.

BONY, J. *French Cathedrals.* Boston, 1951.

——. "French Influences on the Origin of English Architecture." *JWCI*, XII (1949).

——. "Gloucester et l'origine des voûtes d'hémicycle gothique." *BM*, XCVII (1938).

——. "La Technique normande du mur épais." *BM*, XCVIII (1939).

BRÉHIER, L. "L'Histoire de la France à la cathédrale de Reims." *RH*, XXII (1916).

BRIÈRE, G., and VITRY, P. *L'Abbaye de St.-Denis.* Paris, 1948.

BRIGGS, M. S. *The Architect in History.* Oxford, 1927.

BRUYNE, É. DE. *Études d'esthétique médiévale.* Bruges, 1946. 3 vols.

BUCHNER, M. "Das gefälschte Karlsprivileg für St. Denis . . . und seine Entstehung." *Historisches Jahrbuch* (Leipzig), XLII (1922).

BUKOFZER, M. "Speculative Thinking in Medieval Music." *Sp*, XVII (1942).

BULTEAU, M. J. *Monographie de la Cathédrale de Chartres.* 2nd edition. Chartres, 1887–92. 3 vols.

——. "Saint Fulbert et sa cathédrale." *SAELM*, VII (1882).

BULTMANN, R. "Zur Geschichte der Lichtsymbolik im Altertum." *Philologus* (Leipzig and Göttingen), XCVII (1948).

CANIVEZ, J. M. "Les Voyages et les fondations monastiques de St. Bernard en Belgique." *ABSS*, 1928.

CANTOR, M. B. *Vorlesungen über Geschichte der Mathematik.* Leipzig, 1907. 2 vols.

CARTELLIERI, O. *Abt Suger von Saint-Denis.* (Historische Studien, Vol. XI.) Berlin, 1898.

*Catalogue générale des manuscrits des bibliothèques publiques de France.* Paris, 1904.

CHARTRAIRE, E. *La Cathédrale de Sens.* Paris, n.d.

――――. "Le Séjour de St. Bernard à Sens." *ABSS*, 1928.

CHASLES, M. *Aperçu historique sur l'origine et le développement des méthodes en géométrie.* Brussels, 1837.

CHASTEL, A. "La Rencontre de Salomon et de la Reine de Saba dans l'iconographie médiévale." *GBA*, 6th series, XXXV (1949).

CHENEY, C. R. "Church Building in the Middle Ages." *BJRL*, XXXIV (1951–52).

CHOISY, A. *Histoire de l'architecture.* Paris, n.d.

CLASEN, K. H. *Die gotische Baukunst.* Potsdam, 1930.

CLEMEN, P. *Die romanische Monumentalmalerei in den Rheinlanden.* Düsseldorf, 1916.

CLERVAL, J. A. *Les Écoles de Chartres au moyen-âge.* Paris, 1895.

COLOMBIER, P. DU. *Les Chantiers des cathédrales.* Paris, 1954.

CONANT, K. J. *Benedictine Contributions to Church Architecture.* Latrobe, 1949.

――――. "Medieval Academy Excavations at Cluny." *Sp*, XXXIX (1954).

――――. Review in *Sp*, XXVIII (1953).

COOK, G. H. *Portrait of Durham Cathedral.* London, 1948.

COOMARASWAMY, A. K. "Medieval Aesthetics." *AB*, XVII (1935).

COOPER, A. J. (ed.). *Le Pèlerinage de Charlemagne.* Paris, 1925.

CORNFORD, F. M. *Plato's Cosmology.* London, 1948.

CORNOG, W. H. *The Anticlaudian of Alain de Lille.* Philadelphia, 1935.

COULET, J. *Études sur l'ancien poème français du Voyage de Charlemagne en Orient.* Paris, 1907.

COULTON, G. G. *Life in the Middle Ages.* New York, 1931. 4 vols.

――――. "The Meaning of Medieval Moneys." *HAL*, XCV (1934).

――――. *Social Life in Britain.* London, 1918.

COUSSEMAKER, E. DE. *Histoire de l'harmonie au moyen âge.* Paris, 1852.

――――. (ed.). *Scriptores de musica medii aevi.* New series. Paris, 1867.

CROSBY, S. M. *L'Abbaye royale de Saint-Denis.* Paris, 1953.

――――. *The Abbey of St.-Denis.* New Haven, 1942.

――――. "Early Gothic Architecture—New Problems as a Result of the St. Denis Excavations." *JSAH*, VII (1948).

———. "Excavations in the Abbey Church of St.-Denis, 1948." American Philosophical Society, *Proceedings* (Philadelphia), XCIII (1949).

———. "Fouilles exécutées récemment dans la basilique de Saint-Denis." *BM*, CV (1947).

———. "New Excavations in the Abbey Church of Saint Denis." *GBA*, 6th series, XXII (1944).

CROZET, R. "Étude sur les consécrations pontificales." *BM*, CIV (1946).

CURTIUS, E. R. *European Literature and the Latin Middle Ages.* Translated by Willard R. Trask. (Bollingen Series XXXVI.) New York, 1953. (Orig.: *Europäische Literatur und lateinisches Mittelalter.* Bern, 1948.)

———. "Über die altfranzösische Epik." *Romanische Forschungen* (Erlangen), LXII (1950).

DEGENHART, B. "Autonome Zeichnung bei mittelalterlichen Künstlern." *MJ*, III Folge, I (1950).

DEGERING, H. "Theophilus Presbiter." In: *Westfälische Studien . . . Alois Boemer.* Leipzig, 1928.

DEHIO, G. *Untersuchungen über das gleichseitige Dreieck als Norm gotischer Bauproportionen.* Stuttgart, 1894.

———, and BEZOLD, G. VON. *Kirchliche Baukunst des Abendlandes.* Stuttgart, 1892.

DELABORDE, H. F. *Oeuvres de Rigord et de Guillaume le Breton.* Paris, 1882. 2 vols.

DELAPORTE, Y. "Chartres." In: A. Baudrillard (ed.), *Dictionnaire d'histoire et de géographie ecclésiastique*, Vol. XII. Paris, 1951.

———, and HOUVET, E. *Les Vitraux de la cathédrale de Chartres.* Chartres, 1926.

DELISLE, L. "Notice sur un livre à peintures exécuté en 1250 dans l'abbaye de Saint-Denis." *BEC*, XXXVIII (1877).

———. "Traductions de textes grecs faites par des religieux de Saint-Denis au XII° siècle." *Journal des Savants* (Paris), 1900.

DELORME, P. *Le Premier tome de l'architecture.* Paris, 1567. (Facsimile edition, Paris, 1894.)

DEMUS, O. *Byzantine Mosaic Decoration.* London, 1948.

———. *The Mosaics of Norman Sicily.* New York, 1950.

DESCHAMPS, P., and THIBOUT, M. *La Peinture murale en France.* Paris, 1951.

DESHOULIÈRES, F. "L'Église Saint-Pierre de Montmartre." *BM*, LXXVII (1913).

DIDRON, A. N. *Manuel d'iconographie chrétienne.* Paris, 1845.

DIDRON, É. "Artistes du moyen âge." *AA*, I (1844).

———. "Dessins palimpsestes du XIII° siècle." *AA*, V (1846).

DILLMANN, C. F. A. (tr.). *The Book of Enoch.* Oxford, 1893.

DIMIER, M. A. *Recueil de plans d'églises cisterciennes.* Paris, 1949.

DIMIER, M. A. "La Règle de Saint Bernard et le dépouillement architectural des cisterciens." *BRA*, May, 1951 (special number).

DIMOCK, J. F. (ed.). *Life of St. Hugh, Bishop of Lincoln.* Lincoln, 1860.

DOUBLET, J. *Histoire de l'abbaye de S. Denys en France.* Paris, 1625.

DROST, W. *Romanische und gotische Baukunst.* Potsdam, n.d. (1944).

DUBY, G. "Le Budget de l'abbaye de Cluny." *A*, VII (1952).

DU CANGE, CHARLES DU FRESNE, SIEUR. *Glossarium mediae et infimae latinitatis; Editio nova.* Niort, 1883 ff.

DUHEM, P. *Les Origines de la statique.* Paris, 1905.

DUMOUTET, E. *Le Désir de voir l'Hostie.* Paris, 1926.

DUPRAT, C. P. "La Peinture romane en France," II. *BM*, CII (1944).

DURAND, G. *Description abrégée de la cathédrale d'Amiens.* Amiens, 1904.

DYER-SPENCER, J. "Les vitraux de la Ste-Chapelle de Paris." *BM*, XCI (1932).

EDELSTEIN, H. *Die Musikanschauung Augustins nach seiner Schrift "De musica."* Bonn dissertation, 1929.

EDWARDS, K. *The English Secular Cathedrals in the Middle Ages.* Manchester, 1949.

ELORDUY, E. "¿Es Ammonio Sakkas el Pseudo-Areopagita?" *Estudios Eclesiásticos* (Madrid), XVIII (1944).

ENLART, C. *Origines françaises de l'architecture gothique en Italie.* Paris, 1894.

———. "Villard de Honnecourt et les Cisterciens." *BEC*, LVI (1895).

ERDMANN, C. *Die Entstehung des Kreuzzugsgedankens.* Stuttgart, 1935.

———. "Kaiserfahne und Blutfahne." Preussische Akademie der Wissenschaften, *Sitzungsberichte.* Berlin, 1932.

ERLER, A. *Das Strassburger Münster im Rechtsleben des Mittelalters.* Frankfort, 1954.

*Études d'histoire du moyen-âge dédiées à G. Monod.* Paris, 1896.

EVANS, J. *The Romanesque Architecture of the Order of Cluny.* Cambridge, 1938.

EYDOUX, H. P. "Les Fouilles de l'abbatiale d'Himmerod et la notion d'un plan bernardin." *BM*, CXI (1953).

FAWTIER, R. *Les Capétiens et la France.* Paris, 1942.

FELDHAUS, F. M. *Die Technik der Antike und des Mittelalters.* Potsdam, 1931.

FÉLIBIEN, M. *Histoire de l'abbaye royal de Saint-Denys en France.* Paris, 1706.

FELS, E. "Die Grabung an der Fassade der Kathedrale von Chartres." *Kunstchronik* (Munich), VIII (May, 1955).

FISCHER, T. *Zwei Vorträge über Proportionen.* Munich, 1934.

FISQUET, V. *La France pontificale. Chartres.* Paris, n.d.

FLATTEN, H. *Die Philosophie des Wilhelm von Conches.* Koblenz, 1929.

FLICHE, A. "Y-a-t'il eu en France et en Angleterre une querelle des investitures?" *RB*, XLVI (1934).

———, and MARTIN, V. *Histoire de l'Église.* Paris, 1944.

FOCILLON, H. *Art d'Occident, le moyen âge, roman et gothique.* Paris, 1938.

———. *L'Art des sculpteurs romans.* Paris, 1931.

FORSYTH, G. H., JR. *The Church of St. Martin at Angers.* Princeton, 1953.

———. "Geometricis et Arithmeticis Instrumentis." *Archeology* (Cambridge, Mass.), III (1950).

FOURNIER, E. *Nouvelles recherches sur les curies, chapitres et universités de l'ancienne église de France.* Paris, 1942.

FRANCASTEL, P. *L'Humanisme roman.* Rodez, 1942.

FRANKL, P. "The 'Crazy' Vaults of Lincoln Cathedral." *AB,* XXXV (1953).

———. *Frühmittelalterliche und romanische Baukunst.* Wildpark-Potsdam, 1926.

———. "The Secret of the Medieval Masons." *AB,* XXVII (1945).

FRIEND, A. M. "Carolingian Art in the Abbey of St.-Denis." *Art Studies* (Princeton), I (1923).

———. "Two Manuscripts of the School of St.-Denis." *Sp,* I (1926).

FUNCK-HELLET, C. "L'Équerre des maîtres d'oeuvres et la proportion." *Les Cahiers techniques de l'art* (Paris), II (1949).

GALL, E. *Die Gotische Baukunst in Frankreich und Deutschland.* Leipzig, 1925.

———. "Neue Beiträge zur Geschichte vom 'Werden der Gotik.'" *MKW,* IV (1911).

———. *Niederrheinische und normännische Architektur im Zeitalter der Frühgotik.* Berlin, 1915.

———. Review of A. Erler, *Das Strassburger Münster im Rechtsleben des Mittelalters* (Frankfurt, 1954). *Kunstchronik* (Munich), VII (1954).

———. "Über die Maasze der Trierer Liebfrauenkirche . . ." *Form und Inhalt, Kunstgeschichtliche Studien Otto Schmitt* . . . Stuttgart, 1950.

GANDILLAC, M. DE (ed.). *Oeuvres complètes du Pseudo-Denys.* Paris, 1943.

GAUTIER, L. *Les Épopées françaises.* Paris, 1878.

GERBERT, M. (ed.). *Scriptores eccles. de musica.* St. Blasien, 1784.

GHYKA, M. C. *Le Nombre d'or.* 8th edition. Paris, 1931.

GIESAU, H. "Stand der Forschung über das Figurenportal des Mittelalters." In: *Beiträge zur Kunst des Mittelalters. Vorträge der Ersten Deutschen Kunsthistoriker-Tagung auf Schloss Brühl.* Berlin, 1950.

GILSON, É. H. *La Philosophie au moyen-âge.* 2nd edition. Paris, 1947.

———. *La Philosophie de Saint Bonaventure.* Paris, 1924.

———. "Pourquoi St. Thomas a critiqué St. Augustin." *Archives d'histoire doctrinale et littéraire du moyen âge* (Paris), I (1926).

———. Le Sens du rationalisme chrétien." In: *Études de philosophie médiévale.* Strasbourg, 1921.

GILSON, É. H. *The Spirit of Medieval Philosophy*. New York, 1936.

——. *La Théologie mystique de St. Bernard*. Paris, 1947.

GOLDSCHEIDER, C. *Les Origines du portail à statues colonnes*. Doctoral dissertation, 1946. Summarized in *Bulletin des musées de France* (Paris), IX (1946).

GRABMANN, M. "Die mittelalterlichen Übersetzungen der Schriften des Pseudo-Dionysius Areopagita." (*Mittelalterliches Geistesleben*, Vol. I.) Munich, 1926.

GRAF, H. *Opus francigenum*. Stuttgart, 1878.

GRAHAM, R. "An Essay on English Monasteries." *Historical Association Pamphlet* (London), CXII (1939).

GRINNELL, R. "Iconography and Philosophy in the Crucifixion Window at Poitiers." *AB*, XXVIII (1946).

GRODECKI, L. "Fragments de vitraux provenant de St.-Denis." *BM*, CX (1952).

——. Introduction to *Catalogue*, Exposition Vitraux de France. Paris, 1953.

——. "A Stained Glass Atelier of the Thirteenth Century." *JWCI*, X (1947).

——. "Suger et l'architecture monastique." *BRA*, special number (May, 1951).

——. "The Transept Portals of Chartres Cathedral: The Date of Their Construction According to Archeological Data." *AB*, XXXIII (1951).

——. "Le Vitrail et l'architecture au XII⁰ et au XIII⁰ siècle." *GBA*, series 6, XXXVI (1939).

——. *Vitraux des églises de France*. Paris, 1947.

GROSSMANN, W. *Die einleitenden Kapitel des 'Speculum Musicae.'* Leipzig, 1924.

GROUSSET, R. *Histoire des croisades et du royaume franc de Jérusalem*. Paris, 1935.

GUILHERMY, BARON F. DE. *Notes historiques et descriptives sur . . . St.-Denis*. (MS. Bibl. Nat. nouv. acq. 6121.) Paris.

HAEMEL, A. "Überlieferung und Bedeutung des Liber S. Jacobi und des *Pseudo-Turpin*." *Bayerische Akademie der Wissenschaften, Phil.-hist. Klasse*. Munich, 1950.

HAHN, H. *Die Kirche der Zisterzienser-Abtei Eberbach im Rheingau und die romanische Ordensbaukunst der Zisterzienser im 12. Jahrhundert*. Dissertation, 1953. Summarized in *Nassauische Annalen* (Wiesbaden), LIV (1953).

HAHNLOSER, H. R. "Entwürfe eines Architekten um 1250 aus Reims." *XIII⁰ Congrès international d'histoire de l'art*. Stockholm, 1953.

——. *Villard de Honnecourt*. Vienna, 1935.

HALPHEN, L. "Les Entrevues des Rois Louis VII et Henri II." In: *Mélanges d'histoire offerts à Ch. Bémont*. Paris, 1912.

HANDSCHIN, J. "Die Musikanschauung des Johan Scotus Erigena." *Deutsche Viertel-jahrsschrift für Literaturwissenschaft und Geistesgeschichte* (Halle), V (1927).

HARVEY, J. *The Gothic World*. London, 1950.

HASKINS, C. H. *The Renaissance of the Twelfth Century*. Cambridge, Mass., 1927.

———. "Some Twelfth Century Writers on Astronomy: the School of Chartres." In: *Studies in the History of Science*. Cambridge, Mass., 1924.

HAURÉAU, B. *Mémoire sur quelques chanceliers de l'école de Chartres. AIBLM*, 1884.

———. *Notes et extraits de quelques manuscrits latins de la Bibliothèque Nationale*. Paris, 1890.

HEATH, L. *The Thirteen Books of Euclid's Elements*. Cambridge, 1926.

HECKSCHER, W. S. "Relics of Pagan Antiquity in Medieval Settings." *JWCI*, I (1937/38).

HEER, F. *Aufgang Europas*. Vienna and Zurich, 1949.

HEIDELOFF, C. *Die Bauhütte des Mittelalters in Deutschland*. Nürnberg, 1844.

HENRY, F. (ed.). *Enfances Guillaume*. Paris, 1935.

HERRE, C. L. *Die Seele der gotischen Kathedralbaukunst*. Freiburg, 1918.

HOFMEISTER, A. "Otto von Freising als Geschichtsphilosoph und Kirchenpolitiker." (*Leipziger Studien aus dem Gebiet der Geschichte*, Vol. VI.) Leipzig, 1900.

HOLMBERG, J. *Das Moralium Dogma des Guillaume de Conches*. Uppsala, 1929.

HOLMES, U. T. *A History of Old French Literature*. New York, 1948.

HOPPER, V. F. *Mediaeval Number Symbolism*. New York, 1938.

HOUVET, E. *La Cathédrale de Chartres*. Chelles, 1919.

———. *Cathédrale de Chartres, Portail occidental*. Chartres, n.d.

HUBERT, J. *L'Art pré-roman*. Paris, 1938.

———. "Les Peintures murales du Vic et la tradition géométrique." *Cahiers archéologiques* (Paris), I (1945).

HUIZINGA, J. "Über die Verknüpfung des Poetischen mit dem Theologischen bei Alanus de Insulis." *Mededeelingen der Akademie van Weetenschappen, Afdeeling Letterkunde* (Amsterdam), LXXIV (1932).

HUVELIN, P. *Essai historique sur le droit des marchés et des foires*. Paris, 1887.

IMBART DE LA TOUR, P. *Les Élections épiscopales dans l'église de France*. Paris, 1891.

JALABERT, D. "La Flore gothique." *BM*, XCI (1932).

JANNER, F. *Die Bauhütten des deutschen Mittelalters*. Leipzig, 1876.

JANSEN, W. "Der Kommentar des Clarembaldus von Arras zu Boethius' *De Trinitate*." *Breslauer Studien zur historischen Theologie* (Breslau), VIII (1926).

JANTZEN, H. "Über den gotischen Kirchenraum." *Freiburger Wissenschaftliche Gesellschaft*, XV, 1928, new ed., Berlin, 1951.

JOUVEN, G. *Rhythme et architecture*. Paris, 1951.

JUETTNER, W. *Ein Beitrag zur Geschichte der Bauhütte und des Bauwesens im Mittelalter*. Cologne, 1935.

JUNGMANN, J. A. *Missarum Solemnia*. Vienna, 1949.

JUSSELIN, M. "La Maîtrise de l'oeuvre à Notre-Dame de Chartres." *SAELM*, XV (1915-22).

KANTOROWICZ, E. "Deus per naturam, Deus per gratiam." *Harvard Theological Review*, XLV (1952).

———. *Laudes Regiae. A Study in Liturgical Acclamations and Medieval Ruler Worship.* Berkeley, 1946.

KATZENELLENBOGEN, A. "Prophets of the West Façade of the Cathedral of Amiens." *GBA*, series 6, XL (1952).

KAYSER, H. *Ein harmonikaler Teilungs-Kanon.* Zurich, 1946.

KENNEDY, V. L. "The Handbook of Master Peter, Chancellor of Chartres." *Mediaeval Studies* (New York and London), V (1943).

KERN, F. *Kingship and Law in the Middle Ages.* Oxford, 1948.

KIENAST, W. *Deutschland und Frankreich in der Kaiserzeit.* Leipzig, 1943.

KITZINGER, E. "The Mosaics of the Cappella Palatina in Palermo." *AB*, XXXI (1949).

KLETZL, O. *Plan-Fragmente aus der deutschen Dombauhütte von Prag.* Stuttgart, 1939.

KLIBANSKY, R. *The Continuity of the Platonic Tradition during the Middle Ages.* London, 1939.

KNOOP, D., and JONES, G. P. *The Medieval Mason.* Manchester, 1953.

———, ———, and HAMER, D. *The Two Earliest Masonic MSS.* Manchester, 1938.

KOCH, H. *Vom Nachleben des Vitruv.* Baden-Baden, 1951.

KOEHLER, W. "Byzantine Art and the West." *Dumbarton Oaks Papers* (Washington, D. C.), I (1941).

KOSCHWITZ, E. (ed.). *Charlemagne, Voyage à Jérusalem et à Constantinople.* Heilbronn, 1883.

KRAUTHEIMER, R. "Introduction to an Iconography of Medieval Architecture." *JWCI*, V (1941).

KRAUTHEIMER-HESS, T. "Die figurale Plastik der Ostlombardei von 1100 bis 1178." *Marburger Jahrbuch* (Marburg), IV (1928).

KRINGS, H. "Das Sein und die Ordnung." *DVLG*, XVIII (1940).

KUBLER, G. "A Late Gothic Computation of Rib Vault Thrusts." *GBA*, XXVI (1944).

KUNZE, H. *Das Fassadenproblem der französischen Früh- und Hochgotik.* Strassburg, 1912.

KUTTNER, S. "Pierre de Roissy and Robert of Flamborough." *Traditio* (New York), II (1944).

LAIR, J. "Mémoire sur deux chroniques latines." *BEC*, XXXV (1874).

LAMBERT, E. "L'Ancienne Abbaye de St.-Vincent de Laon." *AIBLM*, 1939.

———. *L'Art gothique en Espagne.* Paris, 1931.

———. "La Cathédrale de Laon." *GBA*, XIII, XIV (1926).

———. "Remarques sur les plans d'églises dits cisterciens." In: *MD*.

LANGLOIS, E. (ed.). *Couronnement de Louis.* Paris, 1888.

———. *Table des noms propres . . . dans les chansons de geste.* Paris, 1904.

LAPEYRE, A. "Les Chapiteaux historiés de l'église de Deuil." *BM*, XCVII (1938).

LASSUS, J. B. A. *Album de Villard de Honnecourt.* Paris, 1868.

———. *Monographie de la Cathédrale de Chartres.* Paris, 1867. 2 vols.

LASTEYRIE, R. DE. *L'Architecture religieuse en France à l'époque gothique.* Paris, 1926–27.

LAURENT, H. *Un Grand Commerce d'exportation au moyen-âge: la draperie des Pays-Bas en France et dans les Pays Méditerranéens.* Paris, 1935.

LAURENT, J. "Les Noms des monastères cisterciens." In: *MD.*

LAURENT, M. "Art rhénan, art mosan et art byzantin." *Byzantion* (Paris), VI (1931).

LAVISSE, E. *Histoire de France.* Paris, 1901.

LEBEL, M. L. G. *Histoire administrative, économique et financière de l'abbaye de Saint-Denis.* Paris, 1935.

LECLERCQ, J. *Comment fut construit Saint-Denis.* Paris, 1945.

———. "La Consécration légendaire de la basilique de Saint-Denis et la question des indulgences." *RM*, XXXIII (1943).

———. *Pierre le Vénérable.* Abbaye S. Wandrille, 1946.

———. "Prédicateurs bénédictins aux XIe et XIIe siècle." *RM*, XXXIII (1943).

———. *La Spiritualité de Pierre de Celle.* Paris, 1946.

LECOCQ, A. "La Cathédrale de Chartres et ses maîtres d'oeuvre." *SAELM*, VI (1873).

———. "Histoire du cloître Notre-Dame de Chartres." *SAELM*, I (1858).

———. "Recherches sur les enseignes de pèlerinages et les chemisettes de Notre-Dame de Chartres." *SAELM*, VI (1873).

LECOY DE LA MARCHE, A. *See* Suger.

LEFÈVRE-PONTALIS, E. "Les Architectes et la construction des cathédrales de Chartres." *SNAFM*, 7th series, IV (1905).

———. *L'Architecture religieuse dans l'ancien diocèse de Soissons au XIe et au XIIe siècle.* Paris, 1894.

———. "Comment doit-on rédiger la monographie d'une église?" *BM*, LXX (1906).

———. "Les Façades successives de la Cathédrale de Chartres au XIe et au XIIe siècles." *SAELM*, XIII (1904).

———. "Les Influences normandes dans le nord de la France." *BM*, LXX (1906).

———. "Le Puits des Saints-Forts et les cryptes de la Cathédrale de Chartres." *BM*, LXVII (1903).

LEFRANC, A. "Le Traité des reliques de Guibert de Nogent." In: *Études d'histoire du moyen-âge dédiées à G. Monod.* Paris, 1896.

LEFRANÇOIS-PILLION, L. *Maîtres d'oeuvre et tailleurs de pierre des cathédrales.* Paris, 1949.

LEHMANN, W. *Die Parabel von den klugen und törichten Jungfrauen.* Berlin, 1916.

LEMOSSE, M. "La lèse-majesté dans la monarchie franque." *Revue du Moyen Âge Latin* (Lyons), II (1946).

LÉPINOIS, E. DE. *Histoire de Chartres*. Chartres, 1854. 2 vols.

LESNE, E. "Histoire de la propriété ecclésiastique en France." (*Mémoires et travaux publiés par des professeurs des Facultés Catholiques de Lille*, fasc. VI.) Lille, 1910.

LEVASSEUR, E. *Histoire du commerce de la France*. Paris, 1911.

LEVILLAIN, L. "Essai sur les origines du Lendit." *RH*, CLV (1927).

———. "Études sur l'abbaye de Saint-Denis à l'époque mérovingienne." *BEC*, XCI (1930).

LICHTENBERG, H. *Architekturdarstellungen in der mittelhochdeutschen Dichtung*. Münster, 1931.

LIEBESCHUETZ, H. "Kosmologische Motive in der Bildungswelt der Frühscholastik." *Vorträge der Bibliothek Warburg, 1923–24*. Hamburg, 1926.

———. *Medieval Humanism in the Life and Writings of John of Salisbury*. London, 1950.

LIEBMANN, C. J. "La Consécration légendaire de la basilique de Saint-Denis." *Le Moyen Âge* (Paris), 3rd series, VI (1935).

LIEFTINCK, G. I. "De librijen en scriptoria der Westvlaamse Cisterciënser." In: *Mededeelingen van de Koninklijke vlaamse Academie voor Wetenschappen, Letteren en schone Kunsten van België, Klasse der Letteren XV*. Brussels, 1953.

LOENERTZ, R. J. "La Légende parisienne de St. Denys l'Aréopagite." *Analecta Bollandiana* (Brussels), LXIX (1951).

LONGNON, A. *La Formation de l'unité française*. Paris, 1922.

———. "L'Île-de-France, son origine, ses limites, ses gouverneurs." In: Société de l'histoire de Paris, *Mémoires*, Vol. I. Paris, 1874.

LOOMIS, L. H. "The Oriflamme of France and the War-cry 'Monjoie' in the Twelfth Century." In: *Studies in Art and Literature for Belle da Costa Greene*. Princeton, 1954.

———. "The Passion Lance Relic and the War Cry Monjoie in the *Chanson de Roland*." *Romanic Review* (Lancaster, Pa.), XLI (1950).

LOPEZ, R. S. "Économie et architecture médiévales, celà aurait-il tué ceci?" *A*, VII (1952).

LOT, F. *Le Premier Budget de la monarchie française, le compte générale de 1202–3*. Paris, 1922.

LUARD, H. R. (ed.). *Annales Monastici*. London, 1869.

LUCHAIRE, A. *Études sur les actes de Louis VII*. Paris, 1885.

———. *Histoire des institutions monarchiques de la France sous les premiers Capétiens (987–1180)*. Paris, 1891. 2 vols.

———. *Louis VI le Gros*. Paris, 1890.

———. *Manuel des institutions françaises*. Paris, 1892.

———. *La Société française au temps de Philippe Auguste*. Paris, 1909.

LUDDY, A. J. *Life and Teaching of St. Bernard*. Dublin, 1937.

LUND, F. M. *Ad Quadratum*. London, 1921.

MAILLARD, E. "Recherches sur l'emploi du Nombre d'or par les architectes du moyen-âge." *Congrès d'esthétique et de science de l'art* (Paris), II (n.d.).

MÂLE, E. *L'Art religieux du XII^e siècle en France.* Paris, 1924.

———. *Notre-Dame de Chartres.* Paris, 1948.

MANITIUS, M. *Geschichte der lateinischen Literatur des Mittelalters.* Munich, 1931. 3 vols.

MANTEYER, G. DE. "L'Origine des douze Pairs de France." In: *Études d'histoire du moyen-âge dédiées à G. Monod.* Paris, 1896.

MARLOT, G. *Histoire de la ville, cité et université de Reims.* Reims, 1845.

MARROU, H. I. *Saint Augustin et la fin de la culture antique.* Paris, 1938.

MARTÈNE, E. *Veterum scriptorum amplissima collectio.* Paris, 1729.

MARTIN, R. "La Formation théologique de St. Bernard." *ABSS*, 1928.

MAYER, A. "Liturgie und Geist der Gotik." *Jahrbuch für Liturgiewissenschaft* (Münster), VI (1926).

MAYER, P. (tr.). *Girart de Roussillon.* Paris, 1884.

MEER, F. VAN DER. *Keerpunt der Middeleeuwen.* Utrecht, 1950.

MÉLY, F. DE. "Nos vieilles cathédrales et leurs maîtres d'oeuvre." *Revue archéologique* (Paris), 5th series, XI (1920).

MEREDITH-JONES, C. *Historia Karoli Magni et Rotholandi ou Chroniques du Pseudo-Turpin.* Paris, 1936.

MERLET, R. *La Cathédrale de Chartres.* Paris, n.d.

———. *Dignitaires de l'église Notre-Dame de Chartres.* Chartres, 1900.

———, and CLERVAL, A. *Un Manuscrit chartrain du XI^e siècle.* Chartres, 1893.

*Miracula B. Mariae Virginis in Carnotensi ecclesia facta.* Edited by A. Thomas. *BEC*, XLII (1881).

MOESSEL, E. *Vom Geheimnis der Form und der Urform des Seins.* Stuttgart, 1938.

MOLINIER, A. *Catalogue des manuscrits de la Bibliothèque Mazarine.* Paris, 1886.

———. *Les Sources de l'histoire de France.* Paris, 1902.

———. (ed.). *See* SUGER, *Vie de Louis le Gros.*

MONTFAUCON, B. DE. *Les Monumens de la monarchie française.* Paris, 1729.

MOODY, E. A., and CLAGETT, M. *The Medieval Science of Weights.* Madison, Wis., 1952.

MORTET, V. "L'Expertise de la Cathédrale de Chartres en 1316." *CA Chartres*, LXVII (1900).

———. "Hugue de Fouilloi, Pierre le Chantre, Alexandre Neckam et les critiques dirigées au douzième siècle contre le luxe des constructions." In: *Mélanges Bémont.* Paris, 1913.

———. "La Maîtrise d'oeuvre dans les grandes constructions du XIII^e siècle et la profession d'appareilleur." *BM*, LXX (1906).

———. "La Mesure des colonnes à la fin de l'époque romaine." *BEC*, LVII (1896).

MORTET, V. "La Mesure et les proportions des colonnes antiques d'après quelques compilations et commentaires antérieurs au XII<sup>e</sup> siècle." *BEC*, LVII (1896).

———. "Note historique sur l'emploi de procédés matériels et d'instruments usités dans la géometrie pratique du moyen-âge." *Congrès International de Philosophie*, 2nd session. Geneva, 1904.

———. "Observations comparées sur la forme des colonnes à l'époque romaine." *BEC*, LIX (1898).

———, and DESCHAMPS, P. *Recueil de textes relatifs à l'histoire de l'architecture et à la condition des architectes en France au moyen-âge.* Paris, 1911, 1929. 2 vols.

MUCKLE, J. T. "Robert Grosseteste's Use of Greek Sources." *Medievalia et Humanistica* (Boulder, Colo.), III (1945).

MUETHERICH, F. "Ein Illustrationszyklus zum Anticlaudianus des Alanus ab Insulis." *Münchner Jahrbuch der bildenden Kunst* (Munich), III, series 2 (1951).

NEUSS, W. "Das Buch Ezechiel in Theologie und Kunst." *BGAM*, I, II (1912).

NEWMAN, W. M. *Le Domaine Royal sous les premiers Capétiens.* Paris, 1937.

NORMAND, J., and RAYNAUD, G. (eds.). *Aiol.* Paris, 1876.

OLSCHKI, L. *Der ideale Mittelpunkt Frankreichs im Mittelalter.* Heidelberg, 1913.

OURSEL, C. *La Miniature du XII<sup>e</sup> siècle à l'Abbaye de Cîteaux d'après les manuscrits de la Bibliothèque de Dijon.* Dijon, 1926.

PAINTER, S. *The Scourge of the Clergy, Peter of Dreux, Duke of Brittany.* Baltimore, 1937.

PANGE, J. DE. *Le Roi très-chrétien.* Paris, 1949.

PANOFSKY, E. *Abbot Suger on the Abbey Church of St.-Denis and Its Art Treasures.* Princeton, 1946.

———. *Early Netherlandish Painting.* Cambridge, Mass., 1953.

———. "Die Entwicklung der Proportionslehre als Abbild der Stilentwicklung." *MKW*, XIV (1921).

———. *Gothic Architecture and Scholasticism.* Latrobe, 1951.

———. "Note on a Controversial Passage in Suger's *De Consecratione Ecclesiae Sancti Dionysii.*" *GBA*, 6th series, XXVI (1944).

PARÉ, G. *Le "Roman de la rose" et la scholastique courtoise.* Ottawa, 1941.

———, BRUNET, A., and TREMBLAY, P. *La Renaissance du XII<sup>e</sup> siècle. Les écoles et l'enseignement.* Paris and Ottawa, 1933.

PARENT, J. M. *La Doctrine de la création dans l'école de Chartres.* Paris, 1938.

PARISET, F. "Étude sur l'atelier de la Cathédrale de Strasbourg." *AHA*, VIII (1929).

PETIT, R. P. "Le Puritanisme des premiers Prémontrés." *BRA*, special number (May, 1951).

PÉTRIDÈS, S. "Traités liturgiques de Saint Maxime et de Saint Germain." *Revue de l'Orient chrétien* (Paris), X (1905).

PEVSNER, N. "The Term 'Architect' in the Middle Ages." *Sp*, XVII (1942).

PIETZSCH, G. *Die Musik im Erziehungs- und Bildungswesen des ausgehenden Altertums und frühen Mittelalters.* Halle, 1932.

PITRA, J. B. *Spicilegium Solesmense.* Paris, 1845.

POOLE, R. L. *Illustrations of the History of Medieval Thought and Learning.* London, 1920.

——. "The Masters of the School of Paris and Chartres in John of Salisbury's Time." *EHR*, XXV (1920).

PORCHER, J. "St. Bernard et la graphie pure." In: *MD*.

PORTER, A. K. *Romanesque Sculptures of the Pilgrimage Roads.* Boston, 1923.

POWICKE, F. M. "Ailred of Rievaulx and His Biographer, Walter Daniel." *BJRL*, VI (1921).

——. Review in *Sp*, XII (1938).

PROST, A. "Caractère et significance des quatre pièces liturgiques composées à Metz." *SNAFM*, 4th series, V (1874).

PUIG Y CADAFALCH, J. *La Géographie et les origines du premier art roman.* Paris, 1935.

RABY, F. J. E. *History of Secular Latin Poetry in the Middle Ages.* Oxford, 1954.

——. "Philomena praevia temporis amorem." In: *Mélanges Jos. de Ghellinck.* Gembloux, Belgium, 1951.

RAINE, J. (ed.). *The Historians of the Church of York.* London, 1879.

RAMBAUD, M. "Le Quatrain mystique de Vaison-la-Romaine." *BM*, CIX (1951).

RAUSCHEN, G. (ed.). *Descriptio qualiter Karolus Magnus, clavum et coronam a Constantinopoli Aquisgrani detulerit . . .* In: "Die Legende Karls des Grossen im XI und XII Jahrhundert." (*Publikationen der Gesellschaft für Rheinische Geschichtskunde*, Vol. VII.) Leipzig, 1890.

RAYNAUD, G. (ed.). *Élie de Saint-Gilles.* Paris, 1879.

*Reallexikon zur deutschen Kunstgeschichte.* Stuttgart, 1953 ff.

*Recueil des historiens des Gaules et de la France.* Paris, 1840 ff.

REESE, G. *Music in the Middle Ages.* New York, 1940.

REINHARDT, H. *Der St. Galler Klosterplan.* St.-Gall, 1953.

RENAN, E. *Mélanges d'histoire et de voyages.* Paris, 1878.

RENARD, EDMUND. *Köln.* Leipzig, 1923.

RIANT, P. DE. "Des dépouillées religieuses enlevées à Constantinople au XIII᷎ siècle et des documents historiques nés de leur transport en Occident." *SNAFM*, 4th series, VI (1895).

*Richesses des bibliothèques provinciales de France, Les.* Paris, 1932.

RICÔME, F. "Structure et fonction du chevet de Morienval." *BM*, XCVIII (1939).

RIEGL, A. *Spätrömische Kunstindustrie.* Vienna, 1927.

ROBSON, C. A. *Maurice of Sully and the Medieval Vernacular Homily.* Oxford, 1952.

ROHAULT DE FLEURY, C. *Mémoire sur les instruments de la Passion de N.-S. J.-C.* Paris, 1870.

ROLLAND, P. "La Cathédrale romane de Tournai et les courants architecturaux." *Revue belge d'archéologie et d'histoire de l'art* (Brussels), III (1937).

———. "Chronologie de la Cathédrale de Tournai." *Revue belge d'archéologie et d'histoire de l'art* (Brussels), IV (1934).

RORICZER, MATTHEW. *Das Büchlein von der Fialen Gerechtigkeit.* New edition. Trier, 1845.

ROSE, H. *Die Frühgotik im Orden von Cîteaux.* Munich, 1915.

ROSENAU, H. *Design and Medieval Architecture.* London, 1934.

ROSS, M. C. "Monumental Sculptures from St.-Denis." *Journal of the Walters Art Gallery* (Baltimore), III (1940).

ROUSSEL, E. "La Bénédiction du Lendit au XIVᵉ siècle." *Bulletin de la société de l'histoire de Paris* (Paris), XXIV (1897).

RUEGG, A. *Die Jenseitsvorstellungen vor Dante.* Cologne, 1945.

RUSHFORTH, G. *Medieval Christian Imagery.* Oxford, 1936.

RZIHA, F. *Studien über Steinmetz-Zeichen.* Vienna, 1883.

SABLON, V. *Histoire de l'auguste et vénérable Église de Chartres.* Chartres, 1671.

SALOMON, R. *Opicinus de Canistris.* (Studies of the Warburg Institute.) London, 1936.

SALZMAN, L. F. *Building in England.* Oxford, 1952.

SANDYS, J. E. *A History of Classical Scholarship.* Cambridge, 1921.

SARTON, G. A. L. *Introduction to the History of Science.* Washington, D. C., 1931. 3 vols.

SAUER, J. *Die Symbolik des Kirchengebäudes.* Freiburg, 1902.

SCHEDLER, P. M. "Die Philosophie des Macrobius und ihr Einfluss auf die Wissenschaft des christlichen Mittelalters." *BGPM*, XIII (1916).

SCHMITT, O. "Zur Deutung der Gewölbefigur am ehemaligen Westlettner des Mainzer Doms." In: *Festschrift für Heinrich Schrohe.* Mainz, 1934.

SCHNEIDER, M. *El Origen musical de los animales símbolos en la mitologia y la escultura antiguas.* Barcelona, 1946.

SCHRAMM, P. E. *Der König von Frankreich.* Weimar, 1939.

SCHWARZ, W. "Der Investiturstreit in Frankreich." *Zeitschrift für Kirchengeschichte* (Stuttgart), XLII (new series V) (1923).

SCHWIETERING, J. "The Origins of the Medieval Humility Formula." *Publications of the Modern Language Association of America* (New York), LXIX (1954).

SEDLMAYR, H. "Die dichterische Wurzel der Kathedrale." *Mitteilungen des österr. Instituts für Geschichtsforschung* (Vienna), Supp. Vol. XIV (1939).

———. *Die Entstehung der Kathedrale.* Zurich, 1950.

————. "Das erste mittelalterliche Architektursystem." *Kunstwissenschaftliche Forschungen* (Berlin), II (1933).

————. "Ein zeitgenössischer Fachausdruck für die Raumform 'Baldachin.' " *Österreichische Akademie der Wissenschaften, phil.-hist. Klasse* (Vienna), 1949.

SEYMOUR, C., JR. *Notre Dame of Noyon in the Twelfth Century.* New Haven, 1939.

SHARP, D. E. *Franciscan Philosophy in Oxford.* Oxford, 1930.

SIMSON, O. VON. "Birth of the Gothic." *Measure* (Chicago), I (1950).

————. "Rezensionen zu Hans Sedlmayr's *Die Entstehung der Kathedrale.*" *Kunstchronik* (Munich), IV (1951).

SINGER, C. "The Scientific Views and Visions of St. Hildegard." In: *Studies in the History and Method of Science.* Edited by C. Singer. Oxford, 1917.

SMYSER, H. M. *The Pseudo-Turpin, Edited from Bibliothèque Nationale, Fonds Latin, MS. 17656.* Cambridge, Mass., 1937.

SPITZER, L. "Classical and Christian Ideas of World Harmony." *Traditio* (New York), II (1944), III (1945).

STAHL, W. H. *Macrobius, Commentary on the Dream of Scipio.* New York, 1952.

STEIN, H. *Les Architectes des cathédrales gothiques.* Paris, 1909.

STODDARD, W. S. *The West Portals of Saint Denis and Chartres.* Cambridge, Mass., 1952.

STRAUB, H. *Geschichte der Bauingenieur-Kunst.* Basel, 1949.

STRECKER, K. *Die Gedichte Walters von Châtillon.* Berlin, 1925.

————. *Moralisch-Satirische Gedichte Walters von Châtillon.* Heidelberg, 1929.

STUBBS, W. (ed.). *Rerum Britannicarum Medii Aevi Scriptores.* London, 1825 ff.

SUGER. *De consecratione ecclesiae sancti Dionysii.* In: *Oeuvres complètes,* q.v.

————. *De rebus in administratione sua gestis.* In: *Oeuvres complètes,* q.v.

————. *Oeuvres complètes de Suger.* Edited by A. Lecoy de la Marche. Paris, 1867.

————. *Sugerii vita.* In: *Oeuvres complètes,* q.v.

————. *Vie de Louis le Gros.* Edited by A. Molinier. Paris, 1887.

————. *Vie de Louis VI le Gros.* Edited and translated by H. Waquet. Paris, 1929.

SVOBODA, K. *L'Esthétique de Saint Augustin et ses sources.* Brno, 1933.

SWARTWOUT, R. F. *The Monastic Craftsman.* Cambridge, 1932.

SWARZENSKI, H. *Monuments of Romanesque Art.* London and Chicago, 1954.

TARDIF, J. *Monuments historiques.* Paris, 1866.

TAYLOR, H. O. *The Mediaeval Mind.* New York, 1925.

TEXIER, M. A. *Géométrie de l'architecture.* Paris, 1934.

THALHOFER, V., and EISENHOFER, L. *Handbuch der katholischen Liturgik.* Freiburg, 1912. 2 vols.

THÉRY, P. G. *Études Dionysiennes.* Paris, 1932, 1937. 2 vols.

————. "Existe-t-il un commentaire de J. Sarrazin sur la 'Hiérarchie céleste' du

Pseudo-Denys?" *Revue des sciences philosophiques et théologiques* (Paris), XI (1922).

*Thesaurus Linguae Latinae, Editus auctoritate et consilio academiarum quinque Germanicarum.* Leipzig, 1900 ff.

THIBOUT, M. "À propos de peintures murales de la Chapelle Ste.-Catherine de Montbellet." *BM*, CVIII (1950).

THOMAE, W. *Das Proportionenwesen in der Geschichte der gotischen Baukunst.* Heidelberg, 1933.

THOMAS, A. (ed.). *See Miracula B. Mariae.*

THOMPSON, A. H. "Cathedral Builders of the Middle Ages." *History* (London), X (1925).

TIETZE, H. "Aus der Bauhütte von St. Stephan." *Jahrbuch der kunsthistorischen Sammlungen* (new series), IV, V. Vienna, 1930/31.

TREZZINI, H. *Retour à l'architecture.* Paris, 1946.

UEBERWASSER, W. "Beiträge zur Wiedererkenntnis gotischer Baugesetzmässigkeiten." *ZK*, VIII (1939).

———. "Deutsche Architekturdarstellung um das Jahr 1000." In: *Festschrift für Hans Jantzen.* Berlin, 1951.

———. "Nach rechtem Maasz." *Jahrbuch der preussischen Kunstsammlungen* (Berlin), LVI (1935).

———. "Spätgotische Baugeometrie." *Jahresbericht der öffentlichen Kunstsammlung* (new series, 25-27). Basel, 1928-30.

———. *Von Maasz und Macht der alten Kunst.* Strassburg, 1933.

VACANDARD, E. *Vie de St. Bernard.* Paris, 1910.

VALLENTIN, B. "Der Engelstaat." In: *Grundrisse und Bausteine zur Staats- und zur Geschichtslehre zusammengetragen zu den Ehren Gustav Schmollers.* Berlin, 1908.

VALOIS, N. *Guillaume d'Auvergne.* Paris, 1880.

VELTE, M. *Die Anwendung der Quadratur und Triangulatur bei der Grund- und Aufrissgestaltung der gotischen Kirchen.* Basel, 1951.

VERBEEK, A. *Schwarzrheindorf.* Düsseldorf, 1953.

VERNEILH, F. DE. "Construction des monuments ogivaux." *AA*, VI (1847).

VIARD, J. *Les Grandes Chroniques de France publiées pour la Société de l'histoire de France.* Paris, 1920.

VIELLIARD, J. *Le Guide du pèlerin de Saint-Jacques de Compostelle.* Mâon, 1938.

VIOLLET-LE-DUC, E. E. *Dictionnaire raisonné de l'architecture française du XIᵉ au XVIᵉ siècle.* Paris, 1854-68. 10 vols.

———. *Lectures on Architecture.* Translated by B. Bucknall. London, 1877.

VOEGE, W. *Die Anfänge des monumentalen Stiles im Mittelalter.* Strassburg, 1894.

WALPOLE, R. N. "The Pèlerinage de Charlemagne." *Romance Philology* (Berkeley), VIII (1955).

———. "Philip Mouskés and the Pseudo-Turpin Chronicle." *University of California Publications in Modern Philology* (Berkeley), XXVI (1947).

WALTER, J. "L'Évangeliaire de Marbach-Schwarzenthann de la fin du XIIᵉ siècle." *AHA*, IX (1930).

———. "Les Miniatures du Codex Guta-Sintram de Marbach-Schwarzenthann (1154)." *AHA*, IV (1925).

WAQUET, H. *See* Suger, *Vie de Louis VI le Gros.*

WARD, C. *Medieval Church Vaulting.* Princeton, 1915.

WEBB, C. C. J. *John of Salisbury.* London, 1932.

WEBB, C. F. "The Sources of the Design of the West Front of Peterborough Cathedral." *Archaeological Journal* (London), LVI (suppl. 1952).

WEISE, G. *Die Geistige Welt der Gotik.* Halle, 1939.

WENZEL, H. "Die Glasmalerei der Zisterzienser in Deutschland." *BRA*, special number (May, 1951).

WHITEHILL, W. M. *Liber Sancti Jacobi Codex Calixtinus.* Santiago de Compostela, 1944.

WILLIAMS, G. H. "The Norman Anonymous of 1100 A.D." *Harvard Theological Studies* (Cambridge, Mass.), XVIII (1951).

WILLIS, R. *Architectural History of the Conventual Buildings of the Monastery of Christ Church in Canterbury.* London, 1869.

WILMART, A. "L'Ancienne Bibliothèque de Clairvaux." *Mémoires de la Société académique . . . de l'Aube* (Lyons), LV, LVI (1916).

———. "Poèmes de Gautier de Châtillon." *RB*, XLIX (1937).

———. "La Tradition des grands ouvrages de St. Augustin." In: *Miscellanea Agostiniana.* Rome, 1930.

WITTKOWER, R. *Architectural Principles in the Age of Humanism.* London, 1952.

WOLF, J. "Die Musiklehre des Johannes de Grocheo." In: *Sammelbände der Internationalen Musikgesellschaft*, Vol. I. Leipzig, 1899-1900.

WORMALD, F. "The Development of English Illumination in the Twelfth Century." *Journal of the British Archaeological Association* (London), 3rd series, VII (1942).

WRIGHT, T. (ed.). *The Latin Poems Commonly Attributed to Walter Mapes.* London, 1841.


ADDENDA TO THE SECOND EDITION

CATTIN, G. *Saint Bernard de Clairvaux.* Paris, 1960.

CROSBY, S. M. Review of present volume, in *AB*, XIII (1960).

FRANKL, P. "Reconsiderations on the Chronology of Chartres Cathedral." *AB*, XLIII (1961).

GRODECKI, L. "Chronologie de la Cathédrale de Chartres." *BM*, CXVI (1958).

GRODECKI, L. "Les Vitraux allégoriques de Saint-Denis." *Art de France*, I (1961).

————. "Les Vitraux de Saint-Denis; L'Enfance du Christ." *Essays in Honor of Erwin Panofsky*. New York, 1961.

HAHN, H. *Die frühe Kirchenbaukunst der Zisterzienser*. Berlin, 1957.

KATZENELLENBOGEN, A. *The Sculptural Programs of Chartres Cathedral*. Baltimore, 1959.

KIDSON, P. *Sculpture at Chartres*. London, 1958.

MENÉNDEZ PIDAL, R. *La Chanson de Roland et la tradition épique des Francs*. 2nd edn., revised and brought up-to-date by the author with the assistance of René Louis. Paris, 1960.

PÄCHT, O.; DODWELL, C. R.; and WORMALD, F. *The St. Alban's Psalter*. London, 1860.

References to the plates are in *italic*. References to the text figures are indicated by an asterisk after the page number. Footnote citations of modern scholarship are not indexed.